SYRIA, THE UNITED STATES, AND THE WAR ON TERROR IN THE MIDDLE EAST

SYRIA, THE UNITED STATES, AND THE WAR ON TERROR IN THE MIDDLE EAST

Robert G. Rabil

Foreword by Walid Phares

PRAEGER SECURITY INTERNATIONAL
Westport, Connecticut • London

Library of Congress Cataloging-in-Publication Data

Rabil, Robert G.
    Syria, the United States, and the war on terror in the Middle East
    / Robert G. Rabil ; foreword by Walid Phares.
        p. cm.
    Includes bibliographical references and index.
    ISBN 0-275-99015-X (alk. paper)
    1. United States—Foreign relations—Syria. 2. Syria—Foreign rela-
tions—United States. 3. War on Terrorism, 2001- . 4. United
States—Politics and government—2001- . I. Title.
E183.8.S95R33 2006
327.730569109'045—dc22   2005034115

British Library Cataloguing in Publication Data is available.

Library of Congress Catalog Card Number: 2005034115
ISBN: 0-275-99015-X

First published in 2006

Praeger Security International, 88 Post Road West, Westport, CT 06881
An imprint of Greenwood Publishing Group, Inc.
www.praeger.com

Printed in the United States of America

The paper used in this book complies with the
Permanent Paper Standard issued by the National
Information Standards Organization (Z39.48–1984).

10 9 8 7 6 5 4 3 2 1

To Patricia and Georges Alexander

In Memory of My Father

Georges Elias Rabil

Contents

──────── Acknowledgments ────────

I am grateful to all my colleagues, interviewees, and former and current government officials for their invaluable insights, opinions, and information. I thank the faculty of the department of political science, especially the Chair, Dr. Edward Schwerin, at Florida Atlantic University for their moral and academic support. I am particularly grateful to Dr. Walid Phares for his intellectual and collegial support as well as inspirational and moral encouragement. Florida Society for Middle East Studies deserves my commendation for their professional support. Special thanks go to Saul Gordon, Paul Cutler, and Louis Sandler. I am grateful to Lebanese dignitaries in Diaspora and in Lebanon who were kind enough to share with me their views and analysis on the Middle East. Tom Harb and Adel Suleiman deserve special thanks. I am thankful to my former professor and advisor Avigdor Levy, whose continuous guidance and soothing wisdom keep me even-keeled. I thank Lynne Rienner Publishers for giving me permission to reprint material from my book *Embattled Neighbors: Syria, Israel, and Lebanon.* I thank the Washington Institute for Near East Policy for its support as well as for giving me permission to reprint some of my articles. Robert Satloff, Patrick Clawson, and the editorial staff deserve special thanks.

I am deeply thankful to all my family, in whose unconditional love I find my strength. More specifically, I am profoundly grateful to my father, who recently passed away, for his integrity, honesty, and optimism, which he, in his very simple and loving ways, tried to inculcate in me and strengthen my character. I find myself subconsciously striving to become as good a man as he was. I miss him dearly. Finally, I thank Patricia and Georges Alexander for whom this book is dedicated for coming into my life and filling it with joy, pride, and love.

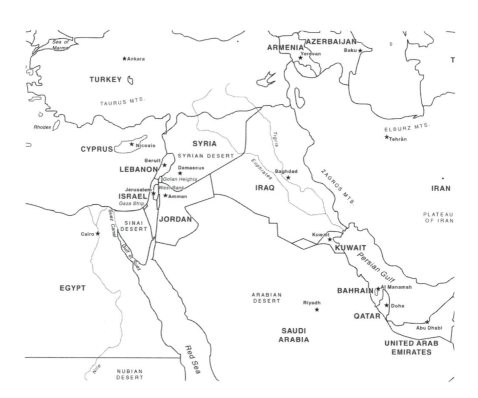

Source: mapcraft.com

Foreword

Since the collapse of the Soviet Union and the end of the Cold War, U.S.-Syrian relations went through different stages and underwent sharply edged changes, in an amazing race between cold but stable relations and rapidly deteriorating ties. The Washington-Damascus web of diplomacy, public policy, and intelligence challenges crossed deserts and jungles: At times, American foreign policy and Syria's strategies overlapped; at other times, especially since 9/11, they diverged radically. Since September 2004, the day a U.S.-French sponsored U.N. Security Council resolution was voted as UNSCR 1559, calling for Syria's withdrawal from Lebanon and the disarming of its local allies in its neighbor, a new cold war started between the two parties: Washington is tightening the pressures on Syria's Ba'th, while Damascus is playing its powerful cards on all available battlefields, from Iraq to Lebanon. The questions at hand in 2006 are these: Are we witnessing a renewal of a cold war between a U.S.-led coalition and a Syrian-led axis in the region? How far can the United States go in pressuring the Syrian regime and its allies into submitting to a reform in its policies and domestic institutions? And, on the other hand, how far can the Syrian regime go in its regional and international involvements, putting itself in the face of U.S.-led policies towards democracy and political change? Which capital will let go of its ongoing agendas and policies first? Is there any chance for a return to the years of accommodations? These and other questions are and will be affecting the present and futures of Syria, Lebanon, Iraq, the Israeli-Palestinian peace process, as well as America's foreign policy in the region, let alone the Arab world. To address these challenging issues, the Middle East studies community in America and the West should muster its resources in a serious effort to accurately describe, project, and prescribe the various parameters of this complex relationship. For it has been established in the past two decades that the expert community in Syrian-American ties, and particularly in the field of Ba'thist strategic thinking, has unfortunately failed in providing an accurate analysis on the subject both in the classroom and to the government over the past few decades. This is why I believe that a new generation of academics and researchers is needed, or, to be fairer, new paradigms are warranted, regardless of their mode of adoption. This new school of Middle East studies in general and levantine politics in particular is surging with the works of solid scholars in the field. Robert Rabil is one of them and is one of the few academics who has been successful in approaching the subject thoroughly and producing a powerful study of its complex and multidimensional aspects.

As an American scholar, trained in prestigious universities, Rabil dispenses endless energies to meet the challenge of academic accuracy. But as an immigrant citizen who was born and raised in the geographical and cultural areas of this subject, he brings along with him the field component. The combination of the two assets of native knowledge and balanced scholarship enable Rabil to be a peculiar contributor to the field and a unique student of Syrian and levantine affairs. Rabil is a native of Lebanon where he received his schooling and served as a volunteer in the Red Cross emergency units. Throughout the difficult years of the war, between 1975 and 1984, he served his civil society despite the dangers surrounding his neighborhood. There, he witnessed first hand the violence of a long war, involving Lebanese factions, Palestinian organizations since 1975, and the Syrian army as of 1976. On April 13, 1975, the Lebanese war began between Palestinian fighters and Lebanese militiamen. Lebanon fractured in enclaves and "areas." In June 1976, Syrian President Hafiz al-Asad ordered his army to invade Lebanon. In July of the same year, he delivered a speech in Damascus, outlining the objectives of the Ba'th regime in Lebanon: confrontation with Israel, support to the Palestinian resistance, obstruction of the partition of the country, and protection of the Arab identity of Lebanon. Syrian forces, which benefited later from an Arab League short-lived mandate for deterrence, clashed with the various military players in the country, containing one after the other. By 1978, Syria's forces have dominated large parts of Lebanon. These events were taking place at the peak of the second stage of the Cold War. The Asad regime was substantially supported by the Soviet Union and positioned itself as an unwavering ally of Moscow in the region, especially after the signing of the Camp David agreement and the pullout of Egypt from the "Arab front" against Israel.

Syria's Arab nationalists, under al-Asad's leadership, were socialists and staunchly anti-Israeli. This dual doctrine put them face to face with the United States, world foe of the Soviet Union and strategic ally of the Jewish state. The Ba'th leadership since its inception in the 1950s, its coming to power in the 1960s, and the coup d'etat of al-Asad in 1970 was poised to be on a collision with Washington's policies in the region. The East-West cold war was merciless: regimes and governments had to be with either one or the other bloc. Despite several attempts by world leaders to form a nonaligned bloc, a majority of the Third World practically ended in the arms of pro-Soviet or anti-American regimes: Castro of Cuba, Nasser of Egypt, and Tito of Yugoslavia are the most notorious examples.

But the shrewd Hafiz al-Asad, coined by many observers as the "most intelligent Arab leader of modern times" always kept back channels to the United States. At the peak of the Cold War, and while his military machine was fed, structured, and trained by Moscow, the Alawite president established secret and sometimes open ties with U.S. intelligence, officials, and diplomats. Syria was the only pro-Soviet ally in the Arab world that maintained "common grounds" with American foreign policy till the end of the Cold War. From the very important backyard of Syria's power, Lebanon, analysts of Syrian politics followed closely al-Asad's web making. Lebanese politicians, those against the Syrians, and those supporting their occupation, emerged as the best connoisseurs of Damascus world views. Phalangist politician Karim Pakradouni, an Armenian, foreign minister Fouad Boutros, a Greek Orthodox, and intelligence official Johnny Abdo, a Maronite, are examples of personalities that knew more about al-Asad's world views than many in his own regime. Muslim politicians in Lebanon had a good grasp on Damascus's goals: Nabih Berri, leader of Shi'ite Amal, Rachid and Omar Karame, Sunni prime ministers, and Walid Jumblat, Druze leader, were among the closest allies of al-Asad, and thus knew his mind very well.

It was from this political and psychological context that a number of Lebanon-originated researchers developed a unique expertise on Syrian politics in general and on the al-Asad regime in particular. Rabil pursued his high school studies in Beirut's suburbs, a sensitive basis for the Syrian military and intelligence presence, but perceived by many as "occupation." For years (especially the 1980s), the inner world of Lebanese and Syrian politics was the daily bread of this young student just before he immigrated to the United States. The understanding of how Syrian power perceives the world has become a second nature to Rabil as well as to many other students of politics. But it was in America where he completed the circle of his research begun in the 1990s and where he built the highest credentials to produce this book. First under the Cold War and after the collapse of the Soviet Union, Rabil was studying Middle East politics and cultures while analyzing U.S. policy towards that region. While his younger years were soaked with a deep understanding of Syro-Lebanese politics, his American academic life provided him with the U.S. foreign policy component towards the levant. With a degree from Harvard University Extension School and a Ph.D. from Brandeis University, Rabil went on to publish his first book, *Embattled Neighbors—Syria, Israel, and Lebanon* (Lynne Rienner, 2003). In this research, Rabil showed Syria's strategies in the triangular equation between the three neighbors. He follows it with a number of articles in various publications. In addition, in the years before 9/11 Rabil was appointed as chief researcher in the U.S. Congress funded Iraq Project. He and his team excavate and review thousands of documents left by Ba'th authorities in Kurdish and Shi'ite areas during the first uprising of 1991 in Iraq. And as the Iraq invasion neared, Rabil was further solicited by media and government to investigate the various possibilities for a post-Saddam Iraq. Most of his assertions regarding the regime change and the necessary policies were right on target, from the issue of the Army, the de-Ba'thification and Shi'a influence in government. Since April 2003, Rabil has published a number of pieces analyzing Iraq, as well as the potential growth of a Syrian involvement, hence a collision course with the United States. I published with Rabil a few pieces, including one in the *Wall Street Journal,* in an attempt to foresee the Ba'thist future in the region, as well as the implications of the Saddam regime change in the region. Rabil, who meanwhile was invited to serve as an adjunct scholar with the prestigious Washington Institute for Near East Policy as of early 2005, has begun the gigantic task of revisiting U.S.-Syrian relations. By mid 2003, Rabil and some of his colleagues noted that Damascus under the young al-Asad was intertwined between the past decades under Hafiz and the years since 9/11.

Breaking the old paradigm in Washington and other Western capitals, Rabil's analysis focused on Syria's very narrow options since the fall of Saddam, but observed its vast fields of maneuver. In a series of articles, including those in the *Daily Star* of Beirut, the *History News Network,* the *National Interest,* and the Washington Institute's *PolicyWatches,* Rabil bypassed the old academic arguments of "realism" imputed to al-Asad, and demonstrated that "something was going inherently wrong" in Damascus. Going against the mainstream Middle East studies establishment, particularly the other experts on Syrian politics, Rabil saw the clouds gathering over Syrian-American relations. At the time, as I was focusing on the discussions in the Security Council of the U.N., preceding the voting of resolution 1559 in September 2004, a matter Rabil was appraised of continuously, he warned of a Syrian miscalculating reaction: It was a few months before the attempt to assassinate former minister Marwan Hamade in Lebanon (Fall 2004) and the assassination of Rafiq Hariri. In our discussions and analysis, Rabil and I projected multiple scenarios of Syrian reactions. We were right on target: Syria chose to play hardball with Washington. Since then, Rabil, who has been hired by Florida Atlantic University as a professor of Middle East studies and the graduate director of the Department of Political Science, concentrated his efforts to produce what became a needed piece of research in the United States: an explanation of Syria's new strategies regarding U.S. policies in the region.

It became evident to the new school of Middle East studies, to which Rabil and I belong, a school that intended to provide a better understanding of the region to the American and international public that a new cold war was brewing. In the post-9/11 era, terrorism became the continental divide in international relations. Regimes and organizations have to choose sides: either rejecting it totally as a tool and philosophy or accepting it, legitimizing it, or even considering its root causes as legitimate. The choice is about a concept in international relations, not about a U.S. administration's doctrine or regime ideologies in the Middle East. In this context, Rabil and the new school of Middle East studies put Syria's regime in the camp of those who have chosen their strategic options. To many other scholars and diplomats, al-Asad's regime can be recuperated. To some, it will be co-opted if the Bush administration is removed from power in the next election. In Rabil's research, it is about American compliance with Syrian claims in the region, not the other way around.

In his series of pieces and talks leading to the book, Rabil measures the Syrian involvement in Iraq, in the Palestinian-Israeli conflict and peace process, and in the Lebanese arena. His conclusions are clear: Damascus is in a countercurrent with the United States. It has opposed the political process following Saddam's fall, without describing clearly its own wishes for its neighbor's future. Damascus has maintained its guidelines of support to the radicals among the Palestinians, after the Oslo agreements, under Arafat, and after his death. Hence it is a permanent policy. Finally, al-Asad's regime opposed UNSCR 1559 at its birth, attempted to break its implementation, and is said to have been involved in violence, including in political assassinations in Lebanon, at least since the U.N., U.S. sponsored resolution. In Rabil's analysis these are all ingredients of a policy heading to a full fledged collision with the U.S. agenda for the region.

Rabil was invited to address government and think tank audiences in Washington on this critical issue: Is Syria, and behind it its strategic allies in Iran and Hizbollah, determined to play the role of a Soviet Union in the region at the peak of a new cold war? Or is the Syrian dictator playing brinkmanship with Washington? U.S. analysts are divided: a majority of traditional "readers" of the al-Asad regime still contend that it is the fault of the United States. According to their thesis, Syria has demonstrated plenty of good resolve: it provided information about terrorists, including al Qaida; it adopted a constructive role in the Arab league; it showed readiness for political reform; etc. But other readers of Syrian politics, including Rabil argued otherwise: Syria's regime wants to project that image while keeping all options open. In fact, the decision makers in the Syrian capital wish for an American collapse in Iraq, a collapse of the Israeli-Palestinian talks, and a collapse of the UNSCR 1559 and the Cedars Revolution in Lebanon.

From reading Rabil's book, without anticipating the conclusions, one can see the historical roots of Syria's policy towards the United States. And from that reading on, one can project the collision: Damascus is struggling to maintain the old order in the region, even by force if needed, while Washington is determined to encourage civil society in the region to produce its own new order based on democracy. Criticism is fusing from all quarters against both the United States and Syria for what is perceived as an unwarranted change. "They could have coexisted" lashes out the older brand of realists in the U.S. foreign policy establishment. They may have responded to Rabil's analysis, but the region has changed, and so have its parameters. Damascus was given more than what it deserves by all realist standards, but it refused to mutate. By the new school parameters, Washington was somewhat late to engage in democracy campaigning. It allowed the senior al-Asad to extend the Cold War in the region one decade and a half after the collapse of the Soviet Union, its protector. Washington's realists throughout the 1990s led Damascus to believe that nothing has really changed: Syria's invasion of Lebanon was permitted by the first Bush Administration in 1990; its challenge of the Oslo peace process tolerated by the Clinton Administration; and its suppression of the Lebanese opposition and support of Hizbollah was not opposed by the West in general.

Rabil's understanding of both U.S. policy and Syrian strategies makes his new book a must in the understanding of the crucial moments to come. The new cold war between Syria's Ba'th and America's new doctrines has already begun on all fronts: Diplomatic at the U.N., Arab League, and worldwide media; military in Iraq, terrorism in Lebanon and the Palestinian arena. The conflict is raging, while the chronicles are staying behind. Unfortunately, little Arab and American scholarship has produced a fresh look at the new battlefields. While a number of authors, published by distinguished presses in America, are stuck in the past, embellishing al-Asad's stereotype of the "new leadership," reality on the ground is developing at a rapid pace: Syrian reformers are now a real factor; the UNSCR 1559 is pounding Syria's vital interest in its past colony of Lebanon; the Hariri assassination may open a breach inside the regime; a general, Ghazi Kenaan, may have committed assisted suicide in Damascus; the new Iraqi government is providing evidence of Syrian involvement in Jihadi operations in the Sunni triangle; Iran's new regime head, Mahmoud Ahmedi Nijad is challenging the United States, Israel, and the West head on, dragging Bashar into his trail; the Palestinians are able to pull deals with the Israelis without Damascus's endorsement; and millions of demonstrators in Beirut have expelled the Ba'thist army from the country, even though its intelligence services are said to be wreaking havoc among Lebanon's anti-Syrian politicians. In short, Syria's world has definitely changed. So has the entire world with America's war on terror.

Robert Rabil is a challenger of old paradigms. His new book will lead in what I expect will become a revolution in the study of U.S.-Syrian relations. In this year of 2006, and throughout the decade, I expect his analysis of the "new cold war" in the region to enlighten decision makers and the public on the fate of a regime, Bashar's Ba'ath, and the fate of a number of countries: Syria, Lebanon, Iraq, and the Palestinians. The book is necessary to understand and project a significant component of U.S. foreign policy in the ongoing war on terror.

Walid Phares
Washington, DC
December 27, 2005

Dr. Walid Phares is a senior fellow with the Foundation for the Defense of Democracies, a professor of Middle East studies at Florida Atlantic University, and the author of *Future Jihad: Terrorist Strategies against America* (November 2005).

Introduction

Over a decade ago Samuel Huntington eloquently proposed a thesis that, with the end of the Cold War, "the fundamental source of conflict in this world will not be primarily ideological or primarily economic. The great division among humankind and the dominating source of conflict will be cultural."[1] Following the September 11 terror attacks on the United States by Muslim extremists and the country's response in the form of a U.S. war on terrorism and a strategy advancing freedom in the Greater Middle East, Huntington's thesis seems to have been validated by some Muslims and Westerners. The invasion by the United States of Afghanistan and Iraq has to some extent been interpreted in religious and cultural terms throughout the Muslim world in general and the Arab world in particular. Muslim religious scholars, considered moderate because they have condemned the September 11 terror attacks, have described Washington's war on terrorism as one against Islam and Muslims. The leading Lebanese Shi'ite cleric, Muhammad Hussein Fadlallah asserted that the "U.S.-led war on terror is, in reality, a war against Islam and Muslims around the world."[2]

This notion of a clash of civilization between the United States and the Muslim world has been surprisingly echoed by the secular Ba'thi regime of Syria. In fact, the Syrian regime has distinguished the clash as essentially anti-Arab, stemming from a historical ongoing hostility to Arab culture and existence. Commenting on the U.S. invasion of Iraq and violence in "Palestine," the Syrian minister for expatriate affairs Bouthaina Shaaban wrote in the Beirut daily, the *Daily Star*:

> The issue is deeper and more dangerous than this. It is a phenomena where Western anti-Semitism is transforming from its conventional form into a new one, where in the 21st century the Arabs have been officially

chosen as the new victim, one country after the other, one people after the
other—falling victims to hatred, killing, ethnic cleansing, torture, and
massacres under the pretext of a multitude of reasons and justifications,
including terrorism. They are not much different from the pretexts used
in the past, and cannot conceal from the observant researcher that at their
very essence they are but different expressions of anti-Arabism and hostility to Arab culture and existence.[3]

In one masterful stroke, Shaaban not only reinforced the notion of
a clash of civilization but also linked the U.S. invasion of Iraq to a
continuous systematic attack on the Arab world by the West. In other words, the invasion was none other than a stage in an ongoing
Western onslaught on the Arabs, with other Arab countries lined
up to become the next targets. Hence, Syria is next according to this
colonial plan to extinguish Arab culture and history. More specifically, the protection of Arab culture and history has become synonymous with the defense of Syria and, by extension, the Syrian
regime. In contrast to what Huntington proposes, to the extent that
each nationalism has its own ideology, the ideological conflict can
still be exploited by regimes suffering legitimacy problems. In Ba'thi
lexicon, it is Arab culture and common history that underpin the
tenets—freedom, unity, and socialism—of Ba'th ideology. Thus the
U.S.-Syrian ideological conflict could animate a "Cold War" between
the two nations, which claim to represent two encompassing cultures. This is how the Syrian regime is portraying its conflict with
Washington. But behind the logic of this Ba'thi Arab nationalist discourse lies an attempt at evoking Arab emotions and outrage with
the objective of undermining U.S. policies in the region and mobilizing Arab and Syrian support for the regime, all in the interest of its
survival.

Nevertheless, to assume that this new "Cold War" has emerged in
a vacuum is to misunderstand the overall dynamics of the development of the U.S.-Syrian conflict. Apprehensions, misunderstandings, and misconceptions have characterized the evolution of
U.S.-Syrian relations. In fact, a regional conflict provoked by mis-
calculation or misunderstanding may be inevitable.

This book attempts to understand the dynamics of U.S.-Syrian
relations by tracing them to Syria's emergence as an independent
state. The aim is to examine and analyze the subject comprehen-
sively by covering its phases with the purpose of identifying patterns and the changes they have produced in U.S. foreign policy
toward Syria. This forms the methodological basis of the book's comprehensive account of the U.S.-Syrian relationship. Behind my
objective of this complex study is an attempt not only to analyze
the experiences and dynamics that have brought the U.S.-Syrian

relationship to a state of "Cold War," but also to highlight the misconceptions and misunderstandings characterizing the relationship so that diplomacy could be properly exhausted without provoking a regional conflict neither Syria nor the United States would benefit from.

Upon analysis, it becomes clear that what lies at the basis of this new "Cold War" between Syria and the United States is a conflict over national security interests, and, more accurately, regime security interests. The U.S.-Syrian relationship went through several phases, each of which, generally speaking, served to intensify the apprehensions and misconceptions between the two countries. Syria's complicity in terrorism and its key regional role lay at the basis of the fluctuations in U.S.-Syrian relations. Even at the height of the peace process (1991–2000), which helped warm U.S.-Syrian relations, Washington's attitude toward Damascus remained ambivalent. This ambivalence, which helped maintain a cautious flexibility in U.S.-Syrian relations, all but dissipated when Damascus began to oppose U.S. invasion and subsequent occupation of Iraq. Similarly, Damascus had come to believe that the regional order Washington was implementing following the first Gulf War (1990–1991) heightened Syria's vulnerabilities. In fact, Damascus saw in the U.S. invasion of Iraq a confirmation of its premonitions.

Washington's war on terrorism and promotion of democracy in the greater Middle East have not only shattered the regional status quo, around which Syria built its reputation as the vanguard of Arab nationalism, but have also threatened the very survival of the regime. Protecting Syria's status quo in a shattered regional order by attempting to survive internal and external threats has become a momentous challenge for the Syrian leadership. It is against this background that the United States and Syria have set themselves on a collision course over terrorism, arms proliferation, Lebanon, the Middle East peace process, and, most importantly, Iraq. It is also partly on account of this that Syrian President Bashar al-Asad has broken with the pragmatist policy pattern established by the late ruler of modern Syria, Bashar's father, Hafiz al-Asad.

Complicating matters has been Syria's belief, shared by many Arabs and Muslims, of a grand plan, contrived in conservative circles in Washington, to subdue the Arabs in favor of a strong Israel. This belief sharpened the apprehensions between the two countries and exacerbated U.S.-Arab relations. Seen through the prism of Syria, the U.S. invasion of Iraq was a prelude to bring the Syrian regime into submission or to its downfall. Thus the United States, and by extension Israel, could dominate the region.

Correspondingly, Washington seeks to implement a Pax Americana at the expense of Arabs in general and Syria in particular. Believing it is fighting for its survival, Syria has abandoned its traditional restraint, increasing the chances of a regional conflict. The Syrian regime, meanwhile, has exploited Arab and Syrian unfavorable public opinion toward the United States to bolster its declining legitimacy. President Asad has emerged as the Arab leader par excellence championing Arab nationalism and opposing U.S. intervention in Iraq.

At the same time, the internal challenges facing the Syrian leadership have been compounded by a reform movement gathering momentum by the day while growing disillusioned with the regime's insignificant reforms. Once the regime felt that the trickle of reform could transform into a deluge that could sweep it away, it sent a stern message that it would not tolerate reforms it could not control. Apparently, the will of the regime's hard-liners prevailed over the impulse of the regime's moderates to reform. Yet, adamant as they are about demanding reform, reformers have found themselves stuck between their nationalist feelings and the regime's selective and insignificant reforms. Theirs has been so far a fight for reform expressed in nationalist terms. Although U.S. efforts to promote democracy in the region have indirectly put pressure on Syria to reform, many reformers have maintained their reservations about U.S. plans and intentions. Significantly, they shared with the regime an alarming belief that Islamists may attempt to assume power under the banner of democracy. Paradoxically, the regime may be playing a dangerous game encouraging Islamic revival. Recognizing that they are at one with the Islamists in opposing the U.S. presence and plans in the Middle East, the Syrian leadership, besides allegedly supporting the insurgency in Iraq, has apparently turned a blind eye to Islamists supporting the ongoing insurgency.

But Syria's vulnerable point may turn out to be Lebanon. To the extent that Syrian activities in Lebanon have under certain circumstances shaped U.S.-Syrian relations, Beirut has been vital to Damascus's domestic and regional politics. Supported internationally, growing Lebanese opposition to Syrian occupation of Lebanon countermanded Syrian plans to entrench its position to control the country's domestic affairs. This conflict polarized Lebanon along confessional/sectarian lines. But Syrian high-handedness and blatant interference in sensitive political matters alienated even the most ardent supporters of the Syrian order in Lebanon. The assassination of former Prime Minister Rafiq Hariri, allegedly by Damascus, launched a grass-roots movement for democracy and freedom.

The Syrian order came crashing down, and Syrian troops withdrew from Lebanon after 29 years of the ruthless reign of Machiavellian politics and terror. The Syrian withdrawal generated new political dynamics for Lebanon full of promises of national reconciliation and integration but fraught with danger revolving around Hizbollah's future role. Most important, the Syrian-imposed security regime all but collapsed, putting Lebanon in a unique position in the Middle East. Lebanon's transition to democracy and the rule of law could transform Middle Eastern politics, which have been dictated by totalitarian and security regimes. Whereas Washington would support such a transition, Damascus would try to maintain the status quo to protect its security regime.

The future of the region and the fate of the U.S. war on terrorism, Lebanon, Iraq, and the Middle East peace process may well depend on how Washington and Damascus deal with each other. Fought under the pretext of an ideology underscoring Arab common culture and history, as well as unity, this new "Cold War" over national and regime security interests could at a maximum provoke a regional war and at a minimum spur profound change in the Middle East.

In carrying out this study, I found it necessary to devote the first chapter to Syria's nationalist struggle for independence and the emergence of modern Syria under the Ba'thi rule of Hafiz al-Asad. The chapter analyzes the impact of Arab nationalism on the collective consciousness of the Syrians. Chapter 2 examines U.S.-Syrian relations against the background of the Arab-Israeli conflict and the Cold War. It also analyzes the implications of the rivalry between the United States and the Soviet Union for U.S. policy in the region, as well as Arab grievances against Western support for Israel. Chapter 3 investigates the emergence of the U.S. ambivalent attitude toward Syria. It also investigates the role of terrorism in shaping the U.S.-Syrian relationship, as well as the Lebanese setting and the emergence of Hizbollah. Chapter 4 examines U.S. foreign policy toward Syria during the peace process (1991–2000). It also scrutinizes the regional security concerns that Syria and the United States had to contend with. Chapter 5 examines the shift in U.S. foreign policy toward Syria following the September 11 terror attacks. It surveys the smooth transition of power in Syria and the new configuration in the region following Israel's withdrawal from Lebanon and the U.S. invasion of Iraq. It also traces the events leading to considering Syria a de facto member in the countries making up the "axis of evil." Chapter 6 scrutinizes the contentious issues gripping the U.S.-Syrian conflict and evaluates the actions and plans undertaken by the two countries vis-à-vis each other, which have set Washington and Damascus on a collision course. It investigates the domestic setting and sociopolitical dynamics in Syria and their impact on the Syrian regime's policies. It also assesses the patterns and prospects for regional conflicts. Chapter 7 examines the Lebanese political setting and the convergence of international and Lebanese interests to free Lebanon from Syrian occupation. It traces the collapse of the Syrian order in Lebanon, and examines the new political dynamics generated by the Syrian withdrawal from the country. It also probes the impact of the collapse of the Syrian-imposed security regime on the potential emergence of a free democratic state in the Middle East and its implication for U.S. foreign policy, regional politics, and the Lebanon-Syria-U.S. triangular relationship. Chapter 8 investigates the Ba'thi regime's responses to mounting international pressure and its humiliating evacuation from Lebanon. It also analyzes the impact of these responses on the regime's attitude toward domestic and regional challenges and threats and their implications for Syria, Lebanon, and the United States. The book's conclusion assesses Damascus's and Washington's policy options and discusses the cultural attack mounted by Syria on the United States, which could make a clash of civilization a self-fulfilling prophecy.

Abbreviations

AIPAC	American Israel Public Affairs Committee
ALC	American Lebanese Coalition
ANM	Arab Nationalist Movement
CENTCOM	U.S. Central Command
CIA	Central Intelligence Agency
DFLP	Democratic Front for the Liberation of Palestine
DOD	Department of Defense
EU	European Union
EUCOM	U.S. European Command
GAP	South Anatolian Project
GCC	Gulf Cooperation Council
IDF	Israel Defense Forces
JPMG	Joint Political and Military Group
LF	Lebanese Forces
MAD	Mutual Assured Destruction
MEDO	Middle East Defense Organization
MFO	Multinational Force and Observers
MNF	Multinational Peacekeeping Force
MOA	Memorandum of Agreement
NATO	North Atlantic Treaty Organization
PFLP	Popular Front for the Liberation of Palestine
PFLP-GC	Popular Front for the Liberation of Palestine-General Command
PKK	Kurdistan Workers Party
PLO	Palestine Liberation Organization
PNF	Progressive National Front
PSP	Progressive Socialist Party
SAL	South Lebanon Army
SALSRA	Syria Accountability and Lebanese Sovereignty Restoration Act
SAM	Surface-to-Air-Missiles
SANA	Syrian Arabic News Agency
SCP	Syrian Communist Party

SDN	Specially Designated Nationals
SOLIDE	Support for Lebanese in Detention and Exile
SSNP	Syrian Social National Movement
UAR	United Arab Republic
UAV	Unmanned Air Vehicle
UNIFIL	U.N. Interim Force in Lebanon
UNTSO	U.N. Truce Supervision Organization
WMD	Weapons of Mass Destruction
WLCU	World Lebanese Cultural Union

CHAPTER 1

Cradle of Arab Nationalism: The Fatherland, the Ba'th, and Modern Syria under al-Asad

The modern state of Syria emerged through a searing nationalist process that made the country the heartbeat of Arab nationalism and the epicenter of the idealized, though illusory, Arab nation. Anticolonialism and Arab unity (based on common culture, language, and history) had become not only the basis of the nationalist movements at the time of the British and French mandates over the Arab countries but also the impulse behind transforming Arab nationalism into one inspired by Germanophilia, or German nationalism. Founded by two Syrians, the Ba'th party typified this strident form of nationalism, which was able to crystallize the notion that the artificial division of the Arab world by the colonialists, along with the corrupt political orders throughout the newly independent Arab states, were at the root of the backward political, social, and economic conditions of the Arabs. These conditions necessitated that a vanguard party, the Ba'th, lead society. This marked the radical transformation of the party. However, Ba'th rivalry as well as internal and regional problems and conflicts paved the way for Hafiz al-Asad to seize power and undo Ba'th radicalization in the interest of Arab cooperation against Israel. Yet, he was pragmatic enough to realize Syria's vulnerabilities and thus sacrifice Arab nationalism at the altar of Syrian national interests in general and regime security in particular. In the process, he built an authoritarian, security state. At the same time, although he robbed the Ba'th party of its ideological raison d'être, he remained adamant about the total return of the Israeli-occupied Golan Heights to Syria as a matter of national interest and national honor.

On account of all this, Arab nationalism grew out of Syria but in the collective consciousness of many Syrians had not grown apart from Syria with the emergence of independent Arab states, with the result that Arab issues remained to a great extent inseparable from Syrian issues. This is the legacy of Syrian nationalism.

The Emergence of Arab Nationalism and the Concept of Greater Syria

The ideational base out of which Arab nationalism grew had its earliest expression in the thoughts articulated by certain activist Muslim intellectuals in response to their growing awareness of the weakness of the Muslim world before European military and political challenges. Those intellectuals opposed European encroachment upon the Arab world, which was under Ottoman Muslim rule. Jamal al-Din al-Afghani (1839–1897), a Persian by birth, regarded religion as a temporal political force that would bring about Muslim unity. He preached "Muslim unity and solidarity in the face of European encroachments."[1] Although al-Afghani transformed Islam into an ideology of a protonationalist type that took the form of pan-Islamism, his pan-Islamist concept emphasized building a new consciousness of Muslim solidarity against colonialism.[2]

Muhammad Abdu (1849–1905), a pupil of al-Afghani, shared the latter's views but went a step further to advocate the freeing of the Muslim mind from the fetters of tradition.[3] H.A.R. Gibb noted that Abdu worked for the "purification of Islam from corrupting influences and practices… and the defense of Islam against European influences and Christian attacks."[4] Abdu believed that Islam is an all-embracing system, and sought to revitalize it through cultural activity, which included modernizing the Arabic language. His goal was to affirm that modern culture was not incompatible with Islam "as long as it does not encroach upon the latter's claim to be an all-embracing system."[5]

Rashid Rida (1865–1935), a pupil of Abdu, who was born in Syria and settled in Egypt, expressed his dissatisfaction with the state of Islam at the time and his desire to reform it. Rida emphasized Arab solidarity (*asabiyya*), which rested on the Arabic language and Arab centrality in Islam. But in contrast to Abdu, Rida worked for a puritanical revival of Islam. Sylvia Haim noted the connection between Rida, al-Afghani, and Abdu which was premised on Islamic reform through the *Salafiyya* movement (the return to the ways of the ancestors). She remarked that "it is in the arguments of the *Salafiyya* that we may trace the first intellectual burgeoning of Arab nationalism."[6]

Abd al-Rahman al-Kawakibi (1849–1902), another follower of Abdu and a Syrian like Rida, who settled in Egypt in 1898, opposed Ottoman as well as European rule over the Arab world (by 1882 Egypt had become a British colony). Al-Kawakibi argued that Ottoman tyranny had caused the decline of Muslim civilization and the stagnation of Islam. He emphasized that Arabs (of the Arabian Peninsula) only can effect the regeneration of Islam. He envisioned an Islamic union spiritually led by an Arab caliph residing in Mecca.[7]

These activists played something of a nationalist role as they revitalized an Islamic movement directed against foreign domination, emphasizing pan-Arab sentiment. But, as Bassam Tibi rightly observed, the movement must be considered an inherent part of the nationalist movement in the Middle East, although in the minds of its own protagonists they were not nationalist but Muslim.[8]

This revitalized Islamic movement planted the seeds of pan-Arabist thought, but its role eventually crumbled before the rising tide of secular nationalism, inaugurated indirectly by the Lebanese Christians' national literary renaissance, which ushered the second and more explicit phase in the development of the Arab nationalist idea. The Arabic literary awakening was the consequence of two related factors: Missionary activities and the reforms of Muhammad Ali. As European powers continued to make political and economic inroads in the Ottoman Empire, particularly in the nineteenth century, they supported their penetration with missionary activities in the Arab Middle East. The cultural and political ideas spread by these missionaries appealed to many in the multinational and multireligious Ottoman Empire, especially to the Lebanese Christians. The political climate under which the Christian missions operated improved drastically when the reforms of Muhammad Ali emancipated the Christians in Lebanon and Syria (1831–1840). The emancipation changed the social structure of Lebanon and Syria and significantly opened them up to Western influence.

The Americans and French led the missionary activities. But, whereas the French pursued a colonialist policy, the Americans, who entertained no colonial ideas, were more interested in revitalizing the Arabic language in order to popularize their religious activities. An unintended consequence of revitalizing the Arabic language was the inauguration of a national literary awakening. It was the literary work of Christian scholars, such as Nasif al-Yaziji (1800–1871), Faris al-Shidyaq (1805–1887), and Butrus al-Bustani (1819–1883), that revived the Arab national culture, thereby arousing national consciousness. According to George Antonius, Ibrahim al-Yaziji (1847–1905), the son of Nasif, was the first Arab nationalist author to compose a poem, eulogizing Arab achievements, denouncing sectarian strife, and inciting Arab insurgency against the Turks.[9]

This trend of cultural nationalism was reinforced by the establishment of the Syrian Protestant College in Beirut in 1866 (later the American University of Beirut), which graduated the first generation of secular Arab nationalists. Although cultural nationalism emphasized the existence of an Arab "nation," it did not call for an independent state. For the Christians, Arab cultural nationalism served as the best means to transcend their minority status and, at the same time, to undermine Arab loyalty to the Ottoman Empire, which was predicated on a religious (Muslim) identity. This set in motion a growing desire for articulating pan-Arab and anti-Ottoman sentiments. Negib Azoury, a Christian Arab, founded a secret society called *La Ligue de la Patrie Arabe* in Paris in 1904; then a year later he published his book *Le Reveil de la Nation Arabe dans L'Asie Turque*. Much in the same vein as Nasif al-Yaziji, Azoury declared the existence of an Arab nation and called for the creation of an Arab empire in the Middle East, not including Egypt, for Azoury did not consider the Egyptians as Arabs.[10]

Meanwhile, the Ottoman state was experiencing a steep decline in its power in large measure due to the activities of the nationalist (separatist) movements in its Balkan territories. A group of Turkish reformers, known as the Young Turks, revolted against the Sultan (1908) and set about to reform the Empire and arrest its decomposition. Turkish nationalism and centralization of the Empire were to be the main vehicles of reform. The Arabs of the Empire perceived the process of Turkification, which intimated the superiority of Turkish elements above all other elements in the Empire, as an open attack on their identity, language, and race. Consequently, they organized several secret societies with a pan-Arabist orientation. Thus, ironically, the Turks strengthened the movement of pan-Arab, nationalist thought.

Among the most important secret societies were *Al-Jam'iyyat al-Arabiyya al-Fatat* (the young Arab society) and *Jam'iyyat al-Ahd* (the society of the covenant). Al-Fatat was founded in Paris in 1911 by Syrian students, and in 1913 its headquarters were moved to Damascus. Al-Ahd was founded in Istanbul in 1913 and was composed entirely of Arab army officers, the majority of whom were Iraqis.[11] Al-Fatat took a leading role in organizing an Arab congress in Paris in 1913. All the participants agreed on the reality of an "Arab nation" distinct from other nations, which "only included the Arabic-speaking Asiatic portion of the Ottoman Empire."[12] Egypt was not included in the "Arab nation." At this point, I would like to say that this overview leads me to conclude that the seeds of the concept of Greater Syria, as the core of the "Arab nation," were sown in this congress. These seeds evolved during World War I and in light of its aftermath to constitute the crux of the Greater Syria concept.

When the Ottoman Empire entered World War I against the British and the French, Arab nationalists faced the inescapable dilemma of having to choose sides. This dilemma marked the third phase in the development of the Arab nationalist idea. Ottoman harsh rule in Syria helped the Arab nationalists in their decision to break away from their Turkish masters. Members of al-Fatat approached Sharif Hussein, the Hashimite ruler of Hijaz, to form an alliance with them and to lead the uprising. Meanwhile, Hussein had established contacts with the British, who had significant interest and influence in all the Arab lands. Between 1915 and 1916 letters were exchanged between Henry Macmahon, the High Commissioner for Egypt and Sudan, and Hussein (known as the Hussein-Macmahon Correspondence). In these letters, the British, in vaguely worded promises, offered Hussein a guarantee of his right to rule Arabia and other Arab lands of the Ottoman Empire if he consented to commit his forces on the side of the war efforts of the Allies.[13]

This British promise to Hussein was substantially contravened by a counterpledge in the form of a secret agreement among Russia, France, and Britain (the Sykes-Picot Agreement) according to which Britain and France were to divide the Arab territories of the Ottoman Empire among themselves after the war. Under this agreement France was to have a great part of Syria, Britain was to have Iraq in addition to the port cities of Haifa and Acre, while parts of Palestine were to be placed under an international administration.[14] Another pledge that raised controversy between the Arab nationalists and Britain, was the Balfour Declaration. On November 2, 1917, Great Britain revealed what came to be known as the Balfour Declaration in the form of a letter addressed to Lord Rothschild. The letter made it known that "His Majesty's Government views with favor the establishment in Palestine of a national home for the Jewish people."[15]

Coming on the heels of the Sykes-Picot treaty revelations, the Arab nationalists were greatly disturbed by the Balfour Declaration. They perceived the Balfour promise as nonbinding and invalidated by the British guarantees to Sharif Hussein. According to the British, the correspondence had excluded Palestine from the territories promised to the Arabs.[16] Despite this misunderstanding, the Arab nationalists fought alongside the British. Prince Faisal, the son of Sharif Hussein, led the Arab revolt that ended triumphantly in Damascus in the fall of 1918, whereupon he established his Arab Military Government. But after driving the Turks out, the British divided the former Ottoman territory of the Arab parts of Asia, with the exception of the Arabian Peninsula, into three military administrations, keeping one under their control and giving the other two to Faisal and the French. This greatly disappointed the Arab nationalists who expected to rule over all these Arab lands.

Consequently, since the Arabian Peninsula remained outside the British division, the Arab nationalists began to focus their political efforts on the remaining land mass that was subjected to this British division and that extended from the Mediterranean in the west to Iraq in the east. This land mass was referred to as "Syria" under the Ottomans and was known in general as Bilad al-Sham by the Arab population (after the Arab conquest in the seventh century). Since the Ottomans structured this land mass, "Syria," into administrative divisions, one of which was called the Province (Vilayet) of Syria, the whole region was subsequently referred to by many Arabs as Greater Syria as well. Greater Syria comprised what is today Syria, Lebanon, Jordan, and Israel. It was within this context that the Arab nationalists began to infuse into the geographical concept of Greater Syria a political meaning, reinforcing it, on the one hand, by the cultural bonds asserted by Arab cultural nationalism, and, on the other, by the sheer political weight of the fact that Arab nationalism had emerged from Greater Syria. The Arab nationalists actualized this by their responses to the unfolding events consequent upon British and French political maneuvering in the region.

Fearing French colonial ambitions in Lebanon and Syria and suspicious of British intentions, Faisal sought to strengthen his regime. He declared his kingdom, the Arab Syrian Government, and sought to enlist Zionist support. Faisal met the Zionist leader, Chaim Weizman, in Aqaba and later on met with other Zionist leaders in London to discuss Arab-Jewish cooperation. As a result, a historic agreement was born in January 1919 that was "mindful of the racial kinship and ancient bonds existing between the Arabs and the Jewish people, and realizing that the surest means of working out the consummation of their national aspirations is through the closest possible collaboration in the development of the Arab State and Palestine...."[17] Nonetheless, in an addendum to the agreement, Faisal made its implementation conditional upon the Arabs obtaining their independence.[18] Apparently Faisal signed the agreement hoping to enlist not only Jewish economic potential in building his state but also Jewish influence with Great Britain to vitiate France's claim to the control of Syria. He also hoped that Zionist political clout could help secure international support for Arab self-determination.

Scores of Arab nationalists strongly rejected Faisal's agreement with the Zionists, in which Arab recognition of a Jewish national home in Palestine was affirmed and Jewish immigration into it was encouraged. Concomitantly, Arab political activity in Palestine converged with that of Syria. A significant number of Palestinian nationalists had already proclaimed their loyalty to the Arab government in Damascus and denounced the Balfour Declaration. In February 1919, Palestinian delegates to a political meeting, referred to as the First Palestinian National Congress, endorsed by a majority a position that considered "Palestine as part of Syria as it has never been separated from it at any time."[19] This position reflected more a concern over the future of Palestine than over the issue of unity with Syria. The underlying assumption was that Palestine, as part of Greater Syria, referred to as "Southern Syria," under the rule of King Faisal, would provide the best reason for invalidating Zionist claims and British rule.

Taking note of Arab nationalist aspirations and concerned with the future of the French and British military administrations in Syria, Faisal attended the Paris Peace Conference and made the case for the independence and unity of Greater Syria. He laid special emphasis on the cultural, geographical, and economic factors that bonded the Arabs of Greater Syria together.[20] Faisal also proposed that a commission of inquiry be sent to Syria and Palestine to find out the aspirations of the population. The proposal was endorsed by President Woodrow Wilson, with the result that an American commission, known as the King-Crane Commission, toured Syria and Palestine in June and July of 1919. Upon his return to Damascus in May, Faisal with the cooperation of al-Fatat (which had transformed itself into the Arab Independence Party) called for a general congress to prepare themselves for the commission of inquiry. The Syrian General Congress, known in Arabic as the *Al-Mu'tamar as-Suri al-Am,* was convened in July and was attended by delegates also from Lebanon and Palestine.

The Congress passed resolutions calling for the independence of Syria with its boundaries covering the land mass of Greater Syria and asking to maintain the unity of the country whereby Lebanon and Palestine remain inseparable parts of Syria. The Congress did not recognize any French governmental right to any part of Syria. In addition, the Congress rejected the "claims of the Zionists for the establishment of a Jewish commonwealth in that part of southern Syria which is known as Palestine."[21] After soliciting opinion from the local population and witnessing the events of the Syrian

General Congress, the King-Crane Commission issued a report that supported some of the resolutions of the Syrian General Congress. It recommended that Palestine and Lebanon remain united with Syria and that Syria be placed for a limited time under either an American or a British mandate. Though the Commission expressed sympathy for the Jewish cause, it recommended restrictions on Jewish immigration and against the project of making Palestine distinctly a Jewish commonwealth.[22]

The resolutions of the Syrian General Congress, along with the recommendations of the King-Crane Commission, constituted a watershed in Syria's history for they enabled the idea of Greater Syria to crystallize as a single political community in the minds of many Arab nationalists. Palestinian nationalism became part of Greater Syria's aspirations for independence and unity, consequently serving as a timeless pretext for many Syrian nationalists to intervene in Palestinian affairs whenever the circumstances behooved them. However, the Syrian General Congress and the King-Crane Commission meant little to Britain and especially to France. In an effort to evade a clash with France over Syria and to keep its commitments under the Sykes-Picot Agreement, Britain decided to withdraw its troops from Syria and Lebanon in September 1919. Faisal and the Syrian nationalists learned of Britain's intentions, particularly at a time when France had dramatically increased the number of its troops in the region. At the urging of Syrian nationalists, Faisal convened another congress in March 1920, at which the call for unity and independence was reiterated. Meanwhile, the Allied powers had decided to meet at San Remo, Italy, in April to decide the fate of the former Ottoman territories. At San Remo, the Allies accorded Britain mandatory jurisdiction over Palestine, and France over Syria and Lebanon. The ostensible purpose of these mandates was to promote the well-being and the development of the indigenous population so as to prepare them to rule themselves and meet the challenges of the modern world. With this international recognition of their rights in Syria, the French moved in on Damascus and dethroned Faisal.

On July 24, 1922, the League of Nations officially approved the British and French mandates and incorporated the Balfour Declaration in the charter of the British Mandate.[23] Not only was Greater Syria dismantled and Arab independence denied, but also the foundation was laid for securing the establishment of a national Jewish home in Palestine. France and Britain had fashioned a new political map in the Middle East roughly conforming to the imperial arrangements of the Sykes-Picot Agreement. This division made a lasting impression on Arab nationalism. It idealized the concept of Greater

Syria as an historic reality by an act of historical retrojection from the present unto the past to prove Greater Syria's political viability. To many Arab nationalists the thinking went as follows: Had Greater Syria not been a united political community, it would not have been divided.

However, the partition of Greater Syria created novel realities. With Faisal dethroned and France ruling Syria and Lebanon while Britain ruled Palestine, Palestinian nationalists faced a new situation where it was more practical for them to fight for the independence of Palestine than to fight for the unity of Palestine with Syria. At the Third Arab Congress, held in Haifa in December 1920, the delegates emphasized the autonomy of the Palestinian Arabs and the need to develop a new strategy dealing exclusively with Palestine. The Palestinian notable Musa Kazim al-Husseini remarked, "Now, after the recent events in Damascus, we have to effect a complete change in our plans here. Southern Syria no longer exists. We must defend Palestine."[24]

In my judgment, this could easily be regarded as the starting point of what was later to become Palestinian nationalism. This development ushered the next phase in the evolution of the Arab nationalist idea.

Syria: The Hub of Nationalist Development

Many Syrian nationalists remained more attached to the idea of Arab unity than the Palestinian nationalists. But their position was greatly circumscribed by the specificity of French rule over Syria and by the character of their leadership. At the time the French took control over Syria, Sunni Muslims constituted 69 percent of the population, heterodox Muslims (Alawis, Druzes, Ismailis) 16 percent, and Christians (Catholics, Uniates, Greek Orthodox) 14 percent.[25] Socioeconomic and cultural differences were inseparable from religious and urban-rural divisions. The mountains and hill districts harbored compact minorities. The Druzes had concentrated southeast of Damascus in Jabal al-Druze and Alawis in the Alawi mountains northwest of Latakia. In the northeast, the Jazira province contained significant communities of Christians and Kurds. Rural-urban and class contrasts more often than not coincided with sectarian differences between urban Sunni Muslims and rural confessional minorities.

The French exploited the ethnic and religious differences in order to contain the spread of Arab nationalism advocated by the urban leadership, drawn from an absentee landowning class and a commercial bourgeoisie. The French put Syria through several territorial alterations between 1920 and 1923 that took the penulti-mate shape in 1924. Syria, then, comprised the former Ottoman provinces of *Sham* (Syria) and Aleppo and the district of Alexan-dretta. But the state excluded the Territory of the Alawis around the Latakia region and the Jabal al-Druze. The Jazira province was not given formal autonomy and was placed under direct French administration. The French also favored the military recruitment of Alawis, Druzes, and other minorities in their newly formed Troupes Speciales du Levant, which subsequently constituted the embryo of the Syrian national army.

However, this exploitative policy that rested on subdividing Syria had the reverse effect of fostering the growth of Arab nationalism rather than undermining it. Political alliances were strengthened among the four cities of Damascus, Homs, Aleppo, and Hama, as well as forged between the urban leadership and members of minor-ity groups. When a local uprising against the French erupted in the Jabal al-Druze in 1925, the Druze leadership cooperated with the urban leadership to expand the uprising, transforming it into a nationalist revolt. The revolt expanded in time and space as it engulfed the major cities in Syria, and came to be known as the Great Syrian Revolt (1925–1927). The French used all means at their disposal to quell it, including shelling Syria's major cities and chasing many nationalists out of Syria. The revolt was very costly for the Syrians. It claimed the lives of thousands and uprooted a staggering number of the population. In addition, it destroyed swaths of agricultural lands in the countryside and towns and para-lyzed commerce, both of which formed the economic basis of the urban leadership.[26] The urban leadership decided to end the revolt not only because of French military might but also because their economic interests had suffered greatly.

With the failure of the Great Revolt, the urban leadership decided to rule out armed struggle as a vehicle for independence. Many Syrian nationalists, including a number who had fled Syria, had resigned themselves to the fact that they should play politics accord-ing to French rules to bring about independence. This pragmatic approach was promoted by a significant number of the urban leader-ship represented now by the National Bloc, which emerged as the main nationalist organization in Syria. The nationalist Bloc leader-ship, headed by Jamil Mardam, reconciled itself to the fact of the mandate and cooperated with the French. They followed what came to be known as the policy of "honorable cooperation," whereby a modus vivendi was struck between them and the French.[27] The log-ic behind this policy meant that the National Bloc would work to secure first small Syria's independence before participating in a

Greater Syria scheme. In turn, the French (High Commissioner) recognized only the nationalist Bloc leaders as the representatives of the Syrian people.

On the surface, the corollary of the policy of honorable cooperation entailed diminished support for the Palestinians until mandatory Syria gained its independence. But on close examination, the nationalist Bloc leaders were concerned that any pan-Arab activity on their part, especially with regard to Palestine, would jeopardize their relations with the British, who might deny these leaders diplomatic support in their future negotiations with the French. More specifically, the nationalist Bloc leaders were keen not to disrupt their newly founded relations with the French, who might marginalize them and thus break their monopoly of power. All in all, this translated into a tepid support for the Palestinians, a support more symbolic than material, pushing to the background the concept of Greater Syria.

When Britain concluded with Iraq a treaty in 1930 promising it independence and entry into the League of Nations, the National Bloc sought to negotiate a similar treaty with France and purposely avoided all pan-Arab activities. Significantly, in December 1931, the National Bloc did not send an official delegation to the Jerusalem Congress organized by the Mufti of Jerusalem, Hajj Amin al-Husseini, to present the Palestinian cause to the Muslim world.[28] But this did not mean that all National Bloc leaders were at one in discouraging pan-Arab activities. Shukri al-Quwatli, the head of the radical faction of the Bloc, the Istiqlal party, remained committed to pan-Arabism and challenged Jamil Mardam, the architect of honorable cooperation. However, al-Quwatli's challenge was meant more to discredit Mardam than to break the National Bloc's negotiations for a treaty with the French. In any event, treaty negotiations proved to be futile, and the Bloc was tarnished with charges of collaboration with the French. This contributed to the emergence of radical nationalist organizations.

Disapproving of French and British colonial rule of the Arab world, a group of radical Arab nationalists, mainly from Syria, organized a conference in 1933 in the Lebanese town of Qarna'il during which they founded the League of National Action. The declared goals of the new organization were Arab unity and independence, emphasizing political, economic, and cultural integration, as well as Arab sovereignty.[29] The League attracted many radical Syrian nationalist youths, who were dissatisfied with the National Bloc leadership. These youths were for the most part students of the most important public high school in Damascus, known as *al-Tajhiz,* and the Law Faculty, two hotbeds of revolutionary ideas. The League organized many youth demonstrations and emerged as an effective instrument in challenging the policies of the National Bloc. Given his pan-Arabist credentials and opposition to Mardam, al-Quwatli was able to woo the League's leaders and thus to put Mardam's leadership on the defensive.

With his honorable cooperation with the French leading nowhere and being under attack from al-Quwatli and the League, Mardam began to look beyond the borders, particularly to Palestine, to rehabilitate his nationalist image and to counterattack his domestic foes. Consequently, Mardam had to set a tough tone against the French and the Zionists. When the Arab Revolt in Palestine (1936–1939) erupted, the National Bloc leadership supported the Palestinian Arabs. But this support was also the outcome of a heightened political awareness of the precarious future of Arab Palestine. The Zionists had built a solid economic and political base there, potentially shifting the locus of power in the country in their favor. The Syrians shared Palestinian concern that the Zionists, with the complicity of Great Britain, had made strides in preparing for the creation of an independent Jewish state, potentially threatening Syrian vital interests. From a political standpoint, the Syrians feared that a Jewish state could serve as an instrument of colonial policies, further undermining Arab unity and progress. From an economic standpoint, the Syrians feared that Zionist enterprises with a high level of agricultural, technical, and commercial expertise could ruin the Syrian economy. Since Palestine constituted the most valuable export market for Syrian products during the Mandate, Jewish competitive products could well find their way into the market, thus driving Syrian enterprises out of business. In addition, Jewish virtual control of the port of Haifa had already negatively affected Syrian transit trade, an important component of the Syrian economy.[30]

Led by the League of National Action and various Islamic benevolent societies (*jam'iyyat*), Syrian pan-Arab nationalists took to the streets of Damascus demonstrating in solidarity with the Arab Revolt. The Palestine Defense Committee was established in Damascus to help the Arab Palestinians. This Committee convened a pan-Arab Congress in the Syrian city of Bludan in 1937 that voted to fight Zionism and coordinate insurrectionary activities. According to Eli Kedourie, the Congress was a landmark in the Arab world's involvement in the Palestine problem, although its resolutions were more anti-Zionist than anti-British.[31] Many Syrian nationalists left for Palestine to participate in the rebellion. Many Palestinian guerrilla leaders wanted by the British escaped to Syria, which gave them political asylum.

However, this support was soon tempered as a result of two main factors. The absentee landowning class and commercial bourgeoisie associated with the National Bloc leadership discouraged the prolongation of the Arab Revolt because it disrupted trade with Palestine, hurting their economic interests. During 1936–1937, the leadership of the National Bloc avoided jeopardizing its resumed negotiations with the newly elected French socialist government of Leon Blum, who was Jewish. The renewal of the moderate policy by the National Bloc further radicalized the Syrian nationalists. For those nationalists, Palestine served as a litmus test for the viability of their pan-Arab ideology. For the veteran nationalists of the Bloc, Palestine manifested the divide between the attraction of pan-Arabism, which enhanced their political posture, and the pull of Syrian provincialism, which safeguarded their interests. This is how Palestine figured in Syrian politics at the time.

As the Arab Revolt in Palestine was losing momentum, the French government refused to ratify the Treaty of 1936 negotiated with the National Bloc and ceded the district of Alexandretta (Hatay) to Turkey in a bid to keep it neutral in the looming World War II. This scrapped whatever remained of the National Bloc's policy of honorable cooperation with the French and reinforced the radical climate within nationalist circles. The pan-Arab nationalist al-Quwatli, supported by the League of National Action, emerged as the new leader of the National Bloc. Under his leadership, Arab Palestine was perceived as an inseparable part of Arab unity and Greater Syria. At the same time, many Syrian nationalists had become dissatisfied even with the radical League of National Action, whose leadership had been co-opted by al-Quwatli. Important leaders of the League, such as Zaki al-Arsuzi (from the district of Alexandretta) and Jalal Sayyid broke with the organization, contributing to its gradual dissolution. Other youth organizations such as the Hama Youth (*al-Shabab al-Hamawi*) eclipsed the League of National Action by outstripping it in fiercely demonstrating against both the National Bloc and the colonial rulers.[32]

Meanwhile, these interwar developments transformed Arab nationalism itself. Whereas the political ideals of early Arab nationalists were grounded in Western liberalism, constitutionalism, and representative democracy, British and French colonization of the Middle East cast a pall over those ideals. Arab nationalists could no longer use Western ideals to support their nationalism, particularly when nationalism became synonymous with decolonization. Germany, on the other hand, presented an ideological basis better suited for Arab nationalism. The Germans based their nationalism on the Volk (the people sharing common history, language, and culture). At the beginning of the nineteenth century, they rallied and fought against the Napoleonic army that conquered their Germanic states, ejecting the French enemy along with his Revolutionary ideals. Basing their nationalism on the German Volk, they succeeded in uniting Germany in 1871. German nationalism appealed to many Arab nationalists.

This German example led to the introduction of a still newer phase in the development of the Arab nationalist idea. The main architect and representative of this phase is without doubt the theoretician Sati al-Husri. Actually, this prominent Arab nationalist is largely credited with transforming Arab nationalism from Anglophilia and Francophilia in the direction of Germanophilia. This Syrian, who was influenced by the German Romantics, drew the parallel between the Arab predicament at the time with that of Germany in the nineteenth century. Al-Husri stated:

> A common language and a common history is the basis of nation formation and nationalism....If we want to define the role of language and history for a nation we can say in short that the language is the soul and the life of the nation, but history is its memory and its consciousness.[33]

Al-Husri's novelty was that he provided the theoretical foundation to prove the existence of the Arab nation through language and history in spite of the partition wrought on it by the colonialists. His focus was Arab unity. If the Germans, through their Volk, were able to overcome their socioeconomic and political problems and thus unite, why, given the similarity of the Arab situation to that of Germany, could not the Arabs do the same? Arabs could unite and thus become strong enough to defeat the foreign powers. This new Germanophile wave of thought in the Arab world intensified Arab opposition to colonialism and, in particular, to Zionism.

Many Arab nationalists did not conceal their hope that Germany might defeat the Allies, thus freeing the Arab world from their grip. In fact, when the Nazis defeated France in 1940 and Syria remained under the control of the Vichy Government, the country was made available to the German Air Force to provide support to Rashid Ali el-Kilani's anti-British revolt in Iraq. Indeed, many Syrian nationalists supported Kilani. While some, such as Michel Aflaq and Salah al-Din Bitar, organized demonstrations in Damascus in solidarity with Kilani, others such as Jamal al-Atasi and Akram al-Hawrani along with some army officers went to Iraq to offer their services to Kilani's government.[34] These nationalists later formed the Ba'th party (as we shall see), which had a tremendous impact on Arab politics. But, at the time, these radical nationalists served as a pressure group on the National Bloc reinforcing its pan-Arab orientation, particularly when it came to the issue of Palestine. When, in 1942, the Zionist leaders adopted the "Biltmore Program," which urged "that the gates of Palestine be opened..., and that Palestine be established as a Jewish Commonwealth,"[35] the Arab nationalist movement in Syria shed all voices of moderation and pragmatism.

Fearing that Syria might fall under Nazi control, the British and the Free French Forces occupied Lebanon and Syria in June 1941. The Free French General, Georges Catroux, in the name of Free France, issued a declaration promising independence to Syria and Lebanon.[36] Other than rejoining the Alawi Territory and Jabal al-Druze to the Syrian government's control in February 1942, the declaration meant little to the Free French who kept their control of Syria, fueling the anger of the Syrian nationalists. Facing an inflexible French ruler, demonstrations broke out in Damascus and other towns in 1945. In May, the French heavily shelled Damascus, prompting British intervention. Following renewed anti-French demonstrations and international pressure and diplomacy, particularly from Britain, the French left Syria, and the country gained its independence in 1946. Finally, the National Bloc achieved its long-sought goal of Syrian independence with al-Quwatli at the head of the Syrian state. But with Syrian independence at hand, the National Bloc could no longer defend its leadership position on nationalist grounds. Already, the radical nationalists had posed a challenge to the National Bloc's monopoly on nationalism.

Al-Quwatli had been a dedicated pan-Arab nationalist opposing Zionism to begin with, but internal and external considerations intensified his anti-Zionism. Internally, socioeconomic problems, represented by a growing gap between the urban merchants and the absentee landlords on the one hand and the peasants and workers on the other, threatened the sociopolitical status quo. At the same time, the situation was complicated by the challenge posed to the leadership of the National Bloc by the rising new modern middle class.[37] Externally, the Syrian government was under pressure from the neighboring Hashimite regimes, particularly Jordan, which became an independent monarchy in 1946, to bring about Greater Syria. The Syrian government perceived Jordan's attempt at unity as a takeover by King Abdullah of Jordan, who wanted to extend his Hashimite rule over Damascus. In addition, since King Abdullah was supported by the British, the Syrian government perceived Jordan's scheme of Greater Syria as a pretext under which Britain would perpetuate its influence in the region. Because of political factionalism within the ruling elites, the external pressure weighed heavily on the fragile Syrian government.[38] Interwoven together, these internal and external pressures threatened the stability of the newly independent state.

Al-Quwatli, then president of Syria, fought back these pressures by adopting a tough anti-Zionist posture to strengthen his position at home. On the one hand, he used the Palestine issue as an instrument to polish his Arab nationalist credentials and as an outlet for domestic pressures. On the other hand, he unequivocally adhered to the anti-Zionist policies formulated by the newly established Arab League (1945). In so doing, he sought the support of Egypt and Saudi Arabia, the two powerful states in the Arab League and opponents of Hashimite schemes, to protect himself from Hashimite ambitions. This anti-Zionist posture was reinforced again by the Syrian fear of the potential danger a Jewish state could pose to Syrian economic interests, which did not change much since the 1930s.

When the U.N. General Assembly passed the resolution of November 29, 1947, to partition Palestine, laying down the boundaries of the proposed Palestinian and Jewish areas,[39] Syria joined other Arab countries in rejecting it. When the Arab League formed "the Liberation Army" with recruits from the Arab world to fight the Zionists (December 1947), Syria was in the vanguard of Arab states providing the Liberation Army with training officers, equipment, and army bases, in addition to its leader, the Syrian military commander Fawzi al-Qawuqji.[40] Syria housed the headquarters of the Arab League's "Military Committee," which had a mandate to "ascertain the defense needs of Palestine and coordinate Arab efforts within that framework."[41] As the war for Palestine loomed nearer, Syria had firmly committed itself to fighting the Zionists.

The Ba'th Party and Syrian Leadership

Against the background of surging Germanophilia and continuing French rule combined with the disintegration of the League of National Action and the onset of World War II, Syria's political climate favored the development of a major political movement. In 1940, Zaki al-Arsuzi, a former leader of the League who left the district of Alexandretta after its cession to Turkey for Damascus, founded the *al-Ba'th al-Arabi* party (the Arab Resurrection/Renaissance).[42] Al-Arsuzi believed that the "Renaissance" of the Arabs would take place once they were freed from colonial rule.[43] Although his movement attracted a small number of dedicated followers, it did not constitute a real political party. The French harried al-Arsuzi, leading to his political inactivity during World War II, though some of his followers remained active.

Another group that fared much better than that of al-Arsuzi's revolved around the two Sorbonne educated teachers at the *Al-Tajhiz*, Michel Aflaq and Salah al-Din Bitar, the first a Greek Orthodox and the second a Sunni Muslim. At the *Al-Tajhiz*, Aflaq and Bitar established themselves as political thinkers and recruited their first disciples. In 1941, the two teachers issued tracts directed against both the French and the National Bloc leaders. By organizing demonstrations supporting Kilani's anti-British revolt in Iraq, Aflaq and Bitar enhanced their nationalist credentials and attracted to their movement additional followers. In 1942, Aflaq and Bitar left teaching and devoted themselves full time to political work, mainly intending to free Syria from French rule. At the time, they issued a number of bulletins and pamphlets in the name of the "Arab Revitalization (*Ihya*) Movement."

In 1943, the movement of Aflaq and Bitar took the name *Harakat al-Ba'th al-Arabi*.[44] A year later, the two began to refer to their movement as the Arab Ba'th party (*Hizb al-Ba'th al-Arabi*) and, in July 1945, applied for a license to function as a legal political party.[45] The Arab Ba'th party did not emerge as a legal party until after the departure of the French in 1946. In 1947, Arsuzi's group merged with the Ba'th party.

Aflaq, especially, and Bitar formulated the doctrine of the Ba'th party, emphasizing three tenets—Arab unity, freedom, and socialism. Aflaq's formulation was heavily couched in metaphysical terms. His message centered fundamentally on Arab nationalism, which is the essential instrument for achieving his primary goal, namely Arab unity. Aflaq wrote in 1940: "The nationalism for which we call...is the same sentiment that binds the individual to his family, because the fatherland is only a large household and the nation a large family."[46] This belief in Arab nationalism as the means to Arab unity is expressed in the opening article of the Ba'th party's constitution of 1947: "The Arabs form one nation. This nation has the natural right to live in a single state and to be free to direct its own destiny."[47] In addition, the Ba'th party (Article 7 of the constitution) defined the boundaries of the Arab nation in the following manner:

> The Arab fatherland is that part of the globe inhabited by the Arab nation which stretches from the Taurus Mountain, the Pocht-i-Kouh Mountains, the Gulf of Basra, the Arab Ocean, the Ethiopian Mountains, the Sahara, the Atlantic Ocean, and the Mediterranean.[48]

However, the struggle for Arab unity is not conceived only in pan-Arab nationalistic terms. It is seen also as a regenerative process leading to the reform of Arab character and society. The revitalization of the Arab society is at the heart of the Ba'th party nationalist doctrine. This is the essence of the eternal mission of the party (*Risallah Khalida*). Aflaq explained the mission in the following words:

> It is our life itself, *it is to agree to experience this life with a deep and true experience, great and massive in proportion to the greatness of the Arab nation, in proportion to the depth of suffering undergone by the Arabs, in proportion to the great dangers which threaten its continued existence. This living and true experience will bring us back to ourselves, to our living realities; it will make us shoulder our responsibilities and will set us on the true path* in order...to fight social injustice, class exploitation, and the eras of selfishness, bribery, and exploitation, in order to combat tyranny, the falsification of the popular will, and the insults to the dignity of the Arab as a citizen and a man; *for the sake of a free society in which every Arab will regain consciousness of himself, of his existence, his dignity, his thinking, and his responsibilities.* The experience in which our struggle takes place is that of the Arab nation dismembered into different countries and statelets, artificial and counterfeit; we struggle until we can reunite these scattered members, until we may reach a wholesome and natural state in which no severed member can speak in the name of all, until we can get rid of this strange and anomalous state. Then will it be possible for the Arabs to unite, for their spirit to be upstanding, their ideas clear, their morality upright; then will there be scope for their minds to create, for they will have become that wholesome natural entity, one nation. This wholesome and true experience, struggling against the existing conditions until we return to the right state, such is the Arab mission.[49]

Freedom, the second tenet of the Ba'th doctrine, comprises personal freedom and national independence, whereby the Arab has the freedom of speech, assembly, and belief and is liberated from colonialism, as well as is freed from foreign control.[50] Socialism, the third tenet, takes on a distinct interpretation. In Europe socialism was internationalist. The nationalist movements of the day (Ba'thism, Zionism) wanted a socialism that would serve their nationalism, so formulas of "nationalist socialisms" were created. This is the Ba'th kind of socialism. In Aflaq's words, socialism, unlike in the West, is not an internationalist movement claiming a materialistic philosophy in order to stand against the Western practice of exploitation, tyranny, and reaction. Arab socialism needs not a materialistic philosophy, for the Arab spirit has no blemish of tyranny. Socialism for the Arab is a part and consequence of the national condition. The Arab nationalist understands that socialism is the best means for the rebirth (renaissance) of his nation and of its nationalism. The Arab struggle rests on Arab unity, which requires socialism. Socialism is a necessity emanating from the heart of Arab nationalism, which guarantees justice, equality, and generous living for all. In this abstract formulation of socialism, Aflaq tends to subordinate socialism to Arab nationalism in order to make political unity a condition for a socialist society.

The Ba'th party does not believe that its objectives can be achieved by gradual or piecemeal reform. It advocates an *Inqilab,* which in contemporary Arab writing means an overturn or a coup. But Aflaq's interpretation of *Inqilab* at the time was more of the order of an organic transformation of society than a sudden seizure of power. Article VI of the general principles of the Ba'th party constitution (1947) states:

> The Party of the Arab Ba'th is revolutionary. It believes that its main objectives for the realization of the renaissance of Arab nationalism and for establishing socialism cannot be achieved except by means of revolution and struggle. To rely on slow evolution and to be satisfied with a partial and superficial reform is to threaten these objectives with failure and loss. Hence the party decides in favor of a) the struggle against foreign colonialism to completely and finally liberate the Arab fatherland, b) the struggle to bring all the Arabs in a single independent state and c) the overthrow of the present corrupt structure, an overthrow which will include all sectors of life, intellectual, economic, social and political.[51]

Aflaq reaffirmed his interpretation of *Inqilab* in a party speech in February 1950. By revolution (*Inqilab*), he said:

> We understand that true awakening of the Arab spirit at a decisive stage in human history....Revolution, then, before being a political program and social program, is that propelling power, that powerful psychic current, that mandatory struggle, without which the reawakening of the nation is not to be understood. This is what we understand by revolution.[52]

Thus, at this time in Ba'th history, "Revolution" meant a transformation of society before a change in the political system.[53] In Aflaq's vision, the Ba'th constituted an elite vanguard (*Tali'ah*) whose task was to transform and revitalize Arab society leading to an independent united state. Nevertheless, despite Aflaq's own interpretation of *Inqilab,* he laid the foundation for a radical transformation of society by an elite represented by the Ba'th party. As John Devlin perceptively observed, "the temptation to the party's followers to see quick action, including the use of military force, as an acceptable means of accomplishing the 'transformation' grew as the years passed, until in the 1960s Aflaq's understanding of *Inqilab* became submerged in the activist belief in forced transformation carried out by an elite represented by the Ba'th party."[54]

Aflaq was influenced by al-Husri's Germanophile ideas of Arab nationalism, but went a step further by adding a mystified notion of socialism to Arab nationalism. Aflaq believed that the party's three objectives were fused in such a manner that one could not be achieved without the other. So, Arab unity, freedom, and socialism, when subsumed under the motto of the Ba'th party—one Arab nation with an eternal mission—can be interpreted to mean a revolution against "reactionary" forces at home and colonialism. The novelty of Ba'thism was that it emerged as an effective organized political movement to preach total Arab unity. Ideas of Arab nationalism and unity were not new at the time. The belief that the Arabs constituted a culturally and politically united nation had been gaining acceptance in intellectual nationalist circles for many years because of the movements of the day, mainly the Arab Nationalist Movement.[55] But it was the Ba'th party that was able to crystallize the notion that the artificial division of the Arab world by the colonialists, along with the corrupt present political order, were at the root of the backward political, social, and economic conditions of the Arabs. This led to a political program that found its expression in anticolonial form of nationalism. Nearly a decade before the appearance of Gamal Abd al-Nasser in Egypt, the Ba'thi leaders emerged as the most stringent anticolonialists in the Arab world.

Political Zionism (the movement to create a Jewish state in Palestine) was ideologically and in every other way incompatible with the Ba'th party, the party that preached Arab nationalism and unity. However, political Zionism did not figure prominently in early Ba'thi writing. Once events in Palestine in 1947 and 1948 began to concern its party leaders, the Ba'th turned its attention south and featured several articles in its mouthpiece, *Al-Ba'th*. The general theme of the articles revolved around the notion that the colonialists were conspiring with the Zionists against the Arabs and that the time had come for the Arabs to unite and save Palestine. At the same time, the party attacked all "reactionary" regimes in the Arab world, especially the one in Syria, for their bankrupt handling of Palestine over the years. Although, one article ended with a note calling for the death of the Zionists, the party seemingly saw in the situation in Palestine at the time an opportunity to advance its political program. The literature of the party consistently emphasized saving Palestine by strengthening the Arab nation through unifying it.[56] Israel gradually began to figure prominently in Ba'thi doctrine as the party went through a process of ideological and structural transformation, culminating in the Ba'thi military coup of 1963.

Initially, Aflaq had subordinated socialism to Arab nationalism to suit his ideology. But socialism began to play a major role in Ba'thi ideology when the Ba'th party united with Akram al-Hawrani's movement of Hama. Al-Hawrani had built a reputation as a radical nationalist during the French Mandate in Syria as well as when he left for Iraq along with some Syrian army officers to support Kilani's anti-British revolt. At the time, al-Hawrani began to forge good relationships with the Syrian officer corps, which evolved into an extensive network of ties when he served as a deputy in the 1940s and when he again joined Syrian army officers in fighting the Zionists in Palestine in the 1948 War. In addition to his credentials as a nationalist, al-Hawrani was notoriously known as the first to lead a campaign against the big feudal families who owned huge estates in rural Syria. As a deputy for Hama in the Syrian parliament, al-Hawrani opposed the National Bloc and consistently attacked the feudal landlords, while fighting for the peasants.[57]

In 1950, al-Hawrani founded the Arab Socialist party, which centered around Hama and immediately drew its strength from the middle and lower social classes. The party called for the distribution of the big landlords' estates to the poor peasants and for a "neutralist" foreign policy.[58] Besides al-Hawrani's strong emphasis on socialism, especially with regard to land reform, he and the Ba'th leaders shared a fair amount of similar nationalistic beliefs. After all, they were in the same political trench fighting the French and the National Bloc. The idea of a merger between the two parties gathered momentum when the leaders of the two parties opposed the military dictatorship of Colonel Adib al-Shishakli (1951–1954), who assumed power in a coup d'etat in December 1949. While in exile in Lebanon, Aflaq, Bitar, and al-Hawrani joined forces, and, according to Devlin, the merger took effect in February 1953.[59] The new party became known as the Arab Ba'th Socialist Party (hereafter the Ba'th party).

The Ba'th party was instrumental in deposing al-Shishakli and returning parliamentary life to Syria. The merger resulted in combining al-Hawrani's populist political base of support in Hama and his network of ties in the army with the political organization of the Ba'th. The benefit of the merger transpired when the Ba'th party won 22 seats out of 142 in the 1954 parliamentary elections. But the real impact of the merger was on the ideology of the Ba'th and its structure. A strong dose of socialism was injected into its doctrine, gradually dissolving Aflaq's own interpretation of the concept. Socialism was no longer subordinate to Arab nationalism; it was becoming a major component of any Arab nationalism. In other words, the Marxist concept of the class struggle began finding its way into the ideology of the Ba'th, eventually putting socialism on a par with Arab unity as essential components of Arab nationalism. Whereas the party before the merger appealed only to the educated of the Syrian cities, it now began to attract a wide range of membership extending to the rural areas. In my judgment, the merger laid the foundation for the radicalization of the Ba'th party. In a move that revealed the paramountcy that the Ba'th put on socialism, the party revised the text of the 1947 constitution by replacing the original name of the party, the Arab Ba'th Party, with the current name, the Arab Ba'th Socialist Party.[60]

During this period of time, the Ba'th maintained its depiction of Israel as a colonialist creation. The party attacked Israel in anticolonial terms, emphasizing Arab unity. Aflaq in a speech in October 1956 stated:

> For decades the colonial powers have striven to delay the resurrection (renaissance) of the Arab nation by impoverishing it, dividing it, and chaining it with many shackles. Then Israel was founded as the last efficacious means to occupy the Arabs, squander their efforts and strength, and cut off the path toward their liberty and unity.[61]

On another occasion Aflaq denounced the creation of Israel:

> In Palestine the colonialists cooperated with the Zionists to evict our people from their land, saying and affirming that Israel was created to stay. Not even a decade had passed since the catastrophe, before the Arab people in Palestine, Egypt, Syria, and every other Arab country answered: Israel was created to vanish and colonialism to vanish with it as well.[62]

Meanwhile, al-Nasser was emerging as the champion of Arab nationalism and attracting the attention of the Ba'thi leaders. The Suez Crisis and War of 1956 substantially boosted the cause of Arab unity, making Nasser's role in bringing it about essential. The Ba'th party sought the unity of Syria and Egypt. In 1958, the greatly anticipated goal of Arab unity was partially achieved when Egypt and Syria merged under the name of the United Arab Republic. But Egypt's assent to the union came only after it secured Syria's political subordination and the dismantling of all political parties, including the Ba'th. During the union, many Ba'thi officers became disgruntled with the way the Egyptians treated them. As if it were not enough that the Egyptians had brought about the dissolution of the Ba'th party, they eyed the Ba'thi officers with suspicion (supposedly the partners in undertaking the unity) and sent scores of them to Cairo.[63] With no party apparatus to sustain them, many Ba'thi officers started to get directly involved in politics. About this time, in 1960, Salah Jadid, Hafiz al-Asad, and Muhammad Umran founded the secret Ba'thi military organization, known as the Military Committee. Meanwhile, chafing under Egyptian lordship, a group of Damascene officers staged a coup d'etat and broke up the union in 1961. In this interim period, the Ba'th was able to reorganize itself again to become a significant force in Syrian political life.

In March 1963, the party and its allies (Nasserite and independent officers) were able to seize power following an Iraqi Ba'th takeover of Iraq in February 1963.

The breakup of the United Arab Republic, followed by the failure of the two Ba'thi regimes in Syria and Iraq to form a federal union, significantly undermined the ideological foundation of the Ba'th party. In addition, many party members no longer respected the party leaders, especially al-Hawrani and Bitar, for they had signed the document approving Syria's secession from the United Arab Republic. Party members with a Marxist inclination were disappointed with the party's past performances and sought to reformulate the Ba'th ideology. Those party members were also encouraged by the contemporaneous ideological developments in the revolutionary Arab regimes (and in the communist world), which to some varying extent emphasized socialist commitments in their nationalism.[64]

Before the 1963 coup, literature critical of Ba'thi ideology circulated in Damascus. Prominent among the Ba'thi contributors were Jamal al-Atasi, Ilyas Murqus, and, significantly, Yassin al-Hafiz. Al-Atasi, a veteran Ba'thi official, criticized bourgeois (political) democracy and emphasized an economic (socialist) democracy that returns national wealth to all the people.[65] Al-Atasi's philosophy revolved around a Marxist concept of socialism that called for the revolutionary forces to change the old system and end exploitation.[66] Murqus attacked the parliamentary system in Syria. Unlike in the West, where parliamentary government is associated with the rise of the bourgeoisie, in Syria the leaders of the ancient regime continued to wield power and influence and to hold sway in parliament.[67] Al-Hafiz, a former communist, criticized Ba'thi ideology especially concerning the question of liberty. He condemned parliamentary government, declaring it a cover for capitalist control. He called for a popular (revolutionary socialist) democracy that would curtail reactionary groups and give the chance to the toiling masses to enjoy complete freedom. Only then could "liberty" be achieved. Al-Hafiz also emphasized keeping the army out of politics.[68]

This ideological ferment formed the basis of a document adopted at the Sixth National Congress in October 1963. The document called "Some Theoretical Propositions" reformulated the doctrine of the Ba'th party. The parliamentary system was no longer accepted as a basis for political action. Power should rest with the toiling classes. And following al-Hafiz's line of thought, the document affirmed that liberty would require a popular democracy, led by a vanguard party, which would limit the political freedom of the bourgeoisie.[69] The Congress decided to proceed with the socialist transformation of society. But it rejected the proposition advanced by Hafiz that the army should be kept out of politics. Instead, the Congress emphasized the military's involvement in politics to bring about popular democracy, stressing the ideological indoctrination of the armed forces.[70] This further politicized the Ba'thi military, which espoused the new ideology.

The new ideology of the Ba'th had a direct impact on Syria's attitude towards Israel. The Palestinian problem became entangled with the social and political problems of Syria, which the Ba'th party wanted to solve. Whereas before support for the Palestinians was formulated only within the context of Arab unity, now that support came to be formulated within the context of Arab unity and socialism. At the Sixth National Congress the ideological document emphasized that the liberation of Palestine depended on the unity and growth of Arab progressive forces.[71] The Congress also advocated (Resolution 21) the creation of a Palestine liberation front whereby the Palestinians would become the vanguard for the liberation of Palestine.[72]

The Marxist notion of "popular struggle" and, when referring to Israel, "people's war of liberation" entered the lexicon of Ba'thi discourse. The radical Ba'thists (or the neo-Ba'thists) came to see popular struggle as the only means to combat Israel. At the same time, popular struggle served as a pretext to marshal support for the regime at a time when the Ba'th party had embarked on a socialist course to transform Syrian society. Popular struggle became the all-inclusive slogan to silence opposition.[73] When the military wing of the Ba'th party assumed power in 1966, the Ba'thi regime's attitude toward Israel grew more militant. The regime translated its espoused ideology into actions. It made good on its ideology of conducting a "people's liberation war" by actively abetting Palestinian guerrilla raids into Israel. In addition, the Ba'thi regime took the position that it was ready to incur huge sacrifices in order to defeat Israel.[74] The Palestine question had become central to the Ba'thi state.

The loss of Syrian territory in the 1967 War did not mitigate but rather sharpened the Ba'thi militant attitude toward Israel. The Ba'thi regime strengthened its commitment to the concept of popular struggle. Not only did the regime continue to support Palestinian guerrilla raids into Israel, but also it established its own loyal Palestinian guerrilla organization, *al-Sa'iqa,* which also functioned as a political arm of Syria within the Palestine Liberation Organization. In addition, the Ba'thi regime proceeded with its policy of transforming Syria's society, essentially nationalizing the Syrian economy and curbing the mercantilistic power of the bourgeoisie.

This radical orientation reached its climax and logical conclusion when the Syrian army intervened in Jordan's civil war in 1970 on the side of the Palestinians. The intervention failed as Jordan subdued the Palestinians and defeated the Syrian army, leading to the ouster of the radical Ba'thi regime of Salah Jadid by then-defense minister Hafiz al-Asad.

Israel figured prominently in al-Asad's ideology. In central disagreement with Jadid, al-Asad advocated a strategy of cooperation with the Arab countries in the interest of confronting Israel. Al-Asad had a Ba'thi nationalist upbringing and was among the politicized army officers who espoused the radical ideology of the Ba'th party. As a Ba'thist, Arab nationalism always weighed heavily in al-Asad's ideology. This was reinforced by his being a minority member of the Alawi sect. On the one hand, pan-Arabism mitigated the contradictions between what constitutes an Alawi, a Syrian, and an Arab, and allowed, especially an Alawi, to be a Muslim by religion, a Syrian by identification, and an Arab by conviction. On the other hand, it seems natural that a minority member would aggressively embrace pan-Arabism in order to dispel any doubts regarding his loyalty entertained by the majority (Sunni) that belonging to a minority group makes one ready to compromise pan-Arab national interests. After all, it was mainly the secular doctrine of the Ba'thi ideology that attracted many members of minority groups.

Al-Asad, like all Ba'thi cadres, believed that Israel not only is an imperialist creation but also is an expansionist state seeking to dominate the region. He was convinced that Zionism's goal was to create a "Greater Israel" extending from the Nile to the Euphrates, with the objective of imposing Zionist hegemony over the Arabs, thus threatening the present and future existence of the Arabs.[75] According to al-Asad, Israel's 1956 invasion of Egypt (along with Great Britain and France), continuous aggression against the Palestinians and Syrians, and acquisition of nuclear weapons were incontrovertible testimonials to Israel's hegemonic nature. The course of events of the Arab-Israeli struggle during the 1970s and 1980s (the invasion of Lebanon) seemed to confirm this perception of Israel on the part of al-Asad. But, at the same time, a more careful look at his position will also show how he slowly and gradually kept modifying and diluting in practice this initial ideological outlook under the pressure of the hard realities of the balance of military and political power between the Israelis and the Arabs. This forms the basis of al-Asad's famous pragmatism.

This pragmatism was manifested early in his rule. He liquidated the extremists of the Ba'th party, who espoused the concept of the popular struggle. He then strove to break Syria out of its regional and international isolation and, internally, to win the support of the bourgeoisie. But, significantly enough, this pragmatism was evinced when al-Asad negotiated the May 1974 Disengagement Agreement with Israel through the United States. In an addendum to the agreement, al-Asad privately pledged to the U.S. Secretary of State Henry Kissinger to prevent Palestinian guerrillas from using Syrian territory to attack Israel.[76] This position has assumed great significance in view of the fact that the Golan front has always been quiet.

Al-Asad's pragmatism has another significant dimension. There is in him a streak of taking bold moves at moments of crisis that go against the grains of Ba'thi ideology. Such moves on his part included the 1976 intervention in Lebanon against the Palestinians and the Lebanese progressive forces, the brutal suppression of the Muslim Brotherhood in Hama in the early 1980s, siding with Iran against Iraq in the first Gulf War (when all Arab countries supported Iraq), and, finally, Syria's participation in the U.S.-led anti-Iraq coalition against Saddam Hussein in the second Gulf War. While these bold moves can be attributed to al-Asad's diligent readiness to adjust and readjust to the realities of the balance of power, they lead inescapably to the subversion of all Ba'thi ideology.

However, the Ba'thi ideology, especially concerning Arab nationalism, had already been greatly weakened. This did not happen only on account of al-Asad's bold moves. In reality, his moves can be perceived as a consequence of Arab nationalism's weakness and not vice versa. Before al-Asad assumed power, the breakup of the United Arab Republic in 1961 and the defeat of the Arabs in the 1967 War had already dealt severe blows to Arab nationalism. This was followed by the Arab defeat in the 1973 War. So the point should be clear that when al-Asad undertook actions against the grain of Ba'thi ideology, the ideology itself was already in limbo. During the Gulf War (1990), this ideology reached its nadir when all pretense of Arab unity and nationalism was shed. What guided al-Asad in his policies was his awareness of the vulnerabilities of the Arab states, especially the vulnerabilities of his own country. Correspondingly, he paid great attention to his country's security imperatives. Herein lies the root of his diligent attempts to adjust to the military and political balance of power, which inadvertently went against the very concept of Arab nationalism. Therefore, a distinction must be drawn between al-Asad's ideology and his pragmatism. Al-Asad's pragmatism took precedence over his ideology when Syria's national security was threatened, but this did not mean that he had completely forsaken his ideology, particularly when it came to Israel. This applied especially well to the Golan Heights.

The Heights were of no less great ideological significance than national interest to al-Asad. In fact, they typify the last symbol of Ba'thi ideology that has not been treaded upon. True, pan-Arabism played a major role throughout al-Asad's Ba'thi rule by being the only ideology capable of transcending tribal, regional, and sectarian differences in Syria. It has given the regime the ideological and inspirational legitimacy to win over the different segments of the population, especially the Sunnis, and to build a consensus on a political program revolving around confrontation with Israel. But, after so many adjustments by al-Asad to the realities of power, coupled with a near bankrupt Arab nationalism, what remains of the ideology of the vanguard party—the Ba'th—in Arab society?

The Ba'th party under al-Asad has been robbed of its ideological raison d'être: Arab unity and nationalism have been sacrificed at the expense of national security. All that remain are the Golan Heights as the last vestige and symbol of Ba'thi ideology in Syria. It is difficult to entertain the idea that al-Asad would have taken the final bold move of his rule and dealt the final blow to Ba'thi ideology, let alone undermine Syria's national interest, by compromising on the total return of the Golan Heights. From the time of the 1974 Disengagement Agreement until his death in 2000, al-Asad, called the Sphinx of Syria, remained adamant about the total return of the Golan Heights from Israel. This is reinforced by two important and interconnected reasons.

The first is the fact that al-Asad belongs to a minority group. Being an Alawi, al-Asad had a psychological need to reassert his Arab nationalism by taking a firm stand on nationalist issues. Being an issue of great national importance, the Golan Heights serve al-Asad as a means to prove again his nationalist credentials. The second reason is the fact that Syria lost the Golan Heights to Israel when al-Asad was defense minister. It is well known that the opposition to Ba'thi rule in Syria, mainly the Muslim Brotherhood, trumpeted the charge that al-Asad is a traitor and the sectarian (Alawi) regime colluded with Israel to surrender the Golan Heights. During the confrontation between the al-Asad regime and the Muslim Brotherhood in the late 1970s and early 1980s, the latter conducted a propaganda campaign that brought up the charge of treason against the Ba'thi regime and its leader. In an article titled "The Treason of Asad in 5 June 1967," which appeared in the mouthpiece newspaper of the Syrian Muslim Brotherhood, *Al-Nadhir,* the sectarian Ba'thi regime was accused of collusion with Israel in the surrender of the Golan Heights.[77] Other articles appearing in *Al-Nadhir* not only attacked al-Asad but also constantly described him with such epithets as "the professional spy," "Islam's number one enemy," and the "seller of the Golan."[78]

After Israel sacked Quneitra, the principal town in the Golan Heights, Patrick Seale remarked that the town "was thereafter to be the badge of Syria's defeat, an emblem of hatred between Syria and Israel and a cross Asad had to bear."[79] Admittedly, that reality was even more bitter to al-Asad, as he had to bear the stigma of treason as well, a cross far heavier to carry than that of defeat. These charges stigmatized al-Asad. The Golan Heights stand not only as an emblem of defeat for al-Asad, but also as the basis for the charge of treason. As a result, the cumulative effect of these two reasons not only hardened al-Asad's outlook regarding Israel, adding to it a personalized dimension mired in guilt and shame, but also made the return of the Golan Heights a matter of national honor. Recovering the entire Heights became a central component of al-Asad's strategy. Herein lay the reason behind al-Asad's intractable attitude concerning the Heights vis-à-vis his peace talks with Israel and the United States. Inasmuch as retrieving the Heights was important, compromising over their total return was unacceptable. This was al-Asad's peace legacy that he left to his son.

The State Under al-Asad

Upon his assumption of power in November 1970, al-Asad understood that the security of his regime would depend on his overall control of Syrian society. He set about creating an authoritarian, security state centering on his leadership. On the one hand, as noted earlier, he removed the Ba'thists who supported the popular struggle against Israel and tried to reverse Salah Jadid's leftist radical transformation of Syrian society. His immediate concerns were to break Syria out of its regional isolation and win the support of the urban bourgeoisie. He partially liberalized trade in order to strike a modus vivendi with the bourgeoisie, especially that of Damascus, who were happy with the overthrow of the Jadid regime. By embracing the Ba'th party's ideological commitment to pan-Arabism, which transcended sectarian differences and gave him the ideological legitimacy to win over the different segments of the population, especially the Sunnis, al-Asad built a consensus on a political program that revolved around confronting Israel.

On the other hand, al-Asad set about to restructure the political system by introducing economic and political reforms. Central to his restructuring was the creation of a formal structure that would legitimize and institutionalize his regime with the objective of controlling Syrian society. In 1971, he appointed a 173-member parliament (an assembly), whose composition included loyal key party leaders and representatives of the armed forces, unions, professional associations, and leftist and nationalist political parties, as well as from the main religious establishments and chambers of commerce and industry. On March 1, 1971, this parliament nominated al-Asad as the sole candidate for the presidency, establishing a pattern of electing him in national referendums with approval hovering around 99 percent of voters. Then in 1972 he established the Progressive National Front (PNF) whose function was to rally the progressive forces in Syria around the Ba'th party in the interest of confronting Israel.[80]

In 1973, al-Asad promulgated a "permanent constitution," which decreed the Ba'th party as "the vanguard party in the society and state."[81] The preamble of the constitution emphasized the revolutionary direction of the Ba'th, establishing a nexus between the national and socialist struggle, the unity of Arab Republics, and the struggle against colonialism and Zionism.[82] These reforms came to be known as the "corrective movement." They created the formal structure of the regime by which Syrian politics have been conducted. The formal structure comprised several institutions and organizations: (1) the presidency to which the constitution gave vast powers, (2) the cabinet, whose ministers represented the Ba'th party and the PNF, (3) the Ba'th party, (4) the leadership of the PNF, (5) the *Majlis al-Sha'b,* or the parliament, and (6) the popular organizations, which according to the constitution comprised the popular forces striving for the progress of society.[83]

However, power resided in an informal structure based on a nexus between the mostly Alawi officers and Ba'th party and regime loyalists, constituting the inner circle of the president and the network attached to it. This group has controlled the functioning of the formal structure. Significantly, the dreaded *Mukhabarat* (security services) play a powerful role extending beyond security matters because Syria has been under a state of emergency since 1963. The government justifies martial law because of the state of war with Israel.[84] But the essence of these reforms was to legitimize the regime and institutionalize it. While the army and security apparatus, the Ba'th party, and bureaucracy constituted the primary base of support for the regime, the formal structure served to expand that base to reach all segments of Syrian society. In a way the formal structure, especially the parliament, the PNF, and the popular organizations, along with the public sector, played a multidimensional role, that of mobilization, control, and representation, leading to the co-opting of potential opposition. The greater its expansion, the more the regime widened its base of support.

By opting for political participation and legality by joining the Ba'th party to form the PNF, the PNF parties have given up much of their independence and, of course, their potential for opposition. In addition, the creation of the PNF caused splits among the parties. Significantly, a sizable faction of the Syrian Communist Party (SCP) headed by Riad al-Turk refused to join the PNF and formed the SCP-Political Bureau. The parliament represented the Ba'th party apparatus and leadership along with the PNF parties, the popular organizations, the religious establishment, and the commerce and industry chambers. In 1990, the parliament was enlarged from 195 to 250 members. One-third of the seats have been reserved for independent deputies. While the PNF has kept its majority and control of the parliament, the independent elements represented social forces, which hitherto had not been represented.

As a rentier state with a "socialist" system, Syria controlled and divided its economy along functional lines. The regime developed the popular organizations into hierarchical, quasigovernmental bodies that uphold the national priorities of the state. The Peasant Union has represented the peasants; the trade unions have represented all workers in the public sector; and the teachers, artisans, writers, and all other unions and associations have represented the segment of society corresponding to their respective functional purpose. These organizations, however, have been the perfect fronts for mobilization and control of Syrian society at large.[85]

The expansion of state institutions and popular organizations went hand in hand with the growth of both the public sector and, of course, the military institutions. However, the regime's attempts at widening its social basis of support have changed its composition with time and, by extension, its relationship with the state. Al-Asad's early reforms had been planned bearing in mind the Ba'th party's attempts at drawing support from non-Alawi rural communities. In fact, during the 1960s and early 1970s rural peasants benefited from land reform, and the public sector benefited from the nationalization of industries. Yet, as I wrote in *Embattled Neighbors,* al-Asad's corrective movement, which had encouraged a limited private-sector role in the economy to appease the urban bourgeoisie, fared well with the expansion of the economy after 1973. Many old Sunni bourgeois families of Damascus took advantage of the new opportunities and cooperated with the regime's elite. Various elements of the private sector prospered as either contractors for the state or middlemen between the state and foreign firms. Political, business, and marriage alliances were formed between the two classes, and a new bourgeoisie emerged. At its core was a military-merchant complex of Alawi officers and Damascene merchants.[86] The alliance between the Alawi officers and Damascene merchants was further strengthened during critical times, thereby enhancing the power of the merchants. During the Muslim Brotherhood insurrection in the early 1980s, the Damascus business community played a significant role in saving the regime by not joining the Brotherhood's inspired antiregime commercial strike, which spread throughout Syria. During the mid-1980s, as Syria faced a serious economic crisis, which brought it to the brink of bankruptcy, the regime adopted market reforms, benefiting the new bourgeoisie. As a result, a web of politico-economic structural interests, benefiting Alawi officers and Sunni merchants, permeated the system.[87] So the regime supported a huge bureaucracy to bring about its socialist contract—provision of work—and obtain a wide societal support, while at the same time it created a new class depending on a market economy for its prosperity.

At this point, I would like to mention that the expansion of the political base of support of the regime did not depend only on co-optation and representation. The regime has had no qualms about using whatever means it has at its disposal to squelch any opposition, from arbitrary arrests, to long-term imprisonment, to assassination. Battling the Muslim Brotherhood (1976–1982), the regime waged an indiscriminate, brute war against them in the city of Hama that left thousands dead.[88]

In addition, the regime filled the formal structure with Sunni appointees and sustained a balance, on the one hand, among the various organs of the formal and informal structures, and, on the other hand, among the elites in a way so as to keep al-Asad's absolute power overarching. The vice presidents Abd al-Halim Khaddam and Muhammad Zuheir Mashariqa, former prime ministers Mahmoud al-Zoubi and Muhammad Mustafa Miro, former deputy prime minister and defense minister Mustafa Tlas, and the foreign minister Farouq al-Shara are all Sunni Muslims. This reflected the genuine need of the regime to conspicuously depict the state as nonsectarian, while at the same time gaining the compliance of the predominant Sunni majority. Through their control of the army, party, and security apparatuses, and their closeness to al-Asad's decision-making process, the Alawi officials in the informal structure have guaranteed the survival of the regime and have controlled the functioning of the formal structure. But their power could be curtailed once they overstep their boundaries. At one time an influential personality, the brother of al-Asad, Rifa't, who commanded the then-praetorian guard, the defense companies (brigades), was

exiled along with high-ranking Alawi officers in 1984 for questioning the policies laid down by al-Asad when he had suffered a heart
attack.[89]

Equally significant, al-Asad promoted his leadership cult to
supersede Ba'th ideology and impose conformity and internal disci-
pline on party members. Besides evolving into an instrument of control and mobilization, the Ba'th party became the bearer of al-Asad's
personal qualities. Hanna Batatu, an authority on the Ba'th party
and its social origins, wrote:

> Under Asad the character of the Ba'ath changed. For one thing, it became,
> in a numerical sense, a mass party....But the growing size of the party
> did not translate into a political force with stronger leverage on the hold-
> ers of real power or greater influence on crucial decision making. What-
> ever independence of opinion its members enjoyed in the past was now
> curtailed, a premium being placed on conformity and internal discipline.
> The party became in effect another instrument by which the regime
> sought to control the community at large or to rally it behind its policies.
> The party's cadres turned more and more into bureaucrats and careerists,
> and were no longer as vibrantly alive ideologically as in the 1950s and
> 1960s, unconditional fidelity to Asad having ultimately overridden fidelity
> to the old beliefs.[90]

As early as May 1971, the new Ba'th Command hailed al-Asad as
Qa'id al-Masirah or "the Leader of the [Nation's] March."[91] Following al-Asad's triumph over the Islamist opposition and the
challenge over his succession that was sparked by his temporary
health incapacity, the Eighth Regional Congress in January 1985
hailed al-Asad as "Our Leader Forever, the Faithful Hafiz al-Asad!"
The Congress then underscored that "loyalty to him is loyalty to
the party and to the people and their cause...and that a breach of
this loyalty, in whatever form...constitutes grave deviation which
the party and the masses reject."[92] Parallel to this, al-Asad was reg-
ularly depicted by the state-controlled media as the "father," the
"first teacher," the "leader forever," the "gallant knight" (compared
favorably to Salah al-Din al-Ayubi, who wrested Jerusalem from
the crusaders in 1187), as well as "a man of the people," among other
accolades. He personified qualities such as steadfastness (*Sumud*),
willingness to struggle (*Nidal*), and willingness to sacrifice
(*Tadhiya*). Portraits, pictures, and banners glorifying his
qualities adorn almost all significant public spaces and busy junc-
tures. One could not but feel his omnipresence and absorb the sub-
liminal message that he was not only to be followed but also to be
emulated.

This is how al-Asad molded modern Syria into an authoritarian, security state, similar to a big prison, centering on his brute power and omnipresent leadership cult. At the same time, al-Asad's Syria, regarding itself as the vanguard of Arab nationalism, fits well the pattern of a country that prides itself on carrying the weight of its history.

CHAPTER 2

The Beginning of U.S.-Syrian Relations: Between the Arab-Israeli Conflict and the Cold War

No account of the relations between the United States and Syria is anywhere near adequate without taking into full consideration the dynamics of the Arab-Israeli conflict and the history of the relationship of the United States to both Syria and Israel and to their fierce enmity, at least since the rise of the state of Israel. As we shall see, U.S.-Syrian relations were shaped by the politics of the Arab-Israeli conflict and the Cold War. It shall also become evident that successive American administrations had to tread a fine line, balancing their commitment to Israel's safety, prosperity, and pre-eminence in a very hostile environment, on the one hand, and protecting their vast vital interests and strategic investments in the Arab world, on the other. In the end, all administrations came around to implementing such balancing policies regardless of their Republican or Democratic affiliations, their conservative or liberal orientations, their initial toughness or softness on Israel and the Arabs, or their confrontational or conciliatory attitude towards the former Soviet Union.

The U.S. relationship with Israel and Syria started on an equal footing after World War II. The United States recognized the independence of Syria before supporting the creation of the state of Israel. The support for Israel was not meant to serve either as a bridgehead to American influence or as an outpost of imperialism. Nor was it a ploy to dictate Syrian policies. The Cold War and Arab nationalist policies, which equated Israel with colonialism, opened the gates of the heartland of the Middle East to the rivalry between the United States and the Soviet Union. The main objective of the

United States was to check Soviet expansion in the region, which fed on Arab grievances against the Western powers and their support of Israel.

Recognition and Neutrality (1944–1953)

Entertaining no colonial ambitions in the Middle East, the United States, unlike Britain and France, was initially regarded favorably by the Arab states. By the end of 1944, the United States granted unconditional recognition to Lebanon's and Syria's independence from France.[1] In the same year the Soviet Union entered into diplomatic relations with those countries as well. The Soviet Union had no overriding interest in the Middle East heartland (Israel, Syria, Egypt, Lebanon, Jordan, and Iraq) as it focused its attention on Greece, Iran, and Turkey in the emerging Cold War. Greece seemed in danger of falling to the Communists as a result of civil war and the pending withdrawal of British troops. The U.S. State Department reasoned that if the tottering Greek government did not receive immediate military and financial aid the Communists would eventually grab power. President Harry Truman reasoned that if Greece fell to the Communists, Turkey would be highly vulnerable to Soviet subversion and the eastern Mediterranean could fall behind the Iron Curtain.[2]

In March 1947, President Truman addressed Congress, requesting assistance for Greece and Turkey. He emphasized: "Should we fail to aid Greece and Turkey in this fateful hour, the effect will be far reaching to the West as well as to the East."[3] This request became known as the Truman Doctrine, which set the stage for the U.S. policy of containing the Soviet Union. In the Middle East's heartland, the Palestine problem had come to the fore of international politics. On November 29, 1947 the U.N. General Assembly voted for the partition of Palestine into two states, one Jewish and the other Arab, with Jerusalem as a separate enclave to be administered by a governor appointed by the international organization. Arab opposition to the plan immediately followed, and in the Syrian capital, Damascus, demonstrators attacked the United States, Soviet, and French legations whose governments had favored the creation of the Jewish state.

With partition plans going nowhere, the United States had a turnabout in its policy; it proposed on March 19, 1948 a U.N. trusteeship over Palestine. This shift in policy betrayed a chasm between the State Department and the presidency over the creation of a Jewish state. Secretary of State George C. Marshall, along with many officials, opposed American recognition of the new Jewish state as the Jewish Agency prepared to declare statehood upon the British withdrawal from Palestine on May 14. Horrified by the Holocaust and believing in the historical right of the Jews to Palestine, President Truman supported the creation of the state. On May 12, in a White House meeting between the President and his executives, Clark Clifford, a domestic presidential adviser, pressed the case for American recognition of a Jewish state over the objections of Marshall. Furious and self-righteous, Marshall made a momentous threat to the President: "If you follow Clifford's advice and if I were to vote in the election, I would vote against you."[4] Marshall reasoned that the President was moved in his decision by domestic considerations, winning the Jewish vote in the upcoming presidential election. He even included his personal comments of the infamous meeting in the official State Department record, hoping that history would prove him right.

The United States recognized the state of Israel but had not extended its recognition to West Jerusalem. Subsequently, the Soviet Union recognized *de jure* the state of Israel. Though President Truman supported the creation of the state of Israel, his administration played a fairly evenhanded role at the Rhodes armistice negotiations, which followed Israel's defeat of the Arab armies that tried to stifle the country's birth. The Rhodes negotiations resulted in armistice agreements between Israel and each of Egypt, Lebanon, Jordan, and Syria, signed, respectively, on February 24, March 23, April 3, and July 20, 1949.[5] Significantly, during the Lausanne conference of late April to early May 1949, meant to complement the Rhodes negotiations, President Truman delivered a stern message to Prime Minister Ben-Gurion, emphasizing the U.S. government's displeasure with the attitude of Israel. His message ended on an ominous note far from any outright support for Israel:

> If the government of Israel continues to reject the basic principles set forth by the resolution of the General Assembly of 11 December 1948 and the friendly advice offered by the U.S. government for the sole purpose of facilitating a genuine peace in Palestine, the U.S. government will regretfully be forced to the conclusion that a revision of its attitude toward Israel has become unavoidable.[6]

With Britain's influence in the Middle East rapidly eroding and the United States by now fully engaged in containing the Soviet Union, the Middle East seemed like an unstable area vulnerable to Communist penetration, as well as a vital interest to the Western world because of its huge oil reserves. The Arab-Israeli conflict had been the major source of tension there. In May 1950, the United

States, along with Britain and France, issued the Tripartite Declaration in which the three powers undertook rationing the arms supply in the region by opposing the development of an arms race between the Arab states and Israel, as well as promoting peace and stability while opposing the use and/or threat of force by any of the states in the region.[7]

In October 1950, the United States, Britain, France, and Turkey formally proposed to Egypt the formation of a Middle East Defense Organization (MEDO), the purpose of which would serve to extend the containment of the Soviet Union to the heartland of the Middle East and end British occupation of Egypt. Britain made the evacuation of its troops from Egypt conditional on its acceptance of MEDO. In addition, MEDO did not entail Egyptian control over the Suez Canal, which was to be internationalized. Egypt promptly turned down the proposal, "arguing that termination of British occupation under such conditions would amount to a substitution of multiple for single occupation."[8] Although no formal request was made for Syria to join, envoys of the four powers informed the Syrian Foreign Minister, Faydi al-Atasi, of the proposal to Egypt.[9] This could not have happened at a worse time in Syria. Early in the year, the Ba'th party, the Arab Socialist party (before the latter joined the Ba'th), and the Islamic Socialist Front all "called for a policy of strict neutrality towards the two world camps."[10] Led by the Islamic Socialist Front, thousands of demonstrators denounced MEDO as an imperialist plot.

Meanwhile, Israel had actually pursued a policy of neutrality between East and West. Relations between Israel and the United States proceeded slowly but steadily on a basis of mutual respect. Israel received moderate U.S. foreign aid and a number of favorable loans extended by the U.S. Export-Import Bank. Though Israel professed neutrality, the Soviet Union interpreted Israel's behavior as courting the West and launched a virulent attack against Zionism and Israel.

Egypt's refusal to enter MEDO and Syria's opposition to it doomed it to failure. However, the stage was set for the Middle East to become a ground of rivalry between the United States and the Soviet Union. The United States had no special relations with either Syria or Israel. Its concern with containing the Soviet Union made it look at Israel and Syria through the prism of Cold War politics.

The "New Look" and Baghdad Pact

The election of a Republican administration in 1953, which emphasized fiscal conservatism, highlighted the need to replace the Containment policy with an effective and less costly one. Thus, the New Look policy, which required a few well-placed U.S. bases around the Soviet Union to provide the nuclear threat of massive retaliation against communist encroachment anywhere around the world, was born, the brainchild of Secretary of State John Foster Dulles and President Dwight Eisenhower.

Dulles expounded the New Look to the Council on Foreign Relations, stating that this "nation would depend primarily upon a great capacity to retaliate, instantly, by means and at places of our own choosing," and emphasized that "we need allies and collective security. Our purpose is to make those relations more effective, less costly. This can be done by placing more reliance on deterrent power and less dependence on local defensive power."[11] Dulles came forward with a proposal for a new alliance between the West and the Middle Eastern countries of the northern tier, Turkey, Iran, and Pakistan. These countries were chosen because they had shown sensitivity to the communist threat and a willingness to cooperate with the West. Preempting the United States, the British, feeling the decline of their influence in the heartland of the Middle East, sought to salvage their interests there by bringing Iraq into the proposal, Iraq being the last bastion of British influence in the region.

Iraq, under Prime Minister Nuri al-Said, embraced the proposal as a political instrument that would secure Iraqi leadership of the Arab world by both providing an opportunity to enlist other Arab states and getting help from the United States and Britain. Iraq concluded an agreement with Turkey in February 1955, known as the Baghdad Pact, which Britain joined in April. Though the United States supported the Baghdad Pact, it did not sign it. The United States had some reservations about British intentions in the region. The United States, unlike Britain, was solely interested in organizing the Middle East as part of the Western alliance in order to contain the Soviet Union.

Egypt fought hard against the Pact and made sure that no Arab state would follow Iraq's footsteps. The fight centered on Syria, which had the potential of tipping the balance in favor of or against the Pact. Syria transpired as a country of note in inter-Arab politics that could decide the outcome of competing political initiatives. Because of the "progressive forces" in Syria, the Ba'th, the Democratic Bloc, and the Communists, opposition to foreign alliances was secured in the Syrian Assembly, and a rapprochement between Egypt and Syria ensued. Gamal Abd al-Nasser, president of Egypt, was emerging as the champion of Arab nationalism. He committed Egypt to a policy of "positive neutrality," which depended on Arab solidarity and Arab collective security, denouncing imperialism and Zionism. Syria gradually and steadily came under his spell.

Consequently, the Pact shifted the center of gravity of the superpowers' rivalry into the heartland of the Middle East. At the same time, because Israel was not included in the Western plans, it opposed the Pact and sought admission to the North Atlantic Treaty Organization (NATO) to counterbalance the Pact's effects on the Arab-Israeli balance of power. The United States, as yet, did not entertain ideas of special relations with Israel. For example, on his May 1953 trip to the Middle East, Secretary of State Dulles nonchalantly remarked on the sensitive issue of the status of Jerusalem, which Israel claimed was under its jurisdiction:

> I felt anew that Jerusalem is, above all, the holy place of the Christian, Moslem, and Jewish faiths. This has been repeatedly emphasized by the United Nations....But the world religious community has claims in Jerusalem which take precedence over the political claims of any particular nation.[12]

The Soviet Insertion in the Middle East

The activities of the West in the Middle East spurred the Soviet Union to launch a counteroffensive. By the early 1950s, the Soviet Union was firmly supporting the Arab side in the Arab-Israeli conflict, as well as supporting Arab nationalism. At this point, the Soviet Union had no interest in Syria save its strategic position, which outflanked Turkey. But its interest in Syria grew following the election of Khalid Bakdash, the Syrian communist party leader, to parliament in 1954. Meanwhile, Israel's attack on the Gaza Strip in February 1955 in response to Palestinian incursions into Israel allowed the Soviet Union to capitalize on al-Nasser's need for arms and his hostility to the Baghdad Pact. Moscow injected itself into the region by concluding a major Soviet-Egyptian arms deal through Czechoslovakia in September. The deal made the Tripartite Declaration obsolete and set the United States and the Soviet Union on a course of competition in the region. Furthermore, the deal completed the Egyptian process of winning over the Syrians. By October 1955, Egypt had signed a common defense treaty with Syria, which was later signed by Saudi Arabia. The Soviet Union embarked on a selective program of economic, technical, and military assistance, concentrating first on Egypt then on Syria.[13]

Syria perceived itself the subject of constant military and political pressures brought upon her by the West in collusion with Jordan, Iraq, Lebanon, and Turkey. Israel was another major concern for Syria, which she had been sparring with along the armistice lines.

Hence, Syria hailed the arms deal as a great victory for the "progressive" forces fighting imperialism. Admittedly, neither Syria nor Egypt considered the arms deal as a catalyst of change in their policy of "positive neutralism" in the Cold War. But, according to Seale, positive neutralism no longer meant putting relations with the two blocs on the same impartial basis. It meant seeking aid where one could, while continuing to fight western imperialism.[14] Mustafa Tlas, a Syrian defense minister and a Ba'thi official, defended the newly formed Arab relations with the Soviet Union as a reaction to Western policies. He recalled in his memoirs that the Western siege against Egypt and Syria, because of their anticolonial stance, left them with no choice but to break the Western arms embargo by concluding deals with the Soviet Union.[15]

The Eisenhower Doctrine and the Middle East

Opposed by numerous Arab countries and overwhelmed by their vast resources, Israel assigned high priority to the pursuit of an alliance with a Western power. Ben-Gurion and his foreign minister, Moshe Sharett, approached the United States, Britain, and France for an alliance, appealing to them for arms. The United States, at first, resisted Israeli requests for arms, only to yield on the condition that France supply Israel's defense requirements. Washington was careful not to antagonize the Arabs, particularly at a time when Israel had been receiving more American aid than the Arab states. Israel stood second only to Greece in receiving U.S. grants and credits to the Near East. From 1945 to 1955, Israel received a total of $370 million, whereas Egypt, the largest Arab recipient of aid, received a total of $30 million for the same period.[16] Before long, the French arms transfer to Israel had become the ingredient of a relationship that later developed into a Franco-Israeli alliance. Meanwhile, in 1954, the leaders of the American Jewish community established the American-Israel Public Affairs Committee (AIPAC) to advance the U.S.-Israel relationship and promote U.S. economic, military, and political support for Israel.

In July 1956, after al-Nasser nationalized the Suez Canal, the British, French, and Israelis led a joint attack on Egypt in late October, which brought the wrath of the United States upon them. This emanated from a cluster of complex considerations. Prominent among them was, on the one hand, the attempt to woo away Egyptian nationalists from the Soviet embrace and, on the other hand, the concern over taking action that could deepen the Soviet embrace. In his memoirs, Eisenhower emphasized the implications of the attack for Arab nationalism:

I must say that it is hard for me to see any good final result emerging from a scheme that seems to antagonize the entire Moslem world. Indeed I have difficulty seeing any end whatsoever if all the Arabs should begin reacting somewhat as the North Africans have been operating against the French.[17]

The United States compelled Israel to withdraw from the Sinai Peninsula and the Gaza Strip, both captured during the Suez War. Syria, for its part, immediately supported Egypt when the three powers invaded it. At the height of the crisis, Syrian President Shukri al-Quwatli flew to Moscow to seek political and military support. Syria was convinced that a Western plot was also being concocted against her. The Syrian Ministry of Foreign Affairs announced to the press that Syria had called on the aggressors to retreat from Egypt and that Syria had discovered a plot contrived against her by the Iraqi government of Nuri al-Said in collusion with the colonialists.[18] Despite the high ground the United States had achieved in the Middle East in the aftermath of the Suez Crisis, the Syrians saw in the Soviet Union a protector that readily provided much needed economic and military assistance in perilous times.

When U.S. expectations of appreciation from the Arabs for intervention in the Suez Crisis in their favor turned hollow, the United States feared a total Soviet victory in the region. In January 1957, Dulles addressed Congress, stressing that "it would be a major disaster for the nations and peoples of the Middle East, and indeed for all the world, including the U.S., if that area were to fall into the grip of international communism." He added that the United States "must do whatever it properly can to assist the nations of the Middle East to maintain their independence."[19] The Eisenhower administration had its way when Congress passed the joint resolution in March 1957, henceforth known as the Eisenhower Doctrine, conceding to the administration request that

> The president is authorized to...employ the armed forces of the United States as he deems necessary to secure and protect the territorial integrity and political independence of any such nation or group of nations requesting such aid against overt armed aggression from any nation controlled by International Communism.[20]

The U.S. president sent Ambassador James P. Richards to the Middle East to inaugurate the new doctrine. Only Lebanon and Iraq endorsed the Doctrine; Syria refused to receive the ambassador. Initially, Syria had rejected the Eisenhower Doctrine on the grounds that intervention in the affairs of a nation over economic interests was a flagrant violation of the sovereignty principle and that the

American assertion that a power vacuum existed in the region was but a pretext for imperialist intervention and hegemony.[21] By August 1957, the relationship between the United States and Syria sank to a new low when the Syrian government charged the United States with an attempt to overthrow it. The Syrian Ministry of Foreign Affairs released a communiqué on August 19 announcing the discovery of the American plot. The communiqué emphasized that the goal of the Eisenhower Doctrine was to seize the independence of Middle Eastern countries and offer them as easy prey to Zionism and imperialism, and that Syria would continue its policy of positive neutrality in the Cold War.[22] Subsequently, the United States and Syrian ambassadors were declared *personae non gratae* in their respective host countries.

The United States rebuffed Syrian accusations, interpreting them as a "smokescreen behind which people that have the leftish leanings are trying to build up their power."[23] In the meantime, Turkey concentrated its troops along the Turkish-Syrian border. Syria feared a Turkish invasion to overthrow its government. The concentration of Turkish troops provoked a Soviet warning to the Turkish prime minister, in which the Soviets stated:

> We shall not conceal the fact that we have met with great concern the report about Turkish troop concentrations on Syria's borders, as well as about the shipments of American arms to Turkey to effect an attack against Syria....We are confident, Mr. Prime Minister, you will agree that the Soviet Union cannot remain indifferent to these events.[24]

The United States denied the charges brought forth by the Soviet Union, as well as tempered the tense atmosphere. Dulles ruled out any aggression in the region, emphasizing that Syria had not been judged to be under the domination of international communism.[25] Although Syria was moving steadily in the direction of the Soviet Union, it was far from becoming a Soviet satellite. In a move to counter the rising influence of the Syrian Communist party in Syria, the Ba'th sought a union between Egypt and Syria, which came into being on February 1, 1958, under the name of the United Arab Republic. The union reflected Syria's and Egypt's defiance of the Western powers. When Iraq was lost as a Western ally in an anti-Western coup d'etat and civil strife broke out in Lebanon in the summer of 1958, the United States intervened militarily by landing its marines in Lebanon. This American show of force stabilized the situation in Lebanon and served to send a message of reassurance to all threatened small countries in the world. But the real message coming out from the region was not lost on the United States; that is, without Egypt's and Syria's consent American policy in the Middle East would be hampered.

A Try at Evenhandedness

The United States suspected that Israel had begun work on a nuclear reactor while continuing to cultivate its strategic alliance with France. Reportedly, the Central Intelligence Agency had transmitted to the administration that Israel, with the help of France, was building a secret plutonium plant.[26] Meanwhile, the Soviet Union continued economic and military support to Syria, by now a well-established pattern. Soviet assistance to and cooperation with Syria increased after it split from the United Arab Republic in September 1961. With the advent of the Kennedy administration to the White House in 1961, economic assistance as an instrument to fend off communism's threat to imperiled countries took precedence over military assistance. On the one hand, President John Kennedy expressed the administration's support for the political independence and territorial integrity of all Arab states.[27] On the other hand, he assured Israel of American support. Breaking rank with the tradition of not supplying Israel with major military equipment, and showing concern for Israel's defense requirements, President Kennedy and later on President Lyndon Johnson ordered the first U.S. "transfers of major weapon systems to Israel—the Hawk air defense missile system and the A-4 Skyhawk combat aircraft."[28]

Following a bloodless coup d'etat in Damascus in March 1963, the Ba'th party controlled the new regime, and under its revolutionary ideology the Syrian government stood in militant opposition to Israel. Simmering tension along the Syrian-Israeli armistice line soon flared into an open conflict in the winter of 1964. The United States called upon both parties to cooperate with the U.N. Truce Supervision Organization.[29] In the meantime, Syria began to support Palestinian guerrilla attacks inside Israel. The advent of the extreme left of the Ba'th to power in February 1966 intensified the conflict along the Israeli-Syrian border. The attitude of the new regime to Israel was best described in the Extraordinary Regional Congress of March 10–27, 1966: "We have to risk the destruction of all we have built up in order to eliminate Israel."[30] The neo-Ba'thists actively abetted Palestinian guerrilla raids into Israel. This assistance served as an unequivocal testimony to Syria's call for a "people's war of liberation."

In order to support its extreme attitude toward the Arab-Israeli conflict and its domestic policy, the neo-Ba'th government cooperated closely with the Soviet Union to obtain Soviet financial and military aid. By contrast, Syria's relations with the United States continued to deteriorate. The United States, however, held both Syria and Israel responsible for the growing violence along the borders.[31] Later it called upon Syria to ensure that its territory not be used as a base for terrorism against Israel.[32]

Heightened tension along the Israeli-Syrian border contributed to the eruption of the June 1967 War, following which Damascus broke off diplomatic relations with Washington. Israel had its first foretaste of strategic cooperation with the United States when it shipped captured Soviet-made weapons to the United States for analysis. During the period before the war, AIPAC and other Jewish groups and organizations led a public campaign in the United States emphasizing the great danger to Israel's existence. Led by AIPAC, the American Jewish community began a serious effort to deepen the relationship between Israel and the United States through democratic lobbying. Yet, notwithstanding the transfers of some offensive weapons, the United States kept considerable constraints on the supply of arms to Israel.

Though the United States tried to maintain an evenhanded approach to its relations with both Israel and Syria, its interest in dealing with Soviet influence in the region cast a pall over its relationship with Syria. Syria, on the other hand, made matters worse. It was ensconcing itself within the Soviet effigy of international politics. Against this background, a Middle East beset by domestic, regional, and international conflicts opened the way for a new turning point in U.S. policy in the area in general and toward Syria in particular.

Turning Points (1967–1979)

The failure of the United States to bring the Arab states into the Western camp and its inability to resolve the Arab-Israeli conflict on the basis of the status quo made U.S. foreign policy in the region inconclusive. The triumph of Israel in the 1967 War and its acquisition of Arab territories changed not only the status quo in the region but also America's concept of how to resolve the conflict. A new rationale developed that occupied Arab territories could be returned in exchange for Arab readiness to make peace with Israel. The United States could still promote its friendship with the Arab states while supporting Israel. The United States could also work for the return of the conquered territories to the Arab states while at the same time giving Israel a qualitative military edge until the Arabs were prepared to make peace. Accordingly, the United States could apply arbitrary pressure on both parties.

Meanwhile, despite the adoption of Resolution 242 by the U.N.,[33] the Soviet Union had replenished the arsenals of Egypt and Syria to the extent that they were eroding Israel's military superiority. The United States loomed for Israel as the only power available to build a strategic relationship with, particularly after France had fallen out with Israel. President Charles de Gaulle grounded the French-Israeli alliance after he castigated Israel for ignoring his warning not to attack Egypt first in the 1967 War and for using French supplied warplanes to stage the famous preemptive strike.

The Johnson administration lived up to the new rationale and acceded to Israel's request for the purchase of 50 Phantom jets and other equipment. Nadav Safran commented that the "transaction represented the first move by the United States to support by military means, not just diplomatic action, the thesis that Israel should hold on to the conquered territories until the Arabs were prepared to make peace."[34] From a different perspective, this arms transfer constituted a point of departure in U.S.-Israeli relations and U.S.-Arab relations: It blurred the distinction between U.S. support for Israel proper and U.S. support for Israel the conqueror of new territories.

By early 1969 the Cold War witnessed a change in diplomacy with the advent of the Nixon administration to the White House. The Vietnam War and the American realization that the sophistication of the Soviet Union's military capability could now neutralize the ability of the United States to check Moscow convinced the new administration to supplement military deterrence with other ways for affecting Soviet behavior. Rapprochement with China, disengagement from Vietnam, and détente with the Soviet Union had become the triad of the administration's new approach to the Cold War. In line with this new approach, the American administration took up two initiatives with regard to the Middle East, in the words of the former Pentagon official and scholar Seyom Brown, "Intense U.S.-Soviet consultations designed to lock the Russians into a joint approach toward an Arab-Israeli settlement; and a new 'even-handed' posture toward the demands of the Israelis and the Arabs."[35] The culmination of both initiatives soon resulted in what became known as the Rogers Plan, the U.S. draft outline prepared by Secretary of State William P. Rogers and presented to the Soviets in October 1969.

The Rogers Plan in essence called for Israel's unilateral withdrawal from Arab occupied territories,[36] confirming Israel's premonition of the two big powers' talks. True, the plan envisaged a contractual peace, but it had not dealt with the issue of securing Israel's borders. Israel, at first, flatly rejected the plan and embarked on a course of strained relations, especially with the U.S. State Department. Even before the superpower talks, a war of attrition had erupted between Egypt and Israel. In January 1970, the Israelis escalated their counterraids across the Suez Canal and deep into Egypt's territory. In response, the Soviets accelerated the delivery of arms to Egypt.

Secretary Rogers believed that even partial identification with Israel would not only hurt American interests in the Arab countries but would also push those countries towards the Soviet Union. Conversely, concerns over the behavior of the United States in the face of Soviet expansion in the Middle East were voiced in the administration. Some members of the defense and intelligence establishment and foreign policy specialists spearheaded by Henry Kissinger, the President's national security advisor, believed that commitment to Israel was no longer burdensome and that a firm support of Israel could deter the Soviet's intention of establishing predominance in the region.

When reports of not only Soviet arms delivery to Egypt such as supersonic (MIG) jets and surface-to-air missiles (SAM) but also of Soviet military personnel manning the SAM sites and piloting the planes reached U.S. intelligence in April, President Nixon ordered an evaluation of the Soviet role in the region and rushed military aid to Israel, short of the supersonic planes (F-4) that Israel had requested. Playing on Israel's need for modern weaponry, Nixon pressured the then Israeli prime minister, Golda Meir, into announcing formally on May 26 Israel's acceptance of U.N. Resolution 242 as a basis for a settlement. Alternatively, President Nixon and Kissinger, in a move that ran counter to the State Department's line, accused the Arabs of "being the aggressors who 'wanted to throw Israel into the sea' and castigated the Soviet Union for supporting them."[37]

By late July and early August, Egypt and Israel, respectively, accepted the American proposal for a cease-fire. Egypt, however, violated the truce by moving SAM batteries into a prohibited zone. Angry over Egypt's violation and over the Soviets' connivance, Nixon reacted by approving the sale of supersonic jets (F-4) to Israel and other electronic-countermeasure equipment for Israeli jets to neutralize the SAMs. This episode marked a decided shift in American foreign policy in the region. The administration began to lean more toward the Israeli position, which loathed making territorial concessions without tangible Arab commitments to live in peace. Against this background, the major turning point in U.S.-Israeli relations had occurred.

A crisis had developed in the Middle East when in September 1970, members of the Popular Front for the Liberation of Palestine (PFLP) hijacked three airplanes and forced them to land on an airstrip in Jordan. The PFLP held 475 hostages, many of them Americans. King Hussein of Jordan appeared helpless before the whole world, as his kingdom was in danger of being overrun by Palestinian guerrillas, who enjoyed the public support of Jordan's Palestinian majority. After the release of most of the hostages except for the Jewish passengers, King Hussein placed the kingdom under martial law and launched a military campaign to crush the guerrillas. Not only the king but also Washington was concerned that Syrians and Iraqis would intervene to help the Palestinians. Washington was adamant about demonstrating its power in the Middle East. President Nixon remarked that the United States would not allow Hussein to be overthrown by a Soviet-inspired insurrection.[38]

When the tide began to turn against the guerrillas, Syria came to their aid. On September 18, Syrian tank units crossed the Jordanian border in the direction of the city of Irbid. The next day Washington ordered a selective alert of American airborne units stationed in the United States and West Germany, and for two days issued warnings to the Soviets that if Syria did not withdraw from Jordan, Israel or the United States itself might intervene.[39] Washington had come to the conclusion that an effective intervention had to involve the Israelis, even before Syrian tanks crossed into Jordan. President Nixon had authorized $500 million in military assistance to Israel plus an additional delivery of supersonic jets, coinciding with Golda Meir's visit to the White House to press for extensive arms deliveries.

In the meantime, King Hussein requested, through the Americans, Israeli air support. Kissinger immediately conveyed this request to Yitzhak Rabin, Israel's ambassador to the United States.[40] After quick deliberations, Israel decided to take action and cooperated with the United States in planning an Israel Defense Forces intervention. Responding to Israel's request, the United States pledged to deliver additional arms and to come to its aid in the event Egypt or the Soviet Union reacted militarily to Israel's intervention. The U.S.-Israeli cooperation, the mobilization of Israeli forces along the Syrian border, the adamant attitude of the Americans to face the Soviets, together with King Hussein's all-out offensive, convinced the Syrians to withdraw from Jordan and the Soviets to avert the risk of a broader war. The king restored order in Jordan, and the United States demonstrated its coercive power in the Middle East.

The Jordanian crisis had a far-reaching impact on U.S.-Israeli relations and, by implication, on U.S.-Syrian relations. At a time when the American position in the Middle East appeared to be beating a retreat, the United States with the help of an unwavering Israel was able to reverse the whole situation. Israel loomed not only as a friend in crucial times, but also as a stabilizing force and a bulwark against Soviet expansion in the region. For the United States, the value of a powerful Israel in the Middle East had weakened the argument that U.S. commitments to Israel would hurt American interests in the Arab world. However, the extent of U.S. commitments had to be weighed against Arab anticipated reaction. Kissinger conveyed a message from President Nixon through Rabin to Israel's Prime Minister Golda Meir: "The President will never forget Israel's role in preventing the deterioration in Jordan and in blocking the attempt to overturn the regime there. He said that the United States is fortunate in having an ally like Israel in the Middle East. These events will be taken into account in all future developments."[41] The groundwork for a strategic cooperation between the United States and Israel had been set up. Though Israel had disagreements with the United States over the Rogers Plan, the State Department no longer applied pressure on Israel by manipulating the supply of arms to it.

Kissinger's Realpolitik

Until the eruption of the October War of 1973, the American administration assumed that war was not a palatable alternative for either Egypt or Syria given Israel's military superiority and given the prospect that under international pressure Israel could return the occupied territories in exchange for Arab commitments to live in peace. Despite indications from various sources that offensive Egyptian-Syrian formations were organized, the attack on Israel came as a surprise to both Israel and the United States.

Kissinger's approach to the crisis rested on two objectives "first, to end hostilities as quickly as possible—but secondly, to end hostilities in a manner that would enable us to make a major contribution to removing the conditions that have produced four wars between Arabs and Israelis in the last 25 years."[42] The underlying assumption was that these objectives could be achieved if neither side had a decisive win. In the course of the war, Kissinger was able to help both Egypt and Israel. He coordinated the American airlift to Israel and relieved Israeli pressure on the surrounded Egyptian Third Army. At the same time he convinced the concerned parties that he was neither pro-Israel nor pro-Arab. Apparently, Kissinger employed an evenhanded approach that many in Israel perceived as a return to the previous policies pursued prior to the 1970 Jordanian crisis. Kissinger had been laying the ground for launching his negotiations to secure political arrangements and some sort of military equilibrium that would be acceptable to all parties.

On his perception of U.S.-Israeli relations, Kissinger wrote in his memoirs:

> ...Israel is dependent on the United States as no other country is on a friendly power. Increasingly, Washington is the sole capital to stand by Israel in international forums. We are its exclusive military supplier, its only military ally (though no formal obligation exists). The Arab nations blame us for Israel's dogged persistence. Israel sees in intransigence the sole hope for preserving its dignity in a one-sided relationship. It feels instinctively that one admission of weakness, one concession granted without a struggle, will lead to an endless catalogue of demands as every country seeks to escape its problems at Israel's expense. It takes a special brand of heroism to turn total dependence into defiance; to insist on support as a matter of right rather than as a favor; to turn every American deviation from an Israeli cabinet consensus into a betrayal to be punished rather than a disagreement to be negotiated.
>
> And yet Israel's obstinacy, maddening as it can be, serves the purposes of both our countries best. A subservient client would soon face an accumulation of ever-growing pressures. It would tempt Israel's neighbors to escalate their demands. It would saddle us with the opprobrium for every deadlock. That at any rate has been our relationship with Israel—it is exhilarating and frustrating, ennobled by the devotion and faith that contain a lesson for an age of cynicism; exasperating because the interests of a superpower and of a regional ministate are not always easy to reconcile and are on occasion unbridgeable. Israel affects our decisions through inspiration, persistence, and a judicious, not always subtle or discreet, influence on our domestic policy.[43]

Although Kissinger summed up the various aspects of the U.S.-Israeli relationship, he spoke out of diplomatic and strategic concerns where the image of Israel, the democratic and "like us" country, did not figure in his exposition. We can deduce from his approach to the crisis and his exposition that despite the special relationship evolving between the United States and Israel, the vital interests of the United States had taken precedence over all other considerations. A peaceful Middle East and a friendly relationship with the Arab countries would serve America's vital interests in the region as much as Israel's special relationship with the United States would.

Through his capacity as a mediator and his step-by-step diplomacy, Kissinger was able to work out bilateral disengagement agreements between Egypt and Israel and then Syria and Israel.

Kissinger engaged in grueling shuttle diplomacy and marathon hours of negotiations with Syrian officials in order to conclude the Israeli-Syrian disengagement agreement, following which Syria resumed its diplomatic relations with the United States. The personality of the Syrian leader, Hafiz al-Asad, took on a dimension of its own in U.S.-Syrian negotiations. Al-Asad had a habit of convening lengthy meetings with his interlocutor along with his principal state officials. Al-Asad's strategy in negotiations had been not to claim or exercise personal authority coupled with involving his principal associates in decision making so as not to act in a vacuum. He had sought consensus prior to making decisions by forcing responsibility of his actions on his associates, heeding genuine concern for domestic reactions.[44]

Kissinger remarked on the nature of his negotiations with the Syrians:

> Time-consuming, nerve-wracking, and bizarre as the procedure was, it had the great advantage from Asad's point of view that he never had to argue for a concession himself, at least in the first instance. That onus was on me. His colleagues were part of the negotiations; they had a chance to object; they almost never did so. Whatever argument persuaded Asad would also have persuaded his colleagues. It was effective domestic politics at the expense of many sleepless nights for me.[45]

The U.S. policy in the Middle East from 1973 to 1976 had revolved around Kissinger's concept of protecting American vital interests in the region through the creation of an enduring Middle East peace. Kissinger explained the U.S. policy: "We must create in the Middle East a lasting peace, not just another cease-fire....For the Arabs there can be no peace without a recovery of territory and the redress of grievances of a displaced people. For Israel, peace requires both security and recognition by its neighbors of its legitimacy as a nation."[46] This attitude of the United States towards the Arab-Israeli conflict, together with the special U.S.-Israeli relationship, made the American administration follow a carrot-and-stick approach in dealing with Israel.

However, whereas the Nixon administration was able to bring pressure to bear on Israel, the successive Ford administration could not. When President Ford called for a reassessment of the U.S.-Israeli relationship in the U.S. Congress in the spring of 1975 after Israel had refused a unilateral withdrawal from strategic positions (mainly from Sinai passes and oil fields) in Sinai within the context of an American attempt at bringing about a second Israeli-Egyptian disengagement agreement, 76 senators scuttled Ford's initiative and reaffirmed the special bond between the two countries. Israel, through AIPAC and its friends in Washington, was able to press its case in Congress, adamantly believing that the concession she was asked to make was dangerous.[47]

Thus at some juncture in U.S.-Israeli relations, where Israel's security was regarded at risk, the American administration's carrot-and-stick approach had its limitations in the form of domestic opposition. But upsetting the President of the United States had its attendant price as well. Following the failure of the American attempt at bringing about a second Israeli-Egyptian disengagement agreement in March, the United States suspended for several months its diplomatic, military, and economic support for Israel. Israeli Prime Minister Yitzhak Rabin noted to Senator George S. McGovern during his spring 1975 visit to the Middle East that Israel had never sought a defense pact with the United States. "Israel seeks a solution that can be maintained on a local basis, not one completely dependent for enforcement on the superpowers," Rabin added.[48] After his meeting with Prime Minister Rabin and Israel's Foreign Minister Yigal Allon, Senator McGovern came out with the understanding that "the kind of commitment Israel desires from the United States is a long-term, Congressionally endorsed promise to maintain a steady and varied supply of modern arms."[49] Accordingly, the gravity of the U.S. decision to suspend support was not lost on Israel. Thus Israel reconsidered its position with regard to the second disengagement agreement with Egypt and concluded that it was in her best interest not to compromise its relationship with its main supporter, the United States, and that Egypt had to be taken out from the Arab-Israeli equation in order to avoid a future war. These conclusions converged with those of the United States.

Israel decided to give up the Sinai passes and oil fields in Sinai in exchange for Egypt's commitment not to resort to force and to seek a peaceful settlement to the Arab-Israeli conflict. But in so doing Israel sought specific security compensations for the concessions it was to make from the United States. The successful conclusion of the second Israeli-Egyptian disengagement agreement (Sinai II) on September 4, 1975, entailed wide ranging American undertakings and commitments to Israel, expressed in two Memorandum of Agreement (MOA). In the first document the U.S. government pledged to Israel to "make every effort to be fully responsive, within the limits of its resources and Congressional authorization and appropriation, on an ongoing and long-term basis to Israel's military equipment and other defense requirements, to its energy requirements and to its economic needs."[50] The second document committed the United States, among other things, to continue not to recognize the Palestine Liberation Organization or negotiate with it so long as it did not recognize Israel's right to exist and did not accept Security Council Resolutions 242 and 338.

The documents were criticized in some American diplomatic quarters as being far too excessive in relation to what Israel was required to give up. Nadav Safran highlighted the criticism by writing: "If so much was given to induce Israel to withdraw some thirty kilometers, it was asked, how much more would have to be given to it, how much indeed could be given to it, to secure its withdrawal to anywhere near the pre-1967 boundaries?"[51] In any event, so long as American vital interests did not diverge from those of Israel and American foreign policy in the Middle East required Israeli concessions, the United States had to pay the attendant price to compensate for those concessions. This had become an established pattern.

The May 1974 Disengagement Agreement: A Foretaste of Middle East Diplomacy

Much has been said about the 1973 War. But whether the origins of the 1973 War lay in the ideology of the Ba'th party or in the stigma of defeat and treason, President al-Asad, like President Sadat, primarily wanted to change the balance of power. Syria's and Egypt's defeat in the 1967 War was humiliating and domestically untenable. In a society that applauds pride and strength, humiliation and weakness are perceived more as mortal enemies than the enemy (Israel) himself. Defense Minister Dayan was correct when he thought that neither Egypt nor Syria would swallow the consequences of their defeat in 1967. The 1973 War broke the stalemate of "no peace, no war" and restored some equilibrium to the balance of power in the region, which had tipped completely in Israel's favor after the 1967 War. Pondering over why Israel was taken by surprise, Muhammad Haykal wrote: "The Israelis completely underestimated the balance of [a certain kind of] power between the Arabs and Israel. A military or political balance between 100 million Arabs and the 3 million Israelis cannot be kept for ever."[52]

Syria was defeated on the battlefield, but since the Syrian regime had made military struggle against Israel a national priority, it had to claim a certain victory for an otherwise flawed policy. Therefore the most militant state against Israel had to vindicate its claim of victory to justify domestically its negotiations with Israel. Vindicating a claim hard to prove put an onus on the negotiations. It was against this background that Secretary of State Kissinger began his shuttle diplomacy between Jerusalem and Damascus to conclude a disengagement of forces agreement.

Egypt's duplicity in the war by hiding from Syria Cairo's true political objectives and its signing of a disengagement agreement before Syria negotiated its own with Israel was a severe blow to al-Asad. Through the Syrian lens, Egypt and the Soviet Union left Syria out on a limb, facing the bulk of Israel's army. The 1973 fighting ended with Israel capturing Syrian territories beyond the 1967 cease-fire line (minor advances on the southern front and significant territory in the north, only 20 miles from Damascus), backed by the strategic area of Mount Hermon. Syria had no other option than to accept American mediation with Israel in order to recover its newly occupied territory. But Syria was in a double bind: Inasmuch as it needed the withdrawal of Israel, it could not settle only for the restoration of the October 6 (prewar) line. It needed a symbolic gain of land captured by Israel in 1967 to safeguard the legitimacy of the regime, to rationalize domestically the negotiations with Israel, to keep pace with Egypt which had recovered a piece of Sinai, and to justify the October war itself.

After signing the disengagement agreement (Sinai I) with Egypt, Israel was not in a hurry to conclude a similar one with Syria. The government came under constant attack from the public at large whose anger over the mismanagement of the war was expressed in several waves of demonstrations. And since the military situation was tenable for Israel along the Golan front, a disengagement agreement with Syria was not high on Israel's military agenda. However, Israel was keenly interested in the return of its prisoners of war, and Secretary of State Kissinger had a clear understanding of Syria's and Israel's predicaments.

After completing the Egyptian-Israeli disengagement agreement, in late January 1974, Israel's prime minister, Golda Meir, informed Kissinger that "there could be no negotiation until there was some sign that Israeli prisoners of war held in Syria would be returned. At a minimum, Israel wanted the names of its POWs and Red Cross visits to verify their treatment."[53] Acting on the assumption that once Syria complied with these terms negotiations would start, Kissinger formulated a proposal that in essence required Syria to reveal the number and names of Israeli prisoners, and in exchange Israel would come up with a disengagement proposal. In early February, Kissinger transmitted his proposal to President al-Asad, emphasizing that he would not proceed with the negotiations until the Arab oil embargo imposed on the West during the 1973 War had been lifted. Meanwhile, combining promises of undertaking a major role for achieving a reasonable peace in the Middle East with a veiled threat of American military intervention, Kissinger convinced the Arab states to lift the oil embargo unconditionally. No linkage was made between lifting the embargo and progress on the Israeli-Syrian disengagement agreement.

President al-Asad at first provided the United States with the number of Israeli prisoners, then the list of names, and agreed to Red Cross visits. In his late February meeting with Kissinger, al-Asad insisted on extracting a guarantee that the final "disengagement line would show he had gained territory from the October war."[54] To pressure the United States and back his diplomacy, he initiated a war of attrition along the new cease-fire line in March.

On April 2, the commission of inquiry established after the war, the Agranat Commission, published its findings, which shook the Labor government and precipitated the resignation of Prime Minister Meir and her government on April 11.[55] Meir's resignation relieved her of many political pressures, and allowed her to focus on the Israeli-Syrian negotiations and the return of Israeli prisoners of war. While Meir's government was acting in an interim period, Kissinger reinvigorated his shuttle diplomacy. Kissinger's priority was to find the separation line that both countries would agree upon and then to bring the elements of the agreement to fall into place.

Kissinger planned to enlist Arab support for his efforts with Syria and to use a carrot-and-stick approach with Israel. Before his shuttle diplomacy took off in late April, President Nixon waived Israel's "repayment on $1 billion of the $2.2 billion in aid to cover arms purchases."[56] This had come in the wake of a U.S. vote for a U.N. resolution that condemned Israel for a retaliatory raid in southern Lebanon. On April 11, Palestinian guerrillas crossed into northern Israel from Lebanon and attacked the town of Kiryat Shmona, prompting an Israeli air retaliation. The U.S. vote in the U.N. outraged Israel, reduced Kissinger's credibility, and heightened Israel's sense of insecurity. Meanwhile, Kissinger received the blessing and support of President Nixon who was anxious for Kissinger to succeed in his mission. Tormented by the Watergate scandal, Nixon sought a breakthrough in the Middle East to enhance his image at home.

Kissinger's shuttle diplomacy took him first to Geneva for talks with the Soviet foreign minister, Andrei Gromyko. He convinced Gromyko to stay out of the substantive Israeli-Syrian negotiations, and to limit the Soviet Union's role to symbolic participation. Since Egypt had started a harsh press campaign against them throughout the month of April, the Soviets were on the defensive and feared a further loss in their influence in the Middle East. Then Kissinger left for Algeria and Egypt to tap Houari Boumedienne's and Anwar Sadat's influence with Syria. Boumedienne had close relations with al-Asad and had good credentials as a revolutionary. Sadat had mended his relations with the United States, and, given Egypt's importance in the calculus of American diplomacy in the Arab world, al-Asad reckoned that Sadat's support could bring the United States closer to his own position. At the same time, al-Asad harbored suspicions that Sadat may have concluded a secret deal with the United States for a separate settlement with Israel and would not come to his aid if the war of attrition escalated into a general war. Hence, al-Asad was inclined to actively involve the Egyptians in the negotiations in order to keep tabs on them. Subsequently, Kissinger girded himself for action and left for Israel and then Syria.

Kissinger realized that an Israeli-Syrian disengagement was essential to protect the Egyptian-Israeli disengagement agreement and to prevent the Soviets from reasserting their influence in the Middle East. He played on the theme with the Israelis that the war of attrition on the Golan Heights could escalate into a resumption of war on the Syrian front with the consequence that Egypt would be forced to join. This would create a general war, reimpose the Arab oil embargo, and threaten American influence in the region. Meanwhile, the Soviets would capitalize on the situation, reposition themselves in Cairo, and reassert their presence in the region. Consequently, U.S. commitment to the defense of Israel would be compromised, increasing Israel's isolation in the world. In addition, to bring pressure to bear on Israel, Kissinger sought President Nixon's help. "A letter from Nixon to Meir on May 4 warned her not to allow Israeli actions to jeopardize the favorable trends in the area. Otherwise the United States, out of friendship for Israel and a sense of responsibility, would have to reexamine the relationship between the two countries."[57] As a result, the Israeli cabinet made an important concession: the Israeli "defense line would be moved behind the October 6 line to the west of Quneitra."[58] The proposal revealed that Israel had crossed a psychological barrier as it was considering, for the first time, pulling back from the prewar line.

Once in Damascus, Kissinger used a negotiating tactic with al-Asad based on disclosing some of Israel's concessions while withholding others, lest al-Asad would ask for more. Al-Asad listened carefully to the proposal, pondering its implications. He had reservations about the plan, but did not flatly reject it. Significantly, he was no longer asking for a deep Israeli withdrawal from the Golan Heights. Regaining Quneitra, the symbol of the 1967 defeat, and the three surrounding hills had become his goal as this would symbolize a tangible gain and could be defended well domestically.

On the morning of May 15, Israel woke up to another Palestinian terrorist attack on the northern Israeli town of Ma'alot. Infiltrating from Lebanon, the terrorists reached Ma'alot and took over a schoolhouse full of children and teachers. After initial bargaining with the terrorists, the Israeli government gave orders to its soldiers to storm the schoolhouse. Before meeting their death, the terrorists murdered 16 school children and wounded 68 others.[59] The gory attack left Israel more insecure and less willing to consider risky concessions. Although Syria dissociated itself from the attack and called for the continuation of negotiations, the deadlock over Quneitra and the gloomy atmosphere in Israel brought the negotiations to the verge of collapse. Kissinger realized that the time had come for the United States to advance its own positions to the concerned parties.

In the meantime, President Nixon was closely following the course of negotiations, desperately hoping for a breakthrough to boost his public image. New revelations and developments surrounding his involvement in the Watergate scandal had brought his public image to a new low. Nixon reaffirmed his full support of Kissinger and urged him to follow through on the negotiations, which appeared to him impeded by Israel's intransigence. The President wanted all aid to Israel cut off unless it changed its position.[60] He even inquired about potential aid to Syria. The intervention by the President had the effect not only of putting the U.S.-Israeli relationship on trial, but also of bringing every future Arab-Israeli deadlock to the American president's doorstep for putting pressure on Israel. This gave additional incentive to Kissinger to come up with an American proposal. Israel, for its part, had seen its fears of Nixon's threat almost confirmed. Not only was there a possible shift in American diplomacy away from Israel, but also that possibility was reinforced by American offers of aid to Syria. The specter of Israel's worsening relations with its main supporter prompted some members of the Israeli cabinet to cooperate with Kissinger.

Kissinger saw tactical advantages in advancing his own plan. He would bring the U.S. proposal close to Israel's demands. Israel would reconsider its position and would go along with the proposal. He presented his government's proposal to Israel's cabinet on May 16. Israel would keep control of the hills on condition that no heavy armaments would be placed there and that the Syrian civilian population would be allowed to return to the city of Quneitra. Subsequently, Kissinger refined the proposal and was able to get

Israel's assent to pulling back to the base of the hills, and Syria's assent to keeping the hills west of Quneitra with Israel as long as no heavy equipment was placed there.

Then, he set out to delineate the zones of limited armaments behind the forward positions of the two sides. The problem of force limitations and the size of the zones of limited armaments arose. Frustrated, Kissinger used the most effective way of putting pressure on both parties. He drafted a departure statement and planned to leave the area. After Egypt interceded with Syria, and after the many hours Kissinger spent on negotiations with the Israelis and Syrians between May 20 and May 25, both sides agreed "on the number of troops and types of equipment in a first zone of limited armaments ten kilometers from each side's forward position."[61] In his talks with the Israelis, Kissinger promised that he would try to place Israel's military supplies from the United States on a long-term basis.[62] Al-Asad accepted a large U.N. force and a wider buffer zone of ten kilometers and limited-force zones of fifteen kilometers.[63] But he was reluctant to limit his ground forces in the limited zones, while accepting the arms limitations. Heavy artillery and surface-to-air missiles would be kept out of range of the other's forward line.

However, the problem was where to draw the forward lines from which the distances of the limited zones would be measured. Israel and Syria disagreed on the exact location of the lines. In addition, neither Syria nor Israel had agreed on the number and name of the U.N. personnel. Al-Asad still refused to concede Israel's demand that he commit himself to preventing Palestinian terrorist attacks from his side of the line. The atmosphere in Israel was ambivalent and tense. In Damascus, Kissinger found al-Asad intractable. He haggled incessantly over the "Syrian forward line, the force limits, the size of U.N. contingent, and the Palestinians."[64] The negotiations were difficult, and both parties appeared to have given up hope. On the morning of May 27, Kissinger readied himself to leave Damascus with a sense of sadness; his mission apparently had failed. Before departing, he held a meeting with al-Asad during which the latter threw a diplomatic bombshell. Out of fondness for the American Secretary of State, al-Asad decided to reconsider the Syrian forward line. He asked Kissinger's view on how far the Syrian forward line could be advanced.

Stunningly, al-Asad reopened the way to follow through on the negotiations, and Kissinger jump-started the negotiations again. He suggested that the line be moved forward another one kilometer. Though the idea was presented as his own, the Israelis had allowed him to offer it, but Kissinger had held the idea back from al-Asad. Al-Asad and Kissinger hit it off well on all issues except on preventing Palestinian guerrilla activity, which al-Asad perceived as an issue of principle. On May 28, the Israeli cabinet, while agreeing on all issues, decided that, unless the terrorism issue was included in the agreement, it would not sign it. It was a difficult problem. Whereas Syria could not publicly dissociate itself from the Palestinians, Israel after Khiryat Shmona and Ma'alot could not avoid tackling Palestinian terrorism. On the same day, Kissinger flew back to Damascus to iron out the last remaining but seemingly intractable difficulty. Al-Asad spoke passionately about the Palestinians and their sad condition, and he thought it was wrong of him to interfere with their struggle. But he gave Kissinger his oral commitment that he would not allow the Golan Heights to become a source of guerrilla attacks against Israel.[65]

Kissinger flew back to Jerusalem to convince the Israelis to accept al-Asad's oral concession. On this issue, he found it essential that the United States assure Israel of American political support for any reaction against possible terrorism attack originating from the Golan Heights.[66] Two days later, on May 31, 1974, Syrian and Israeli military representatives signed the Israeli-Syrian Disengagement Agreement in Geneva. Israel and Syria were to scrupulously observe the cease-fire and refrain from all military actions against each other, in implementation of U.N. Security Council Resolution 338. The agreement was not a peace treaty and was less than the Egyptian-Israeli one. It was a step toward a "just and durable peace on the basis of Security Council Resolution 338 dated October 22, 1973."[67] Israel was to withdraw from the entire land captured in the October war and the few strips of territory conquered in 1967, including the city of Quneitra. The Disengagement Agreement defined three areas of security provisions in order to uphold the scrupulous observance of the cease-fire: The area of separation under the U.N. Disengagement Observers Force (1250 men), which included Quneitra; a second area of equal length (10 kilometers) to both parties from the area of separation, limited to 75 tanks, 36 short-range guns, and 6,000 soldiers for each; a third area, also of equal length (10 kilometers), from the second area, limited to 450 tanks and less than 200 short-range guns. In addition, surface-to-air missiles could be deployed not less than 25 kilometers from the area of separation.[68] The agreement was simple and reciprocative for both parties.

This agreement is important because it was the first one to be signed by Israel and Syria under the auspices of the United States. In addition, it has been scrupulously observed by both parties since its inception. A look at the agreement would show the main factors responsible for its success. First, Secretary of State Kissinger was backed by the President, and he increased American input into the negotiations. The United States not only played the role of moderator but also that of mediator that advanced its own positions. The United States enlisted Arab support for its negotiations with Syria and used a carrot-and-stick approach with Israel, in that the United States compensated Israel for the concessions it was pressured into making. Second, the United States kept the Soviet Union at a distance from the negotiations, allowing for a symbolic Soviet role only. This is important because it conveyed to Arab leaders and particularly to al-Asad that without American support there is no return to the status quo ante. This complemented the overall strategy of the Nixon administration in the Middle East, which set out to demonstrate that the Soviet Union's capacity to foment crises was not matched by its ability to resolve them.[69] The underlying implications of the American strategy were to prod the Arab leaders to approach Washington for assistance in the peace process and to make manifest the Arab's anachronistic concept of the all-or-nothing approach towards Israel. Finally, while the personality of Secretary of State Kissinger was a crucial factor in furthering the negotiations, the singular ingredient of success was the ability of the United States to convey to the Arab negotiator that the United States was able to pressure Israel but that this pressure could not come cheap. This approach softened Syrian intractability. The Syrians understood that they had to limit their expectations from the United States.

A New Beginning?

After Syria resumed its diplomatic relations with the United States, Damascus appeared to have a desire to improve them, a desire that was well received in the American diplomatic quarter. In August 1974, Kissinger welcomed the Syrian foreign minister, Abd al-Halim Khaddam, to the White House, a diplomatic event that had not occurred for the past 15 years in the history of U.S.-Syrian relations.[70] After his spring 1975 visit to the Middle East, Senator McGovern remarked:

> Whatever the drift of their [Syrians] thinking toward Israel, there is a desire for good relations with the United States. Like other Arabs, they exhibit no great affection for the Soviets who supply them with military equipment. A non-Soviet Communist diplomat contended that if Israel returned the Golan Heights, Syria might lose no time in packing off its Soviet advisers.[71]

The American administration was quick in responding to Syria's overture for good relations. The State Department, through the Agency for International Development, provided two loans to Syria totaling $58 million. The loans, one for $48 million and the other for $10 million, were made, respectively, to help Syria expand and modernize its water supply system in Damascus and to increase its agricultural production.[72] Syria placed much emphasis on the economic development of the country and "in having U.S. technical cooperation and capital participation."[73] The American aid was a gesture of the administration's desire for improving its relations with Syria. Although this American approach to Syria had gained ground immediately after the 1973 War and within the context of concluding the May Disengagement Agreement, it grew out of both the U.S. policy in the region and the belief that Syria, by being on good terms with the United States, given its key role in the Arab-Israeli conflict, could enhance the capacity of the United States to bring about its policy objective, a durable peace. Harold H. Saunders, Deputy Secretary for Near Eastern and South Asian Affairs, explained:

> The role that the United States is playing in the search for peace...gives a particular and continuing importance to the relationship between the United States and Syria. It is fair to say that trust and confidence in this relationship will materially enhance the capacity of the United States to play a positive part in the negotiating effort.[74]

This policy of rapprochement was carried on by the Ford and the Carter administrations, especially since the latter had made the reflection of American values in foreign policy one of its central themes. The realpolitik and elliptical approach to foreign policy, which had characterized the State Department under Kissinger, was to be replaced by an open foreign policy, substituting "world order" for "balance of power," and placing human rights issues high on the administration's agenda. Not surprisingly, Carter's quest for idealism in foreign policy clashed with his geopolitical realism, resulting in an ambivalence, which was reinforced by the divergent world views of his principal advisers.

Early in his administration, President Carter met with many Middle Eastern political figures, including the Syrian Deputy Prime Minister and Foreign Minister Khaddam who agreed with the President on the importance of working to reconvene the Geneva conference.[75] The conference refers to the convention in December 1973 in Geneva at which the parties to the Arab-Israeli conflict (Egypt and Jordan, Israel), except Syria, were represented along with the United States and the Soviet Union, the two cochairmen. The conference broke up in a few days. The American administration wanted to include the Soviet Union in its endeavor to find a solution for the Arab-Israeli conflict by committing it to a negotiating process in a way that makes it harder for the Kremlin to oppose a settlement that could emerge. The Soviet Union was more than happy to be a partner in a peace process, after its earlier exclusion by Kissinger.

On October 1, 1977, the United States and the Soviet Union issued a joint statement emphasizing two points:

> [First] the United States and the Soviet Union believe that, within the framework of a comprehensive settlement of the Middle East problem, all specific questions of the settlement should be resolved, including such key issues as withdrawal of Israeli Armed Forces from territories occupied in the 1967 conflict; the resolution of the Palestinian question, including insuring the legitimate rights of the Palestinian people; termination of the state of war and establishment of normal peaceful relations on the basis of mutual recognition of the principles of sovereignty, territorial integrity, and political independence.
>
> [Second] the United States and the Soviet Union believe that the only right and effective way for achieving a fundamental solution to all aspects of the Middle Eastern problem in its entirety is negotiations within the framework of the Geneva peace conference, specially convened for these purposes, with participation in its work of the representatives of all parties involved in the conflict including those of the Palestinian people, and the legal and contractual formalization of the decisions reached at the conference.[76]

On October 6, Secretary of State Cyrus Vance further elaborated U.S. policy in the region by emphasizing three factors: First, the parties involved in the conflict should subordinate their concerns to the overriding goal of convening a Geneva conference; second, the agreed basis for the Geneva conference are Resolutions 242 and 338; finally, the Palestinians must be represented at the conference if a just and lasting peace is to be achieved.[77] Apparently, this new American position jibed more with the Syrian approach on how to resolve the Arab-Israeli conflict than with Israel's. In addition, the joint U.S.-Soviet declaration along with Vance's statement angered the government of Israel and its supporters in the United States. The mention of "legitimate rights" of the Palestinians rather than Palestinian "legitimate interests" and Palestinian representation at Geneva were euphemisms for a claim to statehood. Interestingly enough, Egypt and Israel were not happy with Soviet participation in the peace process. Egypt had already given up on the merit of the Soviet role in the Arab-Israeli conflict and was in the process of mending its relations with the United States. Israel, for its part, was forever wary of superpower talks. This encouraged

Israel and Egypt to upgrade their secret dialogue, which had evolved when Israel was sharing intelligence information with Egypt on a Libyan plot to assassinate the Egyptian president.[78] The newly established Egyptian and Israeli contacts surprised the Americans who eventually changed their plans and sought to bridge the gap between the Egyptian and Israeli positions regarding a peace settlement.

The negotiations between Israel and Egypt and the great effort of the American President Carter, along with his administration, culminated in the Camp David Accords in September 1978 and thereafter in the Israeli-Egyptian Peace Treaty, signed on March 26, 1979. The United States had sufficiently compensated Israel for the concessions it was making, especially the withdrawal from the Sinai peninsula. Congress approved a $4.9 billion aid and loan package to Israel, and, coinciding with the date for signing the Peace Treaty, the United States signed two MOA with Israel. The first included American diplomatic, economic, and military measures designed to support Israel in the event the Peace Treaty was violated, a support which was ultimately opposed by Egypt.[79] The second was an extension of the oil supply arrangement between the United States and Israel.

But this American support for Israel did not keep the administration from offering economic and military support to Egypt. The $1.5 billion package of foreign military sales credits to Egypt requested from Congress by the administration included two squadrons of F-4 Phantom aircraft and appropriate munitions.[80] Israel's foreign minister, Moshe Dayan, remarked "that there has been a 'turn' in U.S. policy concerning Israel," a remark to which the American Secretary of State replied: "I want to state categorically that there has been no change in our policy toward Israel. Our longstanding support for the security and well-being of Israel is firm and unshakable. It remains our policy to work toward a comprehensive peace settlement which is based on U.N. Security Council Resolutions 242 and 338."[81]

It was during the Carter administration that a conceptual framework for U.S.-Israeli strategic cooperation was developed. Andrew Marshall, Dennis Ross, and James Roche, then officials in the Office of Net Assessments of the Department of Defense, formulated the framework, and in 1979 Secretary of Defense Harold Brown and Israeli Defense Minister Ezer Weizman signed the first U.S.-Israeli Memorandum of Agreement on defense cooperation.[82] The U.S. government designated Israel as a non-NATO ally state, making it possible for Israel to receive U.S. technology transfers. In addition, the administration and Congress were ever ready to fight for Israel in the U.N. and to override various efforts to isolate Israel internationally. Nevertheless, while the American administration professed firm support to Israel, its position on the Palestinians and the Arab-Israeli conflict made that support hesitant.

Despite the sharp criticism of Egypt by Syria for signing the Peace Treaty, the Carter administration latched onto the belief that Syria was a key country in the Middle East, with a capacity to influence events beyond its borders. The Syrian leadership still sought to expand its relationship with the United States, emphasizing its need for economic assistance and willingness to cooperate. In 1978, a major "delegation of the Ba'th political party visited the U.S. for the first time in that party's history to meet with American politicians, primarily at the municipal, county, and state levels."[83] In the meantime, the United States and Syria signed a cultural agreement, proposed by the Syrians, and under the auspices of U.S. economic assistance many Syrian educators, engineers, technicians, and scholars visited the United States. In the fiscal years 1978 and 1979, the Carter administration requested, respectively, $90 million and $60 million in economic assistance for Syria.[84]

But this evolution of U.S.-Syrian relations was greatly undermined by Syria's support of terrorism, which set the stage for a new ambivalent relationship between the two countries.

CHAPTER 3

The Emergence of the U.S.-
Syrian Ambivalent Relationship

The evolution of U.S.-Syrian relations was seriously hobbled when Syria appeared on the U.S. State Department's "terrorism list" created in 1979. As a result, Damascus had been barred from receiving any type of assistance from Washington, while the latter had to observe certain limits in dealing with Damascus. Still, Washington maintained a belief in Syria's key regional role and in its capacity to influence events in the region. This led to the emergence of Washington's ambivalent attitude toward Damascus, which first became apparent in Lebanon and then became a hallmark of U.S.-Syrian relations until the U.S. invasion of Iraq in 2003. Ironically, the terrorism issue, which precluded the United States from improving its relationship with Syria, became the issue responsible for bringing the two countries together. At the same time, U.S.-Syrian relations, mainly in the 1980s, were affected by the Cold War and by the complexities and harsh realities of the Middle East in general and Israel's and Syria's struggle for Lebanon in particular.

The Implications of Fighting Evil for the Middle East

Chief among the reasons that have kept relations between the United States and Syria from improving are the sanctions imposed upon Syria. The U.S. Congress passed two acts, the International Security Assistance and Arms Export Control Act of 1976 and the Export Administration Act of 1979, which, respectively, terminated foreign assistance to countries that aid or abet international terrorism and required the secretaries of commerce and state to notify Congress before licensing exports of goods and technology to countries that support acts of international terrorism.[1] A by-product of these laws was the creation in 1979 of a "terrorism list" by the State Department to identify such countries. Syria has been on this list since its creation, and thus has been barred from receiving any type of assistance from the United States. Ironically, Washington has, for the most part, maintained diplomatic relations with Syria, unlike any other country appearing on this list.

Meanwhile, the Carter administration faced serious foreign policy problems that undermined the presidency and the chances for another term. The Iranian hostage crisis and the Soviet invasion of Afghanistan in late 1979 highlighted the ambivalent attitude of the administration, reflected by its divergent world views and its paradoxical attitude on human rights and political realism. Détente with the Soviet Union had come to its end, and the stage was set for the powerful Republican presidential nominee, Ronald Reagan, who exploited to the hilt Carter's ambivalence and weakness in foreign policy, as well as the administration's responsibility for a sluggish economy.

The election of Ronald Reagan to the presidency brought with it a decisive return of U.S. foreign policy to that of the era of the late 1940s and early 1950s, during which time the conflict with Communism was a struggle against evil. Reagan not only metaphorically divided the world between the forces of good and evil, but also rhetorically injected the spirit of American heroism into the struggle against Communism. He projected an image of unshakable faith in America and its ingenuity. The faith reflected the ability of America to harness strength in perilous times leading to victory, while the ingenuity reflected the American genius for unsurpassed innovation. Reagan brushed aside the premises of Mutual Assured Destruction, which depended on deterrence from both sides, denying any American responsibility for the Cold War. After all, the Soviet Union was the "focus of evil in the modern world."[2]

Early in his campaign for the presidency, Reagan disapproved of Kissinger's realpolitik and Carter's human rights policies as weakening the U.S. posture in the world. His policy was to strengthen governments on the side of free democratic capitalism and to weaken governments on the side of Marxism-Leninism. His doctrine stated:

> We must stand by all our democratic allies. And we must not break faith with those who are risking their lives—on every continent, from Afghanistan to Nicaragua—to defy Soviet-supported aggression and secure rights which have been ours from birth.[3]

The Middle East was an arena where, after the defection of Iran from the Western camp and the Soviet invasion of Afghanistan,

Soviet expansion had to be contained. Secretary of State Alexander Haig formulated the policy of "strategic consensus," which prioritized the containment of the Soviet Union over all other considerations. The underlying assumption was that all internecine conflicts in the region sapped the energy of anti-Communist governments and that building a strategic consensus in the region would propel those governments to focus on what united them, at which point the viable threat of the Soviet Union would align those countries with the United States. The Arab-Israeli conflict, however, made direct links between Arab countries and Israel unfeasible, and highlighted the ambivalence over what role Israel might play in the U.S.'s plan for building a regional consensus.

While stumping for the presidency, Reagan blamed the Carter administration for voting in favor of a U.N. resolution that repeatedly condemned Israel (March 1, 1980), America's "staunch Middle East ally for three decades."[4] He admired Israel; nevertheless, once in office, his administration's approach to the Middle East, known as "strategic consensus," caused problems for Israel. Israel could no longer claim the role of the sole strategic ally of the United States for containing the expansion of the Soviet Union since the administration had to count on Arab cooperation as well. Consequently, Arab countries could benefit militarily and economically from the United States at Israel's expense. In addition, the United States might waver in its support for Israeli actions. Following Israel's attack on Iraq's nuclear reactor in June 1981, the State Department condemned the Israeli raid. Then, the State Department presented to Congress a "report of possible Israeli violation of the Mutual Defense Assistance Agreement of July 23, 1953," which prohibited the use of U.S. arms, transferred in this case to Israel, in acts of aggression against any other state without the express consent of the U.S. government.[5]

When Israel bombed the Palestine Liberation Organization (PLO) headquarters in Beirut in July of the same year, inflicting a high number of casualties, the American administration expressed shock and suspended the delivery of supersonic F-16s jets to Israel. But it was the administration's decision to sell Saudi Arabia advanced military equipment including Airborne Warning and Control System (AWACS) aircraft that brought to the fore the discrepancy between America's admiration of and support for Israel on the one hand and America's pursuit of its strategic interests on the other. The Soviet invasion of Afghanistan, the Khomeini revolution, the Iran-Iraq war, and the Soviet presence in South Yemen and Ethiopia underscored the instability of the region and the need for the United States to counteract these advances by enhancing the security of its two major Arab allies, Saudi Arabia and Egypt.

Israel regarded the sale of jets to Saudi Arabia as a threat to its security. The friends of Israel in Congress harnessed their efforts to block the sale proposal. On October 1, 1981, Representative Dante B. Fascell and 23 cosponsors introduced House Resolution 194 disapproving the proposed sale, while Senator Robert Packwood and 49 cosponsors introduced Senate Concurrent Resolution 37 disapproving the sale as well.[6] Congress needed to pass both resolutions in order to block the sale. A battle raged between the administration and Congress, which Reagan once recalled as the toughest battle of his eight years in Washington, spending more time and effort to win on this measure than on any other.[7] On October 7, the House voted in favor of Resolution 194, and the proposed sale seemed in danger of collapsing. Reagan fought back by imposing on the Saudis stringent restrictions as to how the AWACS could be used, thereby giving assurances to the Senate that the sale would pose no realistic threat to Israel.[8] Although the Foreign Relations Committee voted 9 to 8 against the sale, the Senate voted down Resolution 37 to block it by a narrow margin, 52 to 48, and thus the sale proceeded.[9]

The premonitions that Israel had about the negative effects of American policy in the region on U.S.-Israeli relations and especially on Israel's security were being realized. The AWACS controversy stood as a proof of that. Nevertheless, all along, Israeli Prime Minister Menachem Begin continued to suggest an upgrade of U.S.-Israeli strategic cooperation in order to circumvent the now evident erosive trends. Begin emphasized Israel's value to the United States in checking Soviet expansion in the region, as well as Israel's ability to enhance America's security policy vis-à-vis the region. But what Begin was suggesting went beyond what past Israeli administrations looked for in U.S.-Israeli relations. Karen Pushel of the Jaffee Center for Strategic Studies in Israel remarked:

> Begin...expressed his hope for the formalization of closer defense relations with Washington, possibly in the form of a defense treaty. Although he often stated that Israel would not request such a treaty from the United States, Begin left no doubt that, should the United States broach the subject with Israel, he favored a formal alliance that included a defense pact.[10]

Partly to apply "damage control" to U.S.-Israeli relations in the aftermath of the AWACS controversy, and partly out of a conviction that Israel could play a role in securing America's interests in the region, the U.S. administration, over the objections of Secretary of Defense Caspar Weinberger, responded positively to Begin's suggestions, but stayed short of a military alliance. On November 30, 1981, the United States and Israel signed a Memorandum of Understanding (MOU) that enhanced their strategic cooperation. Though the MOU contained significant provisions upgrading U.S.-Israeli strategic cooperation, it reflected primarily an American Cold War strategy that emphasized more concern with Soviet expansion than with Israel's regional security risks.

The MOU stated that the strategic cooperation between the parties "is not directed at any state or group of states within the region," and added that "the parties share the understanding that nothing in this Memorandum is intended to or shall in any way prejudice the rights and obligations which devolve or may devolve upon either government under the Charter of the United Nations or under International Law."[11] Obviously the MOU was a product of the Cold War, revealing divergent motivations for enhancing the strategic cooperation. When Israel annexed Syria's Golan Heights and extended its legal jurisdiction to it in December 1981, the United States opposed Israel's action and endorsed U.N. Resolution 497 of 17 December 1981 demanding Israel to rescind its action.[12] Furthermore, President Reagan instructed his secretaries of defense and state to suspend the implementation of the MOU.[13]

It was against this background that Israel's invasion of Lebanon brought the United States and Syria to the brink of war.

The Brink of War

Following the defeat of the Palestinians in Jordan in 1970, armed Palestinian groups moved to Lebanon, enhancing the power of the Palestinians who came to the country as refugees in 1948. Because of their military power in a weak state, divided by sectarian problems, the PLO and other Palestinian groups [the Popular Front for the Liberation of Palestine, the Popular Front for the Liberation of Palestine-General Command, and the Democratic Front for the Liberation of Palestine] were able to operate in Lebanon unrestrainedly and without impunity, creating a state within a state. Divided into two camps, Lebanon's Christian camp sought to maintain their hegemony over the state and keep the country out of the Arab-Israeli conflict. The Muslim camp, including pan-Arab and leftist forces, sought to alter the status quo and to move Lebanon unequivocally in the direction of pan-Arabism. The PLO naturally sided with the Muslims. Thus, although the Palestinians were not at the root of Lebanon's weak confessional system, they were the catalyst of the system's downfall. Before long, civil war broke out in 1975.

As the civil war intensified and the partition of the country along sectarian lines was becoming a daily reality, Lebanon posed a security problem for Syria as partition of Lebanon could become de jure. Driven by Muslim and Palestinian pressure, the Christians, led by the Maronites, could well be provoked to declare their own independent state, opting for close cooperation with Israel. As the Muslim camp began to gain the upper hand in the civil war, President al-Asad realized that he had to immediately intervene in order to prevent the military downfall of the Christian side. Israel would not sit idly by and witness the creation of a radical country, swarming with Palestinian militants, along its border. At the same time, Syria's military intervention in Lebanon would provoke an Israeli counterintervention.

Meanwhile, however, the situation in Lebanon had alarmed the United States, which at first paid little attention to Lebanon, concentrating its diplomatic efforts on Egypt and Israel. Now the United States could no longer ignore Lebanon, particularly when victory for the left and the Palestinians seemed likely. The Soviet Union had been supporting the winning side, and it would inevitably gain valuable ground in case its clients won. Moreover, as both Syria and Israel perceived Lebanon as crucial to their security, they might clash and lead the region to another war. Therefore the idea of Syrian intervention in Lebanon to rein in the radicals and adjust the military balance appealed to the United States. After a difficult internal debate interspersed with negotiations with Washington, Israel conditioned its consent to the Syrian intervention on certain demands, which it conveyed to U.S. Secretary of State Henry Kissinger. The United States, functioning as an emissary between Jerusalem and Damascus, endorsed Israel's demands and passed them on to the Syrians. Apparently, the Syrians agreed to Israel's conditions, and Washington gave its "green light" for the Syrian army to enter Lebanon. This unsigned, oral U.S.-Israeli-Syrian understanding regarding Lebanon came to be known as the "Red Line" Agreement.[14] On the night of May 31, 1976, Syrian armored columns crossed the border into Lebanon.

Syrian intervention gave only a respite to Lebanon's warring factions as they began to reconsider their plans. Acknowledging that their decision to accede to Syrian intervention was one of stoic resignation because their camp was threatened with defeat, and fearing Syrian ambitions and hegemony in Lebanon, the Christians, led by Bashir Jumayil, began to cooperate closely with Israel. Chafing over the Christians' close cooperation with Israel, Syria decided to whittle away at Christian-Maronite power and began a process of rapprochement with the Palestinians and Muslims.

Meanwhile, during ongoing Egyptian-Israeli peace negotiations, on March 11, 1978, Fatah guerrillas set out from the southern city of Damour on the Lebanese coast and landed on the Israeli coast south of Haifa. When the incident was over, 34 Israelis had been killed and many more wounded. Prime Minister Begin affirmed that "those who killed Jews in our time cannot enjoy impunity."[15] On March 14, Israel retaliated and invaded southern Lebanon with the objective of destroying the military bases of the PLO and weeding them out from there. The invasion was large in scope and destructiveness. Israel seized the whole of southern Lebanon up to the Litani River, after which the operation took its code name, "Operation Litani." Considering the invasion a serious threat to the peace in the region, President Carter told Prime Minister Begin to pull his troops out, and on March 19 he instructed the U.S. ambassador to the U.N. to propose that Israeli troops in southern Lebanon be replaced by a U.N. force. This proposal resulted in the adoption of Security Council Resolution 425, which called for strict respect of Lebanon's territorial integrity and sovereignty, and called upon Israel to "withdraw forthwith its forces from all Lebanese territory." The resolution also established the U.N. Interim Force in Lebanon "for southern Lebanon for the purpose of confirming the withdrawal of the Israeli forces, restoring international peace and security and assisting the government of Lebanon in ensuring the return of its effective authority in the area."[16] Approximately three months from the date of invasion, Israel withdrew from the south of Lebanon, but not before establishing a buffer zone to protect its border from guerrilla attacks.

Following a clash between Christian Lebanese forces and Syrian forces in March–April 1981 in Zahle, the principal Christian town in the Beka Valley, a key strategic area close to the Syrian border, the Israelis, coming to the help of their Christian allies, shot down two Syrian transport helicopters flying to Mount Sanin, overlooking Zahle. In response, Syria introduced surface-to-air missile (batteries) into the Beka Valley, and precipitated what came to be known as the "missile crisis." President Reagan sent his envoy, Philip Habib, to the region to diffuse the crisis. On the way, his mission was expanded to deal with a major flare-up between Israel and the Palestinians along the Lebanese border. With the assistance of the Saudis, Habib was able to temporarily diffuse the crisis. He managed to conclude an "understanding" (i.e., a cease-fire) between Prime Minister Begin, President al-Asad, and Chairman of the

PLO Arafat (the contacts with Arafat went through the Syrians and the Saudis) in late July. According to Patrick Seale, the unsigned understanding provided that Syria would keep its missiles in the Beka Valley, but on the condition that they would not be fired; Israel would continue reconnaissance flights over Lebanon, but would not attack the missiles; and Israel and the Palestinians would stop firing upon each other across the Lebanese border.[17]

Between July 1981 and June 1982, a combination of trends and developments, originating both in the wider context of the Arab-Israeli conflict and in the dynamics of Israel's and Syria's struggle for power in Lebanon, converged to create a situation in which Israel found it expedient to invade Lebanon. Faced with a failed policy aimed at suppressing Palestinian nationalism in the West Bank and Gaza, Begin's government began to deliberate the necessity to clip the PLO's wings (the embodiment of Palestinian nationalism) in Lebanon, while at the same time holding the belief that a limited operation in Lebanon was insufficient. Given its widespread military and political infrastructure in Lebanon, the PLO could recover quickly enough. The Begin government unfailingly probed for information on how the Reagan administration would react to an operation against the PLO in Lebanon, and it frequently received the same ambiguous replies, which it interpreted as an endorsement.[18]

On June 3, 1982, Palestinian extremists (from Abu Nidal's organization and not part of the PLO) shot and gravely wounded Israel's ambassador to Britain, Shlomo Argov, in London. Israel used the incident as a pretext to invade Lebanon on June 6, launching an operation code named "Operation Peace for Galilee," falsely implying that its objective was to push back the PLO 40 kilometers from the Israeli frontier in order to protect the settlements in Galilee. Reagan's administration was greatly disturbed by the scope and breadth of Israel's invasion, as well as by its inability to anticipate this major event. Many in the administration, including Secretary of Defense Caspar Weinberger, Central Intelligence Agency Director William Casey, National Security Advisor William Clark, and Vice President George Bush, were incensed by Israel. Not only did they favor U.N. resolutions condemning Israel, but they also assured Saudi Arabia and other Arab countries that Israel's aggression would not escape with impunity. The Reagan administration immediately dispatched presidential envoy Philip Habib to the region and also voted for Security Council Resolutions 508 and 509, which called for an unconditional Israeli withdrawal. On June 9, while Habib was in Damascus, Israel's air force raided and destroyed the whole Syrian Surface-to-Air-Missiles network in the

Beka valley, raising Syrian doubts about U.S. influence over Israel and aggravating U.S.-Syrian relations.

As Israel intensified its bombing of West Beirut and Israeli armored units entered sections of the city, the United States was hammering out an agreement with the concerned parties (PLO, Syria, Lebanon, and Israel) providing for the evacuation of the PLO. The evacuation was to be monitored by a multinational peace-keeping force (MNF), composed of American, Italian, and French troops. This signaled direct American involvement in Lebanon's treacherous and gory politics. After the successful evacuation of the PLO from Beirut, President Reagan inaugurated his Middle East peace initiative, in which he made America's position on key issues very clear. The U.S. government did not support the establishment of an independent Palestinian state in the West Bank and Gaza, it did not support their annexation or permanent control by Israel, and it did not support Israeli settlement activity. U.N. Resolution 242 remained the basis for America's peace efforts. In return for peace, the "withdrawal provision of the Resolution 242 applies to all fronts, including the West Bank and Gaza."[19] The administration was convinced that Jerusalem must remain undivided and that its final status should be decided through negotiations.[20] The Reagan Plan, as the peace initiative came to be known, boiled down to granting the Palestinians autonomy in the West Bank and Gaza in association with Jordan. The Plan was rejected offhand by Begin who invaded Lebanon to clip the wings of the PLO. As a result, a wide rift between U.S. policy in the region and Israel's was revealed.

After the massacre of the Palestinian refugees in the Sabra and Shatila camps in Beirut in September 1982 by members of the Christian Phalange party, who were guided into the camps by Israel, U.S.-Israeli and U.S.-Syrian relations were further exacerbated.

Significantly, the American involvement in Lebanon suffered a painful blow when 240 U.S. Marines died in a terrorist attack on their headquarters in West Beirut in October 1983. Leftist, pro-Syrian, and nationalist Muslim Lebanese factions perceived the United States as siding with the Phalangists in the Lebanese civil war. The United States had supported the government of Amin Jumayil, a Phalangist Maronite leader. Though fingers were directed to Iran as the sponsor of the Shi'a terrorist who carried out the suicidal attack, Syrian involvement could not be ruled out. Shortly thereafter, Syria was able to rally most feuding Lebanese factions against U.S.-backed Jumayil's government and Israel's occupation.

The United States, backing its diplomacy with the threat of force, fired battleship guns (the carrier *New Jersey*) on Syrian dominated Lebanese positions. Syria fired back and shot down two American war planes, which had engaged in an exchange of fire. This marked the first direct confrontation between Washington and Damascus. However, amid sharp division and opposition to the U.S. role in Lebanon within the American administration, Reagan chose not to escalate the skirmishes to a full war. In addition, Damascus was able to rally and mobilize significant opposition against Jumayil's government, not only weakening the government but also repelling government forces from sections of the capital. Both complexities and treacherous realities of the Lebanese civil war and the Arab-Israeli conflict flew in the face of America's policy in the region. The U.S. redeployed its troops to U.S. ships offshore and put the peace initiative on the back burner. According to some analysts, these violent developments were partly the result of Secretary of State Shultz's determination to punish Syria by concluding a separate Israeli-Lebanese agreement (May 17 Agreement) behind its back and at its expense. In the end, Shultz's contest of wills with al-Asad failed ignominiously (as is made clear by Patrick Seale in the chapter of his book, *Asad of Syria: The Struggle for the Middle East*, titled "The Defeat of George Shultz").[21]

Syria won the struggle for Lebanon and emerged with more gains than any other party. Israel withdrew to the south of Lebanon, and in March 1984, Lebanon under pressure from Syria abrogated the May 17 Agreement signed between Israel and Lebanon. On March 30, the United States terminated its role in the MNF. During this period U.S.-Syrian relations continued to deteriorate but not to the point of no return. Although the U.S. government had tried to maintain to some extent a workable relationship with Syria, various factors entered and exacerbated the already strained relationship. In addition to being on the State Department's terrorism list, Syria's rejection of American peace initiatives, its continuing intervention in Lebanon as an occupier, and Syria's military buildup with the help of the Soviet Union, all combined to frustrate the American administration.

On the other hand, President al-Asad of Syria had not concealed his contempt for the U.S. government. The invasion of Lebanon by Israel not only reinforced his belief that Israel was an expansionist state but also convinced him that America was a partner in Israel's grand plan to control the region.

Al-Asad stated:

Israel's decision to invade Lebanon was taken in association with the U.S., which did not content itself with that association only, but went on to send its fleet to Lebanon to impose the May 17 Agreement...and this confirms that there is no American policy vis-à-vis the region but there is an Israeli decision which the American administration executes.[22]

Al-Asad's contempt for the United States grew out of frustration with America's decisive support for Israel. He believed that America's military and economic aid for Israel disrupted the balance of power in the region and made Israel more aggressive with the Arabs, creating thereby a situation not conducive to peace. On America's intentions on achieving peace in the Middle East, al-Asad said:

> Had the U.S. wanted actually to achieve peace, it would not have given that huge aid to Israel every year, because this huge aid disrupts the balance of power in the region; do they really believe in the U.S. that peace can be achieved when Israel is the superpower in the region? If that is what they believe then this belief lacks logic and objectivity.[23]

But, despite his contempt, al-Asad did not break relations with the United States. He was careful not to burn bridges with Washington. In a symbolic peaceful gesture, Syria released in January 1984 Lieutenant Robert O. Goodman, Jr., who had been captured by the Syrians when his plane was shot down.[24]

Meanwhile, Syria was well under way in its quest for strategic parity with Israel by building its military with the help of the Soviets in order to adjust the strategic imbalance vis-à-vis Israel. The Egyptian-Israeli peace treaty of 1979 and the Iran-Iraq War removed both Egypt and Iraq as potential Arab coalition members in a future confrontation with Israel. In addition, the U.S. support for Israel had further weakened Syria's military standing vis-à-vis Israel. These factors disrupted the balance of power between the Arabs and Israel and spurred Syria to unilaterally pursue its military parity with Israel. The aforementioned episodes in Lebanon only energized Syria to follow through its quest.

The Irony of Fighting Terrorism

As the policy of "strategic consensus" pursued in the region proved to be replete with complexities, Washington decided to focus on the fight against terrorism. After his presidential campaign, President Reagan had often repeated his statements that he would give terrorism no quarters and that he would inflict swift and effective retribution upon those who committed acts of terror. Accordingly, the United States revised its policy, supplanting "strategic consensus" with the battle against terrorism.

Beirut, after the Israeli invasion and the American debacle, had become a playground for terrorists who targeted Westerners, especially Americans. In January 1984, Dr. Malcolm Kerr, the president of the American University of Beirut, was assassinated as he was entering the campus.[25] Before long, a kidnapping spree of foreigners, mostly Americans, pervaded Lebanon. Shi'a radicals, some of whom founded the Islamist party Hizbollah (or the Party of God) and largely votaries of the Khomeini revolution, found out that kidnapping Americans could not only embarrass and take revenge against the great American nation but could also exact a high priced ransom for hostages. William Buckley, Reverend Benjamin Weir, Father Lawrence Jenco, and Terry Anderson topped the growing kidnappers' list.

Shi'a extremists did not confine the perpetration of their actions to Lebanese soil. In June 1985, they hijacked TWA Flight 847 and demanded the release of Lebanese Shi'ites captured by Israel during their invasion of Lebanon. The hijackers made good on their threats by shooting an American passenger and throwing his body off the plane onto Beirut airport's runway. All of a sudden the fate of the American hostages in Lebanon, seven at the time, had become entangled with the arrangements being undertaken to release the TWA passengers. Syria's intercession on behalf of the Americans with the various radical Shi'ite organizations in Lebanon had become essential as a means to facilitate the release of hostages. After all, Syria was the main power broker in Lebanon, maintaining 40,000 Syrian troops there. The combination of Israel's release of a significant number of Lebanese Shi'ites and the efforts of Nabih Berri, the pro-Syrian Shi'ite lawyer and head of Amal, the armed militia of the Shi'ites, who negotiated on behalf of the hijackers, led to the release of the TWA hostages. Afterward, Palestinian terrorists hijacked the Italian cruise ship *Achille Lauro* and demanded the release of some Palestinians from Israeli jails. The terrorists requested Syria's permission to dock the ship at the port of Tartus, a request Syria refused as it cooperated with Italy and the United States. As time passed, the list of hostages captured in Lebanon during the second term of President Reagan had grown in size, and, as a result, America's need for Syria's intercession to free the hostages had grown in comparison.

Ironically, the terrorism issue, which precluded the United States from improving its relationship with Syria, became the issue responsible for bringing the two countries together. By the late 1980s and early 1990s, Syria played a significant role in securing the release of the hostages. In 1989, John H. Kelly, assistant secretary, bureau of Near Eastern and South Asian Affairs, testified before the Committee on Foreign Affairs: "Syria has told us that they will be as helpful as possible on the question of hostages in Lebanon," and added: "I think that Syria was indeed helpful in the case of Charlie Glass who was kidnapped and held for a couple of months."[26] The avenue to freedom for the hostages was through Damascus, where the Syrians basked in the attention of the international press.[27]

Syria's cooperation with the United States pleased the American administration but had little effect on Congress, whose majority remained unswayed in their determination to keep sanctions on Syria so long as it harbored and abetted terrorist organizations on its soil. And, of course, there were limits to the extent to which the administration could go in cooperating with Syria. In addition to being on the State Department's terrorism list, Syria had been denied certification for American international aid as a result of its inadequate effort to stop drug production and/or drug trafficking.[28] When Syrian intelligence was implicated in an aborted attempt (Hindawi affair) to place a bomb on an El Al airliner at Heathrow airport in 1986, the administration added further controls to detailed trade restrictions on exports to Syria.[29] This incident heaped world opprobrium on al-Asad. After much pressure from Britain and the United States, Syria in 1987 expelled the radical terrorist organization of Abu Nidal, Sabri al-Banna, from its soil.[30] Consequently, Syria's relationship with the United States had become contradictory and perplexing: Contradictory, because inasmuch as the United States wanted to punish Syria for its involvement in terrorism, the United States needed Syria's help in dealing with terrorism. Perplexing, because the administration had tried to maintain, if not to improve, its relations with Syria at a time when the U.S. government had to observe limits in its cooperation with Syria considering that Congress was adamant in its negative attitude towards that country. This formed the basis of Washington's ambivalent attitude toward Damascus.

The Emergence of Hizbollah

Initially, many in the Shi'a community welcomed Israel's invasion as a way of ending PLO activities in southern Lebanon. But that initial feeling quickly faded in response to the anti-Israel political climate that the Shi'a community found itself living under due to later developments. Amal had emerged as the strong military arm of the community and had taken the initiative in staking its claim to power in Lebanon. Notwithstanding the close relationship of Shi'a with Syria, Amal's objective of undermining Maronite political hegemony converged with that of Syria, although the two objectives were pursued for different reasons. This automatically tied Amal's struggle to that of Syria against the Maronite-Israeli alliance and thus against Israel.

In addition, Iran's contacts with the Shi'a of southern Lebanon provided the seeds for the emergence of an Islamic movement opposed to Israel. Iran's theocratic leaders strove to expand their revolution by exporting it to Lebanon, building a political base among the Shi'a that supported their radical and anti-Israel ideology. The new movement considered Israel a usurper of Muslim land and a tool in Satan's (the United States) imperialist hands. This was reinforced, on the one hand, by Syria letting into the Beka valley some 2,000 Iranian revolutionary guards who disseminated Iran's radical ideology to the whole Shi'a community, and, on the other hand, by Iran's backing the spread of its ideology by military and financial rewards. This not only had served to turn many Shi'ites into radical Iranian disciples but also had put pressure on the Shi'a mainstream to consider any relationship with Israel as taboo.

Many Shi'ites made a connection between Israel's invasion of Lebanon and their own understanding of the Iranian revolution. The revolution convinced those Shi'ites that armed struggle could win and Islamic fundamentalism could serve as an instrument for achieving political predominance: What could be more behooving to advance an Islamic political movement seeking predominance in a confessional country like Lebanon than embracing the struggle against Israel's invasion? Thus, fighting Israel became the central tenet of an extremist Islamic political movement. It was within this climate that extremist organizations like Hizbollah were created. The current secretary general of Hizbollah, Hasan Nasrallah, claimed that his party was founded by those embracing an Islamist Jihadist (Crusaderist) ideology in response to Israel's invasion of Lebanon in 1982. He also implied that those Islamists, who had belonged to Amal, came to be guided in their decision to establish Hizbollah by their disagreement with Amal over the methods to confront Israel.[31]

While Hizbollah embodied Iran's ideological fervor and received its full support to spread the message of the "Islamic Revolution," Syria found in the Party of God a fortuitous instrument for both preserving its interests in Lebanon and putting military pressure on Israel. Syria, through Hizbollah, could strike indirectly at Israel as well as at anti-Syrian groups in Lebanon. Hizbollah readily accepted Iran's and Syria's support to shrewdly transform its fight against Israel into a nationalist struggle. Deftly and courageously conducted and led by Hizbollah, this struggle not only enhanced the image of the party but also laid the ground for Hizbollah's entrance into the realm of Lebanese politics, a move spurned on ideological grounds not long ago.

Hizbollah is an indigenous organization whose fighters are totally integrated into Lebanese society. Hizbollah listens to its patron, Iran, and defers to Syrian influence in Lebanon. However, secular Syria, theocratic Iran, and Islamist Hizbollah have no neat overlap of their interests. A focal point of their interest is the struggle against Israel, albeit a struggle pursued for different objectives. Whereas Syria seeks to retrieve the Golan Heights, Hizbollah is concerned with its political base of support while at the same time remaining loyal to its patron in general and to its ideology in particular. According to Augustus Richard Norton, Hizbollah's leaders understand that the party's role in Damascus's eyes is utilitarian and transient, and they are ever aware that alliances of convenience may eventually become inconvenient.[32] The implication of all this translates into limits on Syria's influence over Hizbollah.

The cumulative effect of these developments created an anti-Israel politically "correct" environment within the Shi'a community. When on October 16, 1983, an Israeli convoy inadvertently clashed with a Shi'a crowd in the southern city of Nabatiya celebrating the day of Ashura, Shi'a's holiest day, the spiritual leaders of all colors and hues were quick to denounce Israel. Sheikh Muhammad Hussein Fadlallah, the spiritual leader of the new movement, called it a religious duty to destroy Israel. Sheikh Muhammad Mahdi Shamseddine, then the deputy president of the Supreme Shi'ite Council associated with Amal and known for his centrist views, urged resistance against Israel.

Consequently, Amal avoided any contact with Israel, opting instead to embrace a militant posture against it in order to enhance its prestige and fend off any radical threat to its political predominance within the Shi'a community. Before long, Shi'a attacks not only increased on the Israel Defense Forces (IDF) in Lebanon but also became a symbol of the perpetrator's preeminence in the Shi'a community. With its Maronite alliance gone and Lebanon having become a hostile territory overseen by Syria, Israel continued its withdrawal from Lebanon throughout 1984 and 1985. The vacuum created by Israel's withdrawal was speedily filled by Amal and Hizbollah. No longer did Israel entertain ambitious ideas for Lebanon. It reduced its efforts to support its proxy militia, the South Lebanese Army (SLA), which came under the leadership of Colonel Antoine Lahd after the death of Major Sa'd Haddad, in its 10-kilometer wide security zone in southern Lebanon. Still, Shi'a attacks on the IDF and the SLA in the security zone had not subsided, with Hizbollah leading the campaign against Israel.

Support for Israel

The rift in policy between the United States and Israel almost disappeared when the latter withdrew to the south of Lebanon, when Yitzhak Shamir replaced Begin as Israel's prime minister in the fall of 1983, and when the United States had come to the conclusion that its policy in the region had been flawed. As the United States embarked on a course to fight terrorism and as it remained ever wary of the Soviet threat to the security of the region, the United States, as previously, found in Israel a reliable ally in the Middle East. Consequently, Israel's strategic cooperation with the United States substantially resumed. The two countries established the Joint Political and Military Group (JPMG) as a framework to discuss biannually security-related issues. In April 1984 Israeli Defense Minister Moshe Arens and his American counterpart, Caspar Weinberger, signed a MOU on "defense cooperation at three levels: joint planning, combined exercises, and the pre-positioning of arms and ammunition for use by the U.S. military in a time of crisis."[33] President Reagan at the B'nai B'rith International Convention remarked: "We have upgraded and formalized our strategic cooperation. For the first time in history, under our administration, the United States and Israel have agreed on a formal strategic cooperation."[34]

In fact, throughout 1984, the United States and Israel made good not only on developing but also on expanding their strategic cooperation. On the military level, the United States purchased Israeli-manufactured radios, remotely piloted vehicles, antitank weapons, and components for sophisticated aircraft. The United States, in turn, had provided Israel with the latest technology for the development of the Israeli-designed LAVI fighter aircraft, despite strong objections from the Department of Defense.[35] Cooperation also included joint exercises in antisubmarine warfare by Israel's and America's navy. Financial assistance and trade cooperation complemented the military strategic cooperation. The U.S. government restructured the form of assistance to Israel. The 1985 proposed aid of $2.6 billion was to take the form of grants rather than loans.[36] In addition, the United States signed with Israel the Free-Trade Agreement, an unprecedented accord, establishing a free trade area between the two countries.[37]

In 1985, as Israel's economy faced a major crisis with 400% inflation and a burdensome debt (which almost led to an economic collapse), the United States responded by "converting all military and economic support assistance to cash grants instead of loans, and by passing a $1.5 billion supplemental aid package, bringing the total appropriated in 1985 to $4.1 billion in grants."[38] In 1987, the U.S. Congress designated Israel as a major non-NATO (non–North Atlantic Treaty Organization) ally, facilitating specific technology transfers to Israel. Another MOU followed, which upgraded joint defense research and development; Congress provided funding for the Arrow antiballistic missile system. Cooperation between the United States and Israel had culminated with another Memorandum of Agreement, signed in April 1988, regarding joint political, security, and economic cooperation. Key among its articles (Article III) was the reaffirmation of the importance of the following U.S.-Israeli Joint Groups: JPMG, a forum in which the two states discussed joint planning, exercises, and logistics, as well as current political-military issues; the Joint Security Assistance Planning Group, a forum in which the two states reviewed Israel's requests for security assistance; and the Joint Economic Development Group, a forum in which the two states evaluated Israel's requests for U.S. economic assistance and discuss developments in Israel's economy.[39]

Although U.S.-Israeli strategic cooperation had substantially evolved, the United States was careful not to cause a rupture in its relations with key Arab states. The United States kept Israel out of the Persian Gulf's security, and it refrained from ceremonial public display of its strategic cooperation with Israel. President Reagan had placed the responsibility for U.S.-Israel security "cooperation within the U.S. military's European Command (EUCOM), rather than with U.S. Central Command (CENTCOM), which covers the rest of the Middle East and is responsible for securing U.S. interests in the Gulf."[40] Significantly enough, the United States had made Egypt second to Israel in receiving American foreign military and economic aid, thus maintaining a leverage over the most populous Arab state in the world. In 1988, Egypt received $1.3 billion in foreign military sales to support modernization of its military, and $815 million in economic support funds to alleviate the costs of political and economic reforms. These approximate amounts were received by Egypt yearly since it signed the peace treaty with Israel in 1979. It is noteworthy that many U.S. government officials expressed reservations about U.S.-Israel strategic cooperation, arguing that American vital interests were located in the Arab world, not in Israel.

True, U.S.-Israeli relations had developed, resting largely on their mutual interests to ward off Soviet threats to the security of the region, but Israel had more than the Soviet threat on its mind. The political right in Israel, headed by the Likud party, the party of Begin and Shamir, had at the center of its platform the annexation of the West Bank and Gaza and the creation of settlements there. This policy ran counter to that of the American administrations and threatened a deterioration in relations between the United States and Israel. Israel, headed by Likud, feared that the values it shared with the United States, such as commitment to freedom, human rights, and democratic principles, which made it dear to the hearts of all Americans in contrast to other Middle Eastern countries, would not hold water with respect to its policy in the West Bank and Gaza. And those values, even if not maligned, would not be adequate to check a deterioration in relations with the United States. Consequently, barring the Soviet threat or an American foreign policy inimical to Israel, Israel's rationale for developing and expanding its relations with the United States had been partly designed to counteract an expected erosion of the "common values" foundation of American support for Israel.

The late 1980s brought to the fore these concerns of Israel's policy makers. As the Palestinian Intifada erupted in the West bank and Gaza, American public opinion toward Israel began to shift. Myriad images of Palestinian children hurling stones at Israeli soldiers, standing ready to confront and receive the wrath of a powerful adversary, flashed on television screens inside American homes. The image of the "child of the stone" became so powerful and so emotive, particularly when juxtaposed with the "iron fist" or "breaking bone" policies of the Israeli government, that it started to reflect negatively on the whole country. The image of Israel as the oppressed and the threatened had begun to collectively fade from the American memory. Alongside the Intifada, a breaking world event was unfolding: The fall of Communism. Perestroika in the Soviet Union and the subsequent disintegration of the Soviet Union brought the Cold War to an end. Suddenly, American foreign policy in the Middle East had become anachronistic. The end of the Cold War had far-reaching strategic implications not only for the United States but also for Israel and Syria. It was against this background that the new decade, the 1990s, with its momentous events kicked off.

Rewarding Syria

The fortunes of the Christian camp in Lebanon suffered a serious blow in 1988 when President Jumayil prepared himself to leave office. The president, torn between domestic, regional, and international pressures, was unable to present to the Lebanese parliament an agreed-upon list of presidential hopefuls, as mandated by the constitution. Thus he appointed General Michel Aoun to head an executive cabinet until a president was agreed upon and elected. Immediately after his appointment, Aoun opposed Syrian presence in Lebanon. However, many pro-Syrian deputies disapproved of Aoun's appointment, regarding it constitutionally illegitimate, and lent their support to the government of Prime Minister Salim al-Hoss. At the time, Lebanon witnessed two authorities: one formal, led by Aoun and exercising its authority over the Christian area, the other de facto and pro-Damascus, led by al-Hoss and extending its authority over the areas under Syrian control.

In March 1989, General Aoun proclaimed a "liberation war" against Syria and requested help from the Muslims of West Beirut. His liberation war was to take the form of an "intifada" against Syria similar to that of the Palestinians in the West Bank. Aoun also invited Iraqi meddling in Lebanon, which infuriated Syria, by accepting Iraqi military aid. Syria responded by shelling the Christian area and imposed on it a sea-and-land blockade, especially on East Beirut. In view of the constitutional impasse and the escalation of hostilities, Lebanese deputies left for the city of Taif in Saudi Arabia. At the meeting there, the Lebanese deputies, with the intercession of Arab delegates from Saudi Arabia, Algeria, and Morocco, managed to introduce significant amendments to the Lebanese constitution. The new version of the constitution became known interchangeably as the Document of National Understanding and the Taif Accord. In addition, over Aoun's objections the deputies elected Elias Hrawi president, whom Aoun refused to recognize.

General Aoun opposed the Taif Accord as a Syrian scheme to whittle away at Christian-Maronite power and called on the Christian Lebanese Forces to stand by him in order to meet the Syrian challenge. Contemplating the surge of Maronite support for Aoun, the Lebanese forces, in addition to considering Aoun's liberation war against Syria as political suicide, reckoned that under the pretext of meeting the Syrian challenge, Aoun was paving the way for dismantling them. Deadly hostilities broke out between the Lebanese forces and Aoun's forces in Christian East Beirut. The fighting shattered whatever was left of Christian unity. It was against this backdrop that Iraq rocked the region by invading Kuwait in early August 1990. The United States needed Syria's help in forming the international and Arab anti-Iraq coalition to extract Iraq from Kuwait.

Significantly enough, following the visit by John Kelly, the deputy secretary of state for Middle Eastern affairs, to Syria on August 20, the U.S. ambassador to Damascus, Edward Djerejian, announced that Washington wanted to immediately implement the Taif Accord.[41] Equally important, on September 13, Secretary of State James Baker visited Damascus for the first time and discussed with President al-Asad the means of managing both the Gulf and the Lebanese crises.[42] On October 13, the Syrian army, along with a unit of the Lebanese army under the command of Colonel Emile Lahoud, launched an all-out attack on Aoun's forces. The Syrian air force intervened for the first time in the history of the Lebanese conflict and raided Aoun's headquarters. Within hours, East Beirut, the last bastion of Lebanese opposition to Syria, fell. Obviously, the United States had yielded to al-Asad's demand for total hegemony over Lebanon as a price for bringing Syria into the anti-Iraq coalition.

The collapse of East Beirut and the emergence of a "new Lebanon" under Syrian hegemony expedited the implementation of the Taif Accord.[43] In line with the Taif Accord, on May 22, 1991, the Syrian and Lebanese presidents signed a Treaty of Brotherhood, Cooperation, and Coordination calling for the closest coordination in all political, security, cultural, scientific, and other matters between the two countries. On the internal level, the treaty stipulated that neither Lebanon nor Syria shall pose a threat to each other's security under any circumstances. On the external level, the treaty stipulated that each country's foreign policy shall support the other's in matters relating to its security and national interests and that the two governments shall strive to coordinate their Arab and international policies.[44] In a nutshell, since the Syrian-Lebanese relationship is asymmetrical, the agreement would permit Syria to have its own way in Lebanese affairs.

President al-Asad's aim of controlling Lebanon had been largely achieved militarily, politically, and legally, in no small measure with the help of Washington. As it turned out, with Syria controlling Lebanon, Hizbollah had become the most significant instrument at Damascus's disposal to put military pressure on Israel.

CHAPTER 4

The Fulcrum of Elusive Peace

Although an interplay of factors has affected the nature and extent of Syria's relationship with the United States, the Arab-Israeli peace process (1991–2000) became the focus of this relationship. Syria's key role in the region and its capacity to influence the outcome of events beyond its borders kept U.S. foreign policy toward Syria generally constant. Syria's direct or indirect involvement in terrorism by no means pushed U.S.-Syrian relations to the point of hostilities. U.S. foreign policy toward Syria had been ambivalent, for better or for worse. But this ambivalence often translated itself into a tacit bias toward the Syrian position on how to resolve the Arab-Israeli conflict. Whereas the executive branch of the U.S. government defended this bias and tried to improve U.S.-Syrian relations, the legislative branch passed legislation punishing Syria, thereby countermanding the executive branch and undermining the effect of the bias. As a result, U.S. foreign policy toward Syria, while maintaining its continuity, suffered some loss in its political coercive power, affecting Washington's attempt at peacemaking.[1]

The Bush Years: Priorities Reordered

In 1988 George Bush replaced Ronald Reagan as president of the United States. Having served Reagan as vice president, Bush was no outsider to the formulation and execution of the Reagan administration's policies. But, whereas Reagan had been zealous in his cooperation with the new Soviet leader Mikhail Gorbachev to reduce nuclear weapons and put the final nail in the coffin of the Cold War, Bush began his presidency too prudent to follow in the footsteps of his former boss. The Bush administration doubted the intentions of the Soviet leadership and wanted time to confirm the veracity of the Soviets. Although his administration had cooperated with the Soviet leadership, it had pursued a cautious foreign policy that required neither immediate revision nor a reordering of priorities. Within this context, American foreign policy toward the Middle East remained unchanged.

Israel's relationship with the United States continued to evolve, particularly along the lines it had developed and expanded during the Reagan years. The strategic cooperation between the United States and Israel, together with the cautious approach of the American administration toward the Soviet Union to a certain degree dampened the urgency of the Bush administration's seeking immediate solutions in part or in whole to the Arab-Israeli conflict. However, in a departure from the Reagan administration's policies, which kept U.S. objections to the Israeli settlement in the West Bank and Gaza on a low rung on the ladder of U.S.-Israeli relations, the Bush administration considered the settlements to be obstacles to peace and went on to publicly criticize Israel for human rights abuses.[2] At a time when Israel was absorbing Soviet Jewish immigrants, Secretary of State James Baker summed up the position of the administration in the following words:

> Under both Democratic and Republican administrations...American policy has always made a clear distinction between the absorption of Jews into Israel itself, and the settling of them in the occupied territories. Early in the administration, we'd concluded that such settlements constituted a serious obstacle to peace in the Middle East, and as a matter of principle, we believed that we should not in good conscience allow U.S. tax dollars to fund activities contrary to American policy and peace.[3]

America's relationship with Syria remained difficult and contradictory at best, straddling the grounds from sanctions to cooperation. In February 1990, President Bush decided that Syria did not meet the necessary certification standards to control narcotics production or trafficking.[4] In April 1990, the State Department's spokesperson Margaret Tutwiler, briefed the press on the American position on Syria. She elaborated:

> Most of the sanctions imposed in November 1986 remain in place, including strict export controls, the cancellation of Syrian eligibility for Export-Import Bank credits and concessionary wheat purchases, the termination of our bilateral air transport agreement, the prohibition of the sale of Syrian airline tickets, a travel advisory alerting Americans to the potential for terrorist activity originating in Syria, among others....Our relations with Syria have been difficult for a number of years. Notwithstanding Syrian assistance with the release of Robert Hill [American hostage], there remain important impediments to improved U.S.-Syrian relations, particularly the continued presence of terrorist groups in Syria and Syrian-controlled areas of Lebanon.[5]

The state of vetting give-and-take between the United States and the Soviet Union, the stalemate state of "no peace, no war" in the Arab-Israeli conflict, the violence in the West Bank and Gaza, and the situation born of bureaucratic inertia that had kept the U.S. government from reordering its foreign policy priorities were thrown into question when Iraq invaded Kuwait in early August 1990. The Iraqi invasion became the litmus test of Soviet intentions and of America's ability to found a new world order, premised solely on its unipolar power. The State Department had removed Iraq from its terrorism list in 1982 and reestablished full diplomatic relations with the country in 1984, paving the way for the Reagan administration to facilitate the transfer of arms to Iraq. With Iraq fighting Iran, the country that designated the United States as its archenemy, the Reagan administration wanted Iraq to win, as well as to emerge militarily and economically powerful enough to contain Iran's revolutionary ambitions in the region.

Needless to say, when Iraq invaded Kuwait, it violated the sovereignty of an independent state and threatened the security of the Arab Gulf, an oil producing region deemed vital to American interests. The Soviets stood by the Americans and supported a slew of U.N. resolutions—660, 661, 665, 678—which condemned the invasion, placed sanctions against Iraq, and called for its withdrawal from Kuwait. The behavior of the Soviets dispelled any American reservations about Soviet intentions for ending the Cold War. President Bush committed himself to reversing Iraq's aggression by leading an international coalition of forces to extract Iraq from Kuwait. The inclusion of Arab forces in the anti-Iraq coalition became paramount as Saddam Hussein, president of Iraq, tried to portray the coalition's war effort in anti-Islamic, anti-Arab terms. Later he tried to precondition the resolution of the crisis by linking it to a comprehensive regional settlement of outstanding conflicts of occupation, mainly Israel's withdrawal from the occupied territories and Lebanon, and Syria's withdrawal from Lebanon.

Iraq's maneuvers convinced the Bush administration to lure Egypt and Syria into the anti-Iraq coalition and subsequently to isolate the resolution of the crisis from other regional issues. The corollary of this policy entailed the reordering of U.S. priorities in the region, including a rapprochement with Syria, keeping Israel out of the efforts to end the crisis, and supporting an international conference to settle the Arab-Israeli conflict once the liberation of Kuwait was achieved. Syria's regional role had come to the forefront again. Secretary of State James Baker attested to Syria's prominent role in the coalition. In a press conference on September 10, 1990, he stated: "I don't think anything highlights more the isolation of

Saddam Hussein in the Arab world than Syria's opposition to Iraq's invasion and occupation of Kuwait. It has contributed forces to the multinational effort—significant forces. I think its presence is significant."[6] Baker emphasized the importance of face-to-face dialogue with Syrian officials as he prepared himself to travel there, the first visit by a high-level official in years. When members of the press raised the question of Syria's involvement in terrorism and America's "patting them on the back" because they supported the United States in the Gulf crisis, Baker responded that "it's very important…in a situation such as we have in the Gulf that we cooperate with a major Arab country who happens to share the same goals we do."[7] Syria's role did not stop at this point and went further by convincing Iran to resist Saddam's efforts to win its support. Obviously, when American vital interests are at stake, the United States has no compunction either to push aside or to overlook any reservations standing in the way of achieving its goals.

The United States, with Syria's manifest eagerness, pressed ahead with improving its relations with Syria. Suddenly, as the documents examined show, the thorny issue of terrorism, which had marred the U.S.-Syrian relationship, now appeared in a different light. When Baker met President Hafiz al-Asad of Syria on September 14, 1990, in Damascus and raised the subject of terrorism with him, he recalled in his memoirs that al-Asad "made no apologies for supporting terrorism against Israel, which to him was simply part of an armed struggle for liberation from unjust occupation, but insisted that he had agreed to condemn acts of violence elsewhere."[8] Al-Asad maintained that "any person in the land of Syria who is carrying out or planning a terrorist operation outside of the occupied territories will be tried."[9] He also denied any Syrian involvement in the 1988 bombing of Pan American Flight 103 over Lockerbie, Scotland. After the meeting with al-Asad and Syrian officials, Baker and Syria's foreign minister, Farouq al-Shara, held a press conference at which Baker talked about the subject of terrorism and the problems the United States had with Syria on this matter. In a new formulation of the definition of terrorism, Baker was close to al-Asad's interpretation:

> We consider any violent act outside the occupied territory is a terrorist act. But, at the same time, we cannot consider the legitimate struggle against the occupation forces as a terrorist act. Now we are talking about Kuwait, for instance. The Kuwaiti resistance to the Iraqi occupation is legitimate in every sense of the word. We believe that, so far, Syria was put on the terrorist list without any justification. We believe that the Pan Am 103, the disaster of that flight, did not, until this moment, bring hard evidence to who is responsible and for who is behind that terrorist act. But in our

estimation, the accusation addressed to Syria in this respect is meant for political objectives rather than analyzing an objective situation.[10]

Baker's position on Syria's involvement in terrorism was a far cry from the positions of previous administrations. By professing that Syria was put on the terrorism list without any justification, Baker was not only mending fences with Syria, but also drawing the administration closer to the Syrian argument on terrorism. Because the terrorism issue figured so prominently in U.S.-Syrian relations, Baker's position could be interpreted as a harbinger of change. The United States seemed to be moving closer to the Syrian position on resolving the Arab-Israeli conflict. Nevertheless, despite Baker's words, the U.S. government made no attempt to remove Syria from the terrorism list, opting instead to support Syria's hegemony over Lebanon as a reward for its pro-U.S. involvement in the Gulf crisis.[11] On November 23, 1990, President Bush and President al-Asad met in Geneva, where they discussed the restoration of Kuwait's territory and legitimate government, the necessity of implementing the Taif Accords in Lebanon, the importance of moving ahead with the Middle East peace process in accordance with U.N. Resolutions 242 and 338, Syria's help in bringing about the release of all hostages held in Lebanon, and continuing the dialogue on the question of terrorism with the goal of achieving positive results.[12]

Syria went along with U.S. plans to successfully extract Iraq from Kuwait, and by the end of the Gulf War the last of the hostages held in Lebanon, Terry Anderson, saw the first glimpse of freedom when Syrian liaison officers removed the blindfold from his eyes and led him to Damascus.[13]

Meanwhile, Israel, unlike Syria, now presented a vexing problem to the U.S. government. The Bush administration wanted Israel to stay completely out of the Gulf crisis, so that Iraq could neither link it to the Arab-Israeli conflict nor cause a split in the anti-Iraq coalition, which included Arab forces. Israel became more of a liability to U.S. efforts in the region. Nevertheless, when Iraq launched Scud missile attacks against Israel during the American-led campaign against Iraq, Desert Storm, the U.S. government immediately enhanced its strategic cooperation with Israel. The United States sought to improve Israel's security and at the same time to prevent it from striking back at Iraq. According to Shai Feldman an entirely new phase of U.S.-Israeli strategic cooperation occurred in late 1990 and early 1991, which included dramatic developments. Most important, the United States sent Patriot surface-to-air missile units to Israel to intercept and destroy the Scuds in the air, and for the first time members of the U.S. armed forces were sent to operate the Patriot units and help defend the Jewish state.[14]

However, this new phase of cooperation gave way to a situation that not only put a damper on U.S.-Israeli relations, but also placed these relations out on a limb. This new condition developed when the Bush administration tried to make good on its promise to the Arab allies in the anti-Iraq coalition to convene a peace conference after the war as part of an American effort to bring about a comprehensive settlement of the Arab-Israeli conflict. This situation unfolded in the form of a standoff between the Bush administration and Israel and its American Jewish supporters over the $10 billion in loan guarantees, requested by Israel at a time when the United States was shoring up support for the peace process. The standoff underscored (a) Israel's diminished status as a strategic ally for the United States in the aftermath of the Cold War, (b) the divergence of U.S. and Israeli policies on resolving the Arab-Israeli conflict, (c) a renewed desire on the part of the American administration to end the Middle East conflict as satisfactorily as possible for both sides, and (d) a subtle U.S. tilt in the direction of the Arab side of the conflict including Syria.

This problem had its provenance in the reservations the U.S. government had about Israel's settlement activity in the occupied territories. As the coalition forces launched the air campaign against Iraq's forces in Kuwait in January 1991, Iraqi Scud missiles hurled down on Israel, which for the first time in its history refrained from swift retaliation. Though the Bush administration had appreciated Israel's restraint, it was taken aback when Israeli Finance Minister Yitzhak Modai announced that his government would ask for $13 billion in additional aid from the United States—"$10 billion in loan guarantees for settling Soviet Jews, and $3 billion in compensation for the damage inflicted on Israeli cities by Scud attacks."[15] The timing and the size of the request were considered inappropriate and audaciously presumptuous by the Bush administration. As the United States concentrated its efforts on winning the Gulf War and restarting the Middle East peace process, tensions between the United States and Israel over Jewish settlements in the West Bank and Gaza heightened. Ariel Sharon, the Israeli housing minister, aggressively expanded the settlements, and Shamir turned down Baker's suggestion that Israel "curtail the expansion of settlements as a goodwill gesture for peace."[16] The two states did not relent on their positions and went headlong toward collision.

In midsummer 1991, the Bush administration received information that American Israel Public Affairs Committee (AIPAC), headed by Thomas Dine, and its allies in Washington were preparing a campaign to win congressional approval for the loan guarantees regardless of the administration's position. The Bush administration launched a campaign of its own to undercut AIPAC's efforts. It was mainly Baker who approached U.S. congressmen and called upon them to give peace a chance. With the peace conference looming close in the air, around late October, Baker argued that proceeding on the subject of guarantees and settlements would doom the peace process. The administration also perceived that the issue of loan guarantees had become a litmus test of its even-handedness. The congressmen's positions gravitated toward that of the President.

Although Israel had agreed to participate in the Madrid peace conference (see below), the tug-of-war over the loan guarantees and settlements between the two sides continued unabated, particularly after the 120-day deferral period had passed. Shamir, in an angry message to the administration, publicly defied "the gentiles of the world" that "the settlements expansion will continue, and no power in the world will prevent this construction."[17] Shamir's attitude only further exacerbated the relations between the United States and Israel. The U.S. government rejected any idea of compromise short of a settlement freeze, conspicuously linking the loan guarantees with the administration's policies. In late February 1992, Baker appeared before the Senate Operations Subcommittee and pointedly emphasized:

> We simply believe that if we are going to talk about providing assistance of this magnitude over and above the generous assistance that is already provided on an annual basis with no conditions whatsoever—that is, the $3 billion to $4 billion—then we have a right to know, and frankly, we have an obligation to the American taxpayer to know, that we're not going to be financing something directly or indirectly that American policy has opposed for 25 years.[18]

This firm American posture coincided with the recent victory of Yitzhak Rabin in Israel's Labor primaries, sending a message to the Israeli public that America's ties with Israel were at a crossroads, hence, indirectly boosting the chances of a Labor victory in the upcoming summer elections. The standoff over the loan guarantees laid bare the new changed position of Israel after the Cold War. Democratic Senator Robert Byrd of West Virginia, chairman of the Senate Appropriations Committee, addressed the Senate in early April on loan guarantees and U.S.-Israeli relations. He critically scrutinized U.S.-Israeli relations including foreign aid, stressing the overriding interests of the United States. On the issue of settlements, Byrd emphasized that "the stated and demonstrated policy of the state of Israel is in direct contradiction to that of the United States regarding such settlements."[19]

Senator Byrd went further and exposed Israel's transformed image from a bulwark against Soviet expansionism in the Middle East into a liability to stability. He stated:

> We should wake up to the reality which has been slow to dawn on many, including our own Pentagon, that the Cold War is over and the real threat to stability in the Middle East lies in the tension between Israel and its Arab neighbors. And that tension only increases as a result of the continued expansion by Israel of settlements in the occupied territories.[20]

Breaking the Ice: The Madrid Peace Conference

Among the important developments to occur in the aftermath of the Gulf War and the end of the Cold War was the United States' ability to conduct its policy in the Middle East unhindered by the traditional Soviet considerations. In addition, the countries of the region could no longer play on the old superpowers' rivalries there. Capitalizing on this development, President Bush on March 6, 1991, addressed a joint session of Congress outlining his Middle East objectives:

> First, we must work to create shared security arrangements in the region....Let it be clear: Our vital national interests depend on a stable and secure Gulf.
>
> Second, we must act to control the proliferation of weapons of mass destruction and the missiles used to deliver them.
>
> And third, we must work to create new opportunities for peace and stability in the Middle East....A comprehensive peace must be grounded in the U.N. Security Council Resolutions 242 and 338 and the principle of territory for peace. This principle must be elaborated to provide for Israel's security and recognition and at the same time for legitimate Palestinian political rights....The time has come to put an end to the Arab-Israeli conflict.[21]

Late in March, Egypt and Syria issued a call for an international peace conference on the Arab-Israeli conflict. Israel, as in the past, was never enthusiastic about an international conference. In any event, during May the issue of the loan guarantees surfaced and the Bush administration made clear its position on settlements as obstacles to peace.[22] Responding to the President's speech and his administration's stand on settlements, Israel Prime Minister Yitzhak Shamir stated on July 24: "I don't believe in territorial compromise. Our country is very tiny. I believe with my entire soul that we are forever connected to this homeland."[23] What Shamir was really hinting at was a concurrence to negotiations but without prior commitment to the principle of territory for peace.

During this period (as we have seen), the battle over the loan guarantees prompted the President to speak forcefully against the Israeli settlements and the Israeli lobby. At the same time, the President called for a repeal of the U.N. resolution on Zionism, labeling it as racism. Apparently, the Israeli government caved in to American pressure and voted to attend the Madrid Peace Conference on October 20, 1991. On closer examination, however, two other momentous developments contributed significantly to bringing Israel to Madrid: The strategic geopolitical implications of the Gulf War and the impact of the Intifada on Israel.

The Gulf crisis, in the words of Aharon Yariv, a former intelligence chief, appears to have substantiated many lessons and truths for Israel including the following: The U.S. was the superpower, both politically and militarily, hence the inconceivability of any world order without its involvement and leadership; Israel depended on the U.S. and was vulnerable to missile attacks; the despotic regime in Iraq was durable; and Syria had had a change of heart concerning the peace process.[24] Bearing this in mind, Yariv expounded the reasons Israel should participate in the peace process:

> Continued confrontation will inevitably increase tension and sharpen the feelings of mutual enmity and hatred. Estrangement between Israel and most countries in the world will become progressively stronger. A situation of "no peace, no war," accompanied by an escalating arms race, will sooner or later bring about the crystallization of an Arab military coalition that will go to war against Israel....Then, under new circumstances, we shall again face peace negotiations. Shall we then be able to get a better deal than now, when we are in a strong position and enjoy the support of the U.S. as well as many other countries of the world?[25]

The implications of the Intifada for Israel were ponderous as well. As the Palestinian uprising spread in the territories, Israeli Defense Minister Rabin adopted strong measures to quell it in January 1988. He sanctioned what came to be termed as a policy of "breaking bones" to subdue the Intifada.[26] His policy proved futile and counterproductive, as the Intifada continued with a vengeance. The Intifada brought the Palestinian problem before the eyes of the world and most importantly inside the Israeli home. All of a sudden, Israel appeared as an oppressor nation, an image tormenting the conscience of a nation whose history had been replete with oppression. In addition, the Intifada had many damaging effects on the country, including an adverse effect on the esprit de corps in the armed forces. Soldiers faced the psychologically excruciating experience that they were fighting children, an experience with far-reaching dehumanizing effects, on the one hand, and a lowering of the Israel Defense Forces (IDF) morale on the other. This was exacerbated by the Palestinian belief that the IDF was incapable of stopping the Intifada. The peace process loomed as a sound alternative for Israel to fight back the Intifada's effects.[27] As Itamar Rabinovich admitted:

> ...The Palestinians' uprising in the West Bank and in Gaza in late 1987, the *intifada,* had a long and profound effect on the Israeli public. Ever since the 1967 war twenty years before, Palestinians had failed to devise an effective strategy for their struggle against Israel, and whenever Israeli society weighed the costs of keeping the status quo or working out a new compromise, the balance had tilted toward maintaining the status quo. But in 1988, a significant body of opinion in Israel was no longer willing to pay the costs of a perpetuated status quo. It is impossible to understand Yitzhak Shamir's acceptance of the "Madrid framework" or the Labor Party's victory in the 1992 elections without understanding the effect of this change.[28]

For Syria, the march to Madrid was greatly influenced by international, regional, and domestic factors. On the international level, the world's stage was being set for a unipolar power, led by the United States. Syria's old patron, the Soviet Union, was beginning to disintegrate. Its inability to either protect the Iraqi regime or mediate the Gulf conflict had weeded out any influence the Soviets may have had with their client's state in the region. Syria saw the Gulf War as an opportunity to mend its relations with the United States and to reposition itself under the novel circumstances of a unipolar world. The United States, on the other hand, sent positive signals to Syria about a new world order from which Damascus could benefit. Both countries quickly reached an understanding on how to handle the Gulf and the Lebanese crises. In addition, the Syrians, like most Arabs, saw a credible U.S. president unhindered by Jewish pressure. His stand on the loan guarantees was a tangible proof of his administration's evenhandedness.

On the regional level, the alignment of forces in the Gulf War translated itself to a great extent into an alignment of policies after the war. Syria, Egypt, and Saudi Arabia, the states that joined the U.S.-led coalition against Iraq, became more attuned to U.S. policies in the region. This was bolstered by the dawning reality that the actors in the region could no longer play on the historical rivalry of the two superpowers. Equally significant, the Gulf War terminated the once idealized concept of pan-Arabism, under which pretext Arab countries, especially Syria, had meddled in the internal affairs of each other. For the first time in recent history Arab forces joined

Western ones to attack an Arab sister state. The national interests of each Arab state preceded those of pan-Arabism. On the level of inter-Arab relations, the fragmentation of the Arab world in the aftermath of the Gulf War suddenly seemed more dangerous than a negotiated settlement.[29]

In addition, Syria's regional influence with the Arab states and the Palestinians appeared to be beating a retreat. After the Gulf War, the Gulf states signed an agreement with Egypt and Syria, called the Damascus Declaration, that would provide Egypt and Syria with a security role in return for financial remuneration. However, the integration of the United States in the Gulf through bilateral security pacts with the Gulf states reduced, if not scrapped outright, Syria's role there.[30] Significantly enough, Jordan and the Palestine Liberation Organization (PLO) had lost ground in the Gulf War by siding with Iraq. They were resented by the Arab states and the West. At this critical juncture, the United States might capitalize on their weakness and pressure them into signing separate peace agreements with Israel that would leave Syria behind.

On the domestic level, Syria realized that its quest for strategic parity with Israel, while it could deter an Israeli attack, could not give Syria a war option.[31] In time, Syria might even lose its deterrent capability due to the collapse of the Soviet Union and Israel's advanced weapon supply from the United States. With Egypt locked into a peace treaty and Iraq incapacitated, Israel might preemptively attack Syria, the only looming danger for the Jewish state. If Syria could not retrieve its occupied territory by force, the only other option available then would be the peace process. Indeed, in this instance, Syria could well prevent Israel from capitalizing on the region's weakness and launch an attack against it.

On October 30, 1991, under the joint chairmanship of Bush and Gorbachev, the Middle East Peace Conference opened in Madrid with Israel, Syria, Lebanon, and a joint Palestinian-Jordanian delegation in attendance.

Syria's participation in the peace process was a win-win decision. On the one hand, it could show the world that it was not impeding peace, while throwing the ball in Israel's court. If Israel did not join the process, it would appear to be the party impeding peace in the region. If Israel did join the process, it had to agree to the criterion of participation, that is, land for peace. In this instance, Syria would most likely retrieve the Golan Heights. At the same time, Syria would work on improving its relations with the United States while placing the implementation of U.N. Resolutions 242 and 338 in American hands.

This led the U.S. administration to initiate changes in American export laws in favor of Syria and other Arab states that helped the United States win the Gulf War. The documents I examined show that in September 1991, the U.S. Commerce Department made "significant changes in U.S. export regulations applying to Syria and Iran."[32] This had the effect of releasing dual-use technology (militarily applicable) to Syria, giving it a way to circumvent the Export Administration Act (EAA). Representatives Mel Levine and Howard Berman took heed of the changes and petitioned the chairman of the House Committee on Foreign Affairs, Dante B. Fascell, to reconsider the release of export licenses that permit the sale of dual-use items to Syria and Iran.

Although the terms of the EAA protect information regarding the control of exports from disclosure in order to safeguard the "property" rights of American companies and their competitiveness, Section 12(c) of the EAA requires that its full committee meet and determine whether the withholding of that information is contrary to the national interests.[33] In the two letters of May 1 and July 1, 1992, to Fascell, Berman and Levine compared the U.S. export policy toward Syria and Iran with that of Iraq, a policy that provided sophisticated technology to terrorist countries and led to war. The Representatives were concerned with the diversion of some of the technology to military use, as well as with the contribution that such technologies would make to the economic advancement of Syria and Iran. In addition, they reckoned that the administration's policy on Syria and Iran bore all the hallmarks of the logic that characterized the former administration's policy on Iraq: "Presumption that a closer economic relationship can positively influence the behavior of countries which in their every move show no evidence of behaving in a manner we find acceptable."[34]

True, the changes in export laws were made in the aftermath of the Soviet Union's demise; still, they could be viewed as preliminary steps to the removal of sanctions on Syria. Since mid-1990, relations between the Bush administration and Syria had improved substantially and peaked when Syria joined the anti-Iraq coalition. Seemingly, members of Congress were concerned with any promises the administration might have made to Syria in return for its participation in the coalition and its subsequent agreement to attend the Madrid Peace Conference along with holding bilateral talks with Israel, a position Syria had consistently rejected in the past. Not surprisingly, the supporters of Israel in Congress stood in the vanguard to closely observe the administration's dealings with Syria, in an effort to prevent the administration from laying the groundwork to remove Syria from the terrorism and narcotics list, thus making it eligible for American financial and military support.

Various measures and reports were introduced in Congress to highlight Syria's record and urge the administration to make its cooperation with, and consequently its assistance to, Syria contingent upon its satisfying a number of conditions. In the same month, March 1992, that 68 Senators released a letter to Syria expressing their gratitude for Syrian participation in the Gulf War, a House Resolution was introduced in Congress that placed several restrictions on Syria. Section (609) of the 1992 H.R. 4546 ruled that U.S. assistance may not be provided to Syria until the President determined, and so reported to the appropriate congressional committees that (1) Syria had demonstrated its willingness to enter into direct bilateral negotiations with Israel; (2) Syria was not denying its citizens the right or opportunity to emigrate; (3) Syria was no longer supporting groups responsible for acts of international terrorism and was no longer providing a safe haven for terrorists; (4) Syria was withdrawing its armed forces from Lebanon; (5) Syria was no longer acquiring chemical, biological, or nuclear weapons; (6) Syria was fully cooperating with U.S. antinarcotics efforts and was taking steps to remove Syrian officials who were involved in the drug trade; and (7) Syria had made progress in improving its record of respect for internationally recognized human rights. In addition, Section (608) of the same resolution affirmed that it was U.S. policy to oppose Syrian control of Lebanon and ensure that no assistance provided to Lebanon would benefit Syria.[35]

Although Syria had satisfied the first condition, the others had gone to the heart of Syria's domestic politics, conditions regarded as meddling in Syrian national interests. Before long, Chairman Charles E. Schumer of the House Judiciary Committee's Subcommittee on Crime and Criminal Justice directed the subcommittee majority staff to investigate official Syrian involvement in the Lebanese drug trade. While it was not approved by members of the Subcommittee, the report released by the staff accused high ranking Syrian officials such as Defense Minister Mustafa Tlas, Commander of Syrian Military Intelligence, General Ali Duba, and Commander of Syrian Military Intelligence in Lebanon, Ghazi Kanaan, of drug corruption. The report emphasized:

> Although the Administration acknowledges that a few Syrian officials are involved in the Lebanese drug trade, it simply refuses to admit the extent to which drug corruption has been institutionalized in the Syrian military forces now occupying Lebanon. More importantly, the Administration has virtually ignored the important fact that the Syrian government and the

Syrian military, as institutions, directly benefit from their associations with drug traffickers.[36]

Obviously, the administration and Congress had been conducting a tug-of-war over Syria during the delicate time of the ongoing peace process. The administration wanted to improve its relations with Syria by paving the way to removing sanctions on Syria, thereby ridding itself of the legislative shackles to either reward Syria for its participation in the anti-Iraq coalition or to provide it with incentives to enter into a peace agreement with Israel. Farouq al-Shara, Syria's foreign minister, made it clear to Senators James M. Jeffords and Hank Brown during their visit to Syria that if the United States wanted good relations with Syria, it must remove Syria from the terrorism list.[37] Congress, spearheaded by Israel's supporters, had been circumspect with Syria's nature of government and the administration's rapprochement. It toughened the restrictions on Syria in order to constrict the administration's maneuverability and to make sure that Syria would comply with certain conditions before receiving any U.S. assistance. The conditions laid down by Congress heavily intruded upon the domestic politics of Syria, making improved relations between the two countries extremely difficult, if not impossible.

As a result of all these developments, the American Jewish community along with Israel perceived the Bush administration as harsh on Israel. Spokespersons for the former expressed much criticism in the American press and media of the Bush-Baker policies, to which Baker is reputed to have reacted by making his famous comment in reference to the American Jews: "They did not vote for us anyway."

But, contrary to the belief that Bush and Baker were the sole authors of a more critical and tougher American policy on Israel, a group of foreign policy experts, mostly Jews, known as the "Israelites," were behind this policy. According to their logic, Leon T. Hadar wrote:

> Israel's long-term existence could only be assured through the maintenance of American hegemony in the Middle East. However, without a solution to the Arab-Israeli conflict, the U.S. role could be challenged in the long run by the rise of radical forces, especially Muslim fundamentalists, as well as by growing isolationist voices in America who might question the need to pay the costs of intervention in that far-away region. In that case, Israel would be left alone and isolated in the region facing growing threats from militant Islamic governments who perhaps even have nuclear weapons at their disposal.
>
> Hence, since the first days of the Bush administration, the "Israelists" have recommended that Washington work to reach as quickly as possible

some kind of an accommodation between Israel and the Palestinians and the Syrians, even if that would mean painful concessions on the part of the Jewish state.[38]

Oddly enough, a strange coalition between neoconservative Republicans and Democrats developed to counter the policy of the Bush administration on Israel. The committee on U.S. interests on Israel in the Middle East, headed by Frank Gaffney, a neoconservative and former Pentagon official who highlighted Israel's strategic asset during the Reagan years, typified such a coalition. Despite a hopeful Labor election campaign in Israel, which, if successful, held promise of warming the relations between the Bush administration and the government of Israel, AIPAC and other Jewish organizations had other plans on their mind. They believed that their political lot was more secure with the Democratic party than with the Republican, and that they should revert to reactivate their political base of support in Congress rather than largely concentrate on lobbying the executive branch, a lobbying tactic adopted during the Reagan years. Consequently, the Democratic presidential hopeful William Clinton received most of the Jewish vote, contributing not insignificantly to his election.

The tensions between the United States and Israel appreciably dissipated when the Labor government, headed by Prime Minister Yitzhak Rabin, assumed office in Israel. Unlike Shamir's tactics, which mocked the substance of the "land for peace" formula at the Madrid peace conference, Rabin's platform agreed well with the peace process as he became a central figure pressing for peace with all his Arab neighbors, including the Palestinians. Rabin's policies complemented by his leadership traits and excellent credentials smoothed out the rough edges of the U.S.-Israeli relations. He was well aware of the need to re-tailor Israel's national interests within the context of America's, thereby effectively reversing the negative trend set in motion by the end of the Cold War and Shamir's militant policies.

The Clinton Years: Cooperation Versus Limits

President Clinton inherited the framework of the peace process from the Bush administration, giving it his full support. Although a breakthrough between the Palestinians and the Israelis—the Oslo Agreement—had been achieved in Norway without direct U.S. involvement, President Clinton staged a White House lawn signing ceremony where the historic handshake between Yasser Arafat and Yitzhak Rabin took place. Whereas the Israeli-Syrian track of negotiations was perceived as paramount and promising, it proved to be so difficult that it was subordinated to the other Israeli-Arab tracks. President Clinton met twice with the Syrian president al-Asad in January 1994 in Geneva and in October 1984 in Damascus. In his first meeting, the President described Syria as the "key to the achievement of enduring and comprehensive peace." He also expressed his hope that Israel would "respond positively" to al-Asad's call. It should be remembered that al-Asad had called for the peace of the brave, a peace that secures the interests of each side and that emphasizes that if the "leaders of Israel have sufficient courage to respond to this kind of peace, a new era of security and stability in which normal peaceful relations among all shall dawn."[39]

Itamar Rabinovich, Israel's Ambassador to Washington and chief negotiator with Syria, underscored that President Clinton had put the onus on Israel by expressing "hope" that al-Asad's call "would provoke a positive response in Israel."[40] Rabinovich also noted that the President "went along with emphasizing the importance of comprehensiveness in the Arab-Israeli peace process and practically endorsed Syria's policy in Lebanon."[41] In his second meeting, a week after a terrorist bus bombing occurred in Tel Aviv, the President affirmed the resolution of the Arab-Israeli conflict on the basis of U.N. Resolutions 242 and 338 and the principle of land for peace, and added that peace must guarantee security against a surprise attack by any side.[42] But the meeting underscored the philosophical differences between the two heads of state on terrorism. While the issue of terrorism was not openly discussed, Clinton regretted that al-Asad did not publicly denounce the recent terrorist (bus) attack in Israel.[43]

Still, the Clinton administration, virtually like its predecessor, put much emphasis on Syria's key role to regional stability to the point of downplaying the issue of terrorism in the interest of the peace process. Anthony Lake, the national security advisor, emphasized in a lecture delivered at the Washington Institute in May:

> A decisive Syrian-Israeli agreement would allow Jordan and Lebanon to resolve their differences with Israel in a short order. Full normalization of relations between Israel and the Arab states of the Maghreb and the Gulf would follow. An Israel-Syria peace would thus shore up the agreement between Israel and the PLO and greatly advance U.S. efforts to widen the circle of peacemakers, bolster the network of Middle East moderation, and construct a bastion against backlash states.
>
> Syria plays a critical role in the wider sweep of regional peace.[44]

When this administration's policy is juxtaposed against Clinton's expressed hope that Israel respond positively to al-Asad's call, the administration's strategic desire to settle the Israeli-Syrian conflict on terms adequate to Syria becomes clear. This is reinforced by Clinton's continuing emphasis on U.N. Resolutions 242 and 338 as the basis for such a settlement. The endless number of shuttle trips that Secretary of State Warren Christopher made to Damascus, let alone the diplomatic slight he received on one occasion when al-Asad kept him waiting but never met with Christopher, were testimonials to the administration's willingness to travel the extra mile rather than see Syria become a source of regional instability.

But it was the administration's ambiguous language about Syria's involvement in terrorism that demonstrated the administration's complex position on Syria. The State Department's 1994 annual report on terrorism stated:

> There is no evidence that Syrian officials have been directly involved in planning or executing terrorist attacks since 1986. Damascus is publicly committed to the Middle East process and has taken some steps to restrain the international activities of these groups....However, Syria continues to provide safehaven and support for several groups that engage in international terrorism....In addition, Damascus grants a wide variety of groups engaged in terrorism basing privileges or refuge in areas of Lebanon's Bekaa Valley under Syrian control.[45]

In the 1995 report, the State Department emphasized that "Syria continues to use its influence to moderate Hizbollah and Palestinian rejectionist groups....It has, however, allowed Iran to resupply Hizbollah via Damascus."[46] The 1996 and 1997 reports, with slight variations, had the same intent and message.[47] The administration found Syria innocent of the charge of terrorism, but also found Syria an accomplice to the charge. This paradoxical, noncommittal position could best serve the administration when it decided to remove Syria from the terrorism list. So this position had been none other than a lubricating process to smooth out the give-and-take with Syria, whereby, in exchange for Syrian concessions on the peace process, the administration would remove it from the terrorism list. In such an event, the United States could benefit from Syria's key role in order to bolster regional stability, widen the circle of peacemakers, restrict fundamentalism, and rein in terrorism.

The administration had not been alone in devising plans regarding Syria and the peace process. When the idea of stationing U.S. troops on the Golan Heights to monitor an Israeli-Syrian peace accord in the event it occurred circulated in Washington, a campaign that included right-wing organizations and individual activists in the Jewish community, supported and goaded by Israel's Likud party, was organized to bring the idea to naught.[48] Beginning in May 1994, the organized campaign focused on Congress, the media, and the Jewish community, conveying the message that sending American soldiers to the Golan Heights would be a catalyst to severing the U.S.-Israeli relationship. Though in different tones or styles, the message read the same:

> I as an American citizen believe that relinquishing the Golan Heights will necessitate the stationing of U.S. troops who will be exposed to murderous attacks from Arab irregulars. The American people will not accept casualties among the U.S. peacekeeping forces and rightly so. Any such deployment of U.S. troops will begin with good intentions and end with American body bags and vehement American protest demonstrations. This will no doubt lead to a rise in anti-Semitism.[49]

Making such a circumlocution so as to link anti-Semitism with peacemaking was far from diplomatic stonewalling. The writers of the message obviously refused to know, or make known, that such an American role has been, indeed, undertaken. American troops have comprised half of the Multinational Force and Observers in Sinai that monitor Israeli and Egyptian adherence to the security provisions of their 1979 peace treaty. Furthermore, Syria has scrupulously observed the 1974 Disengagement Agreement with Israel on the Golan Heights, and there has been no terrorism incident by Arab irregulars. Nevertheless, as Republicans took over both Houses of Congress in November, the campaign to kill the idea of stationing U.S. troops on the Golan Heights gained momentum. The designated chairman of the Committee of Foreign Affairs, Senator Jesse Helms, lambasted the idea of sending American troops to the Golan Heights to monitor a future peace accord between Israel and Syria.[50]

The Labor government was taken aback by the negativity of the organized campaign. Ambassador Rabinovich wrote: "We saw the campaign as a shrewd effort to controversialize the Israeli-Arab peace process and to provide an American peg for opposing the notion of an Israeli-Syrian settlement. After all, why should an American senator or columnist take exception to the fact that Israel and Syria decided to end their conflict?"[51] However, soon enough, a critical attitude toward Syria prevailed in Congress as Senator Jesse Helms became the chairman of the Senate's Committee on Foreign Relations and Representative Benjamin Gilman became the chairman of the House Committee on International Relations. Gilman at first spoke in favor of placing American troops on the Golan Heights,[52] but then, probably due to pressure from his New York constituency, he became critical of al-Asad's regime.

To the harsh criticism of Syria by Helms and his staff, the *al-Ba'th* newspaper, the mouthpiece of Syrian government, featured several articles responding to Helms and others. In one article, Muhammad Kheir al-Wadi questioned Helms' motives in maligning Syria's reputation, especially when he did not have any relations with the Syrian people, did not know its geographic location and its political weight, and did not know its civilizational role in human history.[53] The article added that Syria did not depend on the Americans the way Israel does for its livelihood. Syria respects the American people.[54] When Syria did not attend the March 13 (1996) Terrorism Summit in Egypt, following suicide bombings in Israel, opposition to Syria, to the chagrin of the administration, increased in Congress. Gilman chaired a hearing before the House Committee on International Relations that questioned whether Syria was a peace partner or a rogue regime. Gilman stated that "the Administrations' efforts to convince Syria to cease and desist from these activities [narcotics trafficking and terrorism] have been paltry, subsumed by the greater desire to achieve a comprehensive peace in the Middle East."[55] He emphasized that as Syria has been acquiring unconventional weapons, has refused to crack down on terrorist groups based in Syria, and has kept its close relationship with Iran, it has renewed the suspicion that it does not desire peace, but rather a "peace process."[56] In the hearing, Patrick Clawson, of the Washington Institute, and Dr. Daniel Pipes, former editor of *Middle East Quarterly,* among others, spoke of Syria as being a "rogue regime," deserving America's toughness rather than "cajoling." This campaign against Syria put a damper on Syria's expectations of improving its relationship with the United States, diminishing Syrian hopes of any financial or military American rewards in the event of an Israeli-Syrian peace agreement. Therefore, while this campaign had not brought Israeli-Syrian negotiations to a halt, it had put serious obstacles in its path.

Even though the Labor government in Israel lost to the Likud party in May 1996, when Benjamin Netanyahu was elected Prime Minister, and the chances of an Israeli-Syrian peace agreement foundered, the campaign against Syria lost no steam. The focus had been mostly from Congress, reinforcing legislation that not only punished Syria but also prevented the President from giving any incentives to Syria. Congressman Schumer introduced Bill (105) H.R. 3080 to waive the determination of the President that Lebanon and Syria were not major drug-transit or illicit drug producing countries under the Foreign Assistance Act of 1961.[57] The bill stated that "notwithstanding the determination of the President that Lebanon and Syria are not major drug-transit countries or major illicit drug producing countries that is contained in the notification submitted to the Congress on November 9, 1997..., Lebanon and Syria shall be deemed to be major illicit drug producing countries or major drug-transit countries."[58]

Though the Foreign Operations, Export Financing, and Related Programs Appropriations Act, 1991, had banned any direct U.S. assistance to eight countries, including Syria, other resolutions had been introduced to strengthen this act, one of which is (105) H.R. 4569. Section (507) of this 1998 House Resolution prohibited direct funding for certain countries, including Syria. The prohibition on obligations or expenditures included direct loans, credits, insurance, and guarantees of the Export-Import Bank or its agents. Furthermore, Section (523) prohibited indirect funding to certain countries, including Syria.[59] The cumulative effects of the tall list of sanctions against Syria indeed punished Syria and shackled the hands of the President, particularly preventing laying the groundwork to remove Syria from the terrorism and narcotics lists.

Meanwhile, the Clinton administration's relationship with Israel had been warm and supportive, but not to the extent of distancing Arab states and the Palestinians. The genuine participation of Israel in the peace process further improved the U.S.-Israeli relationship.[60] Prime Ministers Yitzhak Rabin and Shimon Peres enjoyed a good working relationship with the Clinton administration, despite the fact, already mentioned, that Israel had perceived the administration as supportive of Syria in the sense that the onus of the peace negotiations had been placed on Israel's shoulders. But, as we read from Rabinovich's account, the Israeli government obviously was at one with the administration on the importance of concluding an Israeli-Syrian peace agreement, given the fact that Israel criticized the organized campaign to thwart such an agreement. However, the Israeli government believed that the administration had not done enough to achieve a breakthrough. Rabinovich claimed that, had the United States not been "soft" on Syria, the latter would have signed a peace deal.[61] This argument supports the notion that the United States had obviously been sensitive to Syria's concerns and that the United States had been trying to dovetail Syria's strategic key role in the region with American interests. Though this American position could be interpreted as evenhanded, surely it could not be regarded as blind support for Israel as Arabs often claim.

In fact, it was the peace process that highlighted again, but in a different form, the determining factors of U.S. strategic cooperation. In April 1996, President Clinton and Israel's Prime Minister Shimon Peres issued a joint statement that "anchored their 'strategic partnership' in two main principles: the U.S. commitment to Israel

and a mutual determination to achieve a 'comprehensive peace settlement.'"[62] Joseph Alpher, former director of the Jaffee Center for
Strategic Studies at Tel Aviv University, asserted that "a commend-
able condition for future American strategic support for Israel may
be one which requires that Israel remain pledged to a workable
peace process."[63] When Netanyahu replaced Peres as Prime Minister and challenged the conditions of peace with Syria and the Palestinians, relations between the Clinton administration and Israel's
government became strained. Netanyahu's policies ran counter to
the "land for peace" formula of the peace process, and included the
expansion of Israeli settlements in the occupied territories. However, whereas the Bush administration regarded the settlements
not only as obstacles to peace but also as contradictory to U.S. policy
and as illegal, the Clinton administration regarded them only as no
more than obstacles. The Clinton administration had unfailingly
supported Israel in the United Nations. It had vetoed Security
Council resolutions, which criticized Israeli settlement policies in
the occupied territories, and had voted against General Assembly
resolutions with the same intent.

Toward the Brink of Peace

Although no breakthrough in the Israeli-Syrian peace process
occurred during the tenures of Prime Ministers Yitzhak Rabin and
Shimon Peres, momentous decisions had been made and much had
been achieved between the two countries. When al-Asad met Clinton in Geneva in January 2004, he stated at a joint press conference
that "Syria seeks a just and comprehensive peace with Israel as a
strategic choice that secures Arab rights, ends the Israeli occupation, and enables people in the region to live in peace, security and
dignity." He then added that "we want the peace of the brave...a
peace which secures the interests of each side....If the leaders of
Israel have sufficient courage to respond to this kind of peace, a
new era of security and stability in which normal peaceful relations
among all shall dawn."[64] This constituted an important turning
point in al-Asad's approach to negotiations with Israel. By committing himself to establishing normal relations within the context of
peace, al-Asad was sending Israel a message of his readiness, unlike
before, to discuss normalization. No less important was Israel's
unambiguous admission to Syria in 1994 that Israel's commitment
to withdraw ("full withdrawal") from the Golan Heights referred to
the borders that existed on the eve of the June 4, 1967 war.[65]

In the same year also, in a show of resolve and support for the
peace process, President Clinton made a foray into shuttle

diplomacy in the region in late October with the objective of mediating the Israeli-Syrian talks. This came also within the context of witnessing the signing of the Israeli-Jordanian peace treaty at a desert outpost along their border. At a joint news conference after Clinton's meeting with al-Asad at the Presidential Palace in Damascus, the Syrian president made his opening statement:

> ...I have reaffirmed to President Clinton the continued commitment of Syria to the peace process and her serious pursuit of a comprehensive and just peace as a strategic choice that secures Arab rights, ends the Israeli occupation of the Arab land in conformity with the Security Council Resolutions 242, 338 and 425....I also stressed to President Clinton—emanating from the principle of full withdrawal for full peace—...the readiness of Syria to commit itself to the objective requirements of peace through the establishment of peaceful, normal relations with Israel in return for Israel's full withdrawal from the Golan to the line of June 4, 1967, and from the south of Lebanon.[66]

This was an important development in the peace process. Al-Asad had not only confirmed his readiness to establish normal relations with Israel but also clarified his new perspective on comprehensive peace, which had come to mean withdrawal from the Golan Heights and Lebanon only. However, al-Asad's message to Israel was dampened by his reluctance to criticize in public the recent bombing attacks in Israel, something that the Americans had hoped he might do to soothe an anxious Israeli public. Although al-Asad denied any Syrian involvement in terrorism, his reluctance to denounce the attacks most likely reflected his perception of such acts inside Israel as legitimate forms of resistance, a sign that he was still bound by the older dogmas of the Arab-Israeli conflict.

After the parties agreed on setting a framework for security arrangements so that neither party would make impractical security demands, they reached an agreement on the aims and principles of the security arrangements in May 1995. The final version of the agreement was referred to as the "Non-Paper on the Aims and Principles of the Security Arrangements." Besides being the first agreement reached between Syria and Israel, the importance of the Non-Paper lies in the fact that the two parties had agreed on a resolution of the issue of "equality" and "mutuality" in the security arrangements. This materialized with Syria's concession to forego geographic symmetry.[67]

But this progress was partly parried by Syria's refusal to condemn terrorist attacks on Israel and its support for Hizbollah. In February 1996, the lull in terror attacks during peace negotiations was shattered when Islamist militants exploded bombs in Ashkelon and Jerusalem, killing 25 people. Reportedly, the attacks were an act of revenge for the assassination of Yahya Ayyash, a Palestinian Hamas leader known as "the Engineer," by Israel in early January.[68] Ayyash had designed and helped set off bomb attacks against Israel in recent years.

Other attacks were to follow in early March, raising the death toll to 59.[69] Obviously, the assaults, this time, were clearly both an act of vengeance and a means to derail the peace process. According to Rabinovich, the Syrian refusal to condemn the terrorist attacks made Israeli-Syrian peace negotiations untenable and led Peres to suspend the negotiations on March 4.[70] This brought about the end of the Peres talks with Syria.

In addition to these dramatic and tragic events, other events alienated further the two parties. During and after the negotiations, the cycle of terror was not confined only to suicide bombings in Israel. Hizbollah, in a familiar pattern by now, escalated its attacks on the Israeli army and the SLA in south Lebanon in addition to firing Katyousha rockets into the Galilee. This violence began to bear heavily on Peres, contributing to sharpening his image as "weak on security," an image pointedly projected by the opposition, which had "peace with security" as its election campaign slogan. Apparently, Peres was cornered and had to react with a show of resolve if this violence continued. Meanwhile, the United States organized an international summit in Sharm al-Shaykh in Egypt to deal with combating terrorism. European, Russian, Palestinian, and Arab heads of state attended the summit to lend their support to the peace process and signal their joint dedication to fight against terrorism. The Syrians refused to attend. While this summit was held to some extent to help Peres domestically, the Syrians took exception, interpreting it as a concerted campaign against Damascus and Tehran. In addition, the Syrians saw in the summit an American and Israeli scheme to shift the focus from the peace process to combating terrorism.[71]

Apparently, Syria was using its Lebanese leverage against Israel in an act of defiance. Peres, like Rabin before him, decided to launch an operation, Grapes of Wrath, against Lebanon on April 2, in an effort both to strike at Hizbollah and to put pressure on the Lebanese government and in turn on its Syrian patron. The thinking behind the operation carried the hallmarks of the previous Operation Accountability. Israel's raw power demonstrated time and again its limitations. Grapes of Wrath, conducted among innocent and helpless civilians, resulted in the unintended consequence of shelling a large group of civilians taking refuge at the headquarters of the United Nations in Kafar Qana, killing more than a hundred people.

World public opinion heaped its opprobrium on Israel for the Kafar Qana tragedy. Peres brought the operation to a swift end without achieving anything to help rehabilitate his image at home. Secretary of State Christopher helped bring about a cease-fire. He also managed to organize a committee drawn from Lebanese, Syrian, Israeli, and French diplomats to monitor the cease-fire between Israel and the Hizbollah guerrillas. The parties worked out an agreement, in fact, an extension of the 1993 agreement, which called on Hizbollah not to fire Katyousha rockets into Israel and on Israel not to target civilians in Lebanon.[72] This agreement became known as the April Understanding. One would argue that this agreement helped to legitimize the Islamist party as a resistance movement in the eyes of the Arab world in general and many Lebanese in particular, as Hizbollah continued to attack the IDF in the south of Lebanon.

It was against this background that the Israelis went to the polls on May 29 and gave Likud and its leader, Benjamin Netanyahu, a victory. At this point, one could not dismiss the fact that the campaign of terror led by Hamas, Islamic Jihad, and Hizbollah contributed to the defeat of Peres and therefore to the long hiatus that followed in the Israeli-Syrian negotiations.

The election of Netanyahu cast a pall over the whole peace process. The Arab world watched closely the Israeli election campaign and frowned upon Netanyahu's famous three noes: No to withdrawal from the Golan, no to dividing Jerusalem, and no to a Palestinian state. Insights into Netanyahu's policy on Syria could be gathered early in his term from his meetings with Secretary of State Christopher at the end of June and with President Clinton in July. At the June meeting, he branded Damascus in the same breath as Iran as a terrorist state, while at his July meetings, he tried to persuade the President to adopt a policy of "triple containment." In this way, Netanyahu hoped to add Syria to the existing American policy of "dual containment," and therefore isolate it.[73]

Seemingly, Netanyahu's thoughts and hopes seemed to be based on his book *A Place Among Nations,* in which he calls for a policy of peace deterrence, that is, strengthening the democracies and weakening the dictatorships.[74] As far as Syria was concerned, this policy would bring international pressure to bear on Damascus to force a change in the country's concept of peace. According to Netanyahu, peace had to be resumed with no preconditions, a position he publicly declared from the podium of the Israeli Knesset following his election.[75] Indeed, in his meeting with Christopher, he emphasized his line of policy reflecting his "peace or terror" formula, a formula harking back to Shamir's "peace for peace."[76] In addition, he made clear that he would not be held responsible for the "hypothetical formula" made by the former Labor government concerning full withdrawal from the Golan Heights.

Netanyahu's statements galvanized the Arab world into organizing a summit, the first in six years, in Egypt in a show of collective unity and support for Syria. President Mubarak, sending an indirect message to Netanyahu, said that he "hoped that the display of unity would help to guard against attempts to stray from the path toward peace in the Middle East."[77] As it turned out, Arab fears of Netanyahu's desire to rob the peace process of its significance were confirmed as he proved to be difficult with the Palestinians, albeit he affirmed that he would respect the Oslo accords and work toward their implementation. More specifically, he tried to outmaneuver Syria into agreeing to resume the negotiations without any preconditions, something Damascus was bent on not doing.

Early on in his term, Netanyahu spoke of a "Lebanon First" option, a proposal to enter into negotiations with Lebanon over Israel's withdrawal from the security zone. The proposal was immediately and expectedly rejected by the Lebanese and their Syrian patrons, who shunned any separate solution.[78] He, then, through his defense minister, Yitzhak Mordechai, declared his readiness to implement Security Council Resolution 425. The bottom line was that Israel would not talk about peace or normalization; the pullout price would be security arrangements only.[79] Immediately, Syrian Vice-President Khaddam and Foreign Minister Shara argued that the initiative was part of a plot to isolate Syria, an initiative to evade negotiations over the Golan Heights.[80]

Syria took a firm position regarding the resumption of the negotiations. It made any return to the talks conditional on Israel resuming them from the point at which they were interrupted, thus holding on and protecting the legacy of the previous promises. In an interview with *al-Majalla,* Shara stressed that the fundamental principle for building a just peace was to resume the negotiations from where they stopped. He added that substituting the formula of "peace for peace" for "land for peace" as the principle of the peace process was a Likud stratagem violating international legitimacy and the logic of a just peace.[81]

Against a background where one party predicated the peace process on the principle of "land for peace" and the demand of full withdrawal from the Golan, while the other championed the formula of "peace for peace" along with some withdrawals only, the Israeli-Syrian negotiations plunged into an inauspicious hiatus.[82]

The Last Encounter

After a hiatus of almost four years for Israeli-Syrian peace talks, the election in May 1999 of Ehud Barak, who ran on a platform of peace, as Israel's prime minister revived hopes for peace. Capitalizing on the new political climate, President Clinton was quick in bringing the Israelis and Syrians to resume their peace talks. Not surprisingly, Likud leader Ariel Sharon assaulted liberal U.S. lobbying groups, especially the Israel Policy Forum, a peace group that advocates an active U.S. role in the peace effort, for trying to persuade members of Congress to "overcome 'their natural resistance' to provide Syria money as part of a peace package."[83] Thomas Smerling, director of the Israel Policy Forum's Washington center, said that his group "did not lobby for aid to Syria, but encouraged Congress to see the strategic value of peace with Syria and 'not to foreclose any options before a deal is struck.'" Added Smerling, "Opponents of peace have long viewed Congress as the soft underbelly of Israel's initiative."[84]

This did not discourage President Clinton from focusing on the peace process, even participating as an intermediary. He devised a formula for resuming the negotiations based on the by now famous "constructive ambiguity" approach. He emphasized that both sides had agreed to resume negotiations "from the point they were left off," without further elaboration on the terms for resumption."[85] This phrasing appeared to allow the two parties to save face, with the understanding that each side would underscore different points about the past. In addition, he subsequently devised a seven-page "working paper" defining the parties' agreements and differences. The paper was more in the form of a draft treaty, with the points of dispute bracketed.[86] The parties agreed to structure the talks by setting four committees to discuss specific issues of bilateral relations, security, access to water, and drawing borders. After meeting in Washington in late December and early January, the Syrian delegation left the capital angry with the Israeli delegation, headed by Barak, for sidestepping the key component of peace. They felt that Barak kept evading discussing the demarcation of the June 4, 1967, lines. Indeed, unlike other committees, the border committee barely met.

According to Dennis Ross, Barak had wavered before Shepherdstown talks. As domestic opposition to a Syrian deal began to mount, Barak reversed his initial decision conveyed to the Bush administration that he would confirm to the Syrians Israeli commitment on the June 4 lines (reaffirmation of Rabin's deposit). Consequently, during the talks, Barak raised his requirements for peace by demanding, among other things, resumption of negotiations with Lebanon. Barak apparently needed to show his public he had not rushed to an agreement. As Ross explained, "Barak at Shepherdstown held back for reasons that made sense to him, but he failed to address what the other side needed."[87]

In the meantime, the Syrians leaked a partial and distorted version of the working paper in the form of excerpts to *Al-Hayat,* which published it on January 9, 2000. This upset the Israelis, who pointed out that the published text was inaccurate and biased, but who then proceeded to leak the whole working paper to *Ha'aretz,* which published it on January 13. The revelation of the whole text was received with indignation in Damascus. Its publication made clear where each side stood and revealed before the Syrian public that the Israelis had wrung concessions from the Syrians without getting Israel to declare its commitment to a withdrawal from the Golan Heights to the June 4 lines.[88] Emphasizing that the policy of "constructive ambiguity" had run its course, the Syrians suspended their participation in the next scheduled round of negotiations.[89] At the same time, Hizbollah heightened the tension in the security zone in southern Lebanon by escalating its attacks on Israeli troops and their Lebanese allies, the SLA. Nevertheless, Syria and Israel appeared to retain the desire to resume peace negotiations by alternately signaling in some way or another their readiness.

In late February, Prime Minister Barak threw a political bombshell when he told his cabinet that former prime minister Yitzhak Rabin "had given guarantees that Israel would fully withdraw from the Golan Heights in exchange for security commitments by Syria," apparently confirming what Syria had long maintained.[90] Barak added that he would not "erase the past," hinting that "he, too, would be prepared to meet Syria's demand and withdraw down to, or close to, the shores of the sea of Galilee if Israel's security needs were met."[91] Israeli media perceived Barak's words as a revelation, with Channel 2 News reporting that "it was the first time that an Israeli prime minister has ever admitted that Israel had agreed— conditionally—to a complete withdrawal." A few days later, Barak's apparent overture to Syria acquired a sense of urgency when the Israeli cabinet endorsed the prime minister's vow to withdraw from Lebanon in July, preferably, but not necessarily, in the context of an accord with Syria.[92] Israel appeared determined to strip Syria of its Lebanese card, forcing the former's hand. Damascus would no longer be able to use Hizbollah as a source of leverage against Tel Aviv. Nor could it justify either its military presence in Lebanon or its desire to keep wedding the Lebanese to the Syrian track of negotiations. Simultaneously, Barak was inviting al-Asad back to the negotiating table, by indicating his readiness to withdraw from the Golan Heights, and twisting his arm, by depriving him of a bargaining chip in the negotiations over the Heights.

Barak's revelation followed by his cabinet's vow of unilateral withdrawal from Lebanon set the stage for fast-paced U.S. efforts to try to break the impasse between the two countries. These efforts culminated in a decision to hold a summit meeting in Geneva between President al-Asad and President Clinton on March 26, 2000. In his memoirs President Clinton described his last meeting with President al-Asad and reflected on Israeli-Syrian negotiations:

> Our team had been working to get Barak to make a specific proposal on Syria for me to present. I knew it wouldn't be a final offer, and the Syrians would know it, too, but I thought that if Israel finally responded with the same flexibility the Syrians had shown at Shepherdstown, we might still be able to make a deal. It was not to be.
>
> When I met Assad, he was friendly as I gave him a blue tie with a red-line profile of a lion, the English meaning of his name. It was a small meeting: Assad was joined by Foreign Minister Shara and Butheina Shaban; Madeleine Albright and Dennis Ross accompanied me, with the National Security Council's Rob Malley serving as notetaker. After some pleasant small talk, I asked Dennis to spread out the maps I had studied carefully in preparing for our talks. Compared with his stated position at Shepherdstown, Barak was now willing to accept less land around the lake, though he still wanted a lot, 400 meters (1,312 feet); fewer people at the listening station; and a quicker withdrawal period. Assad didn't want me even to finish the presentation. He became agitated and, contradicting the Syrian position at Shepherdstown, said that he would never cede any of the land, that he wanted to be able to sit on the shore of the lake and put his feet in the water. We tried for two hours to get some traction with the Syrians, all to no avail. The Israeli rebuff in Shepherdstown and the leak of the working document in the Israeli press had embarrassed Assad and destroyed his fragile trust. And his health had deteriorated even more than I knew. Barak had made a respectable offer. If it had come at Shepherdstown, an agreement might have emerged. Now, Assad's first priority was his own son's succession, and he had obviously decided that a new round of negotiations, no matter how it came out, could put that at risk. In less than four years, I had seen the prospects of peace between Israel and Syria dashed three times: by terror in Israel and Peres's defeat in 1996, by the Israeli rebuff of Syrian overtures at Shepherdstown, and by Assad's preoccupation with his own mortality. After we parted in Geneva, I never saw Assad again.[93]

Recounting this episode, Ross explained that "Asad had made up his mind before coming to Geneva that now was not the time to do a deal. Even if Barak got out of Lebanon unilaterally, Israel would not lose interest in having a deal with Syria at some point. That could wait. For al-Asad, he had something more fundamental to deal with. He was preoccupied with succession. He was not healthy enough now to deal with more than one big issue. Managing succession would be demanding enough. And what he saw as Barak's "betrayal" at Shepherdstown had raised the cost of doing an agreement."[94]

On al-Asad, President Clinton reflected: "Although we had our disagreements, he had always been straightforward with me, and I had believed him when he said he had made a strategic choice for peace. Circumstances, miscommunication, and psychological barriers had kept it from happening, but at least we know what it would take for Israel and Syria to get there once both sides were ready."[95]

With the death of al-Asad, who had ruled Syria since 1970, a new chapter in U.S.-Syrian relations has opened.

A New Regional Order?

As we have seen, the Middle East has been an arena for Cold War politics and direct and indirect conflicts between Syria and Israel. The disintegration of the Soviet Union and the Gulf War (1990–1991) had a dramatic impact on the region in general and Syria in particular. Damascus no longer had a patron, the Soviet Union. In addition, the defeat of the Iraqi army at the hands of the American-led coalition in the Gulf War and the subsequent U.N. sanctions placed on Iraq deprived Syria of its Iraqi strategic depth and of an Arab supporter in the event of a future war between Syria and Israel. Damascus found itself at the mercy of a powerful Israel, supported by the only remaining superpower, the United States. At the end of the 1991 Gulf War, Washington's promise of a "new regional order" based on peace between Arabs and Israelis encouraged Syria to join the peace process. But the promise proved somewhat illusory. Although the peace process was launched and new agreements between Israelis and Arab were signed, still the region remained in a state of flux and volatility, affecting Syrian regional security vis-à-vis Israel and, by extension, U.S.-Syrian relations. Central to this was the emergence of the military alliance between Israel and Turkey with the blessing of the United States, which was looked upon by the Syrians as a direct threat to their own security and regional role. Syria responded by improving its strategic cooperation with Iran and supporting Hizbollah as a means of leverage against Israel, while at the same time negotiating peace. Damascus's reaction was also an attempt to prove to the United States, Turkey, and Israel that its regional role was irreducible.

The Gulf War marked the renewal of Turkey's involvement in the rest of the Middle East. Ankara was very concerned with the possibility that Kurdish autonomy and feelings of independence in northern Iraq might spill over into its own Kurdish territories. Throughout Iraq's modern history, the Kurds in the north of the country fought for their autonomy. Following the Gulf War, the political and military situation changed in northern Iraq, which the United States designated as a "no-fly zone." Iraqi Kurds suddenly found themselves for the first time in their history free of the control of central governments. This deeply worried Turkey, and thus it resisted Kurdish independence efforts in Iraq. For the past almost three decades the Kurdistan Workers Party (PKK) had waged war for independence in the east of Turkey. Consequently, Ankara continued to intervene militarily in northern Iraq while paying close attention to Iraq and the region.

Meanwhile, although a member of the North Atlantic Treaty Organization, Turkey feared overall marginalization as a result of the disappearance of the Soviet Union and its threats to the Western alliance. Facing a multitude of regional and internal problems, Turkey sought to improve its relations with the United States and refurbish its armed forces, which are mainly based on U.S. equipment. But Ankara met resistance in the U.S. Congress and at the White House, both of which were lobbied by human rights organizations as well as by Greek American and Armenian American pressure groups. Against a background of fledgling Israeli-Turkish military ties, Israel emerged as the solution to Turkey's dilemma. The Jewish lobby could help Turkey counteract the influence of the Greek and Armenian lobbies and refurbish its armed forces. Indeed, according to Turkish sources, the United States guided Turkey in the direction of Israel.[96] Non-Arab, largely secular, Western-oriented, and democratic (Israel more so), the two countries shared a wide rationale for close relations.

Israel was more than happy to meet Turkey halfway. Isolated in the region despite its participation in the peace process and concerned with threatening developments all around it, Israel unhesitatingly went headlong into a military alliance with Turkey, negotiated by Prime Minister Yitzhak Rabin in 1994–1995. Two agreements were signed in February and August 1996, and in both some provisions remained secret. They provided for joint air and naval exercises, the opportunity for the Israeli air force to train over the mountainous expanses of Anatolia, intelligence cooperation, and substantial Israeli arms transfers to Turkey.[97] Significantly enough, the military alliance brought Israel closer to the borders of Iran, Iraq, and northern Syria. Using Turkey's strategic location, not only could Israel monitor these countries' development of weapons of mass destruction and their military movements, but it could also undertake deep air raids against them to destroy the bases of those weapons.[98]

All this had an impact on Syria's security vis-à-vis Israel. The country saw its once powerful and rival neighbor, Iraq, soundly defeated. The isolation of Iraq left Syria as the only Arab country of note opposing the Jewish state. In addition, in the event of a Syrian-Israeli war, Damascus could no longer expect, as in the past, Iraqi military support. Damascus took careful note of how efficiently the modern technological war against Iraq was carried out. This highlighted Israel's advanced and superior military capabilities in comparison with Syria's, if only because the Jewish state has been the recipient of American advanced weaponry. Undoubtedly, the Gulf War and the consequent destruction of Iraq's military had tipped the balance of power in the region even more decisively in Israel's favor. Syria joined the peace process partly to neutralize Israel's power and partly to position itself within the context of American plans for a new regional order. But, along with that, Syria tried, on the one hand, to strengthen its regional security role, and, on the other, to upgrade its military capabilities.

In March 1991, the six Gulf Cooperation Council (GCC) states signed the Damascus Declaration with Egypt and Syria, apparently creating the Arab anti-Iraq coalition.[99] Actually, the Declaration provided the poor partners in the coalition, Egypt and Syria, with a security role in protecting the rich Gulf states in return for financial remuneration. However, by the end of the Gulf War, fearing that Egyptian and Syrian troops could become a source of tension in the Gulf, the GCC states were quick to strip the agreement of any significance. In fact, the final text of the agreement did not specify any role for Egypt and Syria.[100] In addition, the GCC states went ahead with signing bilateral security pacts with the United States, further eliminating any potential Syrian security role in the Gulf.[101]

What had strategically remained for Syria to improve its regional security was its cooperation with Iran. After the Gulf War, Syria continued to promote its relationship with Iran, the state that Syria supported during the Iran-Iraq Gulf War (1980–1988). While many consider this relationship as a strategic alliance, it is really no more than a form of strategic cooperation dominated by realpolitik. The two states are on the extreme ends of the political spectrum in the region: Syria is secular and Iran is theocratic. Fear of potential Iraqi hegemony in the region in the 1980s made Syria support Iran in the first Gulf War, and Syria's weakness vis-à-vis Israel made Damascus more than happy to cooperate with and welcome Iranian support. More specifically, Iran and Syria frequently found themselves on the same side of the political fence facing regional issues, ranging from an unpredictable Iraq to Gulf security to the Arab-Israeli conflict. One aspect of this cooperation has been Syria benefiting from (and supporting) Hizbollah in Lebanon, Iran's protégé, by waging a guerrilla campaign against the IDF and the South Lebanese Army in the south of Lebanon. Syria has been using this campaign as leverage against the Jewish state.

Syria was concerned with strengthening its regional position, especially at a time when it was deeply involved in negotiating a peace treaty with Israel. This, on the one hand, would allow Syria to negotiate from a position of strength and, on the other hand, could be interpreted as a reminder to the Americans as well as to the Israelis that Syria's strategic regional position is irreducible.

By playing a mediating role between the Arabs and Iran, Syria could only enhance its strategic regional role. More specifically, Syria and Iran seemed to share the belief that Israel is bent on achieving hegemony in the region. In addition, the two countries shared another belief that historically they have been the victims of Western conspiratorial plots. Syria looked at Iran both as a means of leverage against Israel and as a counterweight to its power, especially its nuclear capability. This explains why Syria, unlike other Arab countries, did not see Iran's development of weapons of mass destruction as a threat to the region. At this point, I emphasize that only when Iran acquires the nuclear bomb or when Syria comes under a direct military threat could the Iran-Syria strategic cooperation transform itself into a strategic alliance.

This indicates that Syria's quest for strengthening its regional position grew no less out of its military weakness vis-à-vis Israel than out of its sense of vulnerability and insecurity. In fact, Syria took to heart the fact that Israel's security concept rested on the premise that it should maintain its power and superiority over all the Arabs, especially in the technological field. Accordingly, Syria's military strategists held the belief that Israel operates in an environment of peace in the same manner as in an environment of war, meaning through the logic of power and hegemony.[102] It is against this backdrop that Syria bristled with anger against America as it monitored Damascus's efforts to upgrade its military capabilities, especially those involving the acquisition of ballistic missiles. Indeed, reacting to U.S. attempts to restrict the flow of missiles to Syria (by persuading Russia, China, and South Africa against selling missile technology to Damascus) while Israel was allowed to produce all types of weapons, President al-Asad lashed out: "That is not international legitimacy. That is the law of the jungle, the law of wild animals. They are trying to impose surrender on us."[103]

While the issue of how to neutralize Israel's power, enhanced now by the Israeli-Turkish military alliance, preoccupied Syria, Damascus also had to worry about its relationship with Ankara. Syria had had difficult relations with Turkey. Historically, in 1939, Turkey, with the help of France, annexed the formerly Syrian sanjak (district) of Alexandretta calling it Hatay.[104] Syria did not recognize this transfer until recently (see conclusion). Still, tension between the two countries had emanated largely from two additional conflicts: The first over Turkey's Southeast Anatolian Project (GAP) and its building of dams on the Euphrates river, and the second over Syria's support for the PKK. Since the 1980s the PKK engaged Turkey in armed struggle and terrorist activities. Ankara accused Damascus of harboring the PKK and their leader, Abdallah Ocalan, providing them with bases in Lebanon's Beka valley and in Syria. Ankara believed that the PKK could not continue its terrorist activities without Syria's support.

In 1992 the two countries reached a security agreement, which soon fizzled out as relations between them deteriorated anew. In the mid-1990s Turkey began to make Syria's suspension of all support to the PKK the focal point of their relationship. Syria denied all Turkish accusations and emphasized that the problem was an internal Turkish one, an emphasis repeatedly voiced by the Ba'thi leaders.[105] Discontented with Syria's responses, Turkey threatened action against its neighbor and suspended all official contacts with it.[106] Tension rapidly rose between the two countries in May–June 1996, leading almost to a military confrontation on the border. The assumption to power of Turkey's Islamic leader, Necmetin Erbakan, temporarily defused the crisis.[107] However, Turkey sent a stern message to Syria in the form of bombing attacks against civilian targets planted by Turkish agents in Damascus and other parts of the country.[108]

Paralleling these developments, the rapprochement between Turkey and Israel during the early 1990s culminated in military agreements, at a time when Turkey was also militarily intervening on a regular basis in northern Iraq. Damascus was quick to interpret Turkey's new assertiveness as a product of the emerging Israeli-Turkish alliance. Syria, which shares an 820 kilometer border with Turkey, saw the alliance as a great geopolitical threat to its regional position and its political cohesion. Not only did Syria become sandwiched by two powerful allies, Turkey and Israel, but it also faced a neighbor, Iraq, threatened by sectarian strife and partition. This, Syria feared, could well spill into its own territory, given the sectarian composition of the country's population. Even before the alliance was signed, some Ba'thi leaders believed that there was a plan to partition Iraq, a plan in sync with a Zionist plot to sow divisions within each individual Arab state.[109] In addition, the timing of the alliance during the Syrian-Israeli negotiations convinced some Ba'thi leaders that the objective of the military agreement was to force Syria to sign a peace treaty with Israel on the latter's terms.[110]

The Turkish-Israeli alliance spawned a flurry of activity in the region. Syria mobilized its efforts to seek regional alliances to offset the impact of the Turkish-Israeli alliance on the regional balance of power. Its previous efforts to strengthen its regional role began to meet positive responses from many Arab countries, which themselves frowned on the Turkish-Israeli alliance. Although Israeli and Turkish leaders affirmed that neither country would assist the other in the event of an attack by a third party, the geopolitical aspect of the agreements and their provisions (see above) pointed in another direction.[111] Interestingly enough, Syria's mediation efforts between Iran and the Gulf countries paid off as Saudi Arabia and Iran reached a détente. On the one hand, as a member of the Damascus Declaration, the road was paved for Syria to help bring about a front led by Cairo, Riyadh, and Damascus. On the other hand, Syria deepened its strategic cooperation with Iran.

Contacts between Damascus, Riyadh, and Cairo stepped up. For the first time since the 1991 Gulf War, this tripartite entente managed to convene an Arab summit in June 1996 in Cairo. The parties attending the summit expressed their deepest concern over the Turkish-Israeli military alliance and called upon Turkey to reconsider its position with the objective of canceling it. This Arab stance was emphasized in subsequent meetings between the Damascus Declaration states as they called for Arab cooperation. In addition, in a departure from their tough stance on Iraq, they called for protecting the unity of Iraq.[112] Iran, like Arab states, was also quick to lend its support to Syria. It even proposed the creation of an alliance counteracting that between Turkey and Israel.[113] Syria further improved its strategic cooperation with the Persian state, but short of a military alliance. Following a visit by al-Asad to Tehran in August 1997, the two countries released a joint declaration in which they emphasized their deepest concern over the Turkish-Israeli alliance, which posed security threats to all neighboring countries and regional stability. They also affirmed the necessity of preserving Iraq's territorial unity.[114]

In retrospect, the Turkish-Israeli alliance apparently evoked Arab suspicions of a Western attempt to establish an alliance, similar to that of the historic Baghdad Pact, to impose its will on the region. Given constant Turkish military interventions in northern Iraq, Syria, like the other Arab states, could not but entertain the idea that Turkey, indeed, has never given up its ambitions to control the oil-rich provinces of Mosul and Kirkuk.[115] In the vanguard of Arab states, Syria kept affirming that the Turkish-Israeli alliance was directed against the Arabs, with Syria at the center of the alliance's efforts.[116] Syrian heightened fears of this alliance became all the more telling after these two countries began to flex their muscles against Damascus.

In the fall of 1996, the Israeli media hyped up the possibility of a limited Syrian surprise attack on the Golan Heights. As it turned out, this was fueled in large measure by rumors leaked by a retired Mossad official (Yehuda Gil). But a few months later, the press in Israel began to ask questions about Syria's efforts to quietly acquire ballistic missiles and weapons of mass destruction. Sporadic threats by the government of Israel against Syria accompanied these reports, which centered on Damascus developing Scud assembly lines and chemical and biological weapons. Syria was cautious not to provoke Israel into taking action but was not reticent. On May 1, 1996, while at a press conference in Egypt, al-Asad was asked about the Israeli threats and his country's production of the lethal VX gas which can be carried by missiles. Al-Asad grimly replied that "whoever has nuclear weapons has no right to criticize others for whatever weapons they have. If they [Israelis] want disarmament, let us start with nuclear weapons. We Arabs in general are ready to get rid of the other weapons. We have heard the threats and they did not cause an earthquake, Syria remains unshaken."[117] The conference ended with Syria and Egypt confirming their joint support in facing regional challenges.

Equally significant, Israel, Turkey, and the United States conducted a joint military exercise in the Mediterranean (Operation Mermaid), with Jordan as an observer. Although the exercise was confined to humanitarian purposes, it undoubtedly carried a heavy symbolic message to the region, namely that the United States blessed not only the Turkish-Israeli alliance but also the exercises as a show of force. With the disappearance of the Soviet threat to the region, the Washington-blessed alliance could easily be interpreted by the Arabs as a means to contain and narrow their margin of maneuverability in the area. A few months later in September, tension between Turkey and Syria reached an all-time high as the former massed its troops along the border and appeared ready to invade if Syria did not immediately suspend its support of the PKK. This confirmed Syrian fears that not only was Turkey's sudden hard-line stand a product of the Turkish-military burgeoning alliance but also that Israel was behind this position. The Syrian government's mouthpiece *al-Ba'th* declared on October 2 that "we in Syria are totally sure that this official Turkish position does not reflect the opinion of the Turkish people....It came as a result of full coordination between Ankara and Tel Aviv in accordance with their alliance."[118]

The gravity of the Turkish-Israeli alliance to regional security and particularly to that of Syria was underscored by the Syrian Defense Minister Mustafa Tlas. He stated that "the most serious thing the Arabs are facing is the satanic Israeli-Turkish alliance... the Israeli-Turkish alliance is not only aimed at Syria but at all Arabs."[119] He admitted as well that Israel is also aiming at bringing Jordan into the alliance. Significantly, the Syrians believed that these developments and plans affecting the country's security and regional role would not have happened without Washington's blessing and support. Eventually, Syria caved in to Turkey's pressure and agreed to suspend all support to the PKK, to bring to court any Kurdish rebel found on its territory, and to no longer allow Ocalan in the country. This was spelled out in an agreement signed between the two countries on 20 October.[120]

CHAPTER 5

The Unholy Relationship

Shortly after the failure of the Shepherdstown talks and the Clinton-Asad summit (2000), the Middle East witnessed momentous events that changed the dynamics of the Syrian-Israeli conflict and the configuration of power in the region. After 22 years of occupation, Israel withdrew from south of Lebanon without concluding a peace deal with Lebanon, pulling the rug of legitimacy out from under Syrian feet in Lebanon. No longer could Syria use Hizbollah to militarily pressure Israel with impunity. Nor could Syria any longer hope to wrest concessions from Israel during peace talks. Equally significant, President Hafiz al-Asad passed away after 30 years in power. Although President al-Asad had groomed his son, Bashar, for succession during his last couple of years in power, Bashar's election as general secretary of the Ba'th party and president of Syria was facilitated by a core of supporters, who in turn enhanced their power base in the structure of government. Correspondingly, Bashar found himself not only constricted by the legacy of his father but also by this power base in his regime.

No less momentous were the events and changes in policy that shocked the United States and the world. Initially, the election of president George W. Bush set a new tone for U.S. foreign policy in the Middle East, marked by a minimalist approach to the peace process. Significantly, the sheer magnitude and enormity of the September 11 terror attacks on the United States altered irreversibly not only the American way of life but also foreign policy priorities. Splitting the world between those with "the United States" and those "with the terrorists," President Bush declared a war on terrorism. Syria, as a state sponsor of terrorism, was not included in the "axis of evil," but it was put on notice to reorient its policies and regional alignments. Despite its cooperation on al-Qaeda, Damascus's opposition to the U.S.-led campaign against Iraq not only changed the dynamics of the U.S. ambivalent attitude toward Syria (in favor of the hard-liners) but also marked an ominous break with the pattern that the senior al-Asad established as president of modern Syria. As a result, Syria became a de facto member of the axis of evil.

Shebaa Farms: The Powder Keg of the Middle East

Under the aegis of the United States, Israeli-Syrian peace talks, as Itamar Rabinovich noted, reached the brink of peace. A few meters along the northeastern shore of Lake Tiberias stood against a settlement. These few meters, however, reflected the two countries' difficulty in shedding their ingrained adversarial past vis-à-vis each other.[1] Significantly enough, Israel signed the Oslo accords with the Palestinians in 1993 but remained in south Lebanon. This was Israel's strategic mistake at the time, which Syria and Hizbollah exploited to the hilt.

Damascus used Hizbollah as a means of indirect pressure on Israel during the peace negotiations, and Hizbollah transformed itself into a significant political movement by capitalizing on its resistance to Israel's occupation of south Lebanon. As noted earlier, even the United States helped legitimize Hizbollah as a resistance movement when it brokered the April Understanding of 1996, which served to limit Hizbollah's and Israel's military actions to the security zone, an area along its border in southern Lebanon.

After 22 years of occupation, Israeli prime minister Ehud Barak made good on his campaign promise to withdraw his troops from Lebanon by July 2000 by pulling out of the country ahead of schedule on May 24. Israel's withdrawal was swift and was watched by U.N. observers, who certified Tel Aviv's fulfillment of U.N. Resolution 425. On June 16, U.N. Secretary-General Kofi Annan officially declared that Israel had completed its withdrawal. In the process, the South Lebanese Army (SLA), Israel's proxy army, speedily disintegrated, provoking an exodus of a significant number of Lebanese officers and their families, mainly Christians, into Israel. Other members and affiliates of the SLA surrendered to the incoming forces of Hizbollah, who claimed victory over the retreating Israelis.[2] Barak objected and reiterated his campaign pledge, which was to end Israel's "misguided" involvement in Lebanon. At the same time, he held Damascus and Beirut directly responsible for attacks on Israeli territory launched from Lebanon. Israeli army officers bolstered Barak's warning by suggesting that future retaliatory strikes from Israel "would not exclude" Syrian military installations in Lebanon.[3]

In addition, Israel's ambassador to the United Nations, Yehuda Lancry, delivered a letter from Barak to Secretary-General Annan warning Syria and Iran. An excerpt of the letter reads:

> I [Barak] am referring particularly to Syria's cynical exploitation of the Palestinians in Lebanon to commit terrorist acts against Israel after the withdrawal and the fact that it provides a free hand to Iran, its messengers and protégés—primarily the Hizbollah—to build infrastructures which would undermine regional stability to the point of a possible outbreak of hostilities.[4]

Hizbollah's preeminence spread like wildfire in the Middle East when Israel withdrew from Lebanon, and the Islamist party was credited with dealing Tel Aviv the first defeat ever. True, Israel beat a retreat, but its withdrawal changed the overall dynamics of the triangular Israeli-Syrian-Lebanese relationship. Verified by the U.N., Israel's withdrawal pulled the rug of legitimacy out of the Syrian presence in Lebanon. No longer could Syria use Hizbollah as leverage against Israel without impunity. Nor could Syria any longer hope to wrest concessions from Israel during peace talks. Significantly, Israel apparently severed any future connection between Lebanon's and Syria's peace negotiating tracks. In fact, Lebanese and Syrian officials in March 2000 warned Israel from withdrawing unilaterally without a peace treaty.[5] Suddenly, the configuration of the Israeli-Syrian conflict appeared to change at the expense of Syria's role. Indeed, while enjoying the euphoria of victory, Syria feared that the rules of the game had changed in favor of Israel. Before long, those fears were confirmed when Israel's withdrawal sparked calls for Syrian redeployment in preparation for its withdrawal from Lebanon. Standing at the vanguard of opposition to Syrian presence were the Christians.[6] Out of this fluid situation, a new one emerged centering on Shebaa Farms. Lebanon, apparently at the behest of Syria, claimed that Israel's withdrawal was incomplete since the country still occupied Lebanese land, most notably Shebaa Farms. Shebaa is an area on the southwestern slopes of Mount Hermon (Jabal al-Shaykh), which the Lebanese government and Hizbollah claim is occupied Lebanese territory, while the U.N., after the Israeli withdrawal from Lebanon, considers it a land captured by Israel from Syria in the 1967 Middle East War.[7] In fact, during the run-up to Israel's withdrawal, the speaker of parliament, Nabih Berri, raised the question of Shebaa Farms, obviously at the instigation of Syria. When the issue first arose, few Lebanese, including even senior Hizbollah officials, knew of the case. Syria acknowledged Lebanon's claims to the territory. In addition, when the U.N. rejected Lebanon's claims, arguing that

Shebaa Farms was not covered by Resolution 425 but by Resolution 242, and was therefore subject to Israeli-Syrian negotiations, Lebanon and Syria refused to acknowledge this U.N. position. They have been arguing (along with Hizbollah) that Israel has not completed its withdrawal from Lebanon and thus resistance will continue until all Lebanese territories are liberated.[8]

Ironically, the same people who have been calling for the liberation of Shebaa did not know at the time of Israel's withdrawal that the territory belonged to Lebanon. Obviously, this assertion had in large measure its provenance in the party's utility to Syria. Damascus would keep using Hizbollah as a means of indirect pressure on Israel until Syria retrieved its Golan Heights. Damascus would use Hizbullah to fend off Lebanese opposition to its presence in the country.[9] Indeed, Hizbollah has launched periodic military offensives against Israeli positions in Shebaa, transforming the area into a tinderbox that could explode into a regional war. Seen through the prism of Syria, Hizbollah (with its arsenal of Katyusha rockets) could serve as both a deterrent to Israel's aggression and a daily reminder to Israel that it would not enjoy peace of mind unless it withdrew from the Golan Heights.

Transfer of Power

In the early 1990s, the question of succession began to gain momentum as al-Asad was seen grooming his eldest son, Basil, to succeed him. Basil adopted a military career, throughout which he rapidly advanced in the ranks, and joined the Presidential Guard, a military elite unit charged with protecting the president and the capital. He also got involved in Lebanese affairs and led a campaign against corruption and drug smuggling and trafficking. He was given wide press coverage for his activities, including his supposedly superb equestrian ability. His picture appeared alongside his father's all over the country. Basil supposedly enjoyed wide popularity as a tough but decent and down-to-earth man. To many in Syria, he appeared not only as the heir apparent, but also as the guarantor of political stability who had what it takes to rule.

Obviously, al-Asad promoted his son by delegating to him wide powers to build his base of support. But at the same time, al-Asad did not declare Basil as his heir. In any event, he died in a car accident while speeding to Damascus International Airport in January 1994. The Syrian public sincerely grieved Basil's death as hundreds of thousands participated in the funeral procession first in the capital and then in Qardaha, where the al-Asads hail from. Basil's unexpected death rekindled the undeclared but momentous

issue of succession. Al-Asad's other son, Bashar, studying ophthal-
mology in London at the time of his brother's death, returned home
and received broad media coverage while attending the mourning
ceremonies. Apparently, Bashar emerged as the convenient replace-
ment of his brother for the succession.

Gradually, Bashar began to follow in the footsteps of his late
brother. He joined the Presidential Guard, got involved in Lebanese
affairs, and took an interest in equestrian sports. He also paid significant attention to the importance of technology for Syria's future,
particularly the Internet. Meanwhile, al-Asad began a politico-
administrative process by which he removed too well entrenched
officials that could become future opponents of his son while promoting loyal supporters ready to transfer allegiance to him. At the same
time, Bashar had been steadily promoted in the army, along with
his circle of loyal young officers. And following the same method as
with Basil, al-Asad did not declare Bashar as his heir, although
Bashar's promotion and grooming showed otherwise.[10]

At the same time, Bashar's activities were given wide press coverage, reflecting his elevated status in the higher echelons of the
regime. For example, he was projected as a modern man bent on
reforming the socioeconomic condition of the country, as well as an
advocate of combating corruption. He actively promoted computer
awareness in Syria and emphasized the need of the country to
acquire new technologies. He appeared alongside Defense Minister
Mustafa Tlas at the military graduation ceremonies in Homs and
attended the war games of certain commando units of the Syrian
army along with General Tlas. He also deepened his involvement
in Lebanese state affairs, the former province of Vice-President
Khaddam.

All of these appointments, promotions, and removals reveal the
fact that al-Asad was delegating power to Bashar while he was still
alive with the ultimate objective of preparing a smooth transfer of
power to his son. However, what was happening was extremely haz-
ardous in light of the fact that throughout al-Asad's presidency a
few changes in the makeup of the elites in the military had taken
place before 1994–1995. This indicates that al-Asad was really concerned about a power struggle for succession that could split the
organs of the state, a situation that had occurred before in 1984
when al-Asad's brother, Rifa't, challenged al-Asad's wishes. Certain
rumblings within the civil and military wings of the state and party
that Bashar "does not have it in him to rule" exacerbated this state
of uncertainty in the higher echelons of the regime.[11]

The succession issue became a focal point for al-Asad following
the failure of both the peace talks in Shepherdstown and the

Clinton-Asad summit at Geneva. In contrast to an earlier pattern where al-Asad had been grooming his son for succession without publicly confirming him as heir apparent, the president's bold new moves indicated that he was unequivocally passing the reins of government to Bashar. This was revealed in the power al-Asad vested in his son to wage a campaign against corruption—also a way to elevate Bashar's status in the public eye—and in the decision to hold the ninth convention of the Syrian Ba'th party, which had not been convened for 15 years.

Bashar began intervening in high-profile domestic issues that were once only the sacred domain of his father. After apparently helping to dissolve the government of Prime Minister Mahmoud Zubi for inefficiency and corruption, Bashar confirmed that the Ba'th convention would take place and declared that he recommended people with merit be appointed in the new government.[12] He added that the first mission of the new government would be to modernize the bureaucracy and reduce the level of corruption.[13] These declarations followed frequent public statements about the necessity of introducing changes in all public and private sectors of the Syrian state.

On March 14, 2000, the new prime minister, Muhammad Mustafa Miro, headed a new government, which included twenty-five Ba'thists, five independents, and six representatives of the Progressive National Front.[14] Apparently, the selection process of the members of the new government rested in large part on their professed loyalty to Bashar. One could not dismiss this point, given that the former government was ousted after serving for 13 years.

On June 10, 2000, President al-Asad passed away after 30 years in power. Immediately after his death, Vice-President Khaddam issued legislation promoting Bashar from colonel to lieutenant general—the rank of his father—and appointing him commander in chief of the Syrian armed forces, as well as entitling him to run for the office of president.[15] This was followed by a series of actions that made Bashar the uncontested new leader of Syria. The Ba'th Regional Ninth Congress convened as scheduled, and on its second day, July 18, the ruling Ba'th party unanimously elected Bashar as its secretary general. In addition, Bashar headed a committee of six whose responsibility included overseeing the congress in general and appointing the new ruling Regional Command Council of the Ba'th party in particular.[16] The council wields much power in the party and state. Interestingly enough, the political report of the congress included two points: "Islam is a dogma and a heritage and part of our political life," and "the peace process is the strategic choice" for Syria.[17]

Shortly thereafter, Bashar was elected head of the Regional Command Council and approved unanimously by the parliament as the sole candidate for president in a referendum, in which he eventually won 97.27 percent of the votes. At this point, it is important to elaborate on the appointments, especially to the Regional Command Council, since they indicate the shifting political alliances and by implication the locus of political power in Syria. Out of 21 members, 12 new members were inducted into the council. They included Bashar, Prime Minister Mustafa Miro, Deputy Prime Minister Muhammad Naji Otri, Foreign Minister Farouq al-Shara, Ghiath Barakat, Ibrahim Humeidi, Faruq abu al-Shamat, Majed Shadud, Salam al-Yasin, Muhammad al-Hussein, Walid al-Bouz, and Muhammad Said Bakhtian. Vice-presidents Abd al-Halim Khaddam and Muhammad Zuheir Mashariqa, deputy secretaries of the Ba'th Party Suleiman Qaddah and Abdullah al-Ahmar, parliament speaker Abd al-Qader Qaddura, Defense Minister Mustafa Tlas, Ahmad Dargam, Fa'z al-Naser, and Walid Hamdoun all kept their membership in the council.[18]

It appears that an established core of supporters for Bashar included the original and loyal members of the committee of six, supplemented by Shara, Miro, Atri, and Bakhtian. The latter was a close aide of Bashar and an intelligence chief.[19]

Apparently, the configuration of the new power structure in Syria continued to follow the old pattern institutionalized by the late al-Asad. No organic change had taken place, and it appeared that the new regime would rely on an informal core of loyal military officers, mainly Alawi, and on a formal core of high-ranking state officials, mainly Sunni. Most important, given the new configuration and the pivotal roles played by Khaddam and Tlas in smoothing the transfer of power to Bashar, Khaddam, and Tlas, considered hardliners, especially the first, would play a significant role in protecting and guiding Bashar, but this might come at the expense of the new president's exclusive power. This could impose limits on what Bashar could do internally and externally until he completely consolidated his power.

Hafiz al-Asad departed from life without signing an agreement with Israel and saddled his son not only with an unfinished task but also with a peace process legacy that Bashar could ill afford to deviate from. In addition, the senior al-Asad left his son a security state underpinned by a core of Alawi military and security officials and some Sunni officials, many of whom have been hard-liners and protective of their entrenched interests. Notwithstanding the fact that Bashar will have to be a very skillful political manipulator to sustain a balance of power in his favor during his regime, the configuration of the new power structure suggested that for the time being Bashar will have to toe the line of the regime's stand on foreign policy priorities: recovering the Golan Heights, preserving its "special relations" with Lebanon, and enhancing its regional role.

A New American Outlook

The momentous transition in Syria coincided with a no less momentous transition in the United States, especially with regard to Washington's foreign policy in the Middle East. The election of the Republican candidate George W. Bush as president ended two consecutive Democratic terms and ushered in a new policy agenda. Nowhere was the difference between the incoming Bush administration and the outgoing Clinton administration more pronounced than in U.S. foreign policy, especially regarding the Middle East. In contrast to the Clinton administration, the Bush administration had reservations about making the peace process (as a means to resolve the Arab-Israeli conflict and maintain stability in the Middle East) a cornerstone not only of its Middle East foreign policy but also of U.S.-Syrian and U.S.-Israeli relationships. In fact, early on in office, the Bush administration made it clear that its foreign policy concern in the Middle East was to reinforce the sanctions against Iraq.[20]

The Bush administration had set the tone of a policy best described by the State Department's parlance as a "minimalist" approach to peace talks in contrast to the hands-on approach of the Clinton administration. Following the election of Likud leader Ariel Sharon as prime minister of Israel in early February 2001, largely in response to the failure of peace talks and escalating violence in the Palestinian occupied territories (Al-Aqsa Intifada), the Bush administration formally abandoned former President Clinton's peace proposals concerning the Arab-Israeli conflict. Condoleezza Rice, President Bush's national security adviser, emphasized in an interview: "We shouldn't think of American involvement for the sake of American involvement."[21] Signaling a break with the Clinton administration's hands-on approach to the Palestinian-Israeli conflict, Secretary of State Colin L. Powell stated that "the United States stands to assist, not insist."[22] Reinforcing sanctions against Iraq was Secretary Powell's focal point.

Indeed, in February 2001, Secretary Powell traveled to Middle East capitals on a shuttle diplomacy to reinforce the sanctions against Iraq by rebuilding Arab support for them. With the Al-Aqsa Intifada continuing unabated in the Palestinian occupied territories and stories about the harmful effects of the sanctions on the Iraqi population underscored daily in Arab media, many Arab countries came under pressure from their populations to assist the Palestinians and to support the removal of sanctions against Iraq. In addition, many Arabs began to lose faith in U.S. evenhandedness, citing favoritism toward Israel. Partly on account of all this, several Arab countries, including Syria, began to sign trade agreements with Iraq and fly their planes to Baghdad's international airport in defiance of the sanctions.[23] This made Powell's efforts to solicit strong support for his policy crucial as well as onerous.

Notwithstanding Washington's minimalist approach to the peace process that was all but presumed dead, Syria reemerged as a country of note that could make or break what had been considered as the Bush administration's highest foreign policy priority. Bearing in mind the geostrategic position Syria commands, bordering Iraq, the Bush administration was specifically interested in preventing Saddam Hussein from using revenues of Iraqi oil flowing through Syrian pipelines (which opened after many years of closure) to acquire weapons, whether sophisticated or unconventional. As part of his strategy, Secretary Powell sought to convince President al-Asad to place into a U.N. escrow account those oil revenues flowing into Saddam's pockets. After meeting with President al-Asad on February 26, 2001, Secretary Powell was able to obtain a commitment in this respect from the Syrian president. According to the *New York Times,* the "commitment from the Syrian president was so firm—Mr. Asad stated it three times during the meeting, General Powell said—that the secretary said he had telephoned President Bush to tell him."[24] In the meantime, Washington adopted a neutral position (considered a sign of approval) regarding Syria's prospects of an appointment (as a nonpermanent member) to the U.N. Security Council, despite pressure to oppose the appointment from supporters of Israel in Congress, led by Eliot Engel (D-NY).[25]

This undoubtedly illustrated the premium the Bush administration placed on Syria's key regional role and cooperation, without which the chances of reinforcing sanctions on Iraq appeared dim. However, in the absence of an efficient and clear U.S. policy on Iraq, and hurt financially by sanctions on Iraq, Syria, Turkey, and Jordan increased their trade with Baghdad. In contradiction to what al-Asad promised Powell, approximately 150,000 barrels of oil passed daily through Syrian pipelines, with revenues split between Baghdad and Damascus.[26] Syrian (and Iraqi) officials "maintained that the pipeline was only being tested for future use, implying that they did not regard the shipments as violations of relevant UN export sanctions against Iraq."[27] Secretary Powell was so disappointed by al-Asad's unfulfilled pledge that during his May 2003 visit to

Damascus, he remarked that "I will always have that in my background software and on my hard drive."[28]

Though not liked and in some diplomatic quarters even despised, the senior al-Asad was well respected in Washington. As we have seen, U.S. officials, ranging from Secretary of State Henry Kissinger to President William Clinton, disagreed with him, but almost all came to respect him and trust his word. In sharp contrast, notwithstanding that the peace process was no longer the cornerstone of the U.S.-Syrian relationship, U.S. officials began to doubt Syrian promises.

Put On Notice

The Bush administration's desire for a minimalist approach to the Arab-Israeli conflict quickly submerged under a new and radical transformation of American foreign policy in the wake of the most tragic, horrific, and unprecedented acts of terror ever to have taken place on U.S. soil. Targeting U.S. symbols of economic and military power, Islamic extremists, followers, and/or members of Usama Bin Laden's Al-Qaeda terrorist organization, using hijacked planes as high-explosive bombs, struck the World Trade Center and the Pentagon on September 11, 2001, killing thousands of innocent victims. The sheer magnitude and enormity of this seminal event altered irreversibly not only the American way of life but also U.S. foreign policy priorities. Splitting the world between those "with the United States" and those "with the terrorists," President Bush declared a war on terrorism and moved ahead with building an international coalition to fight terrorists and those countries that harbor them.

President Bush, in his 2002 State of the Union address, singled out Iran, Iraq, and North Korea as countries making up an "axis of evil." Significantly enough, he mentioned in his address Hizbollah as a terrorist organization. Although President Bush left Syria out of his speech, he put the country into a double bind. He highlighted Syria's regional role but put the country on notice to reorient its policies and regional alignments away from harboring Palestinian organizations labeled as terrorist organizations by the State Department and especially away from Iran and Hizbollah or be, by the virtue of its status as a state sponsor of terrorism, a de facto member of the "axis of evil."

The initial objectives of the war, mainly to destroy Bin Laden's Al-Qaeda organization and remove from power the Afghani Taliban rulers who harbored it, were easily accomplished with worldwide support. At the same time, partly because the Bush administration needed Arab participation in the international coalition and partly because escalating violence in the Palestinian occupied territories intensified Arab reservations about Washington's support of Israel, President Bush, on October 2, 2001, endorsed the creation of a Palestinian state. He became the first American President to sanction the creation of an independent Palestinian state. "The idea of a Palestinian state has always been a part of a vision, so long as the right of Israel to exist is respected," President Bush told reporters after meeting with congressional leaders.[29] His comments followed reports from Washington that, prior to the terror attacks on September 11, the Bush administration had been planning a new Middle East initiative. This announcement was followed by a speech by Secretary Powell in which he called on Palestinians to stop terrorism and incitement and on Israelis to stop settlement activity and occupation.[30] However, this did not amount to an enunciation of a Powell plan. Apparently, by taking up the issue of the Arab-Israeli conflict and not offering any policy innovation (sticking to the Mitchell and Tenet recommendations), Powell realized the importance of adopting to a certain extent a hands-on approach (appointing retired Marine Corps General Anthony Zinni as a special envoy to help the parties achieve a durable cease-fire), while at the same time perceiving that the success of any major initiative was highly unlikely.

Syria condemned the September 11 terror attacks on the United States and readily participated in Washington's war on terrorism. In fact, according to U.S. officials, including Secretary of State Colin L. Powell, Syria gave a "treasure trove" of materials on al-Qaeda including information on Syrian members of the organization, mainly Mamoun Darkazanli and Mohammad Haydar Zammar, who was subsequently taken into Syrian custody. Secretary Powell admitted that the Syrians "have said and done some things, and have cooperated with us."[31] Shortly after September 11, Damascus and the Central Intelligence Agency worked on joint intelligence-gathering operations in Aleppo, which had been the subject of Mohammad Atta's dissertation on urban planning. Atta was the leader of the terrorists who committed the September 11 attacks. Damascus also helped save American lives by assisting in foiling terror attacks on U.S. troops and interests in Bahrain and Ottawa.[32]

But, though Damascus supported the U.S. war on terror, it called for a distinction between fighting occupation and acts of terror.[33] Syrian president Bashar al-Asad has been keen on distinguishing what he considers Palestinian resistance to Israel's occupation from international terrorism.[34] Moreover, Syria (along with Arab countries and Iran) has refused the U.S. designation of Hizbollah as a terrorist organization with global reach. In fact, after a meeting between President al-Asad and then-Lebanese Prime Minister Rafiq Hariri, the two decided to object to any "infringement on the movement of resistance under whatever pretext, including that of terrorism."[35] As such, Lebanon declined the U.S. request to freeze the assets of Hizbollah.

In addition, his views on the intifada implicitly support its militarization: "I believe that Palestinians are the people of the intifada, so they can determine the form they want to liberate their land. They have tried the peaceful intifada and the intifada of the stone, and now they are trying the intifada in its current form."[36] Although U.S. officials welcomed Syria's help, almost no one endorsed Syria's stand on terrorism and the intifada. This dashed the hopes of the Syrian leadership who thought that their active participation in the U.S. war on al-Qaeda would help improve U.S.-Syrian relations.[37] Still, Syria and the United States continued their cooperation on intelligence on al-Qaeda. This paradoxical U.S.-Syrian relationship was underscored in the State Department's *Patterns of Global Terrorism 2002*:

> The Syrian Government has continued to provide political and limited material support to a number of Palestinian groups, including allowing them to maintain headquarters or offices in Damascus. Some of these groups have committed terrorist acts, but the Syrian Government insists that their Damascus offices undertake only political and informational activities. The most notable Palestinian rejectionist groups in Syria are the Popular Front for the Liberation of Palestine (PFLP), the Popular Front for the Liberation of Palestine-General Command (PFLP-GC), and the Islamic Resistance Movement (HAMAS). Syria also continued to permit Iranian resupply, via Damascus, of Hizballah in Lebanon. Nonetheless, the Syrian Government has not been implicated directly in an act of terrorism since 1986....The Syrian Government has repeatedly assured the United States that it will take every possible measure to protect US citizens and facilities from terrorists in Syria....The Government of Syria has cooperated significantly with the United States and other foreign governments against al-Qaida, the Taliban, and other terrorist organizations and individuals. It also has discouraged any signs of public support for al-Qaida, including in the media and at mosques.[38]

It was against this background that the Bush administration adopted a new emphasis on the doctrine of preemption in its national security strategy. Although "preemption," defined as the anticipatory use of force in the face of an imminent attack, has long been accepted as legitimate under international law, the new emphasis broadened the meaning to encompass preventive war whereby force may be used (even without evidence of an imminent attack) to ensure that a serious threat to the United States does not "gather" or grow over time.[39] Significantly, preemption was directed against terrorist organizations as well as "rogue" states since the two were linked (according to the strategy and President Bush) by a combination of "radicalism" and "technology." In his September 17, 2002, President Bush asserted that "the gravest danger our nation faces lies at the crossroads of radicalism and technology." Indeed, the link between Saddam Hussein's rogue state and its acquisition (and/or retaining) of weapons of mass destruction (WMD) served as the pretext for the U.S. invasion of the country, though no WMD had been found after the invasion.

Consequently, the war on terrorism, according to the State Department, became guided by four enduring policy principles: First, make no concessions to terrorists and strike no deals; second, bring terrorists to justice for their crimes; third, isolate and apply pressure on states that sponsor terrorism to force them to change their behavior; and fourth, bolster the counterterrorist capabilities of those countries that work with the United States and require assistance.[40]

Apparently, the cumulative effect of all this set in sharp relief the complex and uneasy U.S.-Syrian relationship. Syria, despite its cooperation with the United States on al-Qaeda, not only was put on notice to change its behavior or become a de facto member of the axis of evil but also became a doctrinal subject of the war on terrorism and, by extension, a potential U.S. military target.

De Facto Member of the Axis of Evil

The complex and tense U.S.-Syrian relationship soon gave way to Syria, becoming a de facto member of the axis of evil. Tension between the United States and Syria surfaced once Damascus began to oppose Washington's efforts to remove Saddam Hussein. Syria opposed the use of military force while at the same time it called on Iraq to comply with pertinent U.N. Security Council resolutions. In an interview published on June 18, 2002, President al-Asad warned that "any military attack on Iraq would be a mistake," and said "no country in the world has the right to change the system [of government] in another country."[41] Yet, on November 8, 2002, Syria voted for U.N. Resolution 1441, which cited Iraq as remaining in "material breach" of its obligations and mandated an enhanced weapons inspection regime in Iraq.[42] By voting for the resolution, Syrian officials aimed at saving Iraq from a military strike. Even some officials asserted that Washington had guaranteed Damascus that, if Iraq cooperated with the inspection regime created by the resolution, war would be averted. This was the reason Syria voted for the resolution.[43]

But, soon enough, tension intensified between the two countries as Syria became a leading critic of the U.S.-led campaign against Iraq, which culminated in Operation Iraqi Freedom, launched on March 19, 2003. On March 30, Syrian Foreign Minister Farouq al-Shara told the Syrian parliament that "Syria has a national interest in the expulsion of the invaders from Iraq."[44] If this and similar Syrian statements angered U.S. officials, intelligence reports following the U.S. invasion of Iraq that Syria had provided Iraq with military equipment including night-vision goggles, had given safe haven to senior Iraqi officials, and had allowed Jihadis to cross the border into Iraq, infuriated U.S. officials to the point they were ready to take action against the country. On March 28, 2003 Defense Secretary Donald H. Rumsfeld delivered a stern warning to Syria, "saying it be would held accountable."[45] Although Syrian officials rejected all charges, Damascus had become the focus of concern for and the target of strong rhetoric by the Bush administration.[46] Indeed, Syria became a de facto member of the axis of evil.

Consequently, U.S. Secretary of State Colin Powell visited Damascus in early May 2003 and delivered a blunt and forthright message to Damascus's leadership: Syria should take note of the new reality in the Middle East and accordingly adjust its policies. Significantly, besides making it clear that Washington would not condone any Syrian meddling in Iraqi affairs, Powell emphasized that Damascus must close all offices of terrorist organizations (including dismantling Hizbollah in Lebanon) and expel their leaders, as well as see to it that the Lebanese army extends its authority to the Lebanon-Israel border.[47]

Obviously, Syrian opposition to the U.S. invasion and occupation of Iraq formalized Washington's attitude toward Syria. Not only did the peace process stop being a cornerstone of the U.S.-Syrian relationship, and by extension the modulator of other U.S.-Syrian bilateral issues (arms proliferation, terrorism, and Lebanon), but also every bilateral issue became a bone of contention between the two countries.

Catching the world by surprise, this rising tension between the two countries has become the source of universal and confusing speculation and apprehension. On the surface, this tension had been the product of a stern and blunt message to Syria by the United States: Don't mess with us; we don't mess with you. On a deeper level, however, this tension had been the product of change in the ambivalent attitude of the United States toward Syria. The

fall of Baghdad and the immense challenges facing the United
States in stabilizing and democratizing Iraq have intensified U.S.
concerns about possible Syrian and Iranian meddling with Iraqi
affairs. Exacerbating these concerns was the position of President
Bashar al-Asad of Syria who has emerged as the Arab leader par
excellence championing Arab nationalism and opposing U.S. intervention in Iraq. This position has not only changed the dynamics
of the ambivalent attitude of the United States toward Syria (in
favor of the hard-liners) but has also marked an ominous break with
the pattern that Hafiz al-Asad, Bashar's father, established as president of modern Syria. Ironically, where the senior al-Asad had sacrificed Arab nationalism at the altar of Syria's national interest in
general and regime security in particular, the Syrian leadership
today has been advancing Arab nationalism with the objective of
countering U.S. plans in the region. Why has Damascus staked out
this position? At the center of Damascus's policies are concerns
about U.S. future plans in the region, especially vis-à-vis Syria,
and Damascus's quest for Arab leadership. The Syrian leadership,
advised by the old guard, thinks that the U.S. administration, influenced by the American Jewish lobby and especially by pro-Likud
neoconservatives, is set to divvy up the Middle East into weak, sectarian pro-U.S. states in order for Washington and Tel Aviv to,
respectively, control the region and its resources and impose its
own version of peace. In fact, this Syrian position was in a way an
extension to that expressed by the Syrian leadership (as we have
seen) throughout the late 1990s. No wonder the Syrian leadership
saw in the U.S. invasion of Iraq a confirmation of their premonitions
and fears. Not surprisingly, Damascus has seen the Iraqi issue as
inseparable from the Palestinian issue. President Asad has made
known his feelings in an interview with a Lebanese daily, *As-Safir,*
in which he called for the Arab states to implement the Arab mutual
defense treaty (an Arab Warsaw pact), whereby an Arab state must
defend another.[48]

Similarly, the leadership has believed that in order for the United
States to carry out its plan, it ineluctably needs to deal with Syria,
the heartbeat of Arab nationalism, to make it either a pliant accomplice or an idle bystander. Replying to a question about whether
Syria was on the list of the "aggression plan," President al-Asad
said: "Even if they [U.S. administration] did not include Syria in
the plan, the possibility is always there....I spoke about the subject
of occupying Baghdad in 1258 at the hands of Hulago. But this time
it is not only Baghdad but other Arab countries as well. When I refer
to other Arab countries it is not possible that I except Syria for it is
the closer and always at the center of the struggle against the

invaders. It is the heart of pan-Arabism and is the vanguard."[49] In another interview with the Kuwaiti newspaper *Al-Anbaa*, Asad noted "we are a neighboring country of Iraq and the war will have direct effects on us....So taking the Syrian interest into consideration, it is only natural for us to be against the war whose effects are witnessing now....Targeting Syria has preceded the war, and this is why we knew there will be threats after the war."[50]

At the center of this belief is the notion that a pro-Likud neoconservative group has been behind making the war on terrorism the cornerstone of the Bush administration policy, as well as exploiting the war to fulfill their strategy in the Middle East. The strategy, the Syrians point out, outlined in a report prepared by the Likud-leaning Institute for Advanced Strategic and Political Studies in 1996 and submitted then to Benjamin Netanyahu's newly elect government, emphasizes ensuring Israel's supremacy in the region by relinquishing the comprehensive "land for peace" approach to peace and forging a new basis for relations with the United States. Not only were peace negotiations with Syria to be ended but also Syria itself was to be contained. Emphasizing a move to a traditional balance of power strategy for Israel, the report stated:

> Israel can shape its strategic environment, in cooperation with Turkey and Jordan, by weakening, containing, and even rolling back Syria. This effort can focus on removing Saddam Hussein from power in Iraq—an important Israeli strategic objective in its own right—as a means of foiling Syria's regional ambitions.[51]

Many Syrians and Arabs regard this report as a blueprint for the war on Iraq and potential war against Syria, as well as a testimony to the influence of the neoconservatives in Washington.[52] This perception is buttressed by the fact that the idea of a regime change in Syria has been circulating in neoconservative circles in Washington. Michael Ledeen, an American Enterprise Institute scholar and a neoconservative ideologue, has been vocal in calling for a regime change in Syria. In an interview with Graham Turner's "An American Odyssey," *Daily Telegraph,* June 16, 2003, Ledeen said: "Now, like it or not, we're in a regional war, and we can't opt out of it.... We have to bring down these regimes and produce free governments in all those countries....Undermining the governments of other countries? No big deal." In a speech to the Heritage Foundation on May 6, 2002, Under Secretary of State Bolton grouped Syria with Libya and Cuba as rogue states that support international terrorism and "are pursuing the development of WMD."

Central to this idea is the liberation of Lebanon from Syrian occupation.[53] The mistrust and antipathy with which the Syrians perceive the neoconservatives in, and affiliated with, the U.S. administration were clearly evinced in al-Asad's statements during the Islamic Conference Organization in Malaysia: "A group of extremists...used September 11 attacks...as an excuse to reveal their savage view of human society...based on marketing the principle of force instead of dialogue."[54]

As a result of all these developments, Washington's program of fighting terrorism in the Middle East, reconstructing a democratic Iraq, and peacemaking now confronts Syria's insistence on having a say in all of these issues. Responding to a question over American pressure on Syria, Bashar stated: "We are neither a great power nor a weak country, we are not a country without cards or foundations. We are not a country that can be passed over with respect to the issues."[55]

In addition, feeling the upsurge of popular discontent in the Arab world, President al-Asad turned to the Arab-Israeli and Iraqi conflicts to enhance his credentials as the Arab nationalist leader of note to speak against U.S. policies. The leadership in Damascus apparently is still intoxicated by the defeat and withdrawal of Israel from Lebanon. And yet, paradoxically, al-Asad is cognizant of the dawning reality that changes in Iraq will indirectly put enormous pressure on Syria to change its ways. After all, not only did a Ba'thist sister state collapse, but also the regional status quo itself has been shattered. Importantly, the Americans are next door, and are now part of the Middle East political landscape.

CHAPTER **6**

A New Cold War?

Syria's opposition to American occupation of and subsequent intervention in Iraq, besides making Syria a de facto member of the "axis of evil," set in sharp relief the rift of misunderstandings and apprehensions between the two countries, potentially leading to a confrontation. Syrian president Bashar al-Asad, in a major shift from his late father's pragmatic foreign policy, which was primarily guided by national security (in particular regime security) considerations, has adopted a pan-Arab foreign policy based largely on opposing American occupation of Iraq and supporting what the Syrian government considers as resistance movements, especially Hizbollah. Consequently, the U.S. ambivalent attitude towards Syria, which helped sustain a measure of cautious flexibility in U.S.-Syrian relations, has moved in the direction of the hard-liners in Washington. At the same time, this new Syrian orientation, intended partly to enhance the nationalist credentials of the Syrian government, has been inextricably linked to the government's attempt at entrenching its position to better control internal and external challenges, including preventing dissent in Lebanon and Syria and co-opting and controlling a reform movement growing bolder by the day while becoming disillusioned with the regime's selective and insignificant reform policies.

Meanwhile, frustrated by Syrian behavior, Washington and Paris rose above their disagreements over the Iraq war and sponsored U.N. Resolution 1559, which calls for Syria's withdrawal from Lebanon and Hizbollah's disarmament.

It was against this background that the United States and Syria have set themselves on a collision course over terrorism, arms proliferation, Lebanon, the Middle East peace process, and, most importantly, Iraq. Significantly, the Bush administration is concerned about Damascus's behavior and its implications for U.S.

policy in the region in general and Iraq in particular. Syria thinks that the United States is enforcing a Pax Americana in the region at Syria's expense. Damascus's and Washington's policies and actions have been influenced no less by their own respective ideologies, national (and regime) interests, and domestic politics than by how they have been interpreting the internal dynamics of each other's ideological and domestic politics.

At the same time, the growing frustration of the United States with Syria is encouraging Washington to markedly support and identify with Israel's policies and actions. The unintended consequence of this condition is hastening a Syrian-Israeli conflagration. Believing it is fighting for its own survival, Syria is abandoning its traditional restraint and thus edging closer to war. The future of the region and the fate of the U.S. war on terrorism, Iraq, and the Middle East peace process may well depend on how Washington and Damascus deal with each other in their struggle for the Middle East. This new "Cold War" over national and, more accurately, regime security interests could at a maximum provoke a regional war and at a minimum spur profound change in the Middle East.

Punishing Syria

Amid the tense atmosphere in U.S.-Syrian relations consequent upon Damascus's constant opposition to U.S. efforts in Iraq, the idea of punishing Syria made a comeback in Washington. Congress resurfaced legislation punishing Syria in the form of the 2003 Syria Accountability and Lebanese Sovereignty Restoration Act (SALSRA).[1] The Act calls on Syria "to halt support for terrorism, end its occupation of Lebanon, stop its development of weapons of mass destruction (WMD)" and holds Syria accountable for its role in the Middle East. If implemented, it would impose a ban on U.S. exports to Syria (other than food and medicine), prohibit U.S. businesses from investing there and restrict the movement of Syrian diplomats in the United States.[2] President George W. Bush would retain the right to waive the act's clauses if he deems this necessary. Initially, the administration had deep reservations about the act, which had its provenance in previous legislation introduced in 2002. On April 18, 2002, largely similar bills were introduced in the House (H.R. 4483) and the Senate (S. 2215), both entitled *The Syria Accountability Act of 2002*. Hearings on H.R. 4483 were held by the House International Relations Committee, Subcommittee on the Middle East and South Asia, on September 18, 2002, following which Congress adjourned without floor action on either bill. According to a State Department official, the Bush administration disapproved of the proposed legislation because it "would restrict the President's maneuverability in dealing with Middle East affairs."[3]

Almost a year later, on April 12, 2003, Representatives Ileana Ros-Lehtinen (R-FL) and Eliot Engel (D-NY) introduced SALSRA (H.R. 1828), and on May 1, 2003, Senators Barbara Boxer (D, CA) and Rick Santorum (R-PA) introduced a companion bill (S. 982).[4] In contrast to its oppositional position in 2002, the Bush administration did not initially take a public position on H.R. 1828, which easily gathered support in Congress. Subsequently, in several letters to Congress dated May 2003, State Department officials said that, while they supported the spirit of the act, they opposed its implementation today "in light of this [the] current fluid environment."[5] Apparently, the Bush administration was giving Syria some time to act on Secretary Powell's demands. But, throughout the next few months, Syria did little to satisfy U.S. demands.

Wishful Versus Realpolitik Thinking

Apparently, the Syrian leadership felt it had weathered the storm of U.S. threats that followed the Iraq war. Concerns about "being next" on the American hit list had been replaced by cautious confidence over dealing with the United States without forsaking Syrian priorities. Syria's leadership had most likely thought the growing Iraqi resistance against coalition forces (and the then-upcoming presidential elections in the United States) would restrict American actions. It also believed the United States would eventually be entangled in an Iraqi intifada with or without any Syrian interference. However, Syria has also accepted that U.S. forces will not soon leave Iraq and has decided to avoid any armed confrontation with the United States. Though Syrian officials had been concerned with U.S. plans, they apparently believed the right dose of cooperation could counterbalance the effects of the act. Syria did not expel the leaders of the Palestinian terrorist organizations in Damascus (though some left for Lebanon) but reportedly asked them to maintain a low profile. It tried to keep Hizbollah quiet along the southern Lebanese border. It also pursued limited military redeployments in Lebanon to ease domestic tension there.[6]

Significantly, on June 18, Task Force 20, an American Special Operations team stationed in Iraq, acting on mistaken intelligence information that a convoy of cars and trucks speeding toward the Syria-Iraq border was carrying Iraqi leadership, entered Syria in pursuit of the fleeing Iraqis. The Force attacked the convoy, killing as many as 80 people including civilians living nearby. As it turned out, the convoy was smuggling gasoline.[7] Although Syria did not make a public fuss about the American fiasco, even as the United States held wounded Syrian soldiers for a few days, it reduced its intelligence cooperation with the United States to a minimum.

The Bush administration became frustrated with Syria's lack of cooperation, especially following intelligence reports that Damascus had been playing a spoiler role in Iraq. Hence, the administration gave the go-ahead to Congress to take up SALSRA, and, furthermore, it allowed Under Secretary for Arms Control and International Security John R. Bolton, considered a hard-liner, to testify before the Subcommittee on the Middle East and Central Asia of the House International Relations Committee. Bolton gave a critical testimony, underscoring some concerns about Syria that were similar to those used by the Bush administration to build its case for war against Iraq. He spoke about the danger emanating from the intersection between Syria's sponsoring of terrorism and its quest for unconventional weapons. In addition, he accused Syria of allowing Jihadis to cross into Iraq to kill Americans.[8] He stated:

> We have seen Syria take a series of hostile actions toward Coalition forces in Iraq. Syria allowed military equipment to flow into Iraq on the eve of and during the war. Syria permitted volunteers to pass into Iraq to attack and kill our service members during the war, and is still doing so. Syria continues to provide safe haven and political cover to Hizballah in Lebanon, which has killed hundreds of Americans in the past.[9]

Damascus denied all charges with regard to Iraq.[10] It kept to its policy of saying little, if anything, about its conventional weapons capabilities, insisting on a regional plan to rid the whole region of weapons of mass destruction. Following in the footsteps of the late President Hafiz al-Asad, the Syrian leadership has constantly asserted that Israel's stockpile of conventional weapons, mainly its nuclear weapons, is the real danger to the region. There has been little evidence that Syria is intent on acquiring nuclear weapons. However, according to some analysts, Syria's desire to build up its chemical weapons (sometimes described as "poor man's nuclear weapons") and missile capabilities stems from its need to create a "force equalizer" to counter Israeli nuclear capabilities.[11] Significantly, in an interview with the *Daily Telegraph* President al-Asad came closer than ever before to admitting that his country possessed stockpiles of WMD. He stated: "We are a country which is [partly] occupied and from time to time we are exposed to Israeli aggression....It is natural for us to look for means to defend ourselves. It is not difficult to get most of these weapons anywhere in the world and they can be obtained at any time."[12]

But Damascus has not budged over the issue of Hizbollah and by extension over the whole issue of terrorism. Of all organizations, Hizbollah has been a deep thorn in the American side. U.S. officials have not forgotten or forgiven Hizbollah's terror attacks on the U.S. Marines barracks in Beirut.[13] Then–Assistant Secretary of State Richard Armitage called the party of God the "A Team of terrorists." On the other hand, Hizbollah has not softened its anti-American rhetoric. In fact, prior to the U.S. invasion of Iraq, Hizbollah intensified its rhetoric, further sharpening American apprehensions. Addressing thousands of Shi'ites in Beirut on the day of Ashura, one of the holiest days in Shi'a tradition, Hizbollah Secretary General Hassan Nasrallah, blared his opposition to an American invasion of Iraq. He said that "the peoples of the area will welcome the American invaders with rifles, blood, weapons, martyrdom and suicide bombings and not with roses, aromatic plants, rice and fragrance." He then added "Americans never scared us. When the marines were in Beirut and [American] fleets were in the sea our throats in al-Dahia [a suburb of Beirut] screamed death to America. The region today is being filled with thousands of US soldiers and fleets and our slogans remain: death to America."[14] Why has Syria defied the United States on the issue of terrorism, especially with regard to Hizbollah, thereby harrowing American raw nerves?

Apart from Syria's position calling for a distinction between resistance and terror acts and insisting that the Palestinian offices in Damascus are mainly for media purposes, a good part of the explanation lies in the fact that Syria is unable to confront the powerful Israeli military. Consequently, Syria prefers waging a proxy war. The other part lies in the reality that Hizbollah has managed through its social services and its resistance to Israel's occupation of south Lebanon to weave itself into the social and political fabric of Lebanon's Muslims. Prior to Lebanon's 2005 elections, Hizbollah had nine parliamentary members plus three supporters. Suffering from weak national integration, Lebanon's Muslim majority (including some Christians) have stressed Hizbollah's resistance role.[15] Moreover, Hizbollah has emerged in the eyes of Arabs across the whole region, in contrast to Arab governments, as the only potent force to deal with Israel.[16] Besides using Hizbollah as a means both to fend off opposition in Lebanon and to deter Israel, Damascus has amplified what some in Lebanon say in order to enhance its nationalist image as a supporter of Lebanon's resistance movement and protector of Arab rights.

This position stems in no small measure from Syria's domestic considerations. The Syrian regime has always used the concept of confronting Israel to burnish its nationalist credentials and silence and/or co-opt opposition at home and in Lebanon. The regime has been concerned about a reform movement gathering momentum, thanks in no small measure to radical changes in next-door Iraq, potentially endangering the regime's entrenched interests. It was therefore no surprise that the regime had clamped on the reform movement under the pretext that it omitted from its platform the paramount issue of the Arab-Israeli conflict. Initially, Washington paid little attention to Syria's domestic politics, especially the reform movement and its impact on the regime's policies.

Domestic Considerations: Reform and the Kurdish Question

In his presidential inaugural speech before the Syrian parliament in July 2000, Bashar al-Asad focused on repairing his country's ailing economy, modernizing the bureaucracy, and enhancing democracy. He emphasized the importance of introducing reforms, but, at the same time, he gave no sign that Syria's democratic experience will resemble that of the West. He stated: "Western democracies are the product of a long history....We should have our own democratic experience springing from our history, education and civilized personality...and arising from the needs of our people and reality."[17] What kind of democratic experience was Bashar alluding to?

In official Syrian parlance, this democratic experience is known as *Ta'adudia,* meaning pluralism. Central to this is the concept that reforms will enhance political representation and inclusion and, by extension, freedom. Admittedly, Syria is fairly known for its religious pluralism in contrast to other Middle Eastern states, a vestige of its Ottoman heritage and structure of government (known as the Millet System). The hardening in attitudes toward, as well as persecution and/or harassment of, minorities in the former Ottoman provinces have not, to a greater or lesser extent, become part of the sociopolitical landscape in Syria. Historians and analysts contribute this condition to the fact that Syria itself has been governed by a minority sect, the Alawite, which is regarded by orthodox Sunni Muslims as heretical. Interestingly, as some historians point out, the esoteric Alawi religion contains certain liturgical features that are partly Christian in origin. For example, Jesus Christ occupies a prominent place in Abu Abd Allah Ibn Hamdan al-Khasibi's teaching, a leading tenth century (fourth century by the Islamic calendar) Nusayri jurist. Alawis were previously known as Nusayris, a word with arguably Christian connotations. Others argue that the leadership in Syria has sanctioned cultural and religious freedoms in exchange for political acquiescence. In either case, because of religious pluralism, coexistence among Syria's religious communities has been fairly harmonious.

However, Syria's religious pluralism has not been matched by economic and political pluralism. Will the Syrian leadership, as Bashar promised, introduce reforms that will bring about political and economic pluralism? Will Syria's religious pluralism provide the conditions for accepting political pluralism? And what kind of political pluralism does the leadership and, particularly the reformers, envisage for Syria?

Ta'dudia was first launched by the late president Hafiz al-Asad, who upon his assumption of power established *Majlis Al-Sha'b* (Parliament) and the Progressive National Front—a group of parties affiliated with the ruling Ba'th party—and promulgated a new constitution. The reforms that established these institutions became part of al-Asad's "corrective movement." These institutions, according to the regime, offered political participation and thus represented a pluralistic system. These institutions, in practice, have been none other than a means to broaden al-Asad's basis of support by co-opting and containing political forces. Al-Asad sought to legitimize his regime by institutionalizing it. For example, when Syria's influential merchant class, along with some independent forces, had begun to call for some economic liberalization and political participation, al-Asad, in 1990, enlarged the parliament from 195 to 250 deputies. A third of the seats have been reserved for independent deputies, the majority of whom have been businessmen. Still, on account of their overwhelming majority, the Ba'th party and its affiliate, the Progressive National Front (PNF), have controlled the agenda and decision-making process of the parliament.

Significantly, the call for significant reforms and reform under Asad's tenure had been, respectively, taboo and insignificant. This has changed under Bashar's rule. Bashar's statements and initial actions of political liberalization, such as permitting the publishing of newspapers (*Al-Domari,* the first privately owned published newspaper in over three decades) and releasing political prisoners, fostered an atmosphere of change that was speedily capitalized upon by many Syrians.[18]

In September 2000 a group of 99 Syrian intellectuals issued a statement calling for political reforms.[19] The statement called for ending the state of emergency, issuing a public pardon to all political detainees, establishing a rule of law recognizing freedom of speech, expression, and assembly, and freeing public life from all forms of state surveillance. Obviously, this was a political manifesto, albeit not a revolutionary one. The statement was mildly crafted. It adhered to neither an ideological line nor a position threatening the regime. Interestingly enough though, the signatories included the most prominent intellectuals in Syria (such as Adonis, Sadek Jalal al-Azm, and Haidar Haidar), many of whom were employed by state-run institutions. Before long, public forums addressing reform and revitalization of civil society, hitherto banned, mushroomed in Syria.[20] The Syrian leadership, in fact, took several measures that many Syrians construed as positive reaction to their call for reform.[21] In January 2001, the initial document ballooned into another statement signed by 1000 Syrians of all walks of life.[22] Obviously, religious pluralism in Syria played a role in uniting the voices of reformers by fostering a climate free of sectarian tension and antagonism. In fact, Alawis were at the forefront in signing the statement. In addition to repeating the demands of the first statement, this new document emphasized holding democratic elections at all levels and importantly reconsidering the principle of "the party rules the state and society, and any other principle that alienates people from the political life."[23] This "principle of party rules the state and society" was a direct reference to the Ba'th party, which is constitutionally billed as "the vanguard party in society and state." Simultaneously, the outlawed Muslim Brotherhood, membership of which is still punishable by death under Law 49 of 1980, demanded similar reforms. The boldness of that statement and the speed with which civic forums spread caught the leadership by surprise. Apparently it feared the trickle of reform would turn into a deluge. The leadership struck back by banning all forums without a government license and accused several activists of undermining the constitution and national interest. Prominent state officials, such as then–Vice-President Abd al-Halim Khaddam and then–Minister of Defense Mustafa Tlas (along with other regime hard-liners such as intelligence chiefs Bahjat Suleiman and Hassan al-Khalil) charged the activists with abandoning the struggle for Arab rights since they did not address the Arab-Israeli conflict.[24] Importantly, al-Asad, in an interview with the London-based daily *As-Sharq al-Awsat* on February 8, stated that "the government will stand firmly against any work that might cause harm to the public interest."[25] The dragnet of the regime's antireform measures caught well-known personalities including parliamentarians. Prominent among them were former head of economics at Damascus University Aref Dalila and independent parliamentarians Riad Seif and Mamoun Homsi. The first was sentenced to ten years in prison while the others got five years each.[26] In addition, the regime strictly "controlled the dissemination of information and permitted little written or oral criticism of President Asad, his family, the Ba'th party, the military, or the legitimacy of the

Government."[27] Obviously, the regime sent a clear message to the public that it would not tolerate any reform it could not control. Yet al-Asad was careful not to erode the image of modernity he projected for himself. He continued to address economic and political reform by reconstituting a hyped-up anticorruption campaign, while introducing mobile phones and the Internet. Following the collapse of the Ba'thi regime in Iraq, 287 Syrians petitioned al-Asad in late May, bearing in mind the regime's past actions against activists, calling for "comprehensive national reform." They stressed Syria's urgent need for political reform to supplement economic change without threatening the president's rule.[28] They asked him to implement reforms, including the revocation of martial law and security trials, the immediate release of all political prisoners, and freedom of opinion and assembly. The group stressed the situation Syria is facing: "The occupation of the West Bank and Gaza Strip by Israel and the occupation of Iraq by the United States, have changed the strategic conditions surrounding the homeland and put it between two enemies who possess strength which Syria has never faced before."[29] According to a prominent intellectual, Sadek Jalal Al-Azm, the "reform movement strives to create a political environment similar to that in Turkey where the democratic process would not only legitimize the government but also protect the country from outside threats and pressure."[30] Syrian democrats point out that the United States, prior to invading Iraq, could not tell Turkish Prime Minister Recip Tayyip Erdoghan to "go to hell" when the Turkish parliament voted against U.S. wishes to open a second front with Iraq in Turkey.[31]

The reasons and arguments in favor of a Turkey-like democratic process and structure, overseen and protected by a strong army, however, were not the only ones on the minds of the reformers. Apparently, reformers of almost all ethnic and religious hues, be they intellectuals, professionals, or businessmen, fear that, under certain circumstances, political Islam may make a comeback and thus threaten the political discourse and Syria's stability. The memories of the gory and destabilizing clash between the regime and the Muslim Brotherhood are still fresh in the collective consciousness of the nation. Significantly enough, what made many reformers concerned about the Muslim Brotherhood had been, according to its leadership, its transformation into an organization calling for democratic pluralism while shunning violence. This was underlined in a National Charter adopted by the Muslim Brotherhood in August 2002 in London. The Charter encompassed principles for governing a democratic Syria, including respect for human rights, rights of women, and rejection of all forms of violence.[32] Reformers worry that, under the banner of democracy, the Brotherhood (given its history and Islamist agenda) would try to assume power, something it failed to achieve by violence in the 1970s and 1980s. Ironically, the Syrian leadership shares in the reformers' concerns about political Islam resurgence.[33]

This has become all the more important on account of the complex situation the regime finds itself in regionally and internally. Islamist movements have been making inroads throughout Arab societies, with Syrian society witnessing a religious revival. Religious symbols and feelings increasingly mark the Syrian societal landscape, from proliferation of head scarves worn by young women in Damascus to building enormous mosques (in Aleppo, for example) to swelling enrollment in Islamic schools and foundations. Muslim clerics, meanwhile, have been calling for a larger role in government.[34] This religious revival stemmed from a combination of trends and factors. While the Arab media, especially the *Al-Jazeera* television station, continuously blames the U.S.-led invasion and occupation of Iraq for reviving militant Islam, Syria's depressed economy and high unemployment, coupled with the regime's policy of encouraging a moderate form of Islam, have all combined to create a climate conducive to a religious revival.[35] Interestingly enough, some reformers have accused the government of softening its stand against the Islamic movement, paradoxically citing pressure for reform from the United States and a desire for a rapprochement between the regime and the Islamists because they are facing the same enemy: the United States. In fact, the *Daily Telegraph* featured a story in December 2004 in which it illustrated that the Syrian government has turned a blind eye to Islamists supporting the insurgency in Iraq. The story highlighted that "Mujahideen mosques are springing up all over Syria to arm militants and send them across the border to do battle with the hated Americans."[36] Though this rapprochement could be perceived as an attempt at both undermining American efforts in Iraq and shoring up the Syrian regime's declining popularity, especially among the youth, the regime has asserted its secular credentials. Responding to these accusations, Information Minister Mehdi Dakhlallah said that "the basic attitude of the Baath party is totally secular and against religious interference....There may be some Baath members who have made such alliances. But that is not the prevailing idea among the Baath or among Syrian government officials."[37]

The new petition of the reformers and the swiftness with which the Ba'th regime next door fell apparently reenergized al-Asad to cautiously continue economic and political reform. In July, he issued decree No. 33, which abrogated decree No. 24 of 1986 (and

No. 6 of 2000) that banned foreign exchange.[38] Accordingly, normal civil courts, instead of economic security courts, would handle breaches of the law. He issued a decree providing full pardoning of several exiled and political detainees and permitted Syrians banned from traveling to move freely inside and outside the country.[39] He also issued a decree allowing the establishment of a private university and ordered that the "military" color of school uniforms be changed.[40] In the name of the Ba'th Party Regional Command, al-Asad signed decree No. 408, separating the party from the authority's executive work, emphasizing that the selection of employees should be according to merit rather than party affiliation.[41]

In addition, the Syrian government approved—for the first time since Syria nationalized its banking system—several private banking licenses and specified a period of seven years to restructure the economy (mainly so Syria can join the World Trade Organization and the EU-Mediterranean free trade zone).[42]

At the same time that these reforms were introduced, the government revoked the license of *al-Domari*. Importantly, none of the reformers' main demands were satisfied. Admittedly, the Ba'th party still dominates the political process (two-thirds of Syria's 250 parliament seats are reserved for the Ba'th party and its affiliate, the National Progressive Front).[43] In addition, the composition of the then-new government indicated that reform would not be its top priority. The new government comprised 17 Ba'thists, controlling the most important portfolios (Foreign, Defense, and Interior Ministries), 6 independents, and 7 PNF members.[44] Obviously, the reforms have remained selective and of an ad hoc nature meant to blend dominant state power with economic development without breaking the system. This is the crux of Bashar's democratic experience. In fact, Bashar has so far given no indication that he is willing to introduce reforms that may threaten his regime.

Dissatisfied with the regime's actions, in early February 2004, 700 intellectuals signed and circulated a petition on the Internet including almost the same demands of previous petitions and statements.[45] But this time, the intellectuals aimed at appending one million signatures to the petition and submitting it to the Syrian authorities on March 8, the anniversary of the Ba'th party's rise to power. On March 8, approximately 100 activists, led by the spokesman of The Committees for the Defense of Democratic Liberties and Human Rights, Aktham Nu'aisah, demonstrated before the Syrian parliament. Taken aback by such a bold move, Syrian authorities arrested several activists including Nu'aisah, all of whom were subsequently released.[46]

Meanwhile, capping these few days of tension in the Syrian capital, riots raged throughout Kurdish areas in Syria. Sparked by a brawl during a soccer match in Qamishli on March 12, the riots spread to Hasakah, Dirik, Amouda, Ras el-Ein, and parts of Aleppo and the capital. During a soccer match in Qamishli, a city of 200,000 in the province of al-Hassaka, near the border with Turkey and whose majority is Kurdish, fans of the visiting Futuwwa club fought with supporters of the hometown al-Jihad team, with the former chanting slogans including "Long live Saddam Hussein" and the latter chanting "Long Live Barzani," in reference to the Iraqi Kurdish leader Masoud Barzani. Fearing growing Kurdish separatist feelings, inspired by the Kurds' quasi-independence status in northern Iraq, the government formed a security committee of senior officials to deal with the Kurdish disturbances and grievances, supervised by Ghazi Kanaan, the former intelligence chief in Lebanon. The committee included intelligence chiefs Hisham Bakhtiar and Muhammad Mansoura, and al-Hasaka governor Salim Kabul. At the same time, Syrian police, backed by army troops, reportedly killed over two dozens protestors, who took over and ransacked government buildings and destroyed statues and murals of the Syrian president. The government then imposed curfews and swept the troubled areas, arresting in the process hundreds of Kurds, many of whom were released a few days later. Eventually, quiet was restored and the government sent senior officials to the Kurdish areas to look into and deal with Kurdish grievances.[47]

The Kurds, constituting approximately ten percent of the Syrian population, have not been allowed to study the Kurdish language or form political parties. Importantly, approximately 200,000 of them have been denied Syrian citizenship.[48]

Commenting on the events, President al-Asad, in an interview with the Arabic television station *al-Jazeera,* indicated that Syria dealt swiftly with the situation and that "the question of nationality is 42 years old because some in 1962 acquired the Syrian nationality and some did not and this problem will be solved and the Kurdish people are part and parcel of the Syrian society and history."[49]

The reform movement faces three main challenges. Apparently, the Syrian leadership has not resolved the dilemma over how much change is acceptable before the regime itself is threatened. The dilemma lies in the fact that, unless the institutional and constitutional advantages of the Ba'th party are revoked, reform will be insignificant and inconsistent. The reformers will most likely fail in pushing for significant reform without outside help. Absent support from nongovernmental organizations and governments for reformers, the Syrian leadership will have little incentive to introduce reforms paving the path to a peaceful transition to democracy.[50] Finally, Bashar has to decide whether to partner with the reformers and wean himself from the old guard by putting Syria on a true path of reform or whether to wither in the stagnation of maintaining the status quo.[51] His approach has so far inadequately relied on fixing the system without either undermining his authority or breaking the system itself.

Yet, as a prominent Syrian recently told me, "change is inevitable in Syria despite all the blockage from the government. It is about time. The extent and scope of changes taking place both in the region and in Syria may well in the near future compel the Syrian leadership, mainly the Alawi barons, to reach a compromise with the opposition. The barons may opt to play the role of gatekeepers of a Turkish-like parliamentary model of government from their army barracks. This will form the basis of political pluralism with which we can live."

Dynamics of Confrontation

On account of all these regional and internal challenges, President al-Asad perceives that the security and survival of the regime is related no less to keeping a check on politico-economic changes in Syria, and on political developments in Lebanon, than in Iraq, where he feels helpless. The Syrian regime deep down knows that change is inevitable and is scared stiff. Consequently, it has been hedging its diplomacy by attempting to reconcile incompatible policies. Its cooperation with Washington on al-Qaeda has been markedly offset by charges that Damascus had supplied the now deposed Iraqi regime with military equipment and has allowed Jihadis to cross into Iraq to kill American soldiers, save defying Washington by harboring and supporting organizations labeled as terrorist by the United States.

Damascus can no longer adopt this equivocal position for it is inadvertently leading U.S. frustration with Damascus to an open confrontation. The Syrian leadership has adopted a facade of indifference to the SALSRA. President Bashar al-Asad once indicated that he did not discuss it with U.S. Congressmen who visited Syria, saying: "The issue is an American issue and Congress is an American institution."[52] Damascus may be wagering its diplomacy on America's deep embroilment in the "Iraqi quagmire." But this is simply a losing bet that does not reflect the psyche of the nation. The reluctance of the Bush administration to distinguish between acts of terror and legitimate resistance and to disregard Syria's connivance at the infiltration of Jihadis into Iraq is simply a sheer reflection of the mood of the nation. Consequently, half measures by Damascus are not acceptable to Washington, irrespective of whether Republicans or Democrats control the White House or Congress.

This partly explains why President Bush supported Israel's air strike deep into Syria in early October, the first of its kind in three decades.[53] In fact, the president described the attack as part of an "essential" campaign to defend Israel. A senior administration official said, "We have repeatedly told the government of Syria that it is on the wrong side in the war on terror and that it must stop harboring terrorists."[54]

But Syria's bristling response may have been the opposite of what Israeli and American leaders had hoped. The reply came on the Lebanon-Israel border, where an exchange of fire claimed the life of an Israeli soldier.[55] Through its ambassador in Spain and officials in Damascus, including then–chief of staff General Hassan Turkmani, the Syrian government also vowed to retaliate against any further attacks.[56] No doubt, this Syrian behavior is a reflection that Damascus, believing it is fighting for its own survival, is abandoning its traditional restraint.

Moreover, despite some efforts on the part of the two actors to temper the tense U.S.-Syrian relationship,[57] recent developments have hardened their positions vis-à-vis each other. In a move considered to be a major shift in U.S. policy on the peace process, President Bush, supporting Israel prime minister Ariel Sharon's proposal to unilaterally withdraw from Gaza, endorsed Israel's claim to keep certain settlements in the West Bank and explicitly rejected the "Right of Return" for Palestinian refugees. President Bush cited "new realities on the ground" as a basis for his policy shift, intimating that what he said in public had been said in private.[58] Arabs were outraged. Expressing their disbelief and anger with the Bush administration, Arabs questioned how Bush could forfeit their role as negotiators, insisting that only the two parties themselves (Israelis and Palestinians) can decide final status negotiations.[59] In addition, the Syrian government felt particularly shunned from the peace process because the Bush administration ignored al-Asad's desire, expressed in an interview with the *New York Times,* to resume Israeli-Syrian peace negotiations.[60]

Shortly thereafter, in a move to assuage Arab anger, intensified by a mounting global backlash against the United States after revelations that Iraqi detainees at the notorious Abu Ghraib prison were abused and humiliated, the Bush administration joined the quartet (U.N., European Union, United States, and Russia) in issuing a statement stressing that the "key issues dividing Israelis and Palestinians must be negotiated by both sides."[61]

Arab outrage sparked by this major shift on the peace process came in the wake of President Bush's ambitious initiative to promote democracy in the "Greater Middle East." This initiative, purportedly adapting a model used to press for freedom in Eastern Europe during the Cold War, would call for Arab governments to adopt major political and economic reforms and be held accountable for human rights. Arab governments, mainly Saudi Arabia, Egypt, and Syria, rejected the initiative out of hand. While Egypt and Saudi Arabia rejected the initiative as an attempt to impose Western values on the Arab world (without even consulting the regional parties), Damascus assaulted the initiative as an attempt to control the region and strengthen Israel. In a speech on Teacher's Day, Syrian Vice-President Muhammad Zuheir Mashariqa said "the US marketing of the so-called the Greater Middle East implied goals aimed at weakening Arabs and strengthening Israel. It also disguised motives to dominate the region directly in a way to put it in a state of full subjugation while its resources would be looted."[62]

At the same time, Arab governments chafed at what they perceived as the Bush administration's tacit support for Israel's policy of extrajudicial assassinations of leaders of Palestinian extremist organizations such as the Islamic Resistance Movement (Hamas) and Islamic Jihad, organizations labeled as terrorist by the U.S. government. The assassination of Hamas founder and spiritual leader, Ahmad Yassin, in April 2004 followed by that of Gaza leader Abd al-Aziz al-Rantissi in March, drew emotional protests across the Arab world. While the White House emphasized that it "was deeply troubled" by the killing of Yassin and that it had not been given advance notice of the assassination, it maintained its position that "Israel has the right to defend itself."[63]

While this episode set in sharp relief the controversy over the definition of terrorism and Washington's Middle East diplomacy, it indirectly increased the prospect of a U.S.-Syrian clash over terrorism. For example, Khalid Mishaal became the leader of Hamas following the death of Yassin. Given the fact that Mishaal lives in Damascus (and recently in Lebanon) and that Israel has vowed to kill those responsible for terror acts, the United States may ineluctably find itself under certain circumstances pressured to confront Syria. U.S. officials have been criticizing and warning Syria in such a consistent way, including on domestic matters considered highly sensitive by the regime, that Washington might find itself obliged to make good on its statements, thereby increasing the chances of a confrontation.[64] In an interview on the Arabic television *al-*

Jazeera, President al-Asad warned Israel that Damascus would consider targeting Palestinian groups in Syria as "an aggression that will be handled as an aggression."[65]

Significantly, the Lebanese-Israel border remains a tinderbox, especially under the current tense triangular relationship between Israel, Syria, and Lebanon. Israel has accused Hizbollah of not only enticing Hamas and Islamic Jihad to commit violence against Israelis but also of abetting and training members of these organizations. Hizbollah, for its part, has accused Israel of violating Lebanese air space and of assassinating members of the movement's military wing including most recently Ghalib Awali. Consequently, gun battles raged along the Israel-Lebanon border, prompting General Bini Gants, the chief of the northern areas of the Israeli army, to declare on the Arab television station *al-Jazeera* that, if Hizbollah's attacks continue, Israel would be pushed to launch "a painful and qualitative military operation" against Syria.[66]

Equally significant, in addition to defending what he perceived as Palestinian resistance against Israeli occupation, al-Asad explicitly qualified the insurgency against U.S. troops in Iraq as legitimate resistance. He emphasized: "Certainly, what has happened on the popular level gives legitimacy to the resistance and shows that the major part of what is happening is resistance."[67]

Although al-Asad maintained that Syria has done its utmost to control its border with Iraq and that it has helped the United States in its war against terror,[68] his above statement undoubtedly does not sit well with the Bush administration, especially at a time when U.S. forces in Iraq have been facing multiple threats. Apparently, the evolution of events in the Middle East has strengthened the connection between Iraq, the peace process, terrorism, and Lebanon in a way that they formed a cluster of inherently contradictory phenomena creating their own confrontational dynamics. The possibility for a regional conflagration has never been higher.

Digging In

Keeping to their strategy of hedging their diplomacy, the Syrian leadership's equivocal position on Iraq and Hizbollah soon caught up with them. In addition to imposing sanctions on Syria, the Bush administration found in France an ally to pressure Damascus to withdraw from Lebanon and disband Hizbollah's militia.[69] Because of their lobbying, along with that of Lebanese Diaspora (see below), the U.N. Security Council adopted Resolution 1559 in September 2004, which called on remaining foreign forces to withdraw from Lebanon, insisted on the disbanding of Lebanese militias, and declared support for a free and fair presidential election. Damascus could no longer escape the radar of the world community. Even Arab countries such as those of the Gulf Cooperation Council urged Syria to respect the Resolution.[70] It was at this time when Syria felt under regional and international pressures that a Palestinian Hamas official residing in Damascus was allegedly assassinated by Israel. While Syria warned Israel of the attack, some analysts saw in the attack an Israeli-American message that Damascus should be very careful.[71]

Still, Damascus committed a big mistake by directing its loyalists in Lebanon to extend for three years the term of its ally, President Emile Lahoud, in the face of almost universal Lebanese opposition. Apparently, the Syrians chose continuity over unpredictability by keeping Lahoud. Sticking to their old strategy, the Syrians wanted an ally in Lebanon who could withstand domestic and international pressure by insisting on the resistance role of Hizbollah and "special relations" with Syria. In addition, Damascus would maintain its strategic cooperation with Iran by keeping the Iran-Damascus-Hizbollah axis as an option against growing Israeli and American warnings about Tehran's nuclear plans.

However, what the Syrians had failed to realize was that since the Israeli withdrawal from Lebanon in the summer of 2000 the political dynamics of the country had changed and, by extension, their Lebanese-Hizbollah strategy had outlived its purposes. It was no coincidence that many Lebanese, including Syrian allies, opposed the extension of Lahoud's term. Significantly, Walid Jumblatt, leader of the Druze community, was vocal in his opposition to amending the Lebanese constitution and extending the president's term. In the meantime, Marwan Hamade, a member of parliament and Jumblatt's Democratic Gathering, narrowly escaped an assassination attempt.[72] Even the most ardent of Syrian supporters knew that Syrian intelligence, with that of Lebanon, was behind the attempt. The Syrian record is long on the alleged assassinations of prominent Lebanese political figures, including the Druze leader Kamal Jumblatt in 1976, President-elect Bashir Jumayil in 1982, and President Rene Mouawad in 1989.

Following an outpouring of Lebanese condemnation of the assassination attempt and the fact that Israel was not, as usual, blamed for the assassination attempt, Hamade received a visit from Rustum Ghazale, Syrian intelligence chief to Lebanon, and Lebanon's public prosecutor Adnan Addoum. This signaled the confusion of Syrian intelligence in Lebanon as well as the breakdown of taboos buttressing Syrian power.[73] It was under these circumstances that Ghazi Kanaan, the master of balance-of-power politics in Lebanon, was appointed interior minister. His appointment, along with that of some other Bashar loyalists (including Lahoud and Omar Karame as Lebanon's prime minister) indicated that the Syrian regime had been entrenching itself to better control domestic affairs in both Lebanon and Syria.[74]

But Syria was in for hard times. Unlike the past, Damascus was now under the spotlight of the U.N.[75] Relying on U.N. support, the opposition swelled its ranks and triggered a domestic recrimination of Lahoud that almost forced him out of power and eventually brought down the Syrian order in Lebanon. In fact, the controversial debate over the Syrian presence in Lebanon had polarized the country along confessional/sectarian lines coinciding with party lines, supporting or opposing Syria. Significantly, the Druze leadership, along with some Sunni leaders including former Lebanese Prime Minister Rafiq Hariri, had moved closer to the Maronite-led opposition to Syria, which supported U.N. Resolution 1559. Growing extremely wary of Syrian political (and intelligence) maneuvers in Lebanon, Jumblatt incessantly criticized Syrian heavy-handed involvement in Lebanese affairs, particularly the infiltration of Lebanese institutions by Syrian *Mukhabarat* (intelligence).

On the surface, it is against this background that the Syrian regime has considered helping U.S. troops in Iraq to control the Syria-Iraq border. On a deeper level, however, Damascus (along with Tehran) would not like to see Iraq emerge as a bridgehead for a Pax Americana in the region. It would prefer to see the United States fail and even humiliate itself in Iraq. By directly or indirectly helping the insurgency, Damascus believes it can "kill two birds with one stone," undermining American efforts in Iraq while highlighting its importance in pacifying the country.

In early October 2004, just days after the Syrian leadership had reportedly promised a U.S. delegation to Damascus that it would cooperate with U.S. troops in controlling the Iraq-Syria border, President al-Asad delivered a confrontational speech criticizing U.S. efforts to force Syria from Lebanon, calling them blatant meddling in Lebanese affairs and saying they could push the Middle East toward greater chaos. He stated: "In the Middle East we have become in the heart of the volcano and I say relatively that Syria and Lebanon are the most stable countries in the Middle East.... Do they want to throw all the region without exception in the heart of lava inside the volcano. Have not we learned from September 11 and the Iraqi war...?"[76]

Significantly, the *Washington Post* reported on December 8, 2004 that "US military intelligence officials have concluded that the Iraqi insurgency is being directed to a greater degree than previously recognized from Syria where they said former Saddam Hussein loyalists have found sanctuary and are channeling money and other support to those fighting the established government."[77]

Washington would be wrong to think that the Syrian regime is looking only for a quid pro quo: helping the United States in Iraq so that Washington would reduce its pressure through the U.N. on Syria's presence and support for Hizbollah in Lebanon. Damascus urgently needs to trade with Iraq and resume sales of Iraqi oil. In fact, following the visit by then–Prime Minister of Iraq, Iyad Allawi, to Syria in late July 2004, the two countries agreed not only to form joint committees to control the border but also to promote trade between them, which has been gradually rising since.[78]

No doubt, Washington has reached a critical juncture with its relations with Syria, which may further affect Washington's policies in the Middle East. Washington must capitalize on the evolving situation and articulate a Syria strategy. At this point, it is important to note that a new variable has entered into the equation affecting U.S. foreign policy toward Syria. As we have seen, lobbied by supporters of Israel, and disapproving of Syrian policies and actions, Congress has been adamant about introducing legislation punishing Syria and, consequently, to some extent tying the hands of the President. Following the September 11 attacks, many Lebanese-American organizations and groups have come together to organize a front to support the Bush administration's war on terrorism and to participate in the democratic process of lobbying for a free Lebanon. Some of the objectives of this new lobby converged with those of the supporters of Israel and many conservatives, mainly against terrorism and Syrian occupation of Lebanon.

Toward the Brink?

Faced with growing domestic and regional challenges, Bashar al-Asad broke with the policy pattern his father had established as ruler of modern Syria. Before and after the collapse of the Ba'th regime in Iraq, Bashar has been trying to reconcile a "reformist" domestic policy, indeed a misnomer for regulating economic development, with a pan-Arab foreign policy. He has been trying to survive serious domestic and regional challenges and threats by demonstrating the general anti-U.S. mood of the Arabs in the interest of enhancing his nationalist credentials while at the same time entrenching his position to better control domestic affairs in Lebanon and Syria. The corollary of this strategy has been an incoherent policy, which backfired in Lebanon.

Instead of hedging and filtering its cooperation with Washington, Damascus needs to articulate a comprehensive strategy. It is time for Damascus to decide whether to support or challenge U.S. foreign policy.

Who is kidding whom? The guns of Babylon were silenced without firing a single shot. The edifice of totalitarian national rhetoric crashed down. The status quo has been shattered, bringing down with it overdue failed policies. The upcoming battle for Syria is on both the public diplomacy and economic and political reform fronts. Syria can ill-afford to ignore American, Israeli, and Lebanese public opinions. The United States has embarked on a huge enterprise to pacify and reconstruct Iraq and will appreciate Syria's cooperation and help. The peace camp in Israel needs a breath of life. Lebanon needs its freedom. Syria and Lebanon need urgent reforms, and they need to reexamine their relationship in light of the changes taking place in the region in general and within the confines of their societies in particular. Syria's real withdrawal, including all intelligence agents, and Hizbollah's military wing dismantlement (as stipulated by the Taif Accord, the constitutional compromise upon which the warring factions in Lebanon ended the civil war) could be the first steps in this direction. Championing peace and reform could well be the best weapons at Syria's disposal.

By challenging the United States, the Syrian leadership can depend on neither the Arab states nor the Arab population to secure their survival. The Arab peoples have long forsaken their support for autocratic regimes, and the Arab states have abdicated their pan-Arab role in favor of their own national interests. The political discourse of the day is a muffled "Jordan First-like" policy. But supporting the United States is also problematic. Can Damascus trust an ambiguous Washington sending mixed signals to Syria? Can Damascus support a U.S. policy that sanctions Israeli strikes against Syria? Can Damascus be certain that the United States and Israel will not attempt sooner or later to remove the Syrian Ba'thi regime?

The Bush administration would be wrong to think that SALSRA and Resolution 1559 will dramatically change Syria's behavior unless the United States also addresses Syria's desire to retrieve the Golan Heights and protect its regional interests. Syria, for its part, would be wrong to think that it could circumvent the Act and the Resolution since Damascus has insignificant trade with the United States and has loyalists in Lebanon. After holding off for a few months, President Bush, considering Syrian actions as constituting "unusual and extraordinary threat," issued an executive order on May 11, 2004 imposing sanctions on Syria. The sanctions banned American exports to Syria, except for food and medicine, and barred Syrian air carriers from landing in or taking off from the United States. Significantly, the President imposed additional sanctions not provided in the Act, including freezing the assets of certain individuals and government entities and severing business with the commercial bank of Syria.[79] No doubt, the dimensions of the Act could be far-reaching if Syria does not change its behavior.

Conversely, the Act puts significant pressure on Syria but offers no incentives. So far, Syria's reactions to U.S. policies have manifested themselves in the statements of Syrian Foreign Minister Farouq al-Shara. Once he called the Bush administration the "most violent and stupidest" of all previous administrations, and observed, in reference to the Act, that U.S. officials considered "any law coming out of Congress as descending from Heaven."[80] Equally significant, the idea that America can effect changes in Syria by depending on the appeal of its support for reform and democracy is very much rejected by Syrian reformers.

Similarly, the Syrians would be mistaken to believe that as long as the United States is embroiled in the "Iraqi quagmire" it would leave Syria to its own devices. Indeed, the more the Bush administration finds itself embroiled in Iraq, the more it will be tempted to strike at Damascus.[81] By the same token, Syria, if it does not reorient its policies, may risk being officially added to the list of countries making up "the axis of evil," thereby creating an "evil empire" in the Middle East, bringing together Tehran, Damascus, and possibly Beirut.

Washington, on the other hand, should heed Damascus's concerns by outlining a Middle East political initiative that rewards Syria for its cooperation, including renewing talks on Syria's occupied Golan Heights,[82] while standing firm and clear about its demands from Syria. Washington cannot promote democracy in Iraq and turn a blind eye to democracy in Lebanon. Meanwhile, Washington should make it clear to Damascus that its genuine cooperation with the United States to control the Iraq-Syria border would entail American help in supporting the creation of a significant trade zone between Iraq and Syria, including reopening the oil pipeline between the two countries. At the same time, Washington should put a stop to all talks about removing the Ba'thist regime in Syria, because they are absurd and counterproductive under the current circumstances in Iraq. Progress on the Lebanese and Iraqi tracks should also pave the way for renewed peace talks with Israel regarding the Golan Heights.

Significantly, Washington stands to enhance its policy towards Syria by coordinating with the European Union (EU). The EU maintains a comparative advantage over the United States in the Levant in large part because of Europe's extensive historical ties and geographic proximity, as well as the EU's decade-long engagement through the Euro-Mediterranean Partnership, also known as the Barcelona process, established in 1995. The partnership consists of a series of bilateral association agreements that cover trade, development, and reform issues. Syria is the only Mediterranean country that has not yet signed an associate agreement because it includes a clause committing Damascus not to build or proliferate weapons of mass destruction. Interestingly enough, while Paris and Washington coordinated their efforts to support Resolution 1559, Damascus held talks with the EU foreign ministers over the associate agreement leading to a preliminary agreement, in spite of U.S. sanctions against Syria.[83]

It is now Syria's choice. Its cooperation will be rewarded. Otherwise, the Syrian regime, under the scrutiny and the pressure of the world community led by the United States, will have no other choice but to gradually wither under the weight of its blunders, confusion, and despotic ways. Herein, between U.S. pressure and potential campaigns against Syria and the Syrian regime's attempts at surviving by not only fending off U.S. pressure but also undermining U.S. efforts in the Middle East in general and Iraq in particular lies a new "Cold War," potentially provoking profound changes in the region.

Inasmuch as Damascus needs to define its relationship with the United States, Washington needs to clarify its objectives in the region in general and with regard to Syria in particular. Both countries need to articulate their own strategies and political initiatives. Otherwise, a regional conflict is inevitable. Neither the United States nor Syria will benefit from such a conflict.[84]

Similarly, the ongoing developments in Lebanon, following the assassination of former Prime Minister Rafiq Hariri, have sharpened the apprehensions between Damascus and Washington. For Washington, Lebanon has emerged as a potential democratic model for other Arab countries to emulate. For Syria, the collapse of its order in Lebanon has greatly undermined its regional role, affecting both its domestic and foreign policies.

CHAPTER 7

The New Struggle for Lebanon: Democracy and Syria's Withdrawal

The seeds of the struggle for reclaiming Lebanon from Syrian occupation had been planted as a reaction to Damascus's reign of terror executed by the Syrian-imposed security regime. Lebanese at home and in Diaspora lobbied for the liberation of Lebanon. Yet, it was the convergence of international interests, especially those of Washington and Paris, with Lebanese aspirations, encouraged by the Bush administration's promotion of democracy in the Middle East, that opened cracks in the walls of the security regime in Lebanon.

Meanwhile, growing international and internal opposition to Syrian "trusteeship" over Lebanon, following the assassination of former Prime Minister Rafiq Hariri allegedly by Syria, has unleashed sociopolitical forces taking Lebanon into a new era. Between the opposition's determination to confront Syria and the willingness of pro-Syrian forces to vigorously support the status quo, Syria's authority in the country had become precarious and Lebanon's political future had become unpredictable. It was at this critical juncture in Lebanon's history that many Lebanese from across the country's political and sectarian spectrum joined hands to clamor for democracy and Syria's withdrawal from the country. This "Cedar Revolution" all but crushed the Syrian order in Lebanon, prompting Damascus to withdraw its troops after almost three decades of Syrian Machiavellian politics and reign of terror.

The withdrawal of Syrian troops from Lebanon created a political vacuum, sparking a sectarian struggle for political power. However, the elections in Lebanon have ushered in a new era, full of promises but fraught with danger. The new Lebanese political dynamics engendered a delicate balance between national integration and democratic reform, on the one side, and rogue statehood, on the other. Central to this are two large questions revolving around Hizbollah's future role and Lebanon's ability to withstand subversive activities allegedly carried out by Damascus to destabilize Beirut.

Pressuring Syria: Washington and the Lebanese-American Lobby

It is hardly imaginable that Washington, which mediated the entrance of Syrian troops into Lebanon in 1976 and all but rewarded Lebanon to Syria as a prize for its joining the U.S.-led anti-Iraq coalition during the first Gulf War (1990–1991), would reverse course and become an advocate of a free Lebanon. Washington had consistently perceived Damascus as a force of stability in Lebanon. In fact, some officials have maintained this belief, asserting that a Syrian withdrawal from Lebanon could turn the country into an Iraq-like terror front.

Since the adoption by the U.N. Security Council of Resolution 1559, which calls for the withdrawal of Syrian forces from Lebanon and the disarming of Hizbollah, a debate had raged over the roles played by Syria and Hizbollah in the country. The fault lines had been over whether or not Syria was needed to maintain peace in Lebanon and whether or not Hizbollah had outlived its purpose as an armed resistance movement, especially after Israel's withdrawal from southern Lebanon.

Some analysts, both in Lebanon and abroad, argued that the Lebanese authorities were not yet ready to meet their country's security challenges. They pointed out that Damascus had kept in check the sometimes-violent rivalry between and within Lebanon's confessional groups, as it had the rise of Islamic fundamentalism and armed Palestinian groups. Ironically, this view was echoed in an unlikely quarter, when it was revealed that the head of Israel's National Security Council, Major General Giora Eiland, described a Syrian withdrawal from Lebanon as not in Israel's interest, as it might threaten Lebanese stability and leave Hizbollah unchecked.[1] (Israeli Prime Minister Ariel Sharon's office said he "does not accept" Eiland's recommendations.)

Others had been more circumspect and merely harbored doubts about the day after. Joseph Samaha, the editor of Lebanon's daily *Al-Safir,* wrote: "Nobody can provide a real response to the crucial question of what happens tomorrow." Yet others thought that the United States was not really committed to Lebanese sovereignty and stability, and they worry about Washington using the U.N. resolution to compel Damascus to cooperate with it in Iraq. Syrian President Bashar al-Asad joined the fray by asserting in a recent speech in Damascus that implementation of Resolution 1559 "would serve only to inflame the region further."[2]

One should also add that there was a substantial constituency in Lebanon that argued that a sovereign Lebanese government, having full control over the large Lebanese Army, would be able to control domestic instability. The problem, they argued, was the Syrian presence.

With the stakes in the region so high for the United States, American analysts dealt with the issue more emphatically. Former and current officials and analysts believed that a Syrian withdrawal from Lebanon could have consequences similar to those being observed in Iraq. In fact, their opinion roughly paralleled al-Asad's. Writing in the *Los Angeles Times,* Martha Kessler, a former senior Middle East analyst with the Central Intelligence Agency (CIA), reflected some of the concerns of U.S. officials and analysts. She emphasized that, given the rise of Islamic fundamentalism, Lebanon, like Iraq today, could again attract extremists as it once did; that Sharon could spark Palestinian agitation in Lebanon; that Lebanon still lacks the shared values and spirit of compromise necessary for building durable democratic institutions; and that only Syria can confront extremism and rein in Hizbollah.[3]

Lebanon needs its freedom like any other nation, and, no doubt, it is the Lebanese themselves who have to decide on their own future. However, it is true that extremism has found its way into the country. An example is the Dinniyeh incident in 2000, where the Lebanese Army put down an Islamist revolt led by one Bassam Kanj, who reportedly had close connections with Al-Qaeda. The Palestinian refugee camp at Ain al-Hilweh, in Sidon, is also home to a host of Islamist groups and remains outside the control of the Lebanese government.

Yet one must remember that, generally speaking, extremism has flourished under authoritarian regimes in the Middle East. The Lebanese state, under Syrian supervision, had moved closer to authoritarianism. Civil rights and political liberties were frequently treaded upon. Arbitrary arrests and the denial of freedom of assembly and speech had become the norm when dealing with the opposition. The 40 leading Middle Eastern and North African civil society groups that met in Beirut last September expressed their concern about the Syrian-backed effort to amend the Lebanese Constitution and extend the term of President Emile Lahoud. The groups noted that even "in Lebanon...democracy is endangered by the distortion of the constitutional terms for the sitting president."[4]

On the issue of Palestinian agitation, one needs to consider the fact that Lebanon today is different from Lebanon before the civil war in 1975, if only because the Palestinian leadership and major armed Palestinian groups are no longer in the country. Still, it is the Lebanese government's duty to extend its authority to Palestinian refugee camps and improve the dismal conditions there, though the general consensus is that the decision is not really a Lebanese one to make.

Lebanon's democratic confessional system is not without its flaws and shares uncertainty with liberal democracies. In 1989, Lebanese parliamentarians agreed to a new power-sharing agreement known as the Taif Accord. However, Syria, by keeping its forces in Lebanon, had not complied with Taif's spirit, helping undermine Lebanon's democratic process.

On a recent visit to Lebanon, I felt a general feeling of doubt among the various communities. However, not even the hard-liners among the youths with whom I met spoke of reigniting a civil war. Most Lebanese look back on the war with great resentment and denounce its legacy in their collective consciousness. Lebanon under normal conditions, where it could set its own path, would have a much greater opportunity to strengthen the bonds of shared values and national integration.

The notion that Syria can rein in Hizbollah, and by extension keep the Lebanon-Israel border quiet, is equally flawed. Hizbollah, a nonstate actor, has taken on the responsibilities of a state, particularly in southern Lebanon. How can a government surrender the right to make decisions on peace and war to a nonstate entity, as the Lebanese government has done? Once again, Syria's role in creating such a reality had been significant, and under normal conditions only the Lebanese government should shoulder the duty of defending the nation, mainly by extending its authority to the southern border and disarming Hizbollah.

A prominent Syrian intellectual and reformer once told me: "It really makes no sense what Syria is doing in Lebanon. Damascus at the least can make an agreement with Lebanon over the timetable of withdrawal; after all Lebanon is right there."

No doubt, the September 11 attacks on the United States radically changed the prism through which the Bush administration perceived the Middle East. However, it is fair to argue that had it not been for the efforts of the Lebanese-American lobby, Washington would not have taken this adamant position about Syrian withdrawal from a country that to many U.S. officials remains precarious in terms of its potential ethnic and sectarian strife. After all, Beirut evokes sad memories in the collective consciousness of the American nation by being the site of the first suicide bombing attack against U.S. servicemen and marines. Indeed, it was the convergence of the new political climate in Washington with the emergence of a Lebanese-American lobby that produced the change in American position over Lebanon. As Walid Phares perceptively observed "one without the other wouldn't have produced a decision by Washington to seize the UN Security Council [Resolution 1559] on the Syrian occupation of Lebanon, at least that early in the process."[5]

Lebanese-American organizations and associations are almost as old as the community itself, whose early emigrants arrived on the shore of the United States in the late nineteenth century. Catholic-Maronites and other Christian denominations have composed the bulk of the community, whose overall activities centered on cultural issues and the church as a medium to preserve Lebanese religio-cultural heritage and to bring together old and new generations of Lebanese-Americans. The community experienced a sharp growth in the last quarter of the twentieth century mainly on account of the civil war in Lebanon (1975–1990). Coming from a war-torn country, this new wave of emigrants was much more politicized than previous ones, representing to a greater or lesser extent a wide range of the political spectrum in Lebanon. Syrian total hegemony over Lebanon since 1990 energized a significant number of the community to overtly engage in political activities revolving around opposing Syrian presence in Lebanon.

This "free-Lebanon" political activism took many Lebanese-Americans to the steps of U.S. Congress and Departments, where their concerns initially fell on sympathetic but uninterested ears. Meanwhile, the withdrawal of Israel from Lebanon in the summer of 2000 exposed the weak flank of the Syrian presence in Lebanon. No longer were Syrian troops (as Damascus argued) needed to protect Lebanon and support the Lebanese resistance. Consequently, Lebanese opposition to Syrian presence in Lebanon, led by the Maronite church, intensified. At the same time, political parties, including those banned by the Beirut government, and civil society organizations, including human rights groups, became vocal about Syrian heavy-handed tactics in dealing with the opposition. The Syrian regime, through its proxy Beirut government, tried to discredit the opposition by accusing its leaders of treason as well as attempted to further fragment the opposition by arresting some of its members, all under the pretext of collaborating with Israel. In an unprecedented and sweeping campaign targeting the Lebanese

Forces and the followers of former general Michel Aoun, the Lebanese security apparatus arrested in August 2001 more than 140 individuals.[6]

All of this mobilized Lebanese-American organizations and groups to intensify their "free-Lebanon" efforts in Congress and key think tanks, though their efforts were not coordinated. At the vanguard of these organizations and groups stood the United States Committee for a Free Lebanon (USCFL), headed by Ziad abd al-Nour,[7] the Lebanese-American Council for Democracy (LACD), headed by Aoun supporter Tony Haddad, the Lebanese Information Center, headed by Lebanese Forces supporter Dr. Joseph Jubeily, the American Maronite Union, headed by former Lebanese counsel Sami Khoury, and the World Lebanese Cultural Union (WLCU)-USA, headed by its charismatic figures Joe Beini, Dr. Walid Phares, attorney John Hajjar, and Tom Harb. Meanwhile, largely because of the efforts of Phares, the secretary general of WLCU, the nongovernmental organization representing millions of Lebanese emigrants around the world, transformed itself into a robust transnational movement advocating civil and political liberties in a free Lebanon.

At the same time, the impact of the September 11 attacks on the United States was no less significant on the Lebanese-American community. An urgent need emerged among the various Lebanese-American associations and groups to coordinate their efforts, solidify their contacts with Congress by pursuing a bipartisan approach, and build coalitions with like-minded organizations.[8] Out of this awareness the American Lebanese Coalition (ALC) was founded, with Jubeily as its executive director. With the exception of the USCFL and LACD, the ALC included the aforementioned organizations plus the Detroit-based Assembly for Lebanon, headed by Mel Zuhrob, and the U.S.-Kataeb (Phalange), represented by Joseph Haje. Before long, a significant Lebanese-American lobby emerged, dedicated to supporting the Bush administration's war on terrorism and freeing Lebanon.

As planned, this new lobby focused its efforts on Congress, with Tony Haddad playing a significant role in supporting and lobbying congress members Ileana Ros-Lehtinen and Eliot Engel, who would introduce the Syria Accountability and Lebanese Sovereignty Act of 2003. At the same time, this lobby set about organizing meetings with U.S. officials, while at the same time mobilizing grass-roots support for the legislation. The Bush administration and Congress began to pay attention to Lebanese-American efforts, especially after President Bush launched his initiative to bring democracy to the Middle East. After all, the Lebanese-American community and

its affiliated civil groups in the United States and Lebanon supported the president and his policies. Addressing through a letter
the 41st Annual Convention of the National Apostolate of Maronites
in July 2004 in Orlando, President Bush expressed his gratitude
and support:

> The United States believes that all people in the Middle East deserve to
> live under free and peaceful governments. We are pursuing a forward
> strategy of freedom in the region because the advance of freedom leads to
> peace. As one of the first countries to establish the institutions of democ-
> racy in the Middle East, Lebanon has long served as a bridge between East
> and West....The United States looks forward to elections in Lebanon that
> respect Lebanon's constitutions and a future for Lebanon that is independ-
> ent, fully sovereign, and free of foreign interference or domination. To help
> achieve these goals, I signed into law the Syria Accountability and Leba-
> nese Sovereignty Restoration Act in December 2003....Your efforts make
> America a better place and extend the journey of democracy.[9]

By receiving presidential and congressional support, the Lebanese-American lobby moved next to internationalize the Lebanon
issue by introducing a resolution to the U.N. Security Council. The
biggest challenge was how to get the U.N. and especially France on
board, given the disagreements between Washington and Paris over
Iraq. The WLCU and the ALC led the lobbying efforts, forming a
joint delegation to mobilize support at home and abroad. An American official of Lebanese descent, Walid Maalouf, a former Bush
administration appointee as Alternate Representative of the United
States to the fifty-eighth general assembly of the United Nations
and current appointee to the U.S. Agency for International Development, played a crucial role in arranging high-level meetings of the
U.S. delegation at the U.N. and in Washington. The delegation
pressed for a new U.N. resolution (replacing Resolution 520 of
1982) calling for Syrian withdrawal from Lebanon. With U.S.-
Syrian relations continuously deteriorating, U.S. officials were
more than ready to lend their support.[10]

Shortly thereafter, a WLCU delegation headed to the U.N. and
met with key missions including the French mission. According to
Phares, "the Lebanese delegation assured the French of future
friendship and of common cultural bonds, in addition to a Lebanese
wish to see Paris and Washington acting jointly on Lebanon, even if
Iraqi affairs separated them."[11] Simultaneously, Franco-Lebanese
organizations lobbied the Quai d'Orsay. General Aoun and his loyal
activists, who resided in the French capital, played a significant role
as well. Significantly, this lobbying coincided with a growing French
disappointment over Syrian promises of reform. Equally significant,
Syria's imposition of Lahoud was not received well with then–Prime

Minister of Lebanon Rafiq Hariri, who was compelled to resign from his post. Hariri had been a main associate of French President Jacque Chirac. According to Phares, "dislodging his [Hariri's] political power meant hurting French economic influence. In turn, France sponsored Resolution 1559 with the US."[12] At the same time, WLCU members launched a sustained lobbying campaign in most European capitals including Brussels, the official seat of the European Union.

The WLCU and ALC, meanwhile, drafted the text that would form the basis of Resolution 1559. By September 2004, Washington and France were working on introducing the resolution, which was subsequently approved. The importance of the resolution lies not only in exposing Syria as an occupying power but also in potentially becoming a medium through which international pressure against Syria could be exerted, doubling U.S. efforts to compel Damascus to change its behavior.

Commenting on the "Lebanese-lobby" in Washington in an interview with the Lebanese daily *Al-Nahar,* Syrian Ambassador to the U.S. Imad Mustafa sarcastically stated: "There is a fable about a 'Lebanese-lobby' exerting pressure in the US. Plainly, within the course of the plan to attack Syria, the American-Israeli alliance saw it as advantageous to play the card of Lebanese individuals who amplified the noise about the Syrian presence in Lebanon. They were used as a means towards reaching the desired goal and thus they were pushed to the forefront."[13]

Breaking the Last Straw: Hariri's Assassination

In a dramatic twist of events in Lebanon, former Prime Minister Rafiq Hariri was assassinated in a massive bombing in Beirut on February 14, 2005. The assassination marked the beginning of a new era in Lebanon, the implications of which could be profound for the country and the region. Significantly, this new era decided the fate of the "Second Republic," created by Syria's trusteeship (occupation) over the country in 1990. In fact, the assassination of Hariri was arguably a deliberate attempt by the Syrians to prevent what many in Lebanon perceived as a "white coup" against the pro-Syrian government, leading to the collapse of Syrian authority in Lebanon.

Lebanese politics had been polarized by the extension of the term of the pro-Syrian president Emile Lahoud and by U.N. Resolution 1559, which called for Syrian withdrawal from Lebanon and the disbanding of Hizbollah. In fact, the U.N. resolution not only helped the opposition to Syrian presence broaden its base of support but also gave the opposition an international political cover. Conversely, by losing international recognition of its authority in Lebanon, Damascus's political order in the country had become precarious.

One aspect of this order had been Syria's support of "freely elected" governments endorsing the Syrian presence in Lebanon. Since the overthrow of the "First Republic" in 1990, Damascus manipulated Lebanon's parliamentary elections to prevent the election of vocal or potential opponents, as well as coalitions of independent political candidates. After all, the constitutional amendment to extend the term of the president in the face of almost universal Lebanese opposition was approved by a vote of 96 to 29 with three members not present. Damascus manipulated the elections by gerrymandering electoral districts and enforcing party lists. For example, prior to the parliamentary elections of 2000, Beirut was divided into three districts in order to reduce the number of seats won by Hariri, who had become a fierce critic of Lahoud and then Prime Minister Salim al-Huss. Similarly, Mount Lebanon was divided into four districts, with the Druze areas set apart (along with enforcing a party list), to support the Druze leadership of Talal Arslan against that of Walid Jumblatt, who began to align himself with the Christian Maronites.[14] Led by their patriarch, the Maronite community became vocal in calling for Syrian withdrawal following Israel's pullout of south Lebanon in May 2000. Despite Syrian maneuverings and threats by Syria's and Lebanon's security apparatus, Hariri and Jumblatt fared extremely well in the elections. Hariri even defeated the hitherto long-standing Beiruti leadership of Tamam Salam and Salim al-Huss.

This time around Jumblatt moved to the center of Lebanese opposition, fuming over blatant Syrian intervention in Lebanese domestic affairs and especially over the assassination attempt of his ally, deputy Marwan Hamade, in October 2004. Even the most ardent of Syrian supporters knew that the Syrian intelligence, along with that of Lebanon, was behind the attempt. The fact that Israel was not, as usual, blamed for the assassination spoke volumes about the Lebanese mood.

In the meantime, in response to growing Lebanese opposition to Syria's presence, pro-Syrian forces, numbering in the thousands, demonstrated, apparently at the behest of Damascus, in Beirut in late November to back Syria's presence in Lebanon. The demonstrators were led by the Shi'ite Islamist party Hizbollah and Amal movement, the Syrian Social Nationalist Party, Lebanon's Ba'th party, and scores of Palestinians and Syrian immigrants and workers. In addition, so many pro-Syrian dignitaries and officials supported the demonstration that the opposition accused the government of Prime Minister Omar Karame of supporting the march. Not surprisingly, many Syrian loyalists owed their political fortunes and survival to Syria. Strong loyalists, besides Shi'a parties, Druze and Sunni dignitaries, included former interior minister Suleiman Franjieh, the Maronite Christian leader of North Lebanon whose close alliance and friendship with the Asad family goes back to the time when his grandfather Suleiman Franjieh, before becoming president of Lebanon, found a sanctuary in President al-Asad's hometown of Qardaha. Others include Greek Orthodox business tycoons and officials Issam Fares and Michel Murr, respectively, former deputy prime minister and former minister of the interior.

Chafing over incessant Syrian intervention in Lebanese domestic affairs and Syrian intelligence high-handedness and threats, the opposition called for a meeting at the Bristol hotel in Beirut in December. The gathering was attended by many political activists and parties from across Lebanon's political and communal spectrum. Among those attending were Jumblatt's Democratic Gathering and Progressive Socialist Party, the Christian Qornet Shehwan Gathering, the banned Christian Lebanese Forces, members of General Michel Aoun's Free Patriotic Front, the Democratic Forum, and the Democratic Leftist Movement. Significantly, members of Hariri's parliamentary bloc attended the meeting. The opposition issued a historical document known as the Bristol Declaration, in which they "denounced the amendment of the Lebanese constitution and the extension of Lahoud's term in office under Syrian duress, demanded a fair and just election law and an impartial government to supervise the upcoming elections in May 2005."[15]

This marked the first time since Lebanon's independence that Druzes, Sunnis, leftists, Maronites, and many Lebanese of different sects and political orientations had formed a national cross-communal political bloc similar to the one that had established the national pact of 1943. Shi'ite participation was obviously missing. Meanwhile, Hariri, who resigned as prime minister following a protracted and acerbic fallout with Lahoud, became the target of constant attack by the government, which accused him of whipping up sectarian dissent. Hariri had been a silent critic of Hizbollah and, as of recent, of Syrian high-handedness in Lebanon. Most important, Hariri opposed the parliament's electoral draft law, which would have rearranged the districting of Beirut mainly to undermine his coalition of candidates in the upcoming May elections. Once the Cabinet endorsed the electoral law, Hariri moved closer to the opposition. In fact, he sent MP Bassil Fuleihan to attend the meeting of the Bristol's follow-up committee, which was tasked with coordinating the activities of the opposition.[16]

Significantly, in early February 2005, the opposition met again at the Bristol and, unlike the first time, demanded a "total withdrawal" of Syrian troops from Lebanon.[17] Suddenly, the political order, created by the Syrians in Lebanon, appeared to be on the verge of collapse. Hariri's move toward the opposition completely changed Lebanon's political equation and dynamics, and helped create a national feeling unseen in the country's recent history. If the past is any guide, a coalition of opposition candidates supported by Jumblatt, Hariri, and the majority of Christians would be hard to defeat and, consequently, would change the constitutional equation that legitimized Syria's presence in Lebanon. Given the grave political situation and Syria's long record of alleged political assassinations (Druze Leader Kamal Jumblatt, president-elect Bashir Jumayil, president Rene Mouawad, and Mufti Hassan Khaled), Beirut's political quarters began to buzz with the question of who would be assassinated first: Jumblatt or Hariri. Soon after, Hariri was assassinated.

The swiftness with which the opposition not only blamed Syria but also held the Lebanese government responsible (even bluntly asking it not to participate in Hariri's funeral procession) attested to the new political climate dawning on Lebanon and the determination of the opposition to confront and overthrow Syria's authority in Lebanon.[18] In a dramatic shift of Sunni political attitude, Sunni Muslims held a broad communal meeting, chaired by Mufti Muhammad Rashid Qabani, in which they issued a statement condemning the assassination of Hariri and insisted that "the murder of the martyr Prime Minister Rafiq Hariri targeted the existence, role and dignity of Muslim Sunnis." They added that "they would not be satisfied with deploring this crime...and they have had enough injustice and that patience could no longer be born."[19] In sharp contrast to the bitter reaction of the Sunnis, Druzes, and Christians, the general reaction of the Shi'a community was to fall into the old pattern of blaming Israel. The leading Shi'ite cleric Muhammad Hussein Fadlallah asserted that "plans are set in motion internationally and regionally in order to sink Lebanon in a game, which affords Israel further security at the expense of explosive Arab and Islamic nations."[20] Hizbollah issued a statement that the heinous crime was aimed "at destabilizing Lebanon and planting discord among its people."[21] The Amal Movement stated that the "Zionists are behind the crime, aiming at creating turmoil."[22]

No doubt, the assassination unleashed sociopolitical forces, taking Lebanon to a new level of conflict with unpredictable consequences. Between the opposition's determination to confront Syria and the willingness of pro-Syrian forces to vigorously support the status, Lebanon's political future had become unpredictable. In any event, however, Syria's presence in the country had become untenable. On February 28, 2005, despite a governmental ban on public demonstrations, thousands of Lebanese took to the streets, chanting "Syria out." This nonviolent large-scale demonstration, described by Washington as the "Cedar Revolution," brought down the pro-Syrian government of Omar Karame. Dennis Ross noted that "there is little doubt that the 'Orange Revolution' in Ukraine appears to have had profound effect on the psychology of the Lebanese. Note how the Lebanese have borrowed from Kiev's example by creating a tent city at the site of the assassination and refusing to leave until the government resigns and the Syrians withdraw."[23]

The speed with which Syria's authority in Lebanon had eroded was also reflected by the army's and internal security apparatus's refusal to prevent the demonstrations. No less important, Hizbollah, the most ardent of Syria's supporters, refused to participate in the planned pro-government rally, effectively scuttling the event. At the same time, Syria's closest regional and international friends joined the chorus, calling on the country to withdraw from Lebanon. Saudi Crown Prince Abdullah told al-Asad during his visit to the kingdom that "Syria must start withdrawing soon, otherwise Saudi-Syrian relations will go through difficulties."[24] Even Russia told Syria its troops "should go...a change for a country that abstained when the UN Security Council passed a U.S.-inspired resolution to that effect in September."[25] Responding to a question on Syria's timetable for withdrawal from Lebanon in an interview with *Time*, al-Asad stated:

> It's a technical issue, not political. I could not say we could it in two months because I have not had the meeting with the army people. They may say it will take six months. You need to prepare when you bring your army back to your country....There are two factors. The first is security in Lebanon. The security in Lebanon is much better than before. They have an army, they have a state, they have institutions. The second thing, which is related to Syria, is that after withdrawing we have to protect our borders, because when Israel invaded in 1982, they reached that point. It was very close to Damascus, so we will need [fortifications] for the troops along the border with Lebanon.[26]

Following a joint news conference in early March in London by Secretary of State Condoleezza Rice and Foreign Minister Michel Barnier of France, the U.S. State Department released a joint statement on Lebanon by the two countries:

The United States and France reiterate our call for the full and immediate implementation of UN Security Council Resolution 1559. That means full and immediate withdrawal of all Syrian military and intelligence forces from Lebanon.[27]

In fact, following the resignation of the pro-Syrian government, the opposition issued a statement calling for the dismissal of several Lebanese officials who helped impose the pro-Syrian security regime on the country.[28]

Meanwhile, in response to intense regional and international pressure, President al-Asad delivered a speech on March 5, 2005, before the Syrian parliament addressing the recent regional developments, especially in Lebanon. In much the same style of his father, al-Asad offered a combination of compliance and defiance. Significantly, he based Syria's political approach toward regional events on two pillars: The "protection of national and pan-Arab interests through adherence to our identity, independence, loyalty to our principles and beliefs..., and dealing with the concerned parties with an open mind, without any preconceptions and with a great deal of realism, flexibility and responsibility."[29] In other words, Syria was fighting for Arabism and the identity of Syrians and Arabs. He depicted *al-Sira'* (struggle) as a battle between the forces of colonialism and Zionism against those of Arabs. In fact, he unequivocally framed *al-Sira'* in an ideological context, confirming the new "Cold War" between Damascus and its allies and the Lebanese opposition and the West.

He reiterated his opposition to the Iraqi war on national and strategic grounds whereby "the security and unity of Iraq involves the national security of Syria," as well as insisted that Syria has done what it could to control the Iraq-Syria border. With regards to Lebanon, he stated that Syrian troops would withdraw first to the Beka Valley then to the border in compliance with Resolution 1559 and the Taif Accord. But he offered no timetable for the withdrawal nor did he speak about the Syrian *Mukhabarat* (intelligence) in Lebanon. Significantly, he conveyed a message of intimidation to the Lebanese by underscoring that "Syria's power and its role in Lebanon do not depend on its presence in Lebanon because this power is linked to facts of geography and politics...the heart of Syria that gave Lebanon blood cannot be harmed by certain wrongdoings because you [Syrians] are Syrian Arabs and the sons and grandchildren of Syrian Arabs." He added that all this [withdrawal] "does not mean that Syria will give up its responsibilities toward brothers and friends...but it will remain with them and the battles of honor will remain the symbol of eternal unity....A new 'May 17' [1983 Lebanese-Israeli agreement] is looming on the horizon, so be prepared

for the battle to bring it down as you did two and half decades ago."
By referring to the 1983 agreement, which Syria in concert with its
Lebanese allies succeeded in aborting, al-Asad was sending a clear
signal to Syria's supporters in Lebanon, mainly Hizbollah, the
Syrian Social Nationalist Party, and the Amal Movement to prepare
themselves for a second battle against the Lebanese opposition and
its international supporters, mainly Washington and Paris.

Hours later, in a political move meant to challenge the Lebanese
opposition and show solidarity with Syria, Hizbollah and other
Syrian allies called for a peaceful demonstration on March 8 in Bei-
rut to rally support against what they called "foreign intervention."
Shedding his initial neutral stance following Hariri's assassination,
Hizbollah Secretary General Hassan Nasrallah responded to al-
Asad's signal by stating that the demonstration was to "denounce
Resolution 1559, to show thanks, loyalty and appreciation to the
Syrian leadership, people and army for its achievements in Leba-
non."[30] He ominously added that "the resistance will not give up
its arms because Lebanon needs the resistance to defend it even if
I am optimistic that Israel will soon withdraw from the Shebaa
Farms."[31]

No doubt, Syrian withdrawal from Lebanon had become inevitable. But at the time the extent of Syrian withdrawal remained
unclear. More specifically, notwithstanding Syrian loyalists and
supporters, the question over the scope and breadth of Syria's penetration of Lebanon's institutions, through which Damascus could
retain its influence, remains undecided and an explosive issue.
Equally significant, if Syria fulfills the terms of Resolution 1559 by
withdrawing from Lebanon, will Hizbollah follow suit and disband
its militia or challenge the opposition by remaining a spearhead of
Syrian and Iranian influence and thus plunge the country into
internal strife?

The Swift Collapse of the Syrian Order in Lebanon

Collating the speeches of Hizbollah's Secretary General Hassan
Nasrallah and Syria's President Bashar al-Asad, delivered, respectively, one after the other on March 8 and 5, 2005, largely in
response to growing domestic and international pressure on Syria
to withdraw from Lebanon, one theme becomes salient: The protection of Arab identity.[32] While committing Syria to withdraw from
Lebanon, President al-Asad asserted that his "foreign policy is
guided by the principle of protecting pan-Arab interests by holding
onto Arab identity." Nasrallah asserted that "Lebanon will remain
the country of Arabism, the country of nationalism, the country of

resistance." It is ironic that a Syrian regime, ruled by a junta of Ala-wi barons, and an Islamist party, the brainchild of theocratic Iran, would come together in defending Arab identity and Arabs while the traditional bearer and protector of Arab nationalism and iden-tity, the Lebanese Sunnis, have bolted the pro-Syrian camp, sup-ported by Hizbollah and Iran.

No less ironic was the symbolism of the Hizbollah-organized large demonstration on March 8 in central Beirut to show solidarity with Syria. It is no coincidence that Hizbollah chose the area where the statue of Riad al-Sulh towered over central Beirut as the location of the demonstration. Al-Sulh was the first postindependence Sunni prime minister in Lebanon and a pillar of Arab nationalism.

It was under this Arab nationalist pretext that Hizbollah tried to intimidate the opposition. While calling for an internal and interna-tional dialogue, he threatened the Lebanese opposition by declaring that "Lebanon is an exceptional case. Lebanon is not Somalia nor Ukraine nor Georgia. If some people believe that they can topple Lebanon's government, security, stability and strategic choices through some demonstrations, slogans and media, they are wrong." Moreover, while insisting on the implementation of the Taif Accord, he stressed that "we are here to refuse resolution 1559, in order to protect the resistance as well as its choice...we are here to refuse the settlement...since the Palestinians settlers are our brothers and friends." Notwithstanding the fact that the Palestinian ques-tion has not been an issue in the current crisis with Syria, how will Hizbollah implement the Taif Accord when the Islamist party goes against the letter and the spirit of the accord by affirming that "the resistance will not give up its arms because Lebanon needs the resistance to defend it even if I am optimistic that Israel will soon withdraw from the Shebaa farms."

Apparently, behind Hizbollah's position was an attempt to claim a new domestic role. Recognizing that it will become the focus of domestic and international debates revolving around its disarma-ment following the eventual withdrawal of Syrian troops from Lebanon, Hizbollah decided to align itself with Syria against the opposition by trying to construct under the pretext of national unity a political order supporting the Islamist party's interpretation of the Taif Accord and rejecting Resolution 1559. Lebanon's pro-Syrian camp (and security services) and Hizbollah's praetorian guards would protect this order. On the other hand, if the opposition refused to join a national unity government, Hizbollah and other Syrian supporters in Lebanon would have the high political ground to create a non-neutral government, putting the opposition on the defensive, or, better yet, would try to postpone the elections. In fact,

Nasrallah made it clear in his speech that "if the opposition refuses [to create a government of national unity], I frankly say that there is no meaning for a neutral government." In other words, Hizbollah was not only claiming a new political role in Lebanon, standing in sharp contrast to that espoused by the opposition, but also attempting to making his role the dominant one in the country, that is replacing Syrian occupation with Hizbollah's supremacy.[33]

But Hizbollah (and Syria) apparently underestimated Lebanese frustration with the pro-Syrian order in the country and eagerness for freedom and democracy. Reacting to Hizbollah's show of force and solidarity with Syria, approximately 1.5 million Lebanese took to the streets on March 14, clamoring for freedom and calling for Syria's swift withdrawal. It was the largest demonstration ever in Lebanon's history, not only eclipsing that organized by Hizbollah but also sending a message to the Islamist party that its role in the country has limits. The demonstration hastened the collapse of the Syrian order in Lebanon and apparently convinced the Syrians to withdraw as soon as possible from the country. The demonstration sent shock waves across the Arab world. Arab leaders were apprehensive about the implications of the collapse of the Syrian order in Lebanon by popular will for their rule. Arabs were awed by the determination of the Lebanese to replace a security regime by a democratic government through nonviolent means. No less important was the impact of the demonstration on the international community. Not only did it reinforce the determination of the international community, in particular the United States and France, to keep the pressure on Syria, but also to make sure that the upcoming Lebanese elections were conducted in a free and fair atmosphere. No doubt, Lebanon has emerged for the United States as a potential democratic model in the Middle East for other Arab states to emulate, reinforcing and validating the Bush administration's program of promoting democracy there. Echoing the words of a Lebanese observer "Democracy is knocking at the door of this country. And if it's successful in Lebanon, it is going to ring the doors of every Arab regime," President George W. Bush had already asserted that "elections in Lebanon must be fully and carefully monitored by international observers."[34]

In addition, President Bush in early May renewed economic sanctions on Syria implemented a year ago, saying its government still supports terrorism and is undermining efforts to stabilize Iraq.[35] Meanwhile, a report by a fact-finding mission sent to Beirut by U.N. Secretary General Kofi Annan to look into Hariri's assassination was released by the international organization. The report stated that:

> After gathering the available facts, the Mission concluded that the Lebanese security services and the Syrian Military Intelligence bear the primary responsibility for the lack of security, protection, law and order in Lebanon....It is also the Mission's conclusion that the Government of Syria bears primary responsibility for the political tension that preceded the assassination of former Prime Minister Mr. Hariri.[36]

Al-Asad criticized the U.N.'s report, saying that "it is a report of political character when I was expecting a report of a technical-criminal nature."[37] However, implicated in the assassination and under growing international pressure, the Syrian regime set a date for its withdrawal from Lebanon. In a joint news conference meeting with Syrian Foreign Minister Farouq al-Shara in Damascus, U.N. envoy Terje Roed-Larsen announced Syria's commitment to withdraw all its military and intelligence forces from Lebanon by April 30.[38]

Meanwhile, in a marked shift from its strategy that conflicted with that of the United States on Syria, the European Union, insisting on a full withdrawal from Lebanon and free parliamentary elections, refused to sign the association agreement, which "involves billions of dollars of aid to Damascus as well as the creation of an EU-Syrian free trade zone."[39]

On April 26, al-Shara, in an official letter to U.N. Secretary General Annan, stated that "Syrian Arab Forces stationed in Lebanon at the request of Lebanon and under an Arab mandate have fully withdrawn all their military, security apparatus and assets to their positions in Syria."[40] A U.N. team, led by Brigadier General Elhadji Kandji of Senegal, was dispatched to Lebanon to verify Syria's evacuation. On May 23, U.N. Secretary General Annan stated that "a United Nations mission has verified that Syrian troops and security forces have fully withdrawn from Lebanon."[41]

Syria's withdrawal brought to an end Damascus's three-decades dominance in Lebanon, ushering in a new era for the country full of promises but fraught with danger as well.

Lebanon: The New Republic

The withdrawal of Syrian troops from Lebanon created a political vacuum, sparking a sectarian struggle for political power. In fact, this struggle initially began when the pro-Syrian government of Omar Karame resigned and pro-Syrian and opposition forces haggled over the composition of a new government whose mandate was mainly to oversee the parliamentary elections set to begin in late May. Following *Marathonic* hours of wrangling, a new government was born in April reflecting a delicate balance of sectarian power distribution. However, given the politically charged atmosphere and the rapid erosion of Syrian power, the Hariri family obtained two important cabinet positions, the interior and justice ministries, which were essential for overseeing the elections and leading the probe into Hariri's assassination.[42] The birth of the new government did not mitigate the polarization of Lebanese politics. But this polarization, unlike that recently over Syria, was now over the elections, including choosing an electoral system and forging alliances, all in the interest of staking a claim to political power in the new parliament.

The 1990 Taif Accord, the constitutional compromise that ended the civil war, offered an imperfect compromise between democracy and sectarian peace. The agreement gave equal parliamentary representation to Muslims and Christians, divided proportionally between the two sects' various denominations. Under Syrian pressure, the legislature was later enlarged from 108 to 128 seats, with 64 Christian representatives (34 Maronite, 14 Greek Orthodox, 8 Greek Catholic, 5 Armenian Orthodox, 1 Armenian Catholic, 1 Evangelical, as well as 1 candidate representing various "minorities," including Jews) and 64 Muslim representatives (27 Sunni, 27 Shi'ite, 8 Druze, and 2 Alawite).

Using a system still in place today, voters were assigned to electoral districts originally drawn around Lebanon's six administrative regions, requiring candidates to appeal to a broad cross section of religious communities in order to win office. Candidates generally run as members of a list for their district. In the 1992 and 1996 elections, Damascus gerrymandered certain districts to benefit pro-Syrian candidates. In the 2000 elections, the Taif provisions were entirely ignored, and the country was divided into 14 electoral districts. Overseen by Ghazi Kanaan, then-chief of Syrian intelligence in Lebanon, this division created districts that favored pro-Syrian candidates, bringing together unconnected areas with vast demographic differences. In particular, such gerrymandering joined areas containing denominations of one sect with large areas containing a single majority denomination of another sect. This practice helped dilute anti-Syrian votes, mainly from Maronites. For example, less than half of the 64 Christian representatives were elected from Christian-majority districts; most came from areas annexed to larger Muslim districts, essentially elected by Muslim votes.[43]

Attempting to fill the political vacuum created by the Syrian withdrawal, the opposition and pro-Syrian forces sharpened the sectarian struggle for political power, blurring in the process the lines between the two camps. Angered by the February 2005 assassination of former prime minister Rafiq Hariri, allegedly by Syria, Lebanon's Sunni community rallied around the leadership of Hariri's son Saad. At the same time, Hariri's Sunni archrival, the pro-Syrian Omar Karame, lost his clout with the crushing of the Syrian order in Lebanon. The Hariri family, riding the wave of his martyrdom as a symbol of national unity, sought to become the focal point of national reconciliation and thus position itself at the center of Lebanese politics.

Meanwhile, the Shi'ite community, led by the pro-Syrian Hizbollah, sought to claim a political role in Lebanon commensurate with its demographic strength. Hizbollah became concerned about U.N. Security Council Resolution 1559, part of which calls for its disarmament. The group recognized that it could become a target of the international community, led by the United States. Consequently, it pursued a dual policy of co-opting other communities in the name of national unity and making the elections both a referendum for its role as a resistance movement and a means of showing its political strength. Hizbollah Secretary General Hassan Nasrallah defiantly refused disarmament and urged political reconciliation in Lebanon by reaching out to Christian factions, which have been among the most vocal in calling for Hizbollah to surrender its weapons.[44]

Among the Druze, Progressive Socialist Party chief Walid Jumblatt was central to the unity of the anti-Syrian opposition, given the contrast between his pro-Syrian past and his more recent unwavering stance against Damascus. Once Syria withdrew, however, Jumblatt was hemmed in by his community's numeric weakness and feared a Christian nationalist revival. Consequently, he solidified his alliance with Saad Hariri and mended his relations with Hizbollah. Specifically, he struck a deal with the Sunnis and Shi'ites to base new parliamentary elections on the 2000 electoral law. This would allow Hariri, Nasrallah, and Jumblatt to shape the emergence of the new political order and enable Hizbollah to undermine the candidacy of any Christian calling for its disarmament.

Christians were taken aback by Jumblatt's maneuvering, prompting the League of Maronite Bishops to issue a statement on May 12 condemning the electoral law: "In light of this law, the Christians can elect only 15 MPs out of 64 while the others, almost 50 MPs, are elected by Muslims."[45] Still, Christian factions decided not to boycott the elections for fear of prolonging the parliament's pro-Syrian character. Saad and Jumblatt (with Nasrallah's support) tried to temper Christian discontent by forging alliances with Christian leaders who had been old foes. For example, Saad included in his Beirut electoral list Solange Jumayil, wife of late Phalange president Bashir Jumayil, while Jumblatt (along with Hizbollah) included Edmond Naim of the Christian Lebanese Forces in his Baabda-Alley list. Saad also forged an alliance with Strida Geagea, wife of the imprisoned leader of the Lebanese Forces, to contest the elections in North Lebanon.[46] Christian ranks were further shaken by the apparent defection of General Michel Aoun, who recently returned to Lebanon after 15 years of exile. In disagreement with the mainstream Christian factions, Aoun created his own lists, even allying himself with pro-Syrian politicians such as Michel Murr and Suleiman Franjieh. This development amplified Christian discontent with the overall direction that the anti-Syrian opposition has taken.

Staggered over four dates corresponding to particular districts (May 29 for the Beirut area, June 5 for southern Lebanon, June 12 for Mount Lebanon and Beka, and June 19 for northern Lebanon), the parliamentary elections took place in a free, democratic environment, crowning the new leaders of Lebanon. Saad, Jumblatt, Nasrallah, and Aoun have emerged as the uncontested leaders of their respective communities. The biggest upset was Aoun's victory in Mount Lebanon (North Metn and Jbeil-Keswran) and Beka (Zahleh), where his lists won out over almost all mainstream and historic Christian candidates. Apparently, Christian protest votes were partly responsible for his victory. In general, the elections have ushered in a new era for Lebanon. On a positive note, the polls have helped strengthen national unity by allying certain past opponents. The new political dynamics have also made it nearly impossible for one party to decide Lebanon's governance, thus encouraging compromise, an essential component of the democratic process.[47] On a pessimistic note, these same dynamics could negatively affect national reconciliation. Aoun will no doubt oppose Jumblatt and Hariri's attempts to dislodge pro-Syrian president Emile Lahoud. Moreover, when Lahoud's term ends, Aoun will either run for the presidency himself or nominate an ally. In either case, Aoun may seek Hizbollah's support to counter Jumblatt's opposition. (Jumblatt has already criticized Aoun's victory, using it as an occasion to lament the defeat of Christian moderate leadership.)

The new political dynamics will also make it extremely difficult for any party to support U.N. Resolution 1559. Instead, the government will likely opt for a domestic resolution to the question of Hizbollah's disarmament, one that is favorable to the party.[48] This could entail creating a legitimate pretext under which to protect Hizbollah's weapons, which could bring Lebanon into conflict with the international community.[49]

On the other hand, much will depend on Hizbollah's actions. So far, no one in Lebanon wants to see the party disarmed by force. However, if Hizbollah insists on maintaining its position that armed resistance is necessary to protect against Israeli aggression, then Lebanon may be torn by intercommunal tension and infighting. In fact, Hizbollah is sending mixed messages to both the Lebanese and the international community. On the one hand, Hizbollah has maintained its belief that armed resistance is central to its raison d'être. Nasrallah sees the conflict with Israel as perpetual. While calling for national reconciliation (even borrowing Bashir Jumayil's famous slogan of Lebanon's 10,452 square kilometers), he asserted that Lebanon's territorial integrity include not only the disputed Shebaa Farms but also the disputed Seven Villages, which have been under Israeli control since Israel's independence in 1948.[50] The underlying assumption is that Hizbollah will continue its armed resistance, even if Israel withdraws from Shebaa Farms. On the other hand, Hizbollah has engaged the democratic process and has decided to be part of the new government.

This dual approach will not sit well with many Lebanese, who are looking for a fundamental alteration of the country's post-Syrian politics. One could argue that Hizbollah is facing an identity crisis. In 1992, Hizbollah took a decision to participate in parliamentary elections based on suspending its ideological adherence to transforming Lebanon into an Islamic Republic. Today, Hizbollah is at a critical juncture, with much riding on whether it will forsake its arms or the budding democratic process. As Michael Young perceptively observed, "Even though a reprieve was bought in Tehran this week [The election of hardliner Mahmoud Ahmadinejad as president of Iran will have pleased Hizbollah], Hizbullah's future will remain uncertain for as long as the party cannot define a peaceful role for itself in an exclusively Lebanese context. Sectarian politics, to work, need to be modest; it's Hizbullah's turn to show it agrees."[51]

Interestingly, one of the main factors that brought the Lebanese together upon gaining initial independence was the tacit sectarian understanding that their country was a crossroads between East and West. The success of Lebanon's newly acquired independence may hinge on a similar understanding that it is at a crossroads between democracy and rogue statehood.[52]

The Dynamics of the Lebanon-Syria-U.S. Triangular Relationship

No doubt, the swiftness with which the Syrian order collapsed in Lebanon took the Syrian regime by surprise. Throughout its modern history, Syria meddled in the affairs of Lebanon. In fact, the Ba'thist regime viewed Lebanon as both a foreign and a domestic policy matter, since it combines geostrategic concerns with internal power considerations for Syria. As I wrote in *Embattled Neighbors,* Lebanon served the Asad regime tremendously in many different ways, as a medium of political and military leverage against Israel, as a patronage system to reward the regime's loyalists, and as an outlet to relieve internal politico-economic pressures. Notwithstanding the presence of Syrian troops in Lebanon, by signing a slew of political, economic, and security agreements with Beirut heavily titled in its own favor, Damascus tried to bring Beirut irreversibly within its sphere of influence, if not as an integral part of Syria, then as a quasicolony.[53] Interestingly, in the minutes of the meeting held in September 1993 for the signature of the social and economic cooperation agreement between the two countries, Lebanon was officially described as a *Qutr.*[54] The word has a symbolic meaning in Ba'thi ideology, as it denotes that all Arab states are no more than provinces in a potentially united Arab nation, with the added implication in this context that Lebanon is merely a province of Syria. No wonder Damascus has had no diplomatic relations with Beirut. Damascus does not have an embassy in Beirut. Considering all of this, it is hard to imagine that Damascus will genuinely extricate itself from all Lebanese matters.

In fact, as Syrian troops continued to withdraw from parts of Lebanon, three bomb attacks occurred within eight days in predominantly Christian areas: a March 19 car bomb wrecked the front of a building in New Jdeideh, wounding nine; a March 22 bomb ripped through an elite shopping center in Kaslik, killing three; and a March 26 car bomb in the industrial sector of Sadd el-Bouchrieh wounded five and destroyed several buildings.[55] Respectively, on June 2 and 21, a prominent anti-Syrian journalist, Samir Kassir, was assassinated when his car blew up in the Christian Beirut suburb of Ashrafieh, and a recent critic of Syria, a communist leader, and ideologue, George Hawi, was assassinated by a bomb planted below his car seat. Many Lebanese, especially prominent opposition figures, saw the bombings and the assassinations as an attempt by Syria and its loyalists and/or agents to derail the growing movement for democracy and independence in Lebanon, while at the same time deepening fears of renewed sectarian conflict.[56]

Syria has a long history of using violence to accomplish its purposes in Lebanon. During the 1975–1990 Lebanese civil war, for example, Damascus liquidated those it perceived as obstacles. Syria was allegedly behind the 1976 assassination of Kamal Jumblatt in the attempt to end his leadership of the National Movement (which combined Arabist, leftist, and Muslim forces) and to facilitate a rapprochement between Syria and the Muslim political camp. No less important, Damascus has liquidated those it perceived as potential links to foreign powers, such as president-elect Bashir Jumayil in 1982, who was viewed as an ally of Israel. In 2002, Syria is also thought to have assassinated Elie Hobeika, whose loyalty to Damascus came into question following the September 11 terror attacks, when Hobeika appeared to revive past connections with the CIA. Car bombs in Lebanon became almost daily occurrences during the civil war and were meant to push the country into socio-politico-economic paralysis. The current wave of bombings is reminiscent of this past Syrian use of violence. In addition, there were disturbing indications that Syria was attempting to activate its loyalists inside Lebanon to provoke sectarian troubles. For example, on March 5, a convoy of cars circled Sassin Square in Ashrafieh (the Christian capital of East Beirut during the civil war), carrying pictures of President Bashar al-Asad and firing into the air among a crowd that had gathered there. (It is noteworthy that the shooting of a bus transporting Palestinians in a Christian Beirut suburb sparked the civil war.)

After the civil war, Syria maintained its grip on Lebanon by pursuing a divide-and-rule policy among and between Lebanon's sectarian communities. For example, it balanced the rising power of the late former Prime Minister Rafiq Hariri by supporting traditional Sunni leadership such as Salim al-Hoss and Tamam Salam. It also tried to co-opt sectarian party leaders like Karim Pakradouni in order to fragment communal unity and leadership. As head of the Christian Phalange party, Pakradouni reversed party policy by emerging as an ardent supporter of the status quo, especially of pro-Syrian president Emile Lahoud.

Throughout Israeli-Syrian peace negotiations (1991–2000), Damascus used Hizbollah to put pressure on Israel militarily. In the current scenario, it is distinctly possible that Syria, through Hizbollah, may inflame the Lebanon-Syria border in order to deflect domestic and international attention. Indeed, according to press reports, King Abdullah of Jordan recently warned Israel and the United States about such a likelihood.

Significantly, prominent opposition figures blamed the bombings on Lebanon's security regime and its intelligence patrons in Damascus. Jumblatt even charged that Syria's intelligence services were actively sabotaging Lebanon's security. He stated that "The entire opposition is targeted. It seems that there is a decision somewhere taken with or without President Asad's knowledge to complete a list of assassinations and keep up a subversion campaign."[57] Despite the presence of Syrian troops in Lebanon, Damascus has controlled Lebanon primarily through Lebanese institutions that it fills with pro-Syrian loyalists. In fact, the removal of pro-Syrian officials from their posts was a core demand of the Lebanese opposition. Following a meeting on March 3 in Jumblatt's stronghold of Mukhtara, the opposition called for the removal of Adnan Addoum as state prosecutor, Brigadier General (ret.) Jamil Sayyed as director general of general security, Brigadier General (ret.) Edward Mansour as director general of the state security apparatus, General Ali Hajj as director general of internal security, General Mustafa Hamdan as commander of the army's Presidential Brigade, General Raymond Azar as director of military intelligence, and Colonel Ghassan Tufeili as chief of the military intelligence espionage unit. (Members of the opposition have expressed fear that General Sayyed might be planning a coup d'état. In an audacious and unprecedented move, Sayyed held a press conference in which he attacked the opposition as a "political mafia" that has caused Lebanon's woes.) Admittedly, at the time of this writing, these security chiefs, with the exception of Hamdan, had been sacked.

The recent bombings are not only a sign that Syria and its Lebanese agents are intent on heightening sectarian tension, but also mark the beginning of a new round of intimidation against the opposition, carried out under the pretext of compliance with U.N. Security Council Resolution 1559 and the Taif Accord. Even U.N. Secretary General Kofi Annan warned that he might send a verification team back to Lebanon following reports that Syrian intelligence cells may still be operating in Lebanon.[58]

Syria denied all accusations, insisting that all its military and intelligence apparatus have evacuated Lebanon. Furthermore, Syrian officials drummed up the charge that smuggling of arms and terrorists may have taken place from Lebanon to Iraq via Syria. As a response, Damascus tightened its border inspections with Lebanon to the point of closing the Lebanon-Syria border crossings. This caused long queues of cargo trucks on border checkpoints and led many drivers to throw out their perishable products. Being the only border outlet and overland transit trade for Lebanon's products, Syria apparently had been choking Lebanon's economy. Beirut's media charged that the Asad regime was evidently taking revenge for his country's "humiliating ouster after 29 years of a ruthless reign of terror that no one dared to resist before ex-Premier Rafiq Hariri's assassination."[59] This method of punishing Lebanon by closing the frontiers had been tried before by the senior al-Asad in 1973 when he "determinedly refused to reopen the frontiers unless his Syrian opponents living in Lebanon were deprived of their political freedom and the Lebanese newspapers opposing his government or his policies were censored or shut down."[60] Another sensitive matter with which Damascus has been patronizing Beirut is the question of Lebanese prisoners held in Syrian jails. For years Syria has either equivocated or denied holding Lebanese prisoners. However, though it maintained its position, Damascus released 121 Lebanese prisoners in 1998 and then 46 in 2000. Civil rights organizations, especially Support for Lebanese in Detention and Exile, maintain that over 800 Lebanese are still in Syrian jails. In a marked shift of its original position following pointed criticism from human rights organizations and Lebanese officials, Syria has admitted holding Lebanese prisoners, calling them terrorists. Syrian Prime Minister Mohammad Naji Otri claimed that the detainees were members of the now-dismantled South Lebanese Army that cooperated with Israel Defense Forces prior to their withdrawal from Lebanon in the summer of 2000. Declining to give a figure on their numbers, Otri condescendingly charged that "these people were fighting alongside Israel and killed Syrian soldiers. Obviously, they were punished, like terrorists in Spain or other countries."[61]

Meanwhile, Washington did not stand idly by as Syria engaged furtively in destabilizing and/or punishing Lebanon. The Bush administration constantly stepped up its attacks on Syria. Initially, following the assassination of Hariri, President Bush warned Syria that it must "completely pull out of Lebanon, shut down the offices of Hizbullah in Damascus and stop arms smuggling into Iraq."[62] At the same time, he lashed out at Hizbollah, calling it a "dangerous organization," and that "there is a reason why we've put Hizbullah on a terrorist list. They've killed Americans in the past. We will continue to work with the international community to keep them on that list and we will continue to pressure the group."[63] Then Washington linked the assassinations of Hariri, Kassir, and Hawi to attempts by Damascus to create instability in Lebanon. Secretary of State Condoleezza Rice served a chilling warning on Syria by stating that "there is an atmosphere of instability [in Lebanon] as Syria's activities are part of that context and part of that atmosphere, and they need to knock it off."[64] Rice's comments came amid efforts by the U.N.'s investigation team, led by German prosecutor Detlev Mehlis, probing the assassination of Hariri.[65] Prosecutor Mehlis has vowed to uncover the truth, citing the assassination as "an incomprehensible tragedy not only for you [Lebanon] but for all the civilized world.[66] No doubt, the international community, backed by the United States, will take severe actions against

Damascus if Mehlis's investigation implicates Damascus in the assassination.

Significantly, on June 30, 2005, the U.S. Treasury Department designated Syrian interior minister Ghazi Kanaan and former chief of Syrian military intelligence in Lebanon Rustum Ghazale as Specially Designated Nationals (SDN) under Executive Order 13338. This designation entitles the Treasury Department to freeze their assets on the grounds that they pose a threat to U.S. national security. Coming in the wake of renewing sanctions against Syria, this action was unprecedented in the history of the two countries. According to Matthew Levitt, although several senior Middle Eastern government officials have in the past been connected to terrorism and other illicit dealings, not one has been designated as SDN until now.[67] This demonstrates the gravity and seriousness the Bush administration attaches to Syria's behavior and its implications for U.S. policy in the region.

Lebanon has not emerged only as a potential model of democracy in the region. Significantly, Lebanon's free elections and the almost complete toppling of the state security system (removing six of the seven security chiefs) put Lebanon in a unique position in the Middle East. Lebanon, unlike any other Arab country, has the potential of restoring total civilian control over the state security system, which has undermined the democratic process and circumscribed civil society throughout the Arab world. In this respect, Lebanon could jump-start the regional process of ending the modern Arab era of police and security dominance over state governance while at the same time beginning the process of the rule of law. Correspondingly, Washington will pay special attention to the ongoing developments in Lebanon, offering its help to safeguard and support the country's drive toward democracy. At the same time, it will not shy away from putting more pressure on Syria, including adding more innovative sanctions, if Damascus continues its alleged subversive activities in the country. Similarly, Lebanon has an uphill battle to protect its newly acquired independence and ground its democratic process in the rule of law and liberal democracy. Given Syria's history in Lebanon and recent actions, it seems as if Syria's withdrawal was only a tactical retreat.

CHAPTER 8

Syria Postwithdrawal: Reform or Dictatorship?

Mounting international pressure on Syria coupled with its humiliating evacuation from Lebanon compelled Damascus to refocus on domestic issues, including reform, and to fend off domestic challenges and foreign threats. However, President al-Asad's attempts at dealing with the domestic situation came in the form of putting a show of solidarity and strength directed as much against the domestic opposition and the civil society reform movement as against the West, mainly the United States. Central to his attempts were his decisions to affirm the vanguard role of the Ba'th party and consolidate his rule by completing the transition of power replacing the old guard by a loyal "new guard" sharing his outlook. However, these decisions apparently had their provenance in a Faustian bargain between President al-Asad and the regime's political elite, whereby the vested interests of the latter would be protected in exchange for retiring the old guard among them.[1] More specifically, President al-Asad narrowed the power base upon which he relies to secure his rule to his most trusted Alawi clan members. As a result, this "young guard" may have to be tougher than the old guard in dealing with issues affecting the security of the regime, thereby curtailing substantial reform for the time being and effectively undermining U.S. efforts to promote democracy in the region.

Closing Ranks: Reform Versus Clan Control

Following Syria's humiliating withdrawal from Lebanon and pointed warnings from the Bush administration, coming in the wake of a bill introduced in the U.S. Congress calling for establishing a program to "support a transition to a democratically elected government in Syria."[2] Syrian leaders hoped that reforms introduced at the Ba'th Party's Tenth Regional Congress on June 6 would allow them to fend off both domestic challenges and foreign threats.[3] Addressing the Progressive National Front (PNF), the Ba'thi-led coalition of political parties, in early May, President Bashar al-Asad highlighted the dangers facing Syria by stressing that "Syria has few choices, an American aggression, an Israeli intervention, or activation of the domestic situation."[4] Among the important issues on the Congress's agenda was the status of the Ba'th party itself.

Before the conference, speculation abounded about a "jasmine revolution" that could breathe life into the suppressed Syrian civil society movement, reviving the "Damascus Spring" of reform. Analysts and reformers alike hoped that President al-Asad would launch a peaceful coup against the morbid state of the country by granting a general amnesty for political prisoners and allowing political exiles to return (the regime has allowed some political exiles, such as former president Amin al-Hafiz and Colonel Jassim Alwan, a Nasserist officer who planned a coup d'état against the Ba'th regime in 1963, to return); creating a multiparty system; ending martial law, which has been in effect since 1963; suspending Law 49, which makes membership in the outlawed Muslim Brotherhood punishable by death; and abolishing article 8 of the constitution, which enshrines the Ba'th as the vanguard and ruling party in society. Instead, as Sami Moubayed rightly observed: "The message that emerged from the conference was that the Baath would do what it took to survive, and was here to stay."[5]

Since he assumed office in 2000, Syrian President Bashar al-Asad has struggled to redefine the role of the Ba'th Party. The tenets of Ba'thism—freedom, unity, and socialism—have become obsolete since the party seized power in the 1960s. The ongoing developments in the Arab world have made Arab unity and socialism anomalous features. Notwithstanding the fall of the Ba'thi regime of Saddam Hussein, Arab unity has been early on discredited by the breakup of the merger between Syria and Egypt in 1961. Socialism, on the other hand, had become an outdated economic system lacking ideological vigor and a vehicle to enrich and protect the interests of senior Ba'th figures.

During the party's Ninth Regional Congress, held for the first time in 15 years in June 2000, Bashar emphasized the need to rejuvenate Ba'thism's image. Al-Asad hoped to use the party as a vehicle for rallying broad public support for his policies. He initiated largely open elections in the party branches, allowing junior Ba'thists to contend for seats in the Party Congress. The party also held new elections to its Regional Command and its Central Committee during the Congress. On the Regional Command, the highest body in Syria, newcomers took 12 of 21 seats. Sixty-two of the Central Committee's 90 members were newly elected.[6] These appointments reflected al-Asad's intent to introduce new faces and establish a core of supporters in both offices. In addition, al-Asad reduced military representation on the Regional Command and increased its representation on the Central Committee.

In the wake of the Ninth Party Congress, a younger generation assumed leadership in local party organizations. In July 2003, al-Asad issued a decree separating party and state; appointments to government offices would henceforth be based on merit rather than party affiliation. In early 2004, al-Asad issued another important decree forcing party officials to retire at the age of 60. Meanwhile, debate has raged among Ba'thists and the Syrian public over the future of the party. Some decry al-Asad's policies as weakening the party, while others demand more radical reforms.

It was against this background that many Syrians believed the upcoming Party Congress would discuss a new law for political parties as part of a continuing process to redefine the role of the Ba'th party. Syria outlawed political parties after the Ba'th Party took power in 1963. Beginning a series of reforms, known as the corrective movement, President Hafiz al-Asad ended the one-party system by establishing the Progressive National Front, which included socialist parties led by the Ba'th. He called this parliamentary representation *ta'adudia* ("pluralism"). Though the PNF monopolized political power, real power was wielded by the informal structure of the regime revolving around the president and his network of Ba'th leaders and Alawi military officials. The PNF's monopoly of power has come under significant criticism since Bashar al-Asad assumed power. Bashar recently hinted at freedom for political parties. Reports circulated that parties not based on ethnicity, religion, or subnational allegiances will have a license to participate in the political process.

These reports were partly fueled by the fact that al-Asad's regime has intently courted the Syrian Social Nationalist Party (SSNP). Founded in Beirut in 1932 by the Greek Orthodox Antoun Saade, the radical, secular SSNP called for the reunification of Greater Syria (Syria, Lebanon, Palestine, Iraq, and Jordan, with Cyprus later added to the list). It became popular among the intelligentsia and college students, especially at the American University of Beirut. Syria outlawed the SSNP in 1955, after it was implicated in the assassination of Adnan al-Malki, an influential military figure.

The party gradually reorganized during the last two decades of Hafiz al-Asad's rule.

The SSNP's commitment to Greater Syria dovetailed with al-Asad's desire to project his regional power. Significantly, the party supported Syria's hegemony in Lebanon. In April 2005, Bashar al-Asad allowed the SSNP to join the PNF.[7] Coming barely more than a month before the Ba'th Party Congress, this decision implied that socialism was no longer the basis for PNF membership. Furthermore, al-Asad's decision lent credence to reports that the Ba'th Party would drop socialism from its official name and that the pan-Arab National Command would be dismantled.

The Ba'th Congress was both disappointing and consequential. On the one hand, though President al-Asad focused on the need for economic reforms and combating terrorism, none of the demands and expectations of the reformers had been satisfied.[8] On the contrary, President al-Asad affirmed the dominant role of the Ba'th party, highlighting its pan-Arab credentials. The underlying message, meant no less for Damascus than Washington, was that the Ba'th remained the vanguard party in society as well as the protector of Arab nationalism. He stated:

> The Ba'ath did not invent the idea of pan-Arabism in society, rather the Ba'ath came about as a natural result of a society imbued with all the elements of Arab nationalism. This nationalism, accused by some of chauvinism and racism, is made up of a human civilization capable of absorbing all the cultures, ethnicities, and spiritual affiliations which have formed this society for thousands of years, and consequently it is the foundation of the development and stability of this society. As long as this national existence is part of the reality of this society, the role of the Ba'ath will remain essential.[9]

The only thing that was changed about the Ba'th was al-Asad's emphasis on and substitution of justice and development for socialism. Ironically, at the same time reformers had been aspiring for significant changes, the Syrian government clamped down on civil society leaders and opposition members. On the eve of the Ba'th congress, Syrian authorities, represented by the Political Security Directorate, headed by Muhammad Mansoura, arrested Ali al-Abdullah, a human rights activist, for reading a letter written by the exiled superintendent of the Muslim Brotherhood, Ali Sadr al-Din al-Bayanouni, during a meeting held by the Atasi Forum. A week later, on May 24, the authorities arrested the members of the Atasi Forum, including Atasi family member Souhair, and subsequently closed the Forum.[10] Unlike other such clubs, the regime had not closed the Atasi Forum, which had been active in the Syrian reform movement. Meanwhile, the authorities arrested Mohammad

Ra'dun, head of the Arab Organization for Human Rights–Syria and six Syrians on charges of belonging to the outlawed Muslim Brotherhood and allegedly assassinated Sheikh Muhammad al-Khaznawi, a Kurd and a prominent religious leader who had been critical of the regime and had spoken for Kurdish political rights. Importantly, Sheikh Khaznawi met with leaders of Syria's Muslim Brotherhood in Brussels in February, signaling a possible collusion between the Kurds and the Islamists.[11] Apparently, the regime has been concerned about a possible rapprochement between the Muslim Brotherhood and some dissidents, which could gather momentum under certain circumstances. In this respect, the Muslim Brotherhood has been trying to ingratiate itself with the Kurds and the reform movement by issuing statements supporting their causes. Meanwhile, the Brotherhood issued a statement in the wake of the Ba'th Congress asserting the "necessity of total and fundamental change" in Syria. Significantly, the statement emphasized that "the Syrian regime in its current structure is unable to reform."[12]

The Ba'th Congress concluded by issuing mere policy recommendations on political and economic reform. Among the important recommendations that would be considered were issuing a law for political parties based on strengthening national unity, reviewing martial law by limiting it to national security crimes, and addressing Kurdish grievances by granting Syrian citizenship to no less than 200,000 Kurds who are permanent citizens.[13]

On the other hand, the Congress was consequential because it smoothed the way for Bashar to continue the transition of power, replacing the old guard with loyal, less ideological, more pragmatic party members with an interest in gradual reform who shared his outlook. Since his assumption of power, Bashar has been trying to introduce fresh faces into the government while at the same time widening his base of support. This gathered momentum following both the September 11 terror attacks and the invasion of Iraq. Though he retained influential figures from his father's inner circle, he tapped onto some government positions new faces not necessarily affiliated with the Ba'th party. As Flynt Leverett perceptively observed, "the new president has sought to develop an alternative network of advisers to help him make sense of the new circumstances and develop appropriate policy responses."[14] President al-Asad brought into this network Walid al-Mu'allim, former Syrian ambassador to Washington, appointing him deputy foreign minister and giving him the Lebanese file; Bouthaina Shaaban, a former senior official at the Foreign Ministry, naming her minister of expatriates; and Imad Mustafa, former professor of computer science at

Damascus University, making him Syria's ambassador in Washington. Other figures brought into this inner circle included Iyad Ghazal, appointed head of the Syrian Railway Authority, and Sami al-Khiami, appointed as Syria's ambassador to the United Kingdom.[15] Admittedly, this network has no power base.

The transition, however, was more marked in the country's informal structure, where the country's levers of power remained in the hands of Alawi officials. Before the Congress, Bashar's brother, Maher, has emerged as the strong man of the Republican Guards, whose main function is to protect the presidential palace and the capital. Ghazi Kanaan, former chief of intelligence in Lebanon and confidant of Bashar's father, was appointed minister of the interior in October 2004. Kanaan developed a reputation for his shrewd manner and brutal tactics, though he has come to advocate gradual reform. In February, Bashar's brother-in-law, Asef Shawqat, was appointed chief of military intelligence; he is considered a hard-liner. Bahjat Suleiman, another hard-liner, headed until recently the internal security division of the General Intelligence Directorate, and his influence surpassed that of organization then-chief Hisham Bakhtiar. (It should be noted that, according to the rumor mill in Damascus and Beirut, Maher, Shawqat, and Suleiman supported the assassination of former Lebanese prime minister Rafiq Hariri while Bashar and Kanaan opposed it.) General Muhammad Mansoura replaced Kanaan as head of the Political Security Directorate, and his power is reportedly on the rise. General Zoul Himma Chaliche, Bashar's cousin, is in charge of protecting the president. General Ali Habib replaced Hassan Turkmani as chief of staff in May 2004, while Turkmani replaced Mustafa Tlas as defense minister.[16] All of these officials, with the exception of Turkmani, are Alawis with tribal and/or familial connection to Bashar (as his last name connotes, Turkmani is a Turkman). The only Sunni official with significant power was Vice-President Abd al-Halim Khaddam, whose hard-line policies are infamous.

Changing Guards: From "Old" to "New" Hard-liners

The debacle in Lebanon coupled with the mounting pressure against Syria apparently played into Asad's hands against the old guard in the Congress. As a result, nearly all the old-timers in the regime were led to retirement. Among those retired were Vice-Presidents Abd al-Halim Khaddam and Muhammad Zuheir Mashariqa, former Prime Minister Muhammad Mustafa Miro, former Defense Minister Mustafa Tlas, former Speaker of Parliament Abd al-Qader Qaddura, the two former assistant secretary generals of the Ba'th party, Abdullah al-Ahmar and Suleiman Qaddah, former chief of staff Ali Aslan, former director of Military Intelligence Hassan Khalil, and former director of Political Security Adnan Bader Hassan. At the same time, the membership in the Ba'th party Regional Command Council (RCC) was reduced from 21 to 14. Eight new members were inducted into the RCC. RCC members whose membership was renewed included President al-Asad as Secretary General, Speaker of People's Assembly Mahmoud al-Abrash, Prime Minister Muhammad Naji Otri, head of National Security Bureau Muhammad Said Bakhtian, Foreign Minister Farouq al-Shara, and Finance Minister Muhammad Hussein. The new members included Defense Minister General Hassan Turkmani, Director of General Intelligence Directorate Hisham Bakhtiar, Director of the Presidential Palace Studies Bureau Haitham Sataihi, Governor of Aleppo Osama Adi, President of Ba'th University in Homs Yasser Hourieh, President of Ba'th Party Branch in Suweida Bassam Janbieh, Governor of Edleb Said Elia, and Member of Ba'th Party Branch Command in Deir al-Zur Shahnaz Fakoush.[17]

This shake-up culminated a week later in important changes in the structure of the leadership of Syrian security forces. Bahjat Suleiman, chief of internal security in the General Intelligence Directorate, was transferred from his post to general headquarters. In his place, President al-Asad appointed Brigadier General Fouad Nassif, head of the technical branch in Military Intelligence. Nassif is the son of Muhammad Nassif, a former intelligence chief and a leading figure in the Alawite Kheir Beyk clan, who remains close to the regime's inner core. Brigadier General Ali Mamlouk, deputy director of Air Force Intelligence, replaced Brigadier General Hisham Bakhtiar. Bakhtiar was elevated to a top level post as head of a newly setup national security bureau within the Ba'th party. Brigadier General Hassan Khallouf, head of the Palestine branch in Military Intelligence, was appointed deputy director of General Intelligence Directorate. Brigadier General Said Samour, head of the region's branch in Military Intelligence, was appointed deputy director of Military Intelligence, which is led by Bashar's brother-in-law Brigadier General Asef Shawqat.[18]

On the surface, the Ba'th Congress was a show of solidarity and strength directed against the opposition and the West, mainly the United States. Yet, it signaled the intention of President Bashar to gradually reform while at the same time consolidate his power. In fact, it is safe to argue that the Ba'th Congress was about two mutually inclusive policies. It attempted to lay the ground for uniting a broad spectrum of Syrians to fend off American pressure. Al-Asad also hopes to prevent the creation of a U.S.-supported opposition like Ahmed Chalabi's Iraqi National Congress. In this respect, al-Asad is trying to create a pluralistic nationalist political front that can satisfy some demands for political and economic reform without endangering his rule. The opposition parties most likely to be tolerated have in common a nationalistic outlook and a general antipathy toward the West, especially the United States. The SSNP could become the second-most-popular party after the Ba'th.

On the other hand, the Congress was about further separating the Ba'th Party from the state, while at the same time continuing to rejuvenate Ba'thism, by replacing the old guard with less ideological, more pragmatic party members sharing al-Asad's outlook and having an interest in reform. This coincided with al-Asad's attempt at restoring public confidence in the party and state. It is within this context that changes in the structure of the leadership of Syrian security apparatus had taken place and that the RCC was purged of senior political figures, who were replaced by younger al-Asad loyalists. These moves fit the pattern by which al-Asad has been consolidating his power. At the same time, they also complement al-Asad's attempts to open up the public sector by pursuing a kind of soft privatization and introducing gradual economic reforms to integrate Syria into the global economy.

On a closer examination, however, the changes introduced in the Congress and in its aftermath suggest harsh realities for the future of Syria, its civil society reform movement, and its relationship with the United States. Maintaining the old power structure created by the late al-Asad, Bashar has continued to rely on the country's informal levels of power held disproportionately by Alawi officials. Whereas before the Congress President al-Asad had attempted to solidify his rule by closing ranks with the top leaders of his regime, many of whom had been old guard and hard-liners, the changes introduced at the Congress and in its aftermath show that President al-Asad has rallied those closest to him (or those he thinks he can trust) to further consolidate his rule. The corollary of this, as perceptively observed by Michael Young, is that "the president does not seem to be widening his power base, but narrowing it. He appears to be falling back on those he can trust the most...both within his family and the Alawite community, which leads to two plausible conclusions not mutually exclusive: Assad is accumulating power to impose controlled change in Syria; he is also doing so to guard against what he perceives as growing domestic threats, suggesting democratization is no way a priority."[19] In this respect, it is no idle speculation that the regime would deal with the merchant class in the same manner it has dealt with the reform movement if the former appears to threaten the security of the regime. So far, generally speaking, the Damascene merchant class has been circumspect about criticizing the regime, recognizing that its interests are for the most part meshed with those of the Alawi barons. In addition, it is true that this class is interested in reform and at times has been vocal about improving Syria's economic conditions; yet it is more concerned about stability than unchecked political and economic changes.

In fact, the conditions under which the leaders of Syria's civil society were arrested and the prominent Kurd allegedly assassinated by the Syrian security apparatus underscore that the regime has marked a red line for reformers that they should not cooperate with the Muslim Brotherhood or with Western institutions and governments, especially the United States. Given that these actions, including those that allegedly brought about the debacle in Lebanon, were not carried out by the old guard, it is not unlikely that the new guard may actually be tougher than the old guard in securing the regime's realm. It follows from this that the smooth transition of power from the old to the young guard derived more from a bargain than an internal clash with the old guard to maintain the power structure under which they protect their vested interests. It stands to reason then that the commitment of President al-Asad to the inviolability of the Ba'th party at the Congress was part of that bargain.

Under these conditions, Syria's civil society reform movement can expect little, if any, from the regime at the time being. Political reforms are simply not a priority. Admittedly, all the decisions and changes introduced at the Congress have been part of the regime's efforts to secure its rule and protect its entrenched interests, thereby effectively undermining U.S. efforts to promote democracy in the region. Correspondingly, unless President al-Asad weans himself from the political elite and curtails their vested interests pervading the whole system, Syria is set to clash with the United States over the future of the Middle East. In this respect, Syria's withdrawal from Lebanon was doubly proved to be only a tactical retreat.

Conclusion

Building on the themes of his second inaugural address, in which he emphasized the country's generational commitment to the advance of freedom, especially in the Middle East, President Bush laid out his vision and plan of action for his second term in the State of the Union Address:

> The only force powerful enough to stop the rise of tyranny and terror, and replace hatred with hope, is the force of human freedom....Our aim is to build and preserve a community of free and independent nations, with governments that answer to their citizens, and reflect their own cultures....To promote peace and stability in the broader Middle East, the United States will work with our friends in the region to fight the common threat of terror, while we encourage a higher standard of freedom....To promote peace in the broader Middle East, we must confront regimes that continue to harbor terrorists and pursue weapons of mass murder. Syria still allows its territory, and parts of Lebanon, to be used by terrorists who seek to destroy every chance of peace in the region. You have passed, and we are applying, the Syrian Accountability Act, and we expect the Syrian government to end all support for terror and open the door to freedom.[1]

Syria found itself, unlike in other seminal speeches, specifically mentioned in President Bush's state of the union address. This unequivocally reflected the Bush administration's seriousness with Syria. If Damascus does not change its behavior and reorient its policies, a U.S.-Syrian collision on Iraq, Lebanon, terrorism, weapons of mass destruction, and the peace process may be inevitable. Gripped by myriad problems and an ongoing insurgency in Iraq, Washington may have tied its hands but not to the point of depriving itself of options against Syria. In fact, some neoconservatives have been blunt in underscoring that Washington still has real options against Syria in light of Damascus's intransigence and Iraq's insurgency. Writing in the *Weekly Standard,* William Kristol asserted:

> We have tried sweet talk (on Secretary Powell's trip to Damascus in May 2003) and tough talk (on the visit three months ago by Assistant Secretary of Defense Peter Rodman and Brigadier General Mark Kimmitt). Talk has failed. Syria is a weak country with a weak regime. We now need to take action to punish and deter Assad's regime. It would be good, of course, if Rumsfeld had increased the size and strength of our army so that we now had more options. He didn't, and we must use the assets we have. Still, real options exist. We could bomb Syrian military facilities; we could go across the border in force to stop infiltration; we could occupy the town of Abu Kamal in eastern Syria, a few miles from the border, which seems to be the planning and organizing center for Syrian activities in Iraq; we could covertly help or overtly support the Syrian opposition (pro-human rights demonstrators recently tried to take to the streets of Damascus to protest the regime's abuses). This hardly exhausts all the possible forms of pressure and coercion. But it's time to get serious about dealing with Syria as part of winning in Iraq, and in the broader Middle East.[2]

No doubt, as I noted earlier, Washington needs to articulate a Syrian strategy. But, absent a strategy, any action by Washington entailing dire consequences for the Syrian government could easily backfire precisely because Syria is a weak country with a weak regime. As I have tried to show, the notion that the opposition and/or reformers in Syria would support any campaign by Washington against Syria is a fallacy. In fact, the Muslim Brothers, who pose the most serious threat to the Syrian regime, are at one with the regime against Washington. While denying any contact between his movement and the Syrian government, Ali Sadr al-Din al-Bianouni, the superintendent of the Muslim Brotherhood asserted that "we always stand by our country against any foreign threat."[3]

On the other hand, Syrian reformers have articulated their demands of reform, as illustrated in their manifestos and statements, in nationalist terms. True, they have referred to the regional threats facing Syria, including that from Washington, to prod the regime to undertake reform; still, they have insisted on pressuring the government on their own without U.S. help to carry out reforms. Significantly, reformers (and/or dissidents) have not created a united front facing the regime, though reports about forming a broad opposition front, including the Muslim Brotherhood, have been circulating in Damascus.[4] Nor have they formulated a political agenda earning the support of the Syrian people across the country's political spectrum. This is not to say that opposition outside Syria, mainly Farid Ghadry's U.S.-based Reform Party of Syria, would not have an impact on the reform movement. In fact, Syrian dissidents have had mixed reactions to Ghadry's open identification with the Bush administration. In March 2005, Deputy Assistant Secretary of State for Near Eastern Affairs Elizabeth Cheney held a meeting with Ghadry's group, who also had audiences with European governments. Some, like human rights activist Anwar Bunni, had no objection to the meeting. Bunni remarked: "I'm in favor of any effort to halt human rights violations."[5] But a majority of leading reformers, including Michel Kilo, expressed strong opposition. Kilo stressed: "We're struggling for democracy in Syria to make our country stronger in the face of the U.S. threat, not so that it is torn apart by the Americans."[6]

One could further argue that, although the Ba'th party has been robbed from its ideological reason d'être by none other than the Syrian leadership itself, Arab nationalism is still deeply rooted in Syria. The sheer weight of history on Syria, the country best known as the cradle of Arab nationalism, cannot be disregarded. Consequently, any severe action against Syria not only could undermine the reform movement in the country but also could rally most social forces around the government, bearing in mind that their defense of Syria does not mean support for the regime. This begs the question about the day after in Syria in case the regime collapsed as a result of an American campaign. It is safe to argue that the situation in Syria would be far worse than that in Iraq. Defending Syria against foreign influence, occupation, or control would bring the nationalists and the Islamists together into one common cause. Bearing in mind that Islamists have had a history of political activism in Syria and that the ideational base out of which Arab nationalism grew had its earliest expressions articulated by Muslim activists, it would not be unimaginable that religion would emerge as a political ideology enforcing at one and the same time nationalist and Islamist activism, potentially leading to a symbiotic religiopolitical ideology with a focus on defending Syria. It follows from this that the accusations against the regime of encouraging Islamic revival are not baseless. In fact, after crushing the Muslim Brotherhood insurrection in 1982, the regime has pursued a policy to bolster its Muslim credentials by encouraging a moderate form of Islam through supporting regime-friendly clerics, such as the deputy Muhammad Habash, the Aleppo-based preacher Muhammad Kamil al-Husseini, and the new Grand Mufti Ahmad Hassoun, and the building of many mosques and religious schools.[7] The secular Ba'thi regime of Syria understandably recognizes that the Islamists are its natural allies against their common enemy: the United States. But this poses a double-edged sword for Syria. Syria's secular society has been

growing more conservative thanks, paradoxically, in no small measure to the Syrian government. Ibrahim Hamidi explained that
"there are only two pulpits in the cities and the countryside: the
mosque and government-run cultural centers and media. The
public, therefore, was offered a simple choice: Islam or the official
ideology. Youths began turning en masse to religious schools and
mosques, both as a reaction against official policies and as a means
of coming to grips with the economic and social problems besetting
them."[8] As a result, young conservatives are believing that "Islam
is the alternative," and some of them are reportedly joining funda-
mentalist movements. In fact, Syrian authorities have recently
claimed to dismantle a "terrorist cell" affiliated with the Organization of Damascus Army for Jihad and Unification. This organization, according to the authorities, has been planning to carry out
acts of terror throughout Syria to destabilize the country. The
authorities added that the organization has significant literature
and is well organized.[9]

While it is difficult to gauge the extent and depth of conservatism
in Syria, the Iraqi experience suggests a very likely widespread conservatism, potentially laying the ground for Islamic activism. In
1992, in an attempt to bolster his Islamic credentials and legitimize
his regime following the Gulf War (1990–1991), Saddam Hussein
launched the faith campaign (al-Hamla al-Imaniyah). He encouraged the building of mosques and religious schools. The extent of
conservatism in Iraq had been surprisingly felt by the tenacity of
the ongoing insurgency, which without public support would have
withered.

Syria, for its part, is cognizant of the potential collision with the
United States. Besides trying to entrench its position in Syria and
Lebanon to better control domestic affairs there, it has been
attempting to enhance its regional standing. Recognizing that Arab
countries are pursuing and advancing their national interests
ahead of Arab national interests, Damascus has been trying, on
the one hand, to strengthen its "proxy" defenses by reinforcing its
strategic cooperation with Iran. One aspect of this cooperation has
been Syria's support of Hizbollah as a resistance movement. In addition to allowing Hizbollah to maintain an arsenal of thousands of
Katyousha rockets, Syria indirectly enhanced Hizbollah's military
capabilities by permitting the nonstate actor to obtain, most likely
from Iran, an unmanned air vehicle (UAV). Indeed, Hizbollah
claimed that a drone, named Mirsad-1 (Arabic for Observer) crossed
into "occupied northern Palestine, flying over several Zionist settlements, reaching the coastal settlement of Nahariya (9 kilometers
south of the border) and returning safely to its base."[10] The Israeli

military confirmed a drone had entered Israeli airspace and returned to Lebanon. Significantly, Hizbollah Secretary General Hassan Nasrallah emphasized that the "resistance was working to impose a new equilibrium to confront airspace violations [by Israel]."[11] Furthermore, he indirectly connected Resolution 1559 with the launching of the drone. Without mincing his words, he lashed out at Israel and the United States by asserting that the resolution "includes all Zionist demands but in a UN mask propped by American support...and that Mirsad-1 does not only reach Nahariya but also the deep depth [of Israel]."[12] The underlying message has double meanings. By fighting Israel by proxy, Syria could reach the depth of Israel and any attack on Syria by Israel on the behest of the United States could inflame the Israel-Lebanon border and consequently provoke a regional war. At the same time, Syria's regional role is irreducible and essential.

Significantly, amid rising tensions over the assassination of former Lebanese Prime Minister Rafiq Hariri in February 2005, for which the Syrians were blamed, Secretary of State Condoleezza Rice called on U.S. Ambassador Margaret Scobey to return home from Syria. Simultaneously, the Bush administration condemned the murder and insisted that Syria comply with U.N. Resolution 1559. Apparently, in response to growing U.S. pressure on Damascus, Syrian Prime Minister Muhammad Naji Otri traveled to Tehran. Speaking to reporters, Otri stated that "Damascus and Tehran, both facing intense US pressure, should form a 'united front' against threats from abroad."[13] The underlying assumption of Hariri's assassination and Otri's visit to Tehran was that the Syrian regime would not shy from crossing the rubicon of using terrorism as a means to protect its survival and create havoc in its wake if threatened by defeat. Paradoxically, the swiftness with which Syria's authority has eroded in Lebanon reflected Damascus's growing siege mentality and limits.

On the other hand, Syria has been trying to improve its relations with regional countries mainly to mobilize Arab and Muslim support against any U.S. campaign against Syria and to deprive Washington from regional allies, mainly Turkey, that could serve as a launch pad for a U.S. campaign. Arab leaders have been vocal about opposing American campaigns against any Arab country, let alone Syria. After all, the Arab league opposed the U.S. invasion of Iraq. Most important, Damascus has been making a constant effort to improve its relationship with Ankara. The speedy and impressive rapprochement between the two countries was crowned by the official visit of President al-Asad and his wife to Turkey in January 2005, the first of its kind by a Syrian president. The visit heralded a new era of cooperation on issues of common concerns including trade, security, and the significant Iraq and Kurdish question. Turkish officials warmly welcomed al-Asad and his wife, affirming the potential of the new era. Turkish newspapers, reflecting the mood of the nation, described Syria as "now an ally" and the relationship between the two countries as a "partnership for peace and stability."[14] This stands in sharp contrast to the tense atmosphere between the two countries that almost brought them to war in 1998.

Significantly, al-Asad silently took the initiative to officially drop his country's claim on Hatay after nearly 70 years of resisting to recognize Turkish sovereignty over the province.[15] This important step came in the wake of no less important measures taken by Syria. Following the terrorist bombings in Istanbul in November 2003, Turkey asked Syria to extradite two suspects. The Syrians promptly handed over 22 Turks who were receiving religious education in Damascus, including the two suspects.

Obviously, the swiftness with which this rapprochement is moving indicates that the two countries have more shared views on the Middle East and especially on Iraq than differences.[16] Insofar as this rapprochement is no guarantee of Turkish support of Syria in the event Washington decided to take certain actions against Damascus, it makes it extremely difficult for Ankara to support Washington.

Meanwhile, in line with its strategy to enhance its regional standing, Damascus has sought to widen its international base of support. Besides undertaking a shuttle diplomacy that took him to some European capitals, al-Asad made historic visits to China and Russia, the two permanent members of the U.N. Security Council. In June 2004, he traveled to Beijing to hold political and economic talks with the Chinese leadership. Al-Asad described his visit as "historic in its contents, for Chinese attitudes toward Arab and Syrian national matters and Syrian attitudes toward Chinese national matters have not changed since the two countries began their diplomatic relations in 1956."[17] Emphasizing China's important role in the peace process in the Middle East, al-Asad affirmed that his political talks with the Chinese leadership "revolved around the disturbing and transitional political situation the world is witnessing, while his economic talks centered on improving Syrian-Chinese trade relations, as well as drawing lessons from China's experiences."[18]

In much the same vein, al-Asad traveled to Moscow in late January 2005 to encourage the Russian leadership to reclaim lost regional influence after the collapse of the Soviet Union. Moscow cultivated ties with Damascus during the Cold War, shoring up the country as a counterbalance to the influence of the U.S.-backed Israel. Moscow today has been defending Syria against U.S. and Israeli charges of ties to terrorism. Al-Asad asserted that he was seeking a new path for peace in the Middle East, telling the Russian Izvestia daily that "Russia is a great power, and it carries great responsibilities for world affairs."[19] Meeting with Moscow students, al-Asad called on Russia to play an active role in global politics. He emphasized that "Russia's role is huge and Russia is well respected by third-world countries....These countries are really hoping that Russia will try to revive its lost positions in the world."[20] Al-Asad also focused his talks with the Russian leadership on the mounting crisis surrounding Iran's nuclear power plant, which Russia is helping Iran construct and which is a growing concern for Washington and Israel.

While denying concluding any arms deal with Damascus in light of U.S. and Israeli concerns, Moscow, already at odds with Washington over nuclear ties with Iran, emphasized its concerns over Washington's stance on Syria. Commenting on the rising tension between the United States and Syria and on U.S. accusations regarding Syria's support of the insurgency in Iraq, Foreign Minister Sergei Lavrov stated that "We are concerned with the recent situation around Syria....The language of threats can make the situation only worse....If any concerns (about Syria) remain, they should be backed by concrete evidence and removed through talks."[21] On the other hand, Moscow has joined the international chorus calling for Syria to withdraw from Lebanon. In a sign that Moscow has decided to revive its influence in the Middle East and to upgrade its relationship with Syria, Moscow wrote off 73 percent—$9.8 billion—of Syria's Soviet-era's debts.

Paralleling these Syrian efforts, Damascus has from time to time expressed its desire for resuming the peace process. Following the collapse of the Clinton-Asad summit, Syria, at an Arab summit convened in Beirut on March 27–28, joined other Arab countries in endorsing a peace initiative by Saudi Arabia's Crown Prince Abdullah involving "full Israeli withdrawal from Arab territories occupied since 1967 in return for normal relations with Israel in the context of comprehensive peace."[22]

But feeling sidetracked by the peace plan known as the Road Map, which was officially coordinated by the "Quartet" (the United States, United Nations, European Union, and Russia) and introduced in April 2003, the Syrian government dismissed it as a "Palestinian-Israeli affair." Even President al-Asad went further and stated that "the road map was stillborn."[23] Yet, in an interview with the *New York Times* on December 1, 2003, President al-Asad expressed his desire to resume the peace process, only to feel shunned by the Bush administration because it ignored his desire.[24] Apparently, notwithstanding the Bush administration's deteriorating relations with Syria, the administration was more concerned with Iraq and the Palestinian-Israeli conflict. Then in a meeting with the U.N. Middle East envoy Terje Roed-Larsen, President al-Asad expressed his readiness to reopen peace negotiations with Israel "without conditions."[25] But this time Israel was quick in dismissing the offer as a move designed to alleviate pressure from the United States. A senior foreign ministry official told Agence France Presse that this offer "seems to be a propaganda maneuver by the Syrian side....The Syrians are reacting because they have their backs to the wall after the (U.S.) sanctions and the U.N. vote on Lebanon."[26] Interestingly enough, after Egypt backed Syria's offer and affirmed that Damascus was ready to resume negotiations without prior conditions, the Syrian regime through its mouthpiece Syrian Arabic News Agency (SANA) stressed "Syria's firm stance vis-à-vis the resumption of the peace negotiations and building on what had been achieved."[27]

Commenting on Sharon's government stance on Syria's offer, Asher Susser, director of the Moshe Dayan Center at Tel Aviv University, perceptively stated that "whether or not the Syrian peace offer is a maneuver, Israelis are nowhere near ready to resume negotiations with the Syrians with the political and security situation in the West Bank and Gaza still unnerving and unresolved."[28]

But if Syria's overtures of peace, along with its regional efforts, could be considered as maneuvers to deflect U.S. pressure, the Syrian regime's acerbic verbal attack on the Bush administration by depicting it as a warmonger feeding itself on victimizing Arabs and by questioning its very intentions and morality could be interpreted as an ominous Syrian effort to provoke a clash of civilization between the Arabs and Americans in the interest of Syria's regime survival. This cultural onslaught has been led by none other than the articulate Syrian minister for expatriate affairs, Bouthaina Shaaban. Complementing President al-Asad's nationalist discourse (see Chapter 8), Shaaban elaborated in Beirut's *Daily Star:*

> Thoughtful observation of events in Palestine and Iraq show that the real issue is not one of faulty information sources, because US intelligence and the US administration are not that naïve. Neither is it a failure in media courage and verifying fact, because the US media apparatuses are not that feeble. The issue is deeper and more dangerous than this. It is a phenomena where Western anti-Semitism is transforming from its conventional form into a new one, where in the 21st century the Arabs have been

officially chosen as the new victim, one country after the other, one people after the other—falling victims to hatred, killing, ethnic cleansing, torture, and massacres under the pretext of a multitude of reasons and justifications, including terrorism. They are not much different from the pretexts used in the past, and cannot conceal from the observant researcher that at their very essence they are but different expressions of anti-Arabism and hostility to Arab culture and existence.

It has been proved to all that exercising torture in Iraqi jails is not an individual isolated case. Nor are those responsible just a few. Rather it is a policy in which everyone is involved, and where everyone has taken a part in covering up, denying it as a war crime, and hiding other sides of it, such as the destiny of thousands of prisoners whose names were not registered, and whose bodies were buried in hidden graves. Such policy arises from a racist, condescending view of Arabs, and therefore does not consider Iraqis as human beings equal in feelings, comprehension and sensitivity to Westerners. There is no doubt that those who prepared and misled their people to wage a war of eradication against Iraq are the same people who believe in that racist view towards Arabs and are waging a war of eradication against Palestinians, and supervising the persecution methods secreted by the neo-anti-Semitism in its campaign against Arabs....In the same line of thought falls the US president, administration, and war generals' denials of the war crimes being committed. This includes Bush's continuous justification of Israeli crimes against Palestinian children and the demolishing of Palestinian houses being described as an act of "self-defense." All of this...are nothing but part of a mentality and a policy of a neo-anti-Semitism targeting Arabs. It is a mentality and a policy that is waging a war of elimination, committing massacres, torture, rape and punishments in Palestine and Iraq systematically and in harmony with this new campaign of hatred.[29]

It follows from this logic that the torture of Iraqi prisoners at Abu Ghraib, or other examples of American abuses against Arabs, was a mere consequence of the systematic neo-anti-Semitism permeating the U.S. administration and the armed forces. Notwithstanding the distortion of the use of the term anti-Semitism, its new definition implies that the West in general and the United States in particular have made of the Arabs the persecuted Jews of today. Correspondingly, the assumption is that the elimination of the Arabs and of their culture is sanctioned. This new phenomenon is ominously finding its way into the public discourse in Arab societies, and by implication into the collective consciousness of the Arabs. This phenomenon has serious implications for the world at large, virtually making a clash of civilizations between the Muslim world and the West a self-fulfilling prophecy.[30]

What lies at the heart of the effort of Arab regimes to propagate the notion of neo-anti-Semitism is a calculated attempt to find both a new fig leaf behind which to hide the more sordid aspects of their autocratic rule and a new pretext to secure this rule in a world where extremism has been fed by the whip of their oppression and the lack of public space in their societies. Not surprisingly, these same Arab regimes have been intimidating and imprisoning Arab reformers while also advancing an Arab version of democracy, or what passes for democracy, that contrasts with that in the West. Consequently, the concept of neo-anti-Semitism disingenuously provokes the Arab sense of victimization as an excuse for Arab shortcomings, further exacerbating frustrations in the Middle East, even as the regimes in the region avoid dealing with their deeper causes.

In much the same vein, as long as autocrats determine public space in the Arab world, and as long as Islamists dominate Arab political discourse, reform will, paradoxically, be used to increase the longevity of oppressive rule. Arab rulers have often created a facade of reform to appease the West, but also to hijack the agenda of reformers. Whether in Syria, Tunisia, Egypt, or Saudi Arabia, the pattern is a similar one in that the core demands of reformers —full participation and representation in political systems, ending stifling states of emergency, putting term limits on those holding office—are largely ignored by regimes. Arab rulers are both the judge and jury for deciding the extent and scope of change.

In the name of "security," mainly on account of the Arab-Israeli conflict, they erase public space; in the name of "civility," to satisfy Islamic fundamentalists, they deny full participation and representation in society. In fact, many Arab rulers not only keep reformers weak vis-à-vis the state, but to enhance their Muslim credentials and, therefore, increase their waning legitimacy, they also indirectly align themselves with Islamists.

By so doing, Arab leaders have also given Islamists much more leeway to chip away at relations with the United States and its encouragement of regional reform. For example, in November 2004 a group of Saudi religious scholars asserted that jihad, or holy war, did not qualify as terrorism. They called on Iraqis to support militants waging holy war against the U.S.-led occupation.[31] The same month, the Lebanese Shi'ite cleric, Muhammad Hussein Fadlallah, stated that "President Bush's crusade against Islam had only stopped in theory but not in practice...the U.S.-led war on terror is, in reality, a war against Islam and Muslims around the world."[32]

Such sentiments were ominously echoed by none other than Shaaban who wrote about Western efforts to spur reform: "[W]e witness today calls for democracy and freedom which try to divide the region into ethnicities, tribes, sects and sub-sects under the name of freedom and autonomy. In the process trees, archaeology museums, universities and water are prime but unannounced victims that are scarcely if ever mentioned; besides, of course, thousands of innocent men, women and children who are brutally murdered."[33]

The Palestinian issue has also been an obstacle to change, in that Arab regimes have insisted it be resolved before serious progress can be made on reform. For example, at the end of the 2004 Rabat conference, which brought together G8 and Arab ministers to help promote political and economic modernization and reform, Arab representatives insisted that the final communique include a clause stating that "reform in the region will go hand in hand with support for a just, comprehensive and lasting settlement to the Arab-Israeli conflict."[34] In effect, this seemed little more than a means of postponing change until a future deadline whose timing looks, at best, uncertain today.

Significantly, fending off the impact of change in the Middle East wrought by American efforts to promote democracy there, especially following Iraq's first free elections since 1954 which resonated across the Arab world, the Syrian regime (as illustrated by Shaaban) has been trying to make Washington's efforts to help the Arab world reform synonymous with barbaric acts inflicted on Arabs. Not surprisingly, the Syrian regime has not institutionalized the agenda of reformers. Neither did it delegitimize radical Islam in Iraq nor outlaw the encouragement of violence there.

When all is said and done, Washington and Damascus are on a collision course in the Middle East, with the former pursuing its national strategic interest and the latter trying to survive domestic and regional challenges. However, whereas Washington is trying to generate the momentum for freedom and democracy in the Middle East, Damascus is trying to maintain the security regime that has stifled Arab aspirations and potentials. This is taking place in a region whose status quo has been shattered. More specifically, Syria is operating in an area where Arab power or Arab capacity to influence regional events, including dictating Arab agenda in the Middle East, has been reduced to insignificance. The collapse of the Ba'thi regime of Saddam Hussein all but crumbled the much vaunted but fragmented fertile crescent power base (Syria and Iraq), the birthplace of strident Arab nationalism as illustrated by the Ba'th party. Syria's attempts at shoring up its regional power set in sharp relief the emergence of non-Arab powers in the Middle East, represented by Turkey, Iran, and Israel, each of which could influence the region more than any other Arab country. Add to that the influence of the United States in the region, and Syria's regional role appears all but dissipated. At the same time, with an outdated Soviet style military, a "medieval" economy and increasingly jeopardized political role in Lebanon, Syria has become a shadow of its former self. The dreaded and stern rule of "respected" Hafiz al-Asad whose personality cult fused Arab nationalism and Arab leadership qualities has given way to the rule of Bashar whose lack of a personality cult and declining legitimacy have been affected by its failure to cope with Syrian socioeconomic and political aspirations and challenges. Needless to say, Syria, like most other Arab countries, is facing serious economic, social, and political problems, while at the same time witnessing an explosion of population growth.[35] Similarly, neither is Bashar nor Mikhail Gorbachev ready to introduce a *perestroika and glasnost,* which could unseat his power. Most important, the pattern with which Bashar has been reshuffling his government indicates that the locus of power in Syria remains fluid, further obscuring the process of decision-making in Syria. Decisions are taken behind closed doors with no mere consideration to explain the rationale behind them to the Syrian people. But as Ammar Abdulhammid perceptively observed: "After all these years, one thing is clear: In times of crises, or when it comes to decisions of major significance, Syria's top leaders, for whatever reason, tend to side with the hardliners. Thus, they bear the greatest share of responsibility for Syria's present condition."[36] It is no idle speculation that Bashar's attempts at solidifying his rule are paradoxically entrapping him with the determination of the military and security barons to protect their entrenched interests and thus the status quo.[37]

One could argue that the efforts of the Syrian leadership to confront U.S. plans in the region, which are inseparable from the regime's attempts to survive domestic and regional challenges, are the last sigh of the all but presumed dead Syrian regime. The recent changes in the region, especially in Iraq and Lebanon, and the advent of technology into Syria have breached the walls of the prison Hafiz al-Asad had turned Syria into. The sooner it realizes its terminal disease, the better chances it has to create a new structure of government by which it could safeguard some of its privileges. For example, a Turkey-like form of government is an option acceptable to many Syrians. But a word of caution here is in place. Hastening the death of the Syrian regime is fraught with dangers. Notwithstanding the fact that a dying regime could undertake desperate actions entailing dire consequences, a severe blow in the form of a miscalculated or hubris-laden campaign against Syria could easily bring chaos and anarchy to the country, and, consequently, make Syrian soil a fertile ground for terrorism. This, undoubtedly, will defeat the very purpose of Washington's war on terrorism.

Notes

Introduction

1. Huntington, S. P. (1993, Summer). The clash of civilizations? *Foreign Affairs, 72*(3).

2. Hourani, E. (2004, November 11). Fadlallah accuses US of continuing crusade against Islam. *Daily Star.*

3. Shaaban, B. (2004, June 5). The neo-anti-Semitism of the neoconservatives. *Daily Star.*

Chapter 1: Cradle of Arab Nationalism: The Fatherland, the Ba'th, and Modern Syria under al-Asad

1. Haim, S. (1962). *Arab nationalism: An anthology* (p. 7). Berkeley: University of California Press, Ltd.

2. Tibi, B. (1990). *Arab nationalism: A critical enquiry* (2nd ed., p. 92). New York: St. Martin's Press.

3. Zeine, Z. (1958). *Arab Turkish relations and the emergence of Arab nationalism* (p. 59). Beirut: Khayat's.

4. Gibb, H. A. R. (1947). *Modern Trends in Islam* (p. 33). Chicago: The University of Chicago Press.

5. Tibi, B. (1990). *Arab nationalism: A critical enquiry* (2nd ed., p. 93). New York: St. Martin's Press.

6. Haim, S. (1962). *Arab nationalism: An anthology* (p. 21). Berkeley: University of California Press, Ltd.

7. Ibid., p. 26.

8. Tibi, B. (1990). *Arab nationalism: A critical enquiry* (2nd ed., p. 94). New York: St. Martin's Press.

9. Antonius, G. (1969). *The Arab awakening: The story of the Arab national movement* (p. 54). Beirut: Librairie du Liban.

10. Haim, S. (1962). *Arab nationalism: An anthology* (p. 81). Berkeley: University of California Press, Ltd.

11. Antonius, G. (1969). *The Arab awakening: The story of the Arab national movement* (pp. 108–120). Beirut: Librairie du Liban. Be'eri, E. (1970). *Army officers in Arab politics and society* (p. 327). New York: Praeger. For a detailed account on Arab societies see Tauber, E. (1993). *The emergence of Arab movements.* London: Frank Cass.

12. Tibi, B. (1990). *Arab nationalism: A critical enquiry* (2nd ed., p. 111). New York: St. Martin's Press.

13. Dawn, C. E. (1991). The origins of Arab nationalism. In Rashid Khalidi, Lisa Anderson, Muhammad Muslih, and Reeva S. Simon (Eds.), *The origins of Arab nationalism* (p. 56). New York: Columbia University Press. Khoury, P. S. (1983). *Urban notables and Arab nationalism* (p. 23). Cambridge: Cambridge University Press.

14. See text of Sykes-Picot Agreement in Antonius, G. (1969). *The Arab awakening: The story of the Arab national movement* (pp. 428–430). Beirut: Librairie du Liban.

15. Laqueur, W., and Rubin, B. (Eds.). (1995). *The Israel-Arab reader: A documentary history of the Middle East conflict* (5th ed., p. 16). New York: Penguin Books.

16. The Arab Office. (1976). *The future of Palestine* (p. 99). Westport: Hyperion Press, Inc.

17. See text of Agreement in Laqueur, W., and Rubin, B. (Eds.). (1995). *The Israel-Arab reader: A documentary history of the Middle East conflict* (5th ed., pp. 17–19). New York: Penguin Books.

18. Ibid., p. 19.

19. Porath, Y. (1974). *The emergence of the Palestinian-Arab national movement: 1918–1929* (Vol. 1, p. 81). London: Frank Cass.

20. Antonius, G. (1969). *The Arab awakening: The story of the Arab national movement* (p. 287). Beirut: Librairie du Liban.

21. See text in Ibid., pp. 440–442.

22. See King-Crane Commission recommendations in Laqueur, W., and Rubin, B. (Eds.). (1995). *The Israel-Arab reader: A documentary history of the Middle East conflict* (5th ed., pp. 21–28). New York: Penguin Books.

23. See the text of British Mandate in Laqueur, W., and Rubin, B. (Eds.). (1995). *The Israel-Arab reader: A documentary history of the Middle East conflict* (5th ed., pp. 30–36). New York: Penguin Books; see also Davis, H. M. (1953). *Constitutions, electoral laws, treaties of the states in the Near and Middle East* (p. 328). Durham: Duke University Press.

24. Cited in Porath, Y. (1974). *The emergence of the Palestinian-Arab national movement: 1918–1929* (Vol. 1, p. 107). London: Frank Cass.

25. Khoury, P. S. (1987). *Syria and the French Mandate: The politics of Arab nationalism 1920–1945* (p. 14). Princeton: Princeton University Press.

26. Ibid., pp. 237–238.

27. Khoury, P. S. (1987). *Syria and the French Mandate: The politics of Arab nationalism 1920–1945* (pp. 246–277). Princeton: Princeton University Press.

28. On the Congress see Husseini, M. A. (1957). *Haqaiq An Qadiyat Filistin* [Truths about the Palestinian cause] (p. 197). Cairo: Office of the Arab Higher Committee for Palestine.

29. Diab, I. Al-Din. (1998). *Akram Hawrani...Kama A'ariftahou* [Akram Hawrani...How I knew Him] (p. 45). Beirut: Beisan Press; see also Khoury, P. S. (1987). *Syria and the French Mandate: The politics of Arab nationalism 1920–1945* (pp. 400–401). Princeton: Princeton University Press.

30. Khoury, P. S. (1987). *Syria and the French Mandate: The politics of Arab nationalism 1920–1945* (pp. 284, 480, and 539). Princeton: Princeton University Press; see also Khoury, P. S. (1985, July). Divided loyalties? Syria and the question of Palestine 1919–1939. *Middle Eastern Studies, 21*(3), 324–348; on the Arab and Jewish economy in Palestine see Farsoun, S. K. (1997). *Palestine and the Palestinians* (pp. 88–93). Boulder: Westview Press.

31. Kedourie, E. (1981, January). The Bludan Congress on Palestine, September 1937. *Middle Eastern Studies, 17*(1), 107; Lewis, B. (1990). *Semites and Anti-Semites: A critical enquiry* (2nd ed., p. 148). New York: St. Martin's Press.

32. Al-Khair, H. (1996). *Akram Hawrani: Bayna al-Tanaqulat al-Siyasiya wa al-Inqilabat al-Askaria* [Akram Hawrani: Between political movements and military coup d'etats] (p. 27). Damascus: New Orient Press.

33. Tibi, B. (1990). *Arab nationalism: A critical enquiry* (2nd ed., p. 148). New York: St. Martin's Press.

34. Al-Khair, H. (1996). *Akram Hawrani: Bayna al-Tanaqulat al-Siyasiya wa al-Inqilabat al-Askaria* [Akram Hawrani: Between political movements and military coup d'etats] (p. 31). Damascus: New Orient Press; Seale, P. (1965). *The struggle for Syria: A study of post-war Arab politics 1945–1958* (p. 10). London: Oxford University Press.

35. Laqueur, W., and Rubin, B. (Eds.). (1995). *The Israel-Arab reader: A documentary history of the Middle East conflict* (5th ed., p. 67). New York: Penguin Books.

36. Davis, H. M. (1953). *Constitutions, electoral laws, treaties of the states in the Near and Middle East* (pp. 320–321). Durham: Duke University Press.

37. Ma'oz, M. (1972, Autumn). Attempts at creating a political community in modern Syria. *Middle East Journal, 22*(4), pp. 389–404.

38. For excellent details see Seale, P. (1965). *The struggle for Syria: A study of post-war Arab politics 1945–1958* (pp. 16–36). London: Oxford University Press.

39. See Partition Resolution in Laqueur, W., and Rubin, B. (Eds.). (1995). *The Israel-Arab reader: A documentary history of the Middle East conflict* (5th ed., pp. 95–97). New York: Penguin Books.

40. Kirkbride, Sir A. S. (1956). *A crackle of thorns: Experiences in the Middle East* (p. 153). London: John Murray Ltd. The Liberation Army was also called the Army of Deliverance.

41. Khalidi, W. (1998, Spring). Selected documents on the 1948 War. *Journal of Palestine Studies, 27*(3), 62.

42. Audo, A. (Universite Saint-Joseph) (1988). *Zaki al-Arsouzi: Un Arabe Face a la Modernite* (p. 24). Beirut: Dar al-Mashreq SARL.

43. See also al-Jundi, S. (1969). *Al-Ba'th* (p. 29). Beirut: Dar al-Nahar.

44. This name appeared for the first time in a statement issued by Aflaq and Bitar in support of Shukri al-Quwatli. Documents of the Arab Ba'th Socialist Party. (1963). *Nidal al-Ba'th* [The struggle of the Ba'th] (Vol. 1, pp. 27–28). Beirut: Dar al-Tali'a.

45. Ibid., pp. 104–105.

46. Aflaq, Michel. (1963). *Fi Sabil al-Ba'th* [For the sake of the Ba'th] (p. 45). Beirut: Dar al-Tali'a.

47. Arab Ba'th Socialist Party. (1963). *Nidal al-Ba'th* [The struggle of the Ba'th] (Vol. 1, p. 172). Beirut: Dar al-Tali'a.

48. Ibid., p. 175. See also Haim, S. (1962). *Arab nationalism: An anthology* (p. 236). Berkeley: University of California Press, Ltd.

49. Aflaq, Michel. (1963). *Fi Sabil al-Ba'th* [For the sake of the Ba'th] (pp. 176–180). Beirut: Dar al-Tali'a; first quoted in Haim, S. (1962). *Arab nationalism: An anthology* (p. 248). Berkeley: University of California Press, Ltd.

50. Arab Ba'th Socialist Party. (1963). *Nidal al-Ba'th* [The struggle of the Ba'th] (Vol. 1, p. 173). Beirut: Dar al-Tali'a. This was the second principle of the Ba'th party's constitution.

51. Ibid., p. 175.

52. Ibid., pp. 244–245.

53. See Aflaq, Michel. (1963). *Fi Sabil al-Ba'th* [For the sake of the Ba'th] (p. 178). Beirut: Dar al-Tali'a.

54. Devlin, J. F. (1976). *The Ba'th party: A history from the origins to 1966* (p. 27). Stanford: Hoover Institution Press.

55. For excellent information on the ANM, see al-Hindi, H., and al-Nasrawi, Abd al-Ilah. (2000). *Harakat al-Qawmiyyin al-'Arab: Nash'tuha wa Tataworiha 'ibr Wathaiqaha, 1951–1968* [The Arab Nationalist movement: Its emergence and evolution through its documents, 1951–1968] (Pt. 1, pp. 27–187). Beirut: Institution of Arab Research. Both the Ba'th party and the ANM were heavily influenced by the writings of the pan-Arab nationalist Sati al-Husri. See Tibi, B. (1990). *Arab nationalism: A critical enquiry* (2nd ed., pp. 123–198). New York: St. Martin's Press.

56. See articles in Arab Ba'th Socialist Party. (1963). *Nidal al-Ba'th* [The struggle of the Ba'th] (Vol. 1, pp. 224–247). Beirut: Dar al-Tali'a.

57. See Diab, I. Al-Din. (1998). *Akram Hawrani...Kama A'ariftahou* [Akram Hawrani...How I knew Him] (pp. 25–35). Beirut: Beisan Press; Al-Khair, H. (1996). *Akram Hawrani: Bayna al-Tanaqulat al-Siyasiya wa al-Inqilabat al-Askaria* [Akram Hawrani: Between political

movements and military coup d'etats] (pp. 35–44). Damascus: New Orient Press.

58. For the platform of the Arab Socialist Party see Owen, J. (1996). *Akram al-Hawrani: Dirasa Hawla al-Siyasa al-Suriya ma bayn 1943-1954* (p. 95). Beirut: (n.p.); Diab, I. Al-Din. (1998). *Akram Hawrani...Kama A'ariftahou* [Akram Hawrani...How I knew Him] (pp. 56–57). Beirut: Beisan Press.

59. Devlin, J. F. (1976). *The Ba'th party: A history from the origins to 1966* (p. 64). Stanford: Hoover Institution Press; for different dates on the merger see Seale, P. (1965). *The struggle for Syria: A study of post-war Arab politics 1945–1958* (p. 158). London: Oxford University Press; Khair, H. (1996). *Akram Hawrani: Bayna al-Tanaqulat al-Siyasiya wa al-Inqilabat al-Askaria* [Akram Hawrani: Between political movements and military coup d'etats] (p. 77). Damascus: New Orient Press.

60. See Arab Ba'th Socialist Party. (1963). *Nidal al-Ba'th* [The struggle of the Ba'th] (Vol. 1, p. 172). Beirut: Dar al-Tali'a.

61. Aflaq, M. (1958). *Ma'rakat al-Masir al-Wahid* [The battle of one destiny] (p. 97). Beirut: Dar al-Adab.

62. Ibid., p. 159.

63. Seale, P. (1988). *Asad of Syria: The struggle for the Middle East* (p. 61). Berkeley: University of California Press.

64. See Ben-Tzur, A. (1968, July). The Neo-Ba'th party of Syria. *Journal of Contemporary History* 3(3), p. 170. London: Institute of Contemporary History.

65. Atasi, J. (1963). Arab socialism and the myth of [its] special qualities. *Fi al-Fikr al-Siyasi* (Vol. 1, pp. 170–171). Damascus: Dar Dimashq.

66. Ibid., pp. 152–155.

67. Murqus, I. (1963). Collapse of the Parliamentary system. *Fi al-Fikr al-Siyasi* (Vol. 2, p. 169). Damascus: Dar Dimashq.

68. Al-Hafiz, Y. (1963). About the experience of the Ba'th party. *Fi al-Fikr al-Siyasi* (Vol. 1, pp. 194–197); see also Ben-Tzur, A. (1968, July). The Neo-Ba'th party of Syria. *Journal of Contemporary History* 3(3), p. 171. London: Institute of Contemporary History.

69. See text in Arab Ba'th Socialist Party. (1963). *Nidal al-Ba'th* [The struggle of the Ba'th] (Vol. 6, pp. 232–291). Beirut: Dar al-Tali'a.

70. Ibid., p. 227.

71. Ibid., p. 266.

72. Ibid., pp. 229–230.

73. See Ben-Tzur, A. (1968, July). The Neo-Ba'th party of Syria. *Journal of Contemporary History* 3(3), pp. 174–76. London: Institute of Contemporary History.

74. Ben-Tzur, A. (Ed.). (1968). *The Syrian Baath Party and Israel: Documents from the Internal Party Publications* (pp. 4, 6, 8, and 21). Givat Aviv: Center for Arab and Afro-Asian Studies.

75. See Asad statements in al-Asad, H. (compiled by General Mustafa Tlas). (1984). *Kadhalika Qala al-Asad* [Thus al-Asad said] (pp. 181–183).

Damascus: Tlas press; see also Radio Damascus, May 13, 1988, in *Foreign Broadcast Information Service: Near East and South Asia (FBIS-NES)* (May 16, 1988, p. 34).

76. Kissinger, H. (1982). *Years of upheaval* (p. 1098). Boston: Little, Brown and Company.

77. *Al-Nadhir* (June 17, 1981). (No. 35).

78. *Al-Nadhir* (February 12, 1981). (No. 29); and *Al-Nadhir*, (June 17, 1981). (No. 35).

79. Seale, P. (1988). *Asad of Syria: The struggle for the Middle East* (p. 141). Berkeley: University of California Press.

80. Perthes, V. (1995). *The political economy of Syria under Asad* (p. 162). London: I. B. Tauris. The PNF included the Syrian Communist Party, the Arab Socialist Union (a Nasserist group), the Movement of Socialist Unionists (MSU) (a faction that broke away from the Ba'th party after Syria seceded from the union with Egypt in 1961), The Democratic Socialist Unionist Party (a faction that split in 1974 from the MSU), and the Arab Socialist Party (a Ba'thist faction formed in 1964). See George, A. (2003). *Syria: Neither bread nor freedom* (p. 87). London: Zed Books Ltd.; and on the history and development of parties see 'Othman, H. (2001). *Al-Ahzab al-Siyasiyya fi Suriyya* [Political parties in Syria]. Beirut: Riad El-Rayyes Books.

81. See *Al-Thawra* (February 1, 1973); and Heller, P. B. (1974 Winter). Document: The permanent Syrian constitution of March 13, 1973. *Middle East Journal, 28*(1).

82. Heller, P. B. (1974, Winter). Document: The permanent Syrian constitution of March 13, 1973. *Middle East Journal, 28*(1).

83. *Al-Thawra* (February 1, 1973); and Heller, P. B. (1974, Winter). Document: The permanent Syrian constitution of March 13, 1973. *Middle East Journal, 28*(1); see also Rabinovich, I. (1976–1977). Syria. In Colin Legum (Ed.), *Middle East Contemporary Survey* (Vol. 1). [Hereafter referred to as MECS, published for the Shiloah Center (later on Moshe Dayan Center) for Middle Eastern and African Studies, Tel Aviv University.] New York: Holmes and Meier.

84. U.S. Department of State. (March 31, 2003). *Syria: Country reports on human rights practices—2002.* Washington, DC: Bureau of Democracy, Human Rights, and Labor. Syria's security services are under the control of the government, especially the president. They have overlapping functions so that the regime is not dependent on any one of them. Syria has four main security services. The Political Security Directorate (*Idarat al-Amn al-Siyasi*) monitors organized political activity, including surveillance of political dissidents and foreigners residing in the country. Brigadier General Muhammad Mansoura is the director of the Political Security Directorate. Mansoura replaced former intelligence chief of Lebanon Ghazi Kanaan in October 2004, who in turn was appointed Interior Minister. The General Intelligence Directorate (*Idarat al-Amn al-'Am*) is the main civilian intelligence service. It is divided into three branches. The internal security division is responsible for surveillance of the

population in general. The two other divisions are external security and the Palestine division, which monitors the activities of Palestinian groups in Syria and Lebanon. Brigadier General Ali Mamlouk is the director of the General Intelligence Directorate. His deputy director is Hassan Khallouf. Mamlouk replaced Brigadier General Hisham Bakhtiar in June 2005, who in turn was appointed director of a newly setup national security bureau within the Ba'th party. Brigadier General Bahjat Suleiman headed until recently the important post of internal security division. He was replaced by Brigadier General Fouad Nassif in June 2005. The Military Intelligence (*Shu'bat al-Mukhabarat al-'Askariyya*) is generally responsible for military surveillance and intelligence. Headquartered at the Defense Ministry complex in Damascus, it is headed by Brigadier General Asef Shawqat, Bashar al-Asad's brother-in-law, who has recently (February 2005) replaced General Hassan al-Khalil. Finally, Air Force Intelligence (*Idarat al-Mukhabarat al-Jawiyya*) is responsible for domestic and international operations, mainly against Islamists. It is headed by Major General Ibrahim Hwayjah. It is not certain whether Brigadier General Ezzedine Ismail replaced Major General Ibrahim Hwayjah. Almost all these security officials are Alawis and close to the Asad family. See Syria's intelligence services: A primer. (July 1, 2000). *Middle East Intelligence Bulletin, 2*(6); Rabil, R. G. (2003). *Embattled neighbors: Syria, Israel and Lebanon* (pp. 139–141, 272–273). Boulder, CO: Lynne Rienner Publishers; U.S. Department of State, *Syria*; and *As-Safir* (June 10 and 17, 2005).

85. Perthes, V. (1995). *The political economy of Syria under Asad* (pp. 170–171). London: I. B. Tauris; on the political economy of Syria, see also Hinnebusch, R. (1990). *Authoritarian power and state formation in Baathist Syria: Army, party, and peasant*. Boulder: Westview Press.

86. See Rabil, R. G. (2003). *Embattled neighbors: Syria, Israel and Lebanon* (p. 123). Boulder, CO: Lynne Rienner Publishers. Based on discussions with Sadek al-Azm, who coined the term "military-merchant complex" on September 19, 1999. It is noteworthy that Bashar al-Asad's wife Asma is the daughter of Dr. Farid al-Akhras, a scion of a prominent Sunni family from Homs.

87. See Hinnebusch, R. A. (1995, April). Syria: The Politics of Peace and Regime Survival. *Middle East Policy, 3*(4).

88. See Middle East Watch. (1991). *Syria unmasked: The suppression of human rights by the Asad regime* (pp. 18–21). New York: Vail-Ballou Press.

89. Seale, P. (1988). *Asad of Syria: The struggle for the Middle East* (pp. 421–440). Berkeley: University of California Press.

90. Batatu, H. (1999). *Syria's peasantry, the descendants of its lesser rural notables, and their politics* (p. 326). Princeton, NJ: Princeton University Press.

91. Ibid., p. 176.

92. Ibid., p. 176.

Chapter 2: The Beginning of U.S.-Syrian Relations: Between the Arab-Israeli Conflict and the Cold War

1. Department of State. (1965). *Foreign relations of the United States: Diplomatic papers 1944* (Vol. 5, pp. 774–813). Washington, DC: Government Printing Office (GPO).

2. Truman, H. S. (1955). *Memoirs: Year of decisions* (Vol. 2, p. 100). New York: Doubleday.

3. Paterson, T. G. (Ed.). (1989). *Major problems in American foreign policy Volume II: Since 1914, documents and essays* (p. 299). Lexington: DC Heath and Company.

4. Clifford, C. M. (1991). *Counsel to the President: A memoir* (p. 13). New York: Random House.

5. It is noteworthy that during the Rhodes negotiations, Colonel Husni al-Zaim seized power in Syria by carrying out a coup d'etat on March 30, 1949. Al-Zaim tried to improve Syria's relations with the United States, which was leading the Conciliation Commission for Palestine in Lausanne to promote a peaceful resolution of the Arab-Israeli conflict, while at the same time probing Soviet intentions in the region. Contacts between al-Zaim and the United States had taken place before the coup. A Central Intelligence Agency (CIA) agent in the Middle East, Miles Copeland, reported in his book *The game of nations,* that Stephen Meade, the assistant military attaché of the U.S. legation in Damascus, had established contact with al-Zaim, then chief of the general staff of the Syrian army, who brought up the idea of a coup. According to Copeland, al-Zaim transmitted his program to the United States, which entailed, among other points, the institution of social and economic reforms and doing "something constructive about the Arab-Israel problem." In his conversations with Meade, al-Zaim envisaged a plan of action in which technical and military aid to Syria figured substantially. Copeland, M. (1969). *The game of nations* (p. 42). London: Weidenfeld & Nicholson. For Meade's contacts with al-Zaim, see Little, D. (1990, Winter). Cold War and covert action: The United States and Syria, 1945–1958. *Middle East Journal, 44*(1); and Rathmell, A. (1995). *Secret war in the Middle East: The covert struggle for Syria, 1949–1961* (pp. 36–44). London: I. B. Tauris. See also al-Azm, K. (1973). *Mudhakkirat* [Memoir] (Vol. 2, p. 183). Beirut: Al-Dar al-Taqaddumiya lil-Nashr.

6. Department of State. (1977). *Foreign relations of the United States: Diplomatic papers: 1949* (Vol. 6, pp. 1072–1074). Washington, DC: GPO.

7. Department of State. (1957). *American foreign policy 1950–1955: Basic documents* (Vol. 2, p. 2237). Washington, DC: GPO.

8. Safran, N. (1969). *From war to war: The Arab-Israeli confrontation, 1948–1967* (p. 103). Indianapolis: The Bobbs-Merrill Company, Inc., Publishers.

9. Seale, P. (1965). *The struggle for Syria: A study of post-war Arab politics 1945–1958* (p. 112). London: Oxford University Press.

10. Ibid., p. 103.

11. Dulles, J. F. (1964, January 27). The evaluation of foreign policy, address to the Council on Foreign Relations, January 12, 1954. In *Department of State Bulletin, 50*(1283), 107–110.

12. Department of State. (1957). *American foreign policy 1950–1955: Basic documents* (Vol. 2, p. 2170). Washington, DC: GPO.

13. See Howard, H. N. (1974). The Soviet Union in Lebanon, Syria and Jordan. In I. J. Lederer and W. S. Vucinich (Eds.). *The Soviet Union and the Middle East: The post-World War II era* (pp. 138–141). Stanford: Hoover Institution Press.

14. Seale, P. (1965). *The struggle for Syria: A study of post-war Arab politics 1945–1958* (pp. 236–237). London: Oxford University Press.

15. Tlas, General M. (1997). *Mar'at Hayati: Al-Aqd al-Awal—1948–1958* [Mirror of my life: The first decade—1948–1958] (2nd ed., p. 514). Damascus: Tlas Press.

16. Department of State. (1957). *American foreign policy 1950–1955: Basic documents* (Vol. 2, p. 2236). Washington, DC: GPO.

17. Eisenhower, D. D. (1963). *Mandate for change: The White House years 1953–1956* (p. 252). New York: Doubleday.

18. Ministere Syrienne des Affaires Etrangeres. (1956, Novembre 29). *Expose du Ministre des Affaires Etrangeres en Conference de Presse sur les Fausses Rumeurs propagees au Sujet de la Syrie* (pp. 1–2). Damas: Bureau des Documentations Syriennes et Arabes.

19. Dulles, J. F. (1957, January). *Economic and military cooperation with nations in the general area of the Middle East* (pp. 2–5). Washington, DC: GPO.

20. Department of State. (1961). *American foreign policy: Current documents 1957* (pp. 816–817). Washington, DC: GPO.

21. Ministere Syrienne des Affaires Etrangeres. (1957, Janvier 10). *Declaration du Gouvernment Syrien au Sujet du Projet du President Eisenhower* (p. 1). Damas: Bureau des Documentations Syriennes et Arabes.

22. Ministere Syrienne des Affaires Etrangeres. (1957, Aout 19). *Expose du Ministre des Affaires Etrangeres au Sujet de la Decouverte du Complot Americain contre la surete de L'etat* (pp. 1–4). Damas: Bureau des Documentations Syriennes et Arabes.

23. Department of State. (1961). *American foreign policy: Current documents 1957* (p. 1036). Washington, DC: GPO.

24. Ibid., p. 1042.

25. Secretary Dulles' News Conference of September 10. (1957, September 30). In *Department of State Bulletin, 37*(953), 528.

26. See Donovan, J. (1964). *U.S. and Soviet policy in the Middle East: 1957–1966* (p. 171). New York: Facts on File, Inc.; for more information on Israel's Dimona nuclear reactor see Peres, S. (1995). *Battling for peace.* New York: Random House.

27. Department of State. (1964). *American foreign policy: Current documents 1961* (pp. 671–672). Washington, DC: GPO.

28. Feldman, S. (1996). *The future of U.S.-Israel strategic cooperation* (p. 9). Washington, DC: The Washington Institute for Near East Policy; see also Ma'oz, M. (1995). *Syria and Israel: From war to peacemaking* (p. 86). New York: Oxford University Press Inc.

29. Department of State. (1967). *American foreign policy: Current documents 1964* (pp. 685–686). Washington, DC: GPO. The Armistice Agreement between Israel and Syria provided that the territories captured by Syria in the 1948 War be demilitarized. Article V of the agreement stipulated that the Demilitarized Zone (DMZ) be excluded for the armed forces of both countries and be supervised by the U.N. Truce Supervision Organization (UNTSO). The text of the Armistice Agreement was reproduced in Bar-Yaacov, N. (1967). *The Israel-Syrian Armistice: Problems of Implementation, 1949–1966* (pp. 339–346). Jerusalem: Magnes Press, Hebrew University. For more details see Rabil, R. G. (2003). *Embattled neighbors: Syria, Israel and Lebanon* (pp. 14–20). Boulder, CO: Lynne Rienner Publishers.

30. Ben-Tzur, A. (Ed.). (1968). *The Syrian Baath Party and Israel: Documents from the Internal Party Publications* (p. 19). Givat Haviva: Center for Arab and Afro-Asian Studies.

31. Department of State. (1969). *American foreign policy: Current documents 1966* (p. 525). Washington, DC: GPO.

32. Ibid., pp. 530–531.

33. An outcome of compromise, accommodating both the Arab and Israeli positions, Resolution 242 was sufficiently ambiguous to allow the Arab states and Israel to read into it what they wanted. In the preamble, the resolution emphasized "the inadmissibility of the acquisition of territory by war and the need to work for a just and lasting peace in which every state in the area can live in security." It then affirmed:

> The fulfillment of Charter principles requires the establishment of a just and lasting peace in the Middle East which would include the application of both the following principles: (i) Withdrawal of Israeli armed forces from territories occupied in the recent conflict; (ii) Termination of all claims or states of belligerency and respect for acknowledgment of the sovereignty, territorial integrity and political independence of every state in the area and their right to live in peace within secure and recognized boundaries free from threats or acts of force.

While Egypt and Jordan accepted the resolution, Syria rejected it.

34. Safran, N. (1978). *Israel: The embattled ally* (p. 431). Cambridge: Harvard University Press.

35. Brown, S. (1994). *The faces of power: Constancy and change in United States foreign policy from Truman to Clinton* (p. 259). New York: Columbia University Press.

36. See Quandt, W. B. (1977). *Decade of decisions: American policy toward the Arab-Israeli conflict, 1967–1976* (pp. 89–90). Berkeley: University of California Press.

37. Safran, N. (1978). *Israel: The embattled ally* (p. 444). Cambridge: Harvard University Press.

38. Nixon, R. M. (1978). *RN: The memoirs of Richard Nixon* (p. 920). New York: Grosset & Dunlap; for detailed information on Jordan's crisis see Kissinger, H. (1979). *The White House years*. Boston: Little, Brown and Company, Inc.

39. Kissinger, H. (1979). *The White House years* (pp. 594–631). Boston: Little, Brown and Company, Inc.

40. Rabin, Y. (1996). *The Rabin memoirs* (p. 187). Berkeley: University of California Press.

41. Ibid., p. 189.

42. *Department of State Bulletin.* (1973, November 12). *69*(1794), pp. 583–594.

43. Kissinger, H. (1982). *Years of upheaval* (pp. 483–484). Boston: Little, Brown and Company.

44. See Zisser, E. (1998, February). Decision making in Asad's Syria. *Policy Focus* (No. 35). Washington, DC: The Washington Institute For Near East Policy.

45. Kissinger, H. (1982). *Years of upheaval* (p. 1067). Boston: Little, Brown and Company.

46. Bureau of Public Affairs, Department of States. (1975). *U.S. Policy in the Middle East December 1973–November 1974* (No. 12, p. 1). Washington, DC: GPO.

47. McGovern, Senator G. S. (1975). *Realities of the Middle East* (p. 22). Washington, DC: GPO.

48. Ibid.

49. Ibid.

50. Safran, N. (1978). *Israel: The embattled ally* (pp. 557–558). Cambridge: Harvard University Press.

51. Ibid., pp. 559–560.

52. Heikal, M. (1975). *The road to Ramadan* (p. 43). London: Williams Collins Sons.

53. Kissinger, H. (1982). *Years of upheaval* (p. 939). Boston: Little, Brown and Company.

54. Ibid., p. 954.

55. Safran, N. (1978). *Israel: The embattled ally* (p. 530). Cambridge: Harvard University Press.

56. Quandt, W. B. (1993). *Peace process: American diplomacy and the Arab-Israeli conflict since 1967* (p. 210). Berkeley: University of California Press.

57. Ibid., p. 211.

58. Kissinger, H. (1982). *Years of upheaval* (pp. 1062–1063). Boston: Little, Brown and Company.

59. Dayan, M. (1976). *Moshe Dayan: Story of my life* (p. 586). New York: William Morrow.

60. Kissinger, H. (1982). *Years of upheaval* (p. 1078). Boston: Little, Brown and Company.

61. Ibid., p. 1093.

62. Safran, N. (1978). *Israel: The embattled ally* (p. 531). Cambridge: Harvard University Press; Quandt, W. B. (1993). *Peace process: American diplomacy and the Arab-Israeli conflict since 1967* (p. 213). Berkeley: University of California Press.

63. Quandt, W. B. (1993). *Peace process: American diplomacy and the Arab-Israeli conflict since 1967* (p. 213). Berkeley: University of California Press.

64. Kissinger, H. (1982). *Years of upheaval* (p. 1096). Boston: Little, Brown and Company.

65. Kissinger, H. (1982). *Years of upheaval* (p. 1104). Boston: Little, Brown and Company; Quandt, W. B. (1993). *Peace process: American diplomacy and the Arab-Israeli conflict since 1967* (p. 214). Berkeley: University of California Press.

66. Kissinger, H. (1982). *Years of upheaval* (p. 1104). Boston: Little, Brown and Company.

67. Ibid., pp. 1253–1254.

68. Ibid., pp. 1253–1254; Shalev, A. (1994). *Israel and Syria: Peace and security on the Golan* (Map 4). Boulder: Westview Press.

69. Kissinger, H. (1994). *Diplomacy* (p. 738). New York: Simon & Schuster.

70. Bureau of Public Affairs, Department of States. (1975). *U.S. Policy in the Middle East December 1973–November 1974* (No. 12, p. 29). Washington, DC: GPO.

71. McGovern, Senator G. S. (1975). *Realities of the Middle East* (p. 16). Washington, DC: GPO.

72. Bureau of Public Affairs, Department of State. (1976). *U.S. Policy in the Middle East: November 1974–February 1976* (No. 4, p. 94). Washington, DC: GPO.

73. Ibid., p. 93.

74. Ibid., p. 93.

75. *Department of State Bulletin* (1977, November). 77(2002), p. 636.

76. Ibid., pp. 639–640.

77. Ibid., pp. 637–638.

78. Brown, S. (1994). *The faces of power: Constancy and change in United States foreign policy from Truman to Clinton* (pp. 341–342). New York: Columbia University Press.

79. See text of MOA in Department of State. (1983). *American foreign policy: Basic documents 1977–1980* (pp. 684–685). Washington, DC: GPO; see also Egypt's opposition of MOA, Department of State. (1983). *American foreign policy: Basic documents 1977–1980* (p. 686).

80. *Department of State Bulletin* (1979, October). 79(2031), p. 52.

81. Ibid., p. 52.

82. See Feldman, S. (1996). *The future of U.S.-Israel strategic coopera-tion* (p. 10). Washington, DC: The Washington Institute for Near East Policy.

83. *Department of State Bulletin* (1979, April). *79*(2025), p. 40.

84. Ibid., p. 40.

Chapter 3: The Emergence of the U.S.-Syrian Ambivalent Relationship

1. See Prados, A. B. (1992, May 12). Syrian-U.S. Relations. *Congression-al Research Service* (p. 11). Excerpts from this chapter originally appeared in Rabil, R. G. (2003). *Embattled neighbors: Syria, Israel and Lebanon*. Boulder, CO: Lynne Rienner Publishers.

2. See Ronald Reagan's address in Orlando, Florida, March 8, 1983, in *Weekly Compilation of Presidential Documents, 19*(10), 364–370.

3. Paterson, T. G. (Ed.). (1989). *Major problems in American foreign pol-icy Volume II: Since 1914, documents and essays* (p. 682). Lexington: DC Health and Company.

4. Ibid., p. 681.

5. Department of State. (1984). *American foreign policy: Current docu-ments 1981* (p. 685). Washington, DC: GPO.

6. Ibid., p. 815.

7. Reagan, R. (1990). *An American life* (p. 416). New York: Simon & Schuster.

8. Department of State. (1984). *American foreign policy: Current docu-ments 1981* (p. 824). Washington, DC: GPO.

9. Ibid., p. 826.

10. Quoted from Feldman, S. (1996). *The future of U.S.-Israel strategic cooperation* (p. 11). Washington, DC: The Washington Institute for Near East Policy; Puschel, K. L. (1992). *U.S.-Israel strategic cooperation in the post-Cold War era: An American perspective* (p. 35). Tel Aviv: Jaffee Center for Strategic Studies.

11. Department of State. (1984). *American foreign policy: Current docu-ments 1981* (pp. 772–773). Washington, DC: GPO.

12. Ibid., p. 723.

13. Ibid., p. 724.

14. According to Ze'ev Schiff, the agreement contained three key ele-ments: "(1) The Syrian army would not enter southern Lebanon and would not cross a line starting south of Sidon, on the coast, and running east to Aysiya and from there towards the Syrian border; (2) the Syrian army in Lebanon would not be equipped with surface-to-air missile batteries; (3) and the Syrian army would not use its air force against the Christians in Lebanon." Schiff, Z. (1993). *Peace with security: Israel's minimal security requirements in negotiations with Syria* (p. 26). Washington, DC: Washing-ton Institute for Near East Policy. For more details on this episode see Rabil, R. G. (2003). *Embattled neighbors: Syria, Israel and Lebanon*

(pp. 50–53). Boulder, CO: Lynne Rienner Publishers; see also Seale, P. (1988). *Asad of Syria: The struggle for the Middle East* (pp. 279–280). Berkeley: University of California Press.

15. Hamizrachi, B. (1988). *The emergence of the South Lebanon security belt* (p. 112). New York: Praeger.

16. Text of resolution is available at http://www-UN.org/documents/sc/res/1978/scres78.htm.

17. Seale, P. (1988). *Asad of Syria: The struggle for the Middle East* (p. 371). Berkeley: University of California Press; see also Rabil, R. G. (2003). *Embattled neighbors: Syria, Israel and Lebanon* (pp. 59–69). Boulder, CO: Lynne Rienner Publishers.

18. After Prime Minister Begin and Defense Minister Ariel Sharon probed Secretary of State Alexander Haig about the U.S. reaction in the event Israel invaded Lebanon, Haig maintained an attitude that "unless there is a major, internationally recognized provocation, the United States will not support such an action." In addition, Haig remarked in public that "the time has come to take concerted action in support of both Lebanon's territorial integrity...and a strong central government." These attitudes were construed by Begin as an endorsement of Israel's invasion under the right circumstances. See, respectively, Haig, A. M., Jr. (1984). *Caveat: Realism, Reagan, and Foreign Policy* (pp. 326–328). New York: Macmillan; and Haig's statements before the Chicago Council on Foreign Relations on May 26, 1982. In *U.S. Department of State Bulletin* (1982, July), pp. 44–47.

19. Department of State. (1985). *American foreign policy: Current documents 1982* (p. 756). Washington, DC: GPO.

20. Ibid., p. 756.

21. Seale, P. (1988). *Asad of Syria: The struggle for the Middle East* (pp. 394–420). Berkeley: University of California Press.

22. Al-Asad, H. (compiled by Mustafa Tlas). (1984). *Kadhalika Qala al-Asad* [Thus al-Asad said] (p. 260). Damascus: Tlas Press.

23. Ibid., p. 265.

24. Department of State. (1986). *American foreign policy: Current documents 1984* (pp. 546–547). Washington, DC: GPO.

25. Ibid., p. 556.

26. Hearing before the Subcommittee on Europe and the Middle East of the Committee on Foreign Affairs House of Representatives. (1989). *The situation in Lebanon July 1989* (pp. 118–119). Washington, DC: GPO; see also Hearing before the Subcommittee on International Operations of the Committee on Foreign Affairs House of Representatives. (1990). *American hostages in Lebanon*. Washington, DC: GPO; Department of State. (1991). *American foreign policy: Current documents 1990* (p. 622). Washington, DC: GPO.

27. For vivid accounts on American hostages in Lebanon, see memoirs of hostages, one of which is Anderson, T. A. (1993). *Den of lions: Memoirs of seven years.* New York: Crown Publishers, Inc.

28. Department of State. (1989). *American foreign policy: Current documents 1988* (p. 216). Washington, DC: GPO.

29. Prados, A. B. (1992, May 12). Syrian-U.S. Relations. *Congressional Research Service* (p. 13). According to Patrick Seale, a Jordanian by the name of Nizar Hindawi placed powerful plastic explosives in the bag of his fiancée Ann Murphy, who was traveling to Israel. After dropping his fiancée at Heathrow airport, Hindawi went to a room in Kensington's Royal Garden Hotel reserved for personnel of Syrian Arab Airlines. Following his interrogation by British authorities, Hindawi stated that he was an opponent of King Hussein of Jordan and that he had sought Syrian support. "In Damascus in January 1986 he had met the head of air force intelligence Muhammad al-Khuly, and one of his officers, Colonel Haytham Sa'id. A month later Sa'id gave him a Syrian service passport in the name of 'Issam Share' and instructed him to place a bomb on an El Al aircraft in London." See Seale, P. (1988). *Asad of Syria: The struggle for the Middle East* (pp. 475–477). Berkeley: University of California Press.

30. Department of State. (1989). *American foreign policy: Current documents 1988* (p. 227). Washington, DC: GPO.

31. See the interview of Hizbollah's Secretary General, Hasan Nasrallah. (1996, March 18). *al-Wasat,* p. 30.

32. Norton, A. R. (2000, Autumn). Hizbollah and the Israeli withdrawal from Southern Lebanon. *Journal of Palestine Studies, 30*(1), 3. For more details on Hizbollah, see also Norton, R. A. (1999). *Hizballah of Lebanon: extremist ideals vs mundane politics.* New York: Council on Foreign Relations.

33. Feldman, S. (1996). *The future of U.S.-Israel strategic cooperation* (p. 13). Washington, DC: The Washington Institute for Near East Policy.

34. Department of State. (1986). *American foreign policy: Current documents 1984* (p. 531). Washington, DC: GPO.

35. Ibid., p. 531.

36. Ibid., p. 532.

37. Ibid., p. 533.

38. Byrd, Senator R. (1992, Summer). Senator Byrd on loan guarantees and U.S.-Israeli relations. *Journal of Palestine Studies, 21*(4), 135–136; quoted from *Congressional Record* (1992, April 1).

39. Department of State. (1989). *American foreign policy: Current documents 1988* (pp. 414–415). Washington, DC: GPO.

40. Feldman, S. (1996). *The future of U.S.-Israel strategic cooperation* (p. 14). Washington, DC: The Washington Institute for Near East Policy.

41. Pakradouni, K. (1992). *La'nat Watan: Min Harb Lubnan Ila Harb al-Khalij* [Curse of a Fatherland: From the Lebanese War to the Gulf War] (p. 223). Beirut: Trans-Orient Press.

42. Ibid.

43. The accord reduced the prerogatives of the Maronite president and enhanced the positions of both the Sunni prime minister and the Shi'ite speaker of parliament. It called for (1) building the armed forces to

shoulder their national responsibilities in confronting Israeli aggression, (2) dismantling all militias, (3) implementing U.N. Resolution 425, and (4) taking the necessary measures to liberate all Lebanese territory from Israeli occupation. The accord also provided that the Syrian forces shall assist the legitimate Lebanese forces in establishing the state's authority within a period not exceeding two years and that the two governments shall decide on the future redeployment of Syrian forces. See text of Taif Accord in Nasrallah, F. (1992). *Prospects for Lebanon: The questions of South Lebanon*(pp. 71–74). Oxford: Centre for Lebanese Studies.

44. See text of the treaty in *An-Nahar* (1991, May 23). For an analysis of the agreement see Rabil, R. G. (2003). *Embattled neighbors: Syria, Israel and Lebanon* (pp. 128–129). Boulder, CO: Lynne Rienner Publishers.

Chapter 4: The Fulcrum of Elusive Peace

1. This chapter relied on excerpts originally appearing in Rabil, R. G. (2003). *Embattled neighbors: Syria, Israel and Lebanon*. Boulder, CO: Lynne Rienner Publishers. and in Rabil, R. G. (2001, Summer). The ineffective role of the US in the US-Israeli-Syrian relationship. *Middle East Journal, 55*(3).

2. Middle East Watch. (1992, Summer). Human Rights Watch World Report 1992: The Israeli-Occupied West Bank and Gaza Strip. *Journal of Palestine Studies, 21*(4), 123. This report was reproduced from *Human Rights Watch* (1991, December).

3. Baker, J. A., III. (1995). *The politics of diplomacy: Revolution, war and peace 1989–1992* (p. 542). New York: G.P. Putnam's Sons.

4. Department of State. (1991). *American foreign policy: Current documents 1990* (p. 111). Washington DC: Government Printing Office (GPO).

5. Ibid., pp. 621–622.

6. Ibid., p. 622.

7. Ibid., p. 623.

8. Baker, J. A., III. (1995). *The politics of diplomacy: Revolution, war and peace 1989–1992* (p. 426). New York: G.P. Putnam's Sons.

9. Ibid., p. 426.

10. Department of State. (1991). *American foreign policy: Current documents 1990* (p. 626). Washington DC: Government Printing Office (GPO).

11. See Pakradouni, K. (1992). *La'nat Watan: Min Harb Lubnan Ila Harb al-Khalij* [Curse of a Fatherland: From the Lebanese War to the Gulf War] (pp. 205–224). Beirut: Trans-Orient Press.

12. Department of State. (1991). *American foreign policy: Current documents 1990* (p. 627). Washington DC: Government Printing Office (GPO).

13. Anderson, T. A. (1993). *Den of lions: Memoirs of seven years* (pp. 343–345). New York: Crown Publishers, Inc.

14. Feldman, S. (1996). *The future of U.S.-Israel strategic cooperation* (p. 15). Washington, DC: The Washington Institute for Near East Policy.

15. Baker, J. A. (1995). *The politics of diplomacy: Revolution, war, and peace 1989-1992* (p. 544). New York: G. P. Putnam's Sons.

16. Ibid., p. 547.

17. Quoted from Hadar, L. T. (1992, Summer). The last days of Likud: The American-Israeli big chill. *Journal of Palestine Studies, 21*(4), 81; Shields, M. The Gulf War fades. *Washington Post* (1992, March 6).

18. Quoted from Hadar, L. T. (1992, Summer). The last days of Likud: The American-Israeli big chill. *Journal of Palestine Studies, 21*(4), 82; Friedman, T. L. (1992, February 26). Senators press Baker on help to Israel. *New York Times.*

19. Byrd, Senator R. (1992, Summer). Senator Byrd on loan guarantees and U.S.-Israeli relations. *Journal of Palestine Studies, 21*(4), 131.

20. Ibid., p. 138.

21. See text of speech in the *Washington Post* (1991, March 7).

22. See Friedman, T. L. (1991, May 23). Baker cites Israel for settlements. *New York Times;* Friedman, T. L. (1991, May 24). Bush backs Baker view of Mid-East barriers. *New York Times.*

23. Quoted from Quandt, W. B. (1993). *Peace process: American diplomacy and the Arab-Israeli conflict since 1967* (p. 44). Berkeley: University of California Press.

24. See Yariv, A. (1992). *War in the Gulf: Implications for Israel* (p. 382). Boulder: Westview Press; and for details see pp. 382–397.

25. Ibid., p. 395.

26. Quandt, W. B. (1993). *Peace process: American diplomacy and the Arab-Israeli conflict since 1967* (p. 364). Berkeley: University of California Press.

27. See Shalev, A. (1991). *The Intifada: Causes and effect* (pp. 163–175). Boulder: Westview Press.

28. Rabinovich, I. (1999). *Waging peace: Israel and the Arabs at the end of the century* (p. 36). New York: Farrar, Straus, and Giroux.

29. For a detailed account on the impact of the Gulf War on the Arab world see Faour, M. (1993). *The Arab world after Desert Storm.* Washington, DC: United States Institute of Peace Press.

30. Ibid., pp. 84, 87, 107.

31. Safran, N. (1992). Dimension of the Middle East problem. In Roy Macridis (Ed.). *Foreign policy in world politics* (8th ed., p. 393). Englewood Cliffs: Prentice Hall.

32. Hearing before the Committee on Foreign Affairs House of Representatives. (1992, July 22). *To consider release of dual-use export licenses to Iran and Syria pursuant to Section 12(c) of the Export Administration Act* (p. 19). Washington, DC: GPO.

33. Ibid., pp. 2, 19.

34. Ibid., p. 22.

35. See 1992 H.R. (House Resolution) 4546, 102 (102nd Congress) H.R. 4546, *Congressional Information Service.*

36. Staff Report issued on November 23, 1992 by the Subcommittee on Crime and Criminal Justice of the Committee on the Judiciary. (1993).

Syria, President Bush, and drugs—The administration's next Iraqgate
(p. 1). Washington, DC: GPO.

37. A Report to the Committee on Foreign Relations United States
Senate by Jeffords, Senator J. M., and Brown, Senator H. (1993). *Trip to
Croatia, Syria, Jordan, Israel and Egypt* (p. 10). Washington, DC: GPO.

38. Hadar, L. T. (1992, Winter). High Noon in Washington: The shootout
over the loan guarantees. *Journal of Palestine Studies, 21*(2), 77–78; the
foreign policy experts included Richard Haass, Dennis Ross, Aaron Miller,
and Daniel C. Kurtzer.

39. Curtius, M. (1994, January 17). Asad calls for "normal" relations with
Israel. *Boston Globe.*

40. Rabinovich, I. (1998). *The brink of peace: The Israeli-Syrian negotiations* (p. 129). New Jersey: Princeton University Press.

41. Ibid., p. 129.

42. Excerpts from Remarks by President Clinton and President Hafiz al-
Asad of Syria. (1994, October 28). Assad and Clinton speak: Shared quest
for peace. *New York Times,* p. A21.

43. Ibid., p. A20.

44. Rabinovich, I. (1998). *The brink of peace: The Israeli-Syrian negotiations* (p. 145). New Jersey: Princeton University Press.

45. Department of State. (1995, April). *Patterns of Global Terrorism 1994*
(pp. 23–24).

46. Department of State. (1996, April). *Patterns of Global Terrorism 1995*
(p. 28).

47. See Department of State. (1997, April). *Patterns of Global Terrorism
1996;* and Department of State. (1998, April). *Patterns of Global Terrorism
1997.* The 1997 report claimed that Syria continues to provide a safe haven
and support for radical terrorist groups including the Popular Front for the
Liberation of Palestine–General Command (PFLP-GC), the Palestine
Islamic Jihad (PIJ), the Palestinian-Islamic Resistance Movement
(HAMAS), and the Kurdistan Workers Party (PKK).

48. Among those involved were Frank Gaffney, who ran a conservative
think tank in Washington—the Center for Security Policy, and Yossi Ben-
Aharon, the predecessor of Rabinovich as chief negotiator with Syria. It is
noteworthy that key Republicans such as Dan Quayle, William Bennet,
and Jack Kemp have supported Gaffney.

49. Rabinovich, I. (1998). *The brink of peace: The Israeli-Syrian negotiations* (p. 166). New Jersey: Princeton University Press.

50. Greenhouse, S. (1994, December 9). Dole may moderate Helms conservatism. *New York Times,* p. 3.

51. Rabinovich, I. (1998). *The brink of peace: The Israeli-Syrian negotiations* (p. 165). New Jersey: Princeton University Press.

52. Greenhouse, S. (1994, December 9). Dole may moderate Helms conservatism. *New York Times,* p. 3.

53. Al-Wadi, M. K. (1995, March 28). Helms...wa al-Nazzara al-Israiliya
[Helms...and the Israeli binoculars]. *al-Ba'th.*

54. Ibid., p. 1.

55. Hearing before the Committee on International Relations House of Representatives. (1996). *Syria: Peace partner or rogue regime?* (p. 31). Washington, DC: GPO.

56. Ibid., p. 32.

57. See 1997 H.R. 3080, 105 H.R. 3080, *Congressional Information Service.*

58. Ibid.

59. See 1998 H.R. 4569, 105 H.R. 4569, *Congressional Information Service.*

60. It is noteworthy that human rights considerations were of second importance in formulating U.S. foreign policy in the region. Rarely has the U.S. criticized Israel for human rights abuses. When it had done so, during the Bush administration, Human Rights Watch claimed that the criticism "has been less effective than it could have been for two principal reasons. Foremost is the Administration's unwillingness to link, at least publicly, Israel's human rights record with the amount of aid it receives or the favorable trade relations it enjoys....Second, the United States has long made clear that its concern for human rights abuses committed by Israel is subservient to the goal of bringing Israel and her neighbors into a peace process." See Middle East Watch. (1992). Human Rights Watch World Report 1992 (p. 123). The Human Rights Committee's 1998 report on Israel confirmed Israel's "serious shortcomings in meeting its obligations under the International Covenant on Civil and Political Rights." The Committee also deplored the controversial guidelines in Israel's Landau Commission (which has since been revised) as constituting violations. See Human Rights Watch. (1998). *Israel's Record of Occupation: Violations of Civil and Political Rights.* New York: Human Rights Watch. The 1995 State Department report on Israel human rights practices stated that Israel's main human rights problems "have arisen from its policies and practices in the occupied territories....The redeployment of the IDF from most major Palestinian population areas...are significantly reducing the problems." The 1995 State Department report on Syria wrote that, despite some improvements, the government continues to restrict or deny fundamental rights. Serious abuses include the widespread use of torture in detention, arbitrary arrest, fundamentally unfair trials in the security courts, and serious others. See U.S. Department of State. (1996, March).

61. An interview by the author with Professor Itamar Rabinovich, November 12, 1998.

62. Lippman, T. W. (1996, May 1). Anti-terrorism accord signed. *Washington Post*, p. A23; Clarke, D. L. (1997, Spring). US security assistance to Egypt and Israel: Politically untouchable? *Middle East Journal, 51*(2).

63. Alpher, J. (1995–1996, Winter). Israel: The challenge of peace. *Foreign Policy 101*, pp. 142–143.

64. Curtius, M. (1994, January 17). Assad calls for "normal" relations with Israel. *Boston Globe.*

65. It is important to note the distinction between 1923 international boundary lines, the 1949 armistice lines, and the June 4, 1967 lines. The 1923 lines, delineated by the French and British Mandates over Syria, Lebanon, and Palestine, kept the Jordan River and Lake Tiberias (also known as the Sea of Galilee and Lake Kinneret) within Israel (Palestine). The armistice lines passed through the Demilitarized Zone (DMZ, an area of less than 100 square miles), which was actually composed of the three sectors conquered by Syria in the 1948 War west of the international boundary. The northern sector consisted of an area next to Tel Dan along the Israeli-Syrian frontier. The central sector straddled the Jordan River between Lake Huleh and Lake Tiberias. The southern sector consisted of an area that ran from the northeastern shore of Lake Tiberias to its southeastern shore, extending to the international boundary lines. The area southeast of Lake Tiberias constituted the bulk of the southern sector. It should also be recalled that the question of sovereignty over the DMZ was never resolved between Israel and Syria. During the period before the eruption of the 1967 War, the DMZ was partitioned de facto by both countries. Most important, Syria remained along the northeastern shore of Lake Tiberias and in the Al-Hamma area, southeast of the Lake. These constitute the June 4, 1967 lines, meaning the lines that existed on the eve of the 1967 War. See Rabil, R. G. (2003). *Embattled neighbors: Syria, Israel and Lebanon* (pp. 6–10). Boulder, CO: Lynne Rienner Publishers.

66. See excerpts from remarks by President Clinton and President Hafiz al-Asad. (1994, October 28). Asad and Clinton speak: Shared quest for peace. *New York Times,* p. A21.

67. For Muallem's remarks on the agreement see "Fresh light on the Syrian-Israeli peace negotiations." (1997, Winter). *Journal of Palestine Studies, 26*(2), 92. For Rabinovich's remarks see Rabinovich, I. (1998). *The brink of peace: The Israeli-Syrian negotiations* (p. 178). New Jersey: Princeton University Press; cf. Interview with Ambassador Rabinovich on November 12, 1998. Author note: thanks to the Ambassador I have a copy of the agreement. Also see text of the agreement in *Al-Hayat,* November 22, 1999.

68. See Schmemann, S. (1996, February 26). Revenge is claimed for the killing of a Hamas bomber. *New York Times.*

69. See Schmemann, S. (1996, March 5). 4th Terror blast in Israel kills 12 at mall in Tel Aviv: Nine-day toll grows to 59. *New York Times.*

70. Rabinovich, I. (1998). *The brink of peace: The Israeli-Syrian negotiations* (p. 266). New Jersey: Princeton University Press; Savir, U. (1998). *The process: 1,100 days that changed the Middle East* (pp. 284–285). New York: Random House.

71. On Sharm al-Shaykh summit see Jaafar, K. M. (1996, March 18). Al-Salam Wa al-Intihariyoun: Al-Muwajaha al-Quatila [Peace and suicide bombers: The deadly confrontation]. *al-Wasat,* pp. 10–19; Muallem, W. (1997, Winter). Fresh light on the Syrian-Israeli peace negotiations. *Journal of Palestine Studies, 26*(2), 81–82.

72. Associated Press. (1996, May 9). US arranges talks on Lebanon truce. *Boston Globe,* p. 11.

73. For details on Netanyahu's policy guidelines see Susser, L. (1996, July 25). Where is Netanyahu leading Israel? *Jerusalem Report,* pp. 12–16.

74. Netanyahu, Benjamin. (1993). *A place among nations: Israel and the world.* New York: Bantam Books.

75. Jehl, D. (1996, June 23). Struggle for peace, Egyptian urges Arab. *New York Times,* p. 8; see also *Al-Hayat* (1996, June 3).

76. Susser, L. (1996, July 25). Where is Netanyahu leading Israel? *Jerusalem Report,* p. 12.

77. Jehl, D. (1996, June 23). Struggle for peace, Egyptian urges Arab. *New York Times,* p. 8.

78. For details see Matar, J. (Beirut). (1997, May 15). A diplomatic Babel. *Jerusalem Report,* pp. 26–27.

79. For details see Susser, L. (1998, February 19). New approach to a deal in Lebanon. *Jerusalem Report,* p. 22.

80. Ibid., p. 22.

81. See Farouq al-Shara's interview with *al-Majalla* (1998, November 11), pp. 28–29.

82. As revealed by Dennis Ross, Netanyahu was serious about trying to do a deal with the Syrians and wanted to open a secret, private channel to al-Asad. In fact, he used an American businessman and friend, Ronald Lauder, as a go-between to al-Asad beginning in the summer of 1998, going to Damascus with messages from Netanyahu. It was over this period that "Lauder said they had basically reached agreement on all issues—the border, security arrangements, peace, and Lebanon—and had boiled them down to ten points which they would have finalized except for Asad's insistence on reviewing maps on the border and the security arrangements and Bibi's refusal lest he lose all deniability. Then came Wye and the agreement with the Palestinians, Lauder explained, and Bibi did not have the political cover to pursue the effort further." See Ross, D. (2004). *The missing peace: The inside story of the fight for Middle East peace* (p. 511). New York: Farrar, Straus, and Giroux. For details on the ten points see p. 513.

83. Sontag, D. (2000, March 1). Sharon cautions West against aid to Syria in any peace deal. *New York Times.*

84. Ibid.

85. Perlez, J. (1999, December 9). Israel and Syria to reopen talks, Clinton reports. *New York Times.*

86. Sanger, D. E. (2000, January 8). Clinton offers Israel and Syria seven-page "Working Paper" to study Golan Heights contract. *New York Times.*

87. See Ross, D. (2004). *The missing peace: The inside story of the fight for Middle East peace* (pp. 536–565). New York: Farrar, Straus, and Giroux.

88. For more details and analysis see Rabil, R. G. (2003). *Embattled neighbors: Syria, Israel and Lebanon* (pp. 218–221). Boulder, CO: Lynne Rienner Publishers.

89. Al-Maalouf, Rafiq Khalil. (2000, January 18). I'lan Ta'jile Mufawadat Shepherdstown [Announcing the postponement of Shepherdstown negotiations]. *Al-Hayat.*

90. Sontag, D. (2000, February 28). Rabin vowed to pull back from Golan, Barak says. *New York Times.*

91. Ibid.

92. Sachs, S. (2000, March 6). Israeli cabinet vows July Lebanon pullout. *New York Times.*

93. Clinton, W. J. (2004). *My life* (pp. 903–904). New York: Alfred A. Knopf.

94. Ross, D. (2004). *The missing peace: The inside story of the fight for Middle East peace* (p. 588). New York: Farrar, Straus, and Giroux.

95. Clinton, W. J. (2004). *My life* (pp. 909–910). New York: Alfred A. Knopf.

96. See Necmetin Erbakan's interview with *al-Wasat.* (1996, December 30). Erbakan: Liha-dhihi al-Asbab Ata'awan Ma'a Israil [Erbakan: For these reasons I cooperate with Israel] (pp. 16–17).

97. See Nachmani, A. (1998, June). The remarkable-Turkish Israeli tie. *Middle East Quarterly, 5*(2), 24–25.

98. For an analytic assessment of the Turkish-Israeli cooperation see Eisenstadt, M. (1997). Turkish-Israeli cooperation: An assessment. *Policy-Watch* (No. 262). Washington, DC: The Washington Institute for Near East Policy.

99. The GCC was established in 1981 and included Saudi Arabia, Kuwait, Bahrain, Qatar, the United Arab Emirates, and Oman.

100. See text of final agreement in *An-Nahar* (1991, August 7).

101. See *Mideast Mirror* (1991, September 18), p. 19, and (1991, October 28), p. 24; see also *The Washington Post* (1992, June 23), p. 15.

102. Maksoud, General A. K. (1996, May–June). Al-Stratigiyah al-Istailiya fi al-Tis'inat [Israel's strategy in the nineties]. *Al-Fikr Al-Askari*, p. 79.

103. *Mideast Mirror* (1992, March 12), quoted from Faour, M. (1993). *The Arab world after Desert Storm* (p. 86). Washington, DC: U.S. Institute of Peace Press.

104. See Khoury, P. S. (1987). *Syria and the French Mandate: The politics of Arab nationalism 1920–1945* (pp. 499–514). New Jersey: Princeton University Press.

105. Even al-Asad himself followed this line. See *al-Thawra* (1997, September 19).

106. It should be noted that Damascus refused to extradite Ocalan at Turkey's official request in early 1996.

107. Erbakan and his Refah party encouraged the promotion of Turkey's relations with its Muslim neighbors. In a symbolic statement Erbakan told *al-Wasat* that he shall remove the Turkish-Syrian border. See Erbakan's interview with *al-Wasat* (1996, January 1), pp. 10–12.

108. See *Al-Hayat* (June 10, 1996), quoted from *Middle East Contemporary Survey (MECS)—1996*, p. 632.

109. See Abd al-Halim Khaddam's interview with *al-Wasat* (1995, November 20), pp. 12–14.

110. See statements of Syria's assistant foreign minister, Adnan Umran, on the Turkish-Israeli military agreement in *al-Thawra* (1996, April 11).

111. Interview with Dr. Martin Kramer, director of the Moshe Dayan Center for Middle Eastern and African Studies, Tel Aviv University, on November 18, 1998.

112. See *Tishrin* (1997, June 25) and (1998, June 17).

113. *Al-Hayat* (1996, June 20).

114. See text of Declaration in *Tishrin* (1997, August 2).

115. The Treaty of Lausanne of July 1923 did not deal with the future of the province of Mosul, integrated de facto by Iraq but claimed by Turkey. However, in a separate accord between Great Britain, Turkey, and Iraq in June 1926, the three states agreed that the province would remain under the sovereignty of Iraq.

116. Khaddam bluntly repeated his accusation that the Turkish-Israeli alliance threatened the security and stability of the region and was directed against the Arabs. He asserted that Syria would oppose all schemes to dismantle Iraq. He also affirmed that there was no reason for Syria to strain its relations with Turkey and that the country's crisis with the Kurds should be resolved internally. See Khaddam's interview with *al-Quds al-Arabi* produced in *Tishrin* (1997, June 15).

117. See press conference in *Tishrin* (1997, May 2).

118. *Al-Ba'th* (1998, October 2); quoted from *Middle East Economic Survey (MEES)* (1998, October 5), p. C2.

119. *Middle East Economic Survey (MEES)*, October 5, 1998, pp. C2–C3.

120. See *Middle East International* (1998, October 30), p. 9; for the text of the agreement see *Middle East Quarterly* (1999, June), p. 24.

Chapter 5: The Unholy Relationship

1. See Rabinovich, I. (1998). *The brink of peace: The Israeli-Syrian negotiations* (p. 266). New Jersey: Princeton University Press; Rabil, R. G. (2003). *Embattled neighbors: Syria, Israel and Lebanon* (pp. 218–221). Boulder, CO: Lynne Rienner Publishers; Muallem, W. (1997, Winter). Fresh light on the Syrian-Israeli peace negotiations. *Journal of Palestine Studies, 26*(2); and Quandt, W. B. (2001, Winter). Clinton and the Arab-Israeli conflict: The limits of incrementalism. *Journal of Palestine Studies, 30*(2); Ross, D. (2004). *The missing peace: The inside story of the fight for Middle East peace*. New York: Farrar, Straus, and Giroux.

2. See *Al-Hayat* (2000, May 24); and *New York Times* (2000, May 24).

3. Orme, W. A., Jr. (2000, May 24). Barak declares end to "tragedy" as last troops leave Lebanon. *New York Times*.

4. See Warning from Barak. *New York Times* (2000, May 24).

5. Syria's protégé, President Emile Lahoud of Lebanon, said in an interview with *Al-Hayat* that "an Israeli unilateral withdrawal will not work… it will lead to another war." See Lahoud's interview with *Al-Hayat* (2000, March 11). He appeared to warn Israel that a unilateral withdrawal without prior negotiations with Beirut and Damascus could lead to a new conflict, as Palestinian refugees in Lebanon would resume their attacks on Israel, a condition that precipitated Israel's 1978 invasion of Lebanon in the first place. As is well known, Lebanon refused to grant citizenship to the Palestinian refugees, estimated at over 300,000, who came to Lebanon during the wars of 1948 and 1967. Lebanon always demanded that the Palestinian refugees be repatriated. Lahoud critically questioned: "How would it be possible to guarantee Israel's borders when thousands of armed refugees are present in the Palestinian camps, demanding the right to return amid a total absence of any answers about their fate and future." Warning from Barak. *New York Times* (2000, May 24).

6. Rabil, R. G. (2001, September). The Maronites and Syrian withdrawal: From "isolationists" to "traitors"? *Middle East Policy, 8*(3).

7. "Shebaa Farms, located south of the Lebanese village Shebaa, is 14 km in length and about 2 km in width, at altitudes ranging from 400 to 2,000 meters. It is composed of plots of some 14 agricultural farmlands that have been used before 1967 by farmers from the village of Shebaa." Kaufman, A. (2002, Autumn). Who owns the Shebaa Farms? Chronicle of a territorial dispute. *Middle East Journal, 56*(4).

8. See Lebanese Prime Minister Salim al-Huss's speech delivered at the U.N. General Assembly on September 14, 2000. U.N. Official Records, A/55/PV.14, 14.9.2000. See also issues of *Al-'Ahd,* the official organ of Hizbollah, May 2000. First quoted from Kaufman.

9. Other potential cases similar to Shebaa include several villages such as Nkhaile, al-Ghajar, and the "seven villages."

10. Major General Ali Haydar, commander of the Special Forces, was arrested in the summer of 1994 and stripped of his post, which was assigned to Major General Ali Habib. His closest supporters were also ousted from their posts. Haydar hails from the powerful Alawi Haddadin clan, a traditional supporter of the regime, and he was instrumental in subduing the Moslem Brotherhood. His fall from grace was reportedly the consequence of his criticism of al-Asad for deviating from Ba'thi principles and joining the peace process. In the same year, Major General Muhammad al-Khuli was appointed commander of the air force. His appointment came as a surprise to many since Khuli had been implicated in the attempt to blow up an El Al airplane at London Heathrow airport in 1986. Because of that attempt and under international pressure, mainly from the United States and Britain, Khuli was dismissed from his post as chief of the Air Force Security Directorate. By bringing him back into his inner circle, al-Asad indicated that his need to reinforce his regime with a loyal associate overrode his concern with the possible anger of the United States and Britain. This was so in spite of the fact that Syria was trying to enhance its image and improve its relations with both powers. Al-Asad undertook that step

because he knew he could rely on a grateful Khuli to support his policies, particularly with regard to the succession issue.

This process of establishing Bashar as the successor gathered steam from the mid-1990s to the late-1990s. Reportedly, Major General Adnan Makhluf, commander of the presidential guard, and a relative to Al-Asad by marriage, was dismissed from his post in 1995 following disagreements with Bashar. He was replaced by a young officer with no political power, Major General Ali Hussein, making Bashar the strong man of the guard. In the same year, two longtime loyalists of Al-Asad, Generals Ibrahim Safi and Shafiq Fayyad were promoted, respectively, to commanders of the Second Corps (Syrian forces in Lebanon) and Third Corps. Their former posts as commanders of the First Division and Third Division, were filled by young Alawi officers whose loyalty went to Bashar. Other appointments of Bashar loyalists had taken place in 1995 and 1996 as well.

In 1997 Bashar had a retroactive promotion from major in 1995 to lieutenant colonel. His speedy promotion, which started with the rank of captain in 1994, was attributed to his excellent achievement in the army. Al-Asad's son-in-law Asef Shawqat was appointed to the Military Intelligence Department headed by General Ali Duba, making him the second strong man in that all-important department and presumably in line to replace Duba upon his retirement. Major military changes took place in 1998 as well. General Hikmat Shihabi, Army Chief of Staff and a Sunni, was retired and was replaced by an Alawi, General Ali Aslan. Some analysts claim that Shihabi did not get along well with Bashar. Meanwhile, four major generals were promoted to generals: Abd al-Rahman al-Sayadi, Ali Habib, Toufic Jaloul, and Farouq Issa Ibrahim, all considered longtime loyalists to al-Asad. In addition, Major General Mahmoud al-Shaqa, an Alawi and commander of the Syrian forces in the Gulf War, was appointed head of Civilian Intelligence. See Rabil, R. G. (2003). *Embattled neighbors: Syria, Israel and Lebanon* (pp. 139–141). Boulder, CO: Lynne Rienner Publishers.

11. Rabil, R. G. (1999, October 27). Interview with a prominent Damascene personality.

12. Seale, P. (2000, March 7). Bashar al-Asad li-al-Hayat: Mu'tamar al-Ba'th Hadha al-Am wa Zakayt Ba'd al-Akfiya' lil-Hukuma al-Jadida [Bashar al-Asad to Al-Hayat: The Ba'th Congress this year and I recommended some meritorious people to the new government]. *Al-Hayat*.

13. Ibid.

14. For the names and titles of the members of the new government, see *Al-Hayat* (2000, March 15).

15. See *Al-Hayat* (2000, June 12).

16. See Hamidi, I. (2000, June 20). Bashar al-Asad Raasa "Lajna Sudasiya" Li-Edarat Mu'tamar "al-Ba'th" [Bashar al-Asad heads a "committee of six" to manage the "Ba'th" Congress]. *Al-Hayat*. The committee of six included Bashar, Vice-Presidents Abd al-Halim Khaddam and Muhammad Zuheir Mashariqa, deputy secretaries of the Ba'th Regional and Central Command Councils, respectively, Suleiman Qaddah and Abd allah

al-Ahmar, and Defense Minister Mustafa Tlas. Tlas played as pivotal a role as Khaddam by organizing meetings between high-ranking military officials and Bashar and rallying unequivocal support for him.

17. Ibid.

18. Hamidi, I. (2000, June 21). Mu'tamar al-Ba'th Yantakheb Bashar wa Yudkhel 12 'dwan Jadidan [Ba'th Congress elects Bashar and brings in twelve new members]. *Al-Hayat.*

19. Bakhtian served as director of the National Security Bureau, which coordinates party and government bodies. Hamidi, I. (2000, June 21). Mu'tamar al-Ba'th Yantakheb Bashar wa Yudkhel 12 'dwan Jadidan [Ba'th Congress elects Bashar and brings in twelve new members]. *Al-Hayat.* It is noteworthy that the council did not include Ali Aslan, chief of staff, and Asef Shawqat, military intelligence chief and Bashar's brother-in-law, both considered the military muscle of Bashar's new regime. This was more or less countervailed by beefing up the Central Command Council of the Ba'th party (90 members), by bringing into it military officers constituting a third of its total number and including Maher al-Asad, Bashar's brother, and Manaf Tlas, the secretary of defense's son. In addition, Ali Duba, the former strong man of military intelligence, was ousted from the Central Command Council. Equally significant, Bashar's attempts to continue to consolidate his power involved promoting several loyal supporters in the military, among whom was none other than his brother, Maher, and discharging several military officers whose loyalty to Bashar was in doubt. See Rabil, R. G. (2003). *Embattled neighbors: Syria, Israel and Lebanon* (p. 273). Boulder, CO: Lynne Rienner Publishers.

20. See statements by then newly appointed Secretary of State Colin Powell and National Security Adviser Condoleezza Rice, respectively, in Erlanger, S. (2000, December 18). A higher threshold for U.S. intervention means adjustments abroad. *New York Times,* and (2000, January–February). Promoting the National Interest. *Foreign Affairs.* Excerpts of this section originally appeared in Rabil, R. G. (2003). *Embattled neighbors: Syria, Israel and Lebanon* (pp. 108–112). Boulder, CO: Lynne Rienner Publishers.

21. Perlez, J. (2001, February 9). Bush officials pronounce Clinton Mideast plan dead. *New York Times.*

22. Perlez, J. (2001, March 20). Powell stresses responsibility of Mideast policy. *New York Times.*

23. See *Al-Hayat* (2001, March 11).

24. Perlez, J. (2001, February 27). Powell proposes easing sanctions on Iraqi civilians. *New York Times.*

25. See *Al-Hayat* (2001, March 31).

26. Sipress, A., and Lynch, C. (2002, February 14). U.S. avoids confronting Syrians on Iraqi oil. *Washington Post.* Iraqi oil flowed into Syrian pipelines from November 2000 to March 2003. Various reports had different figures about how many barrels of oil were shipped through the 550-mile pipeline, with estimates ranging from 120,000 to 230,000 barrels a day. See *Los Angeles Times* (2002, January 29); and *Washington Post* (2003, May 12).

27. Prados, A. B. (2003, October 10). Syria: U.S. Relations and Bilateral Issues. *Congressional Research Service* (p. 7). Washington, DC: The Library of Congress.

28. Ibid. See also *Washington Post* (2003, May 3).

29. CBS News. (2001). Bush backs Palestinian state. www.cbsnews.com/ stories/2001/09/03/world/main313042.shtml.

30. See Secretary Powell's Louisville speech on the State Department Web site, www.state.gov/secretary/rm/2001.

31. MacFarQuhar, N. (2002, January 14). Syria repackages its repression of Muslim militants as antiterror lesson. *New York Times.*

32. Hersh, S. M. (2003, July 28). The Syrian bet: Did the Bush administration burn a useful source on Al-Qaeda. *The New Yorker;* Sale, R. (UPI Intelligence Correspondent). (2003, July 17). US Syria raid killed 80. *Washington Times;* Risen, J. (2001, October 30). New allies help CIA in its fight against terror. *New York Times.*

33. For a complete view of Syria's stand on the issue of terrorism, see its official position with respect to U.N. Security Resolution 1373, which created a U.N. committee to combat terror, in *Al-Hayat* (2002, January 3).

34. According to the U.S. State Department [Title 22 of the United States Code, Section 2656f(d)], "the term terrorism means premeditated, politically motivated violence perpetrated against noncombatant targets by subnational groups or clandestine agents, usually intended to influence an audience."

35. See *Al-Hayat* (2001, November 8).

36. See Bashar al-Asad's interview with Al-Arabia Television Station on June 11, 2003.

37. According to Seymour M. Hersh, "Among other things, the Syrians wanted a back channel to Washington—that is, a private means of communicating with the President and his key aides." Hersh, S. M. (2003, July 28). The Syrian bet: Did the Bush administration burn a useful source on Al-Qaeda? *The New Yorker.*

38. U.S. Department of State. (2003, April). *Patterns of global terrorism 2002* (p. 81). Washington, DC: Office of the Secretary of State.

39. For the text of the National Security Strategy of the United States of America see www.whitehouse.gov/nsc/nss.html. For implications of the strategy for U.S. foreign policy see O'Hanlon, M. E., Rice, S. E., and Steinberg, J. B. (2002, December). The new National Security strategy and preemption. *Brookings Institute,* Policy Brief #113.

40. U.S. Department of State. (2004, April). *Patterns of global terrorism 2003* (p. ix). Washington, DC: Office of the Secretary of State.

41. Prados, A. B. (2003, October 10). Syria: U.S. relations and bilateral issues. *Congressional Research Service* (p. 5). Washington, DC: The Library of Congress.

42. Ibid., p. 6.

43. Discussion with a high-level Syrian official stationed at the Syrian Embassy in Washington, DC, November 16, 2002.

44. Prados, A. B. (2003, October 10). Syria: U.S. relations and bilateral issues. *Congressional Research Service* (p. 6). Washington, DC: The Library of Congress.

45. See "Rumsfeld warns Syria on military shipments," http://www.cnn.com/2003/WORLD/meast/03/28/sprj.irq.war.main/; and Slevin, P. (2003, March 29). US warns of interference in Iraq. *Washington Post*.

46. Syrian Foreign Minister Farouq al-Shara roundly rejected U.S. charges as baseless. See MacFarquhar, N. (2003, April 14). Syria's Foreign Minister calls US charges "baseless." *New York Times*.

47. See Young, K. (2003, May 5). US warns Syria it is watching its actions. *Washington Post*; see also *The Daily Star* (2003, May 5). Representatives of Islamic Jihad, the Islamic Resistance Movement (Hamas), the Popular Front for the Liberation of Palestine, and the Popular Front for the Liberation of Palestine–General Command have all offices in Damascus. The Syrian leadership denies U.S. charges that these offices engage in terrorist activities. President Bashar al-Asad said that "these are not offices, really. They are houses where these groups do media activities." See al-Asad's interview with Newsweek-Washington's Post Lally Weymouth, *Washington Post* (2003, May 11).

48. *As-Safir* (2003, March 27).

49. Ibid.

50. See President Bashar al-Asad's interview with *Al-Anbaa* (2003, June 11).

51. See the full report bearing the title "A clean break: A new strategy for securing the realm" at http://iasps.org/pubs/stratpubs.htm#pap. Among the contributors to the report were Richard Perle, Douglas Feith, James Colbert, Charles Fairbanks, Jr., and David Wurmser.

52. This point of view has been consistently aired in the Arab media, especially on *Al-Jazeera* and *Al-Arabiya* television stations. According to Raghida Dergham, "The hawks and radicals within and without the US administration set out the policies with the end of invading and occupying Iraq as one of the gateways to strike and shatter Syria, which is all part of the strategy to ensure Israel's supremacy and protect it from establishing peace with its neighbors." See Dergham, R. (2003, October 10). Why will traditional calculations in the region fail? *Al-Hayat*.

53. Near the end of the Clinton presidency, a study group wrote a document called "Ending Syria's occupation of Lebanon." Among the signatories of the documents were Richard Perle, Douglas Feith, Ziad abd al-Nour, and Elliot Abrams, all with connections to the Bush administration. Michael Ledeen, an American Enterprise Institute scholar, and a neoconservative ideologue, has been vocal in calling for a regime change in Syria. In an interview with Graham Turner's "An American Odyssey," *Daily Telegraph* (2003, June 16), Ledeen said: "Now, like it or not, we're in a regional war, and we can't opt out of it....We have to bring down these regimes and produce free governments in all those countries....Undermining the governments of other countries? No big deal."

54. Hamidi, I. (2003, October 17). Al-Asad Yantaqed "majmou'a min al-Muta'assibin'" fi al-'idara wa Ra'is al-Arkan Yad'u ela al-Jahiziyya Lirad Ay Adwan [Al-Asad criticizes a "group of extremists" in the administration and the Chief of Staff calls for readiness to respond to any aggression]. *Al-Hayat.*

55. See President Bashar al-Asad's interview with *Al-Hayat* (2003, October 7).

Chapter 6: A New Cold War?

1. See the text of the Act at http://thomas.loc.gov/cgi-bin/query/D? c108:2:./temp/~c1084wdYcM::.

2. It is interesting to note that Washington, keeping to its old pattern, has not included human rights considerations in its legislation against Syria.

3. Prados, A. B. (2003, October 10). Syria: U.S. relations and bilateral issues. *Congressional Research Service* (p. 13). Washington, DC: The Library of Congress.

4. The Senate bill imposed similar sanctions to those contained in H.R. 1828 with the exception of not including a ban on Syrian aircraft landing in or flying over the United States.

5. The author received a copy of one letter.

6. Ibrahim, A. (2003, July 17). Syrian army continues troop deployment. *The Daily Star.*

7. See Hersh, S. M. (2003, July 28). The Syrian bet: Did the Bush administration burn a useful source on Al-Qaeda. *The New Yorker;* and Sale, R. (UPI Intelligence Correspondent). (2003, July 17). US Syria raid killed 80. *Washington Times.* Some analysts and intelligence officers think that the incursion was meant to end U.S.-Syrian intelligence cooperation. Patrick Lang, a former Defense Intelligence Agency official, said that "many in the government believe that incursion was an effort by ideologues to disrupt cooperation between the US and Syria." See Kristof, N. D. (2003, July 15). 16 Words and Counting. *New York Times;* see also Goldstein, R. (2003, October 30). Cheney's Hawks "Hijacking Policy." *Sydney Morning Herald.*

8. See Bolton's complete testimony at http://wwwa.house.gov/international_relations/108/bol091603.htm.

9. Ibid.

10. Following Bolton's testimony, Paula Zahn of CNN had an interview with Syrian Foreign Minister Farouq al-Shara on September 25, 2003, in which he denied American accusations that Syria was allowing Jihadis to cross into Iraq.

11. See *Washington Post* (2003, April 17).

12. See *Daily Telegraph* (2004, June 1).

13. According to the State Department's *Patterns of global terrorism,* "Hizballah is dedicated to liberating Jerusalem and eliminating Israel,...

is closely allied with, and often directed by, Iran but has the capability and willingness to act alone. Although Hizballah does not share the Syrian's regime's secular orientation, the group has been a strong ally in helping Syria advance its political objectives in the region. First designated in 1997. Known or suspected to have been involved in numerous anti-US and anti-Israeli terrorist attacks, including the suicide truck bombings of the US Embassy and US Marine barracks in Beirut in 1983 and the US Embassy annex in Beirut in September 1984. Three members of Hizballah—'Imad Mughniyah, Hasan Izz-al-Din, and Ali Atwa—are on the FBI's list of 22 Most-Wanted Terrorists for the hijacking in 1985 of TWA flight 847 during which a US Navy diver was murdered. Elements of the group were responsible for the kidnapping and detention of US and other Westerners in Lebanon in the 1980s." U.S. Department of State. (2004, April). *Patterns of global terrorism 2003* (pp. 121–122). Washington, DC: Office of the Secretary of State.

14. See Nasrallah's speech in *Al-Hayat* (2003, March 14). Shortly thereafter CNN interviewed Nasrallah, who claimed that Hizbollah has no operational links with Iraq and the party has no plans to attack Americans unless they attacked it first.

15. The glorification of resistance, as led by Hizbollah, has been widening across Lebanon's ethnic and religious communities. Renowned Lebanese singers, including Wadi' al-Safi, have dedicated songs eulogizing the resistance movement. A television series revolving around the role of resistance in the south of Lebanon aired on the first day of the Muslim religious holiday, Ramadan. Significantly, Hizbollah fared extremely well in the municipal elections in Lebanon, winning overwhelmingly in the Beka valley and the southern suburbs of the capital. For details on the municipal elections see *An-Nahar* (2004, May 20, 21, 22).

16. In sharp contrast to the impotency of Arab states, as perceived by Arabs, Hizbollah was able to strike a deal, mediated by Germany, with Israel to swap prisoners. Arabs hailed and applauded Hizbollah's achievement, which they considered as a victory over Israel. For example, Lebanese prisoners were welcomed by thousands, many of whom attended a festival arranged by Hizbollah, including ironically government officials. See *An-Nahar* (2004, January 30).

17. See the entire inaugural speech in *Tishrin al-Usbu'I* [Tishrin Weekly] (2000, July 18).

18. In November 2000, Syrian authorities released 600 political prisoners. See *Al-Hayat* (2000, November 18).

19. See the text of Statement 99 in *Al-Hayat* (2000, September 27). It is noteworthy that, according to Alan George, the first seed of Syria's civil society movement (*Harakat al-mujtama' al-madani*) was planted even earlier, at a May 28, 2000 meeting at the Damascus home of film director Nabil al-Maleh. The meeting was organized by the 60-year-old writer and long-standing dissident Michel Kilo, who had been jailed in 1980–1983 at the height of the countrywide rebellion against the regime. Also present were the poet and writer Adel Mahmoud and the film director Muhammad

Qa'arisili. "The subject of the meeting was: 'How could we revive the cultural and democratic movement in Syria?'" recalled Kilo. "This was, if you want, the inaugural meeting of the civil society movement in Syria." The group continued to meet informally but subsequently established itself formally as a Constituent Board for the movement, that was named the Committees for the Revival of Civil Society in Syria (*Lijan Ihya' al-Mujtama' al-Madani fi Suriya*). See George, A. (2003). *Syria: Neither bread nor freedom* (p. 33). London: Zed Books.

20. It is important to note that Riad Seif, a deputy in parliament and outspoken critic of the regime, played a key role in promoting civil forums. In fact, Seif, unlike Kilo and his associates, who sought establishing a political-cultural movement, favored an "overtly political campaign which might attract support from reformers within the regime." In July 2000, Seif launched an explicitly political discussion group, or a forum, in his offices in Damascus. Subsequently, he and his associates issued a statement proposing the formation of an association to be named "Friends of Civil Society in Syria." The statement affirmed the need "to revive the institutions of civil society and achieve balance between their role and that of the state in the context of a real partnership between them in the higher national interest." See George, A. (2003). *Syria: Neither bread nor freedom* (p. 35). London: Zed Books.

21. On November 15, 2000, President al-Asad issued a decree releasing 600 prisoners, many of whom were Muslim Brotherhood members, and most of the rest were leftists. On November 22, he issued a general pardon for nonpolitical prisoners to mark the thirtieth anniversary of his father's "corrective movement." He also ordered the closure of the notorious Mezzeh prison in Damascus. During this lax period, a couple of human rights organizations reemerged, including the Committees for the Defense of Democratic Freedoms and Human Rights in Syria and the Syrian Human Rights Association. The first one had been created in 1989 but suppressed in 1991 when its chairman, Aktham Nu'aisah, and other key figures were arrested. See George, A. (2003). *Syria: Neither bread nor freedom* (p. 41). London: Zed Books.

22. See text of Statement 1000 in *Al-Hayat* (2001, January 12).

23. Ibid.

24. See Vice-President Abd al-Halim Khaddam's statements in *Al-Hayat* (2001, February 19). See also Defense Minister Mustafa Tlas's statements in *Al-Hayat* (2001, April 12).

25. See President Bashar al-Asad's interview with *As-Sharq al-Awsat* (2001, February 8).

26. It is noteworthy that civil society activists arrested in August and September 2001 were tried in criminal and state security courts. Though Seif and Homsi were tried in a criminal court, they were denied confidential access to their lawyers throughout their detention. Other activists were tried in secrecy by the Supreme State Security Court under the authority of the Emergency Law. See U.S. Department of State. (2003, March 31). *Syria: Country Reports on Human Rights*

Practices-2002, Washington, DC: Bureau of Democracy, Human Rights, and Labor.

27. Ibid. It is interesting that although the regime amended the Press Law to permit the reestablishment of publications that circulated prior to 1963, the same amendments also "stipulated imprisonment and stiff financial penalties as part of broad, vague provisions prohibiting the publication of "inaccurate" information, particularly if it "causes public unrest, disturbs international relations, violates the dignity of the state or national unity, affects the morale of the armed forces, or inflicts harm on the national economy and the safety of the monetary system."

28. See the text of the petition in *As-Safir* (2003, June 3).

29. Ibid.

30. Telephone interview by the author with Professor Sadek Jalal Al-Azm (2003, September 6).

31. See Glass, C. (2003, July 24). Is Syria next? *London Review of Books.*

32. See Amnesty International. (2003). *Syria* (Report No. 2003). Available at www.web.amnesty.org/report2003/syr-summary-eng; and see also George, A. (2003). *Syria: Neither bread nor freedom* (p. 92). London: Zed Books.

33. According to Amnesty International, scores of people were arrested during 2002 for political reasons, including former political activists affiliated with the Muslim Brotherhood. See Amnesty International. (2003). *Syria* (Report No. 2003). Available at www.web.amnesty.org/report2003/syr-summary-eng.

34. For a detailed account on religious revival in Syria, see Wilson, S. (2005, January 23). Religious surge alarms secular Syrians. *Washington Post;* and especially Hamidi, I. (2005, June 18). Dimashq Ta'lun 'an Khalaya Takfiriyah wa Da'awat ila Juhud Tanwiriyah...Syria al-'Ulmaniyah Tazdad Islamiyah [Damascus reports on infidel (unbelief) cells and calls for awareness efforts...Secular Syria grows Islamic]. *Al-Hayat.*

35. In an attempt to encourage moderate Islam, the Syrian government supported the building of some 80,000 mosques, over 22 higher-education institutions for teaching Islam, and many regional Shari'a schools. Hamidi, I. (2005, June 18). Dimashq Ta'lun 'an Khalaya Takfiriyah wa Da'awat ila Juhud Tanwiriyah...Syria al-'Ulmaniyah Tazdad Islamiyah [Damascus reports on infidel (unbelief) cells and calls for awareness efforts...Secular Syria grows Islamic]. *Al-Hayat.*

36. See *Daily Telegraph* (2004, December 2).

37. Ibid.

38. Statement by Syria's official news agency, Syrian Arab News Ageny (SANA) (2003, July 8).

39. See http://www.arabicnews.com/ansub/Daily/Day/030717/2003071701.html.

40. Sipress, A. (2003, May 12). Syrian reforms gain momentum in wake of war. *Washington Post.*

41. See SANA (2003, July 7); and see http://www.arabicnews.com/ansub/Daily/Day/030729/2003072909.html.

42. See www.arabicnews.com/ansub/daily/day/030526/2003052608.html.

43. While denying any connection to the collapse of the Ba'th party in Iraq, the regional command of the Ba'th party in Syria had been exploring ways to reform the party. In this respect, the 21 members of the regional command formed four committees to tackle the reorganization of the party, reform the principles of the Ba'th in relation to its tenets (freedom, unity, and socialism), and discuss democracy. Their assessment will be based on questionnaires already mailed to approximately 1.8 million members. See Hamidi, I. (2004, March 8). Al-Ba'th al-Suri Yahya Thukra Tasalomihi al-Hukm Min Doune Mazaher Ihtifalia wa Ba'idan 'An al-Rafiq al-Iraqi [The Syrian Bath commemorates the anniversary of its assumption of power without festivities and distant from the Iraqi comrade]. *Al-Hayat*.

44. See the composition of the new government in *Al-Hayat* (2003, September 19).

45. The petition was published in *An-Nahar* (2004, February 10).

46. See *Al-Hayat* (2004, March 9). Commenting on the petition's demand to lift emergency rules, Syrian officials asserted that these rules are rarely invoked, mainly in national security matters. Aktham Nu'aissi was shortly thereafter rearrested. In October 2004, the Ludovic-Trarieux International Human Rights Prize Committee in Brussels rewarded its human rights prize to Nu'aissi, compelling the Syrian government to grant him permission to travel.

47. See *An-Nahar* (2004, March 18, 19); and *Al-Hayat* (2004, March 15, 20, 27).

48. In 1962 a census taken in the al-Jazira province failed to register thousands of Kurds. Human Rights Watch has documented systematic discrimination against the Kurdish minority in Syria, including arbitrary denial of citizenship to generations of Syrian-born Kurds. See Human Rights Watch. (1996, October). *Silenced Kurds*.

49. President Bashar al-Asad's interview with *al-Jazeera* was aired on May 1, 2004.

50. Farid Ghadry, founder of the Reform Party of Syria, has been vocal in calling for international support for the reform movement in Syria. Based in Washington, DC, Ghadry's partial agenda is to "educate those in Syria about democracy (since the understanding of democracy within Syria is limited); to maintain pressure on the Syrian regime by reporting on corruption and abuse; to capture the loyalty of the Syrian army; to promote understanding of US foreign policy in the region; and to harness the power of liberal democrats as a counterbalance to Islamists and Baathists." See Ghadry, F. (2005, Winter). Syrian reform: What lies beneath. *Middle East Quarterly*.

51. Reportedly former Defense Minister Mustafa Tlas and former Vice-President Abd al-Halim Khaddam had significant influence over President al-Asad. They played an important role in paving the way for al-Asad to

become president. Immediately after the death of Bashar's father, the late president Hafiz al-Asad, Khaddam issued legislation promoting Bashar from colonel to lieutenant general—the rank of his father—and appointing him commander in chief of the Syrian armed forces. Khaddam and Tlas were behind amending a provision in the Syrian constitution, which stipulated that the president be at least 40 years old. Bashar then was in his early thirties. They also helped elect Bashar as the secretary-general of the Ba'th party. See, respectively, *Al-Hayat* (2000, June 11, 20, 21).

52. See Bashar's statement in *Al-Hayat* (2003, July 2).

53. The bombing was conducted in retaliation for a Palestinian suicide attack in the northern city of Haifa. Islamic Jihad, which maintains an office in Damascus, claimed responsibility for the attack. This attack marked the end of the tacit understanding between Syria and Israel over the "red lines" that each side had expected each other to respect.

54. Anderson, J. W. (2003, October 6). Israeli airstrike hits site in Syria. *Washington Post.* Secretary of State Colin Powell had already accused Syria of "not doing enough to end what he said was its support of 'terrorist activity' including cross-border infiltration by saboteurs into Iraq." See Haddadin, H. (Reuters). (2003, September 15). Powell says Syria is not doing enough on terrorism. *Washington Post.*

55. Moore, M. (2003, October 7). Israeli killed in border attack. *Washington Post.*

56. See *Al-Hayat* (2003, October 12, 20).

57. The Bush administration maintained its ambassadorial diplomatic relations with Syria by appointing Margaret Scobey as U.S. ambassador there. Syria is alone among countries on the State Department's terrorism list to have a U.S. ambassador. President al-Asad appointed Imad Mustafa as Syrian ambassador to the United States. Mustapha, who is in his early forties, is known as a supporter for reform and better relations with the United States. His appointment was seen as an attempt by the Syrian government to improve its image in the United States.

58. Slevin, P. (2004, April 15). Bush backs Israel on West Bank. *Washington Post;* and Kessler, G. (2004, May 4). Jordan's call for U.S. policy on West Bank is rebuffed. *Washington Post.*

59. Kessler, G. (2004, May 4). Jordan's call for U.S. policy on West Bank is rebuffed. *Washington Post.* See also Erakat, S. (2004, April 25). Why did Bush take my job? *Washington Post.*

60. See MacFarquhar, N. (2003, December 1). Syrian pressing for Israel talks. *New York Times.*

61. Kessler, G. (2004, May 5). US retreats from Bush remarks on Sharon Plan. *Washington Post.*

62. See "Vice President highlights Syria's policy towards Greater Middle East initiative" at http://www.arabicnews.com/ansub/Daily/Day/040319/2004031907.html.

63. Moore, M., and Anderson, J. W. (2004, March 23). Emotional protests in slaying of Sheikh. *Washington Post.*

64. In his daily briefing, following protests and disturbances in Lebanon and Syria, U.S. State Department deputy spokesman stated, "We would note that the recent suppression of protests, both in Syria and in Lebanon, over the last couple of days: In Lebanon, students protested peacefully at several universities against the continuing domination by Syria of Lebanon and the continued Syrian military presence there, those protests were suppressed by police; in Syria, citizens of Kurdish descent have been protesting the lack of equal rights and in the ensuing violence, the authorities have not only killed and injured demonstrators, but also clamped down hard on normal life in cities where there is a Kurdish majority. We have made our concerns known, and we reiterate our call upon the Government of Syria to stop suppressing non-violent political expression in Syria and Lebanon." See statement at http://www.state.gov/r/pa/prs/dpb/2004/ 30526.htm.

65. The interview with *Al-Jazeera* was aired on May 1, 2004. For excerpts of the interview see *Al-Hayat* (2004, May 2).

66. See General Gant's interview on *Al-Jazeera* (2004, July 20). Excerpts of the interview can be accessed at http://english.aljazeera.net/NR/exeres/ 7732C490-4F79-4328-8C9D-186AF002F1D2.html.

67. Interview with *Al-Jazeera* (2004, May 1).

68. Syria has been making the point that it has been a target of terrorism itself. Syrian authorities have stressed this point following explosions and gunfire that broke out on April 7, 2004 in Mezzah, the diplomatic quarter of Damascus. See *An-Nahar* (2004, April 28). Damascus has not seen such incidents since the Syrian regime brutally put down an uprising by the Muslim Brotherhood in 1982. These incidents came on the heels of discovering an alleged al-Qaeda plot to carry out a chemical attack in Jordan. Significantly, Jordan security services announced that two trucks laden with explosives were seized in early April. The trucks reportedly entered the Kingdom from Syria. Syrian authorities immediately denied that the vehicles came from Syria. See Hamzeh, A. S. *Jordan Times* (2004, April 8). Commenting on the incidents, the Syrian ambassador to Washington said that "we are not clear who may have been targeted. It may have been one of the Western embassies, or may be the perpetrators were unhappy with Syria's cooperation against al-Qaeda. It could be part of the same wave of attempted terrorist attacks that were planned in Jordan." See Wilson, S. (2004, April 28). Syrian capital is rocked by blasts. *Washington Post.* The rumor mill among some analysts has it that Syria itself had staged the incidents. The government has recently acknowledged that the explosions were the work of a small group of Islamic militants, some of them from the Israeli-occupied Golan Heights. See Wilson, S. (2005, January 23). Religious surge alarms secular Syrians. *Washington Post.*

69. It is noteworthy that the United States was vocal in calling for free and fair presidential elections in Lebanon, though Syria has influenced the outcome of the elections. During the swearing-in ceremony of the new U.S. Ambassador to Lebanon Jeffrey D. Feltman, Marc Grossman, Under Secretary of State for Political Affairs stated: "Over the coming year,

Lebanon will hold presidential and parliamentary elections. These elections must be free and fair. They should be held in accordance with the established Lebanese constitution, and they should be held without interference from any other country." See Statement at http://www.10452lccc.com/daily%20news%20bulletin/swearing .ceremony22.7.04.htm.

70. Following a GCC meeting in Saudi Arabia, Kuwait's foreign minister Muhammad Sabah al-Salem al-Sabah said: "The council (GCC) supports international resolutions, including the last decision issued by the Security Council calling for the withdrawal of all forces from Lebanon." See Assaf, N., Fleihan, K., and Rizk, Z. A. (2004, September 15). Arab foreign ministers affirm Lebanon's right to a free political decision. *The Daily Star.*

71. Syria warns Israel over attack. (2004, September 27). *The Daily Star.* It is noteworthy that this attack inside Syria was the second of its kind. In October 2003, Israel's air force, for the first time in almost three decades, struck a base for Islamic Jihad, purportedly in retaliation for an Islamic Jihad suicide bombing in Haifa.

72. Hamadeh blames Lebanese authorities for attempt to assassinate him. (2004, October 7). *Naharnet.* See article at http://www.naharnet.com/ domino/tn/Newsdesk.nsf/Story/EC1A0FBD19F2AFAAC2256F.

73. Young, M. (2004, October 7). All fall down? Syria's regime takes an option out on its future. *The Daily Star.*

74. The Syrian cabinet reshuffle included appointing Dr. Ghassan Tayarah as Minister of Industry, Dr. Maher Hussami as Minister of Health, Dr. Mohammad Ziyad al-Ayoubi as Minister of Awkaf (Islamic Trusts), Dr. Amer Hosni Lutfi as Minister of Trade and Economy, Mr. Muhammad al-Ghofri as Minister of Justice, and Dr. Diyala al-Haj Omar as Minister of Labor and Social Affairs. Most importantly, Ghazi Kanaan was appointed Minister of Interior and Mehdi Daklallah, editor of the Syrian state-run daily *al-Ba'th,* Minister of Information. Kanaan and Daklallah are considered supporters of reform and close to al-Asad. Prime Minister Muhammad Naji Otri continued to head the cabinet. Defense Minister Hassan Turkmani retained his post, which he was appointed to by al-Asad in May, replacing the longtime defense minister Major General Mustafa Tlas. See *Al-Hayat* (2004, October 4).

75. On October 1, 2004, U.N. Secretary General Kofi Annan issued a report pursuant to Security Council Resolution 1559, in which he observed that the requirements of the resolution have not been met. He noted that the only significant foreign forces deployed in Lebanon are Syrian and several armed elements remain in south Lebanon, the most significant of which is Hizbollah. See United Nations Security Council (S/2004/777), "Report of the Secretary-General Pursuant to Security Council Resolution 1559 (2004)," available at http://ods-dds-ny.un.org/doc/UNDOC/GEN/ NO4/531/35/PDF/N0453135. The Lebanese government responded by emphasizing that the report failed to mention the historic responsibility born by Israel's occupation policies in Palestine, Syria, and Lebanon; the amendment to the constitution was approved in the parliament by a vote

of 96 to 29 with three members not present; the withdrawal of Syrian forces is determined by bilateral agreements between the two countries, especially in the absence of a comprehensive peace in the region; and Hizbollah is a party resisting occupation. See Lubnan Arsala Mulahazatihi 'Ala Taqrir Anan [Lebanon sent its comments on Anan's report] (2004, October 7). *An-Nahar.*

76. The complete text of President al-Asad's speech was published by SANA on October 9, 2004.

77. Ricks, T. E. (2004, December 8). Rebels aided by allies in Syria, U.S. says. *Washington Post.*

78. See *As-Sharq Al-Awsat* (2004, July 25).

79. The order of President Bush implementing the Act emphasized that the "President will consider additional sanctions against the Government of Syria if it does not take serious and concrete steps to cease its support for terrorist groups, terminate its weapons of mass destruction, withdraw its troops from Lebanon, and cooperate fully with the international community in promoting the stabilization and reconstruction of Iraq." See text of order at http://www.whitehouse.gov/news/releases/2004/05/20040511-7.html. It is interesting to note that the timing of the order coincided with the Arab foreign ministers approving a framework for reform, paving the way to reconvene an Arab summit that was postponed on account of disagreements over reform and terrorism. It is noteworthy that in an interview with the *Daily Telegraph* President al-Asad came closer than ever before to admitting that his country possessed stockpiles of WMD. He stated: "We are a country which is [partly] occupied and from time to time we are exposed to Israeli aggression....It is natural for us to look for means to defend ourselves. It is not difficult to get most of these weapons anywhere in the world and they can be obtained at any time." See *Daily Telegraph* (2004, June 1).

80. *Al-Hayat* (2003, July 28).

81. So far Syrian attitudes towards U.S. plans in the region in general and in Iraq in particular show that Damascus does not like to see Iraq emerge as a bridgehead for a Pax Americana in the region. Therefore, it would like to see the United States fail and even become humiliated in Iraq without it being partitioned or fallen into complete anarchy, thereby directly affecting its national security. It is within this context that the recent development in the Syrian-Iraqi relationship must be examined. In late July 2004, the Syrian leadership officially recognized and welcomed Iyad Allawi, the Prime Minister of Iraq's interim government. The two parties agreed to restore diplomatic relations between the two countries and to establish a joint committee dealing with guarding the borders. Seemingly, Allawi is trying to strike a balance between maintaining good relations with the United States without appearing to be an American stooge, and reassuring the regional countries of neighborly relations, which would include "unique" roles in building Iraq. For more details see Phares, W., and Rabil, R. G. (2004, July 30). Prime Minister's coalition-building serves Iraqis well. *Chicago Sun-Times.*

82. Damascus has repeatedly offered to resume peace talks with Israel. The recent offer was conveyed to U.N. Middle East envoy Terje Roed-Larsen in late November 2004. Sharon's government rejected Damascus's offer. Some Israeli officials have dismissed the offer as "nothing more than a maneuver designed to alleviate international pressure on the regime in Damascus." Agence France Presse. (2004, December 1). Egypt backs Syrian peace overture to Israel. *The Daily Star.*

83. See Agence France Presse (2004, September 22). Syria, EU reach agreement on weapons. *The Daily Star.*

84. See Rabil, R. G. (2003, November 5). Holding Syria to account. *In the National Interest, 2*(43).

Chapter 7: The New Struggle for Lebanon: Democracy and Syria's Withdrawal

1. See Rabil, R. G. (2004, December 3). Expecting the worst in Lebanon is self-fulfilling. *Daily Star.*

2. SANA printed text of al-Asad's speech on October 9, 2004.

3. Kessler, M. (2004, November 1). Danger in pushing Syria out of Lebanon. *Los Angeles Times.*

4. Rabil, R. G. (2004, December 3). Expecting the worst in Lebanon is self-fulfilling. *Daily Star.*

5. Phares, W. (2004, November 29). The road to UNSCR 1559 calling on Syria to pull out from Lebanon. *Lebanonwire.*

6. See *Al-Hayat* (2001, August 8). For more details see Rabil, R. G. (2001, September). The Maronites and Syrian withdrawal: From "isolationists" to "traitors"? *Middle East Policy, 8*(3).

7. As mentioned in a previous chapter, Ziad abd al-Nour is a signatory of the document entitled "Ending Syria's occupation of Lebanon." Other signatories included Richard Perle, Douglas Feith, and Elliot Abrams, all with connections to the Bush administration.

8. In fact, the Maronite Union had already initiated "a series of alliances as of the late 1990s, peaking in June 2000 in a U.S. Senate sponsored forum gathering including main Human Rights bodies and think tanks. That particular meeting was attended by Dr. Elliot Abrams, who would become the National Security Middle East director under President Bush's first term." See Phares, W. (2004, November 29). The road to UNSCR 1559 calling on Syria to pull out from Lebanon. *Lebanonwire.*

9. As an attendee to the convention, the author received a copy of the letter.

10. Members of the WLCU-ALC delegation included Joe Baini, Joseph Jubeily, John Hajjar, Tom Harb, and Walid Phares.

11. Phares, W. (2004, November 29). The road to UNSCR 1559 calling on Syria to pull out from Lebanon. *Lebanonwire.*

12. Phares, W. (2004, October 22). Hariri's resignation, a step toward Syrian isolation in Lebanon. *Lebanonwire.*

13. See Mustafa's interview in *An-Nahar* (2005, February 3).

14. For details on Syria's manipulation of Lebanese elections see Gambill, G. C., and Aoun, E. A. (2000, August). Special Report: How Syria orchestrates Lebanon's elections. *Middle East Intelligence Bulletin,* 2(7); and Gambill, G. C. and Nassif, D. (2000, September). Lebanon's Parliamentary elections: Manufacturing dissent. *Middle East Intelligence Bulletin,* 2(8).

15. See *An-Nahar* (2004, December 14).

16. Choucar, W. (2005, January 29). Franjieh accuses Hariri of being a "Sectarian." *Daily Star.*

17. Raad, N. (2005, February 3). Opposition demands total Syrian withdrawal from Lebanon. *Daily Star.*

18. See *An-Nahar* (2005, February 15, 16).

19. See *As-Safir* (2005, February 15).

20. Khatib, H. (2005, February 15). Cabinet holds extraordinary session, officials warn of threat to national unity. *Daily Star.*

21. Ibid.

22. Ibid.

23. Ross, D. (2005, March 2). Lebanon's lessons for Arab leaders. *Financial Times.*

24. Reuters. (2005, March 3). Saudis back calls for Syrian pullout from Lebanon. *New York Times.*

25. Ibid.

26. Syria's president Bashar Asad talks with Time columnist Joe Klein about his plans to withdraw the Syrian Army from Lebanon in matter of months. (2005, March 1). *Time.*

27. U.S. Department of State. (2005, March 1). Joint statement by the United States and France on Lebanon.

28. The opposition called for the resignation of the following pro-Syrian Lebanese officials: (1) State Prosecutor, Adnan Addoum, (2) Chief of the General Security Department (known as Surete General), Brigadier General Jamil Sayyed, (3) Director-General of the State Security apparatus, General Edward Mansour, (4) Chief of the Internal Security Forces, General Ali Hajj, (5) Chief of the Military Intelligence, Brigadier General, Raymond Azar, (6) Commander of the Army's Presidential Brigade, Brigadier General Mustafa Hamdan, (7) Chief of the "Eavesdrop Apparatus" in Military Intelligence, Colonel Ghassan Tufeili. See *An-Nahar* (2005, March 3).

29. SANA translated the speech into English and posted it on its Web site. See it on www.sana.org/english/headlines/5-3/Assad's%20speech.htm. For the original Arabic text see *Al-Hayat* (2005, March 6).

30. See *Daily Star* (2005, March 7); and *An-Nahar* (2005, March 7).

31. See *Daily Star* (2005, March 7); and *An-Nahar* (2005, March 7).

32. For Asad's speech before Syrian parliament see Syrian Arab News Agency (SANA), March 5, 2005. For Nasrallah's speech see *As-Safir,* March 9, 2005.

33. Significantly, preempting the opposition once Syria pledged to complete its withdrawal from Lebanon by the end of April, Hizbollah's deputy chief, Sheikh Naim Qassim, in an interview with *Financial Times* on April 7 declared that "We will discuss [Hizbollah's] arms after Shebaa but on a condition that a credible alternative is found to protect Lebanon. A reservist army doesn't mean the resistance becomes part of the army but it's a formula of co-ordination with the army. It's resistance by another name." So even if Israel withdrew from the disputed Shebaa Farms, save mentioning that Israel had already withdrawn from south of Lebanon, Hizbollah will keep its weapons under a new formula to "defend" Lebanon.

34. See President Bush's speech at the National Defense University on March 8, 2005, available at http://www.cnn.com/2005/ALLPOLITICS/03/08/bush.transcript/.

35. Bush originally banned all U.S. exports to Syria except for food and medicine on May 11, 2004. The measures also include a ban on flights to and from the United States; authorization to the Treasury Department to freeze assets of Syrian citizens and entities involved in terrorism, weapons of mass destruction, the occupation of Lebanon or terrorism in Iraq; and restrictions on banking relations between U.S. banks and the Syrian national bank.

36. See Report of the Fact-Finding Mission to Lebanon inquiring into the causes, circumstances, and consequences of the assassination of former Prime Minister Rafiq Hariri, 25 February–24 March 2005, by Peter Fitzgerald, Head of the United Nations Fact-Finding Mission in Lebanon, New York, March 24, 2005. Interestingly, the Report stated that, according to testimonies, in a meeting between President al-Asad and Hariri in Damascus, "Mr. Hariri reminded Mr. Assad of his pledge not to seek an extension for Mr. Lahoud's term, and Mr. Assad replied that there was a policy shift and that the decision was already taken. He added that Mr. Lahoud should be viewed as his personal representative in Lebanon and that "opposing him is tantamount to opposing Assad himself." He then added that he (Mr. Assad) "would rather break Lebanon over the heads of [Mr.] Hariri and [Druze leader Walid] Jonblatt than see his word in Lebanon broken."

37. El-Ghoul, A. (2005, March 31). Assad slams UN's report on Hariri assassination. *Daily Star.*

38. See *An-Nahar* (2005, April 4).

39. Rasmussen, W. (2005, April 8). EU adds to Syria's international woes. *Daily Star.*

40. See *Naharnet* (2005, April 27); and *An-Nahar* (2005, April 27).

41. Syrian forces have verifiably been withdrawn from Lebanon, Annan says. (2005, May 23). *UN News Service.*

42. The formation of the government was as follows: (1) Najib Mikati, Prime Minister, Sunni, close to President Emile Lahoud and Syria, (2) Elias Murr, Deputy Prime Minister and Defense Minister, Greek Orthodox, close to President Lahoud, (3) retired General Hassan Saba', Interior Minister, close to Hariri family, (4) Ghassan Salameh, Minister of Education and

Culture, Catholic, close to Hariri family (he declined the nomination), (5) Mahmoud Hamoud, Foreign Minister, Shi'a, close to President Lahoud and Speaker of Parliament, Nabih Berri, (6) Damianos Kattar, Minister of Finance and Economy, Maronite, close to Mikati, (7) Adel Hamieh, Minister of Public Works and Displaced, Druze, close to both Druze leaders Walid Jumblatt and Adel Arslan, (8) Alain Tabourian, Minister of Telecommunications, Youth and Sports, Armenian, close to President Lahoud, (9) Judge Khaled Kabbani, Minister of Justice, Sunni, close to Hariri family, (10) Bassam Yamine, Minister of Energy and Industry, Maronite, close to Suleiman Franjieh, (11) Charles Rizk, Minister of Information and Tourism, Maronite, close to president Lahoud, (12) Mohammad Khalifeh, Minister of Public Health and Social Affairs, Shi'a, close to Berri, (13) Tarek Mitri, Minister of Environment and Administrative Development, Orthodox, close to President Lahoud and Mikati, and (14) Trad Hamadeh, Minister of Labor and Agriculture, Shi'a, close to Hizbollah.

43. This section of the chapter originally appeared in an article by the author for the Washington Institute for Near East Policy. See Rabil, R. G. (2005, June 17). Lebanon: At the crossroads between democracy and rogue state. *Washington Institute for Near East Policy, PolicyWatch 1004.*

44. Hizbollah Secretary General Hassan Nasrallah has consistently defied mounting international pressure to disarm his party. Addressing a rally in south Lebanon during elections, Nasrallah threatened to "cut off any hand that reaches out to our weapons because it is an Israeli hand." In addition, he warned that the "resistance has more than 12,000 rockets that can target northern Israel at any time." See *As-Safir* (2005, May 26).

45. See The Maronite Statement in full in the *Daily Star* (2005, May 12).

46. The main opposition alliance put together by Hariri, Jumblatt, and Geagea included in its platform a demand to release LF leader Samir Geagea. The first order of business undertaken by the newly elected parliament was an overwhelming vote to free Geagea after more than 11 years in jail.

47. The composition of the new parliament is as follows: (1) Future Current Bloc (Hariri), 36 seats, (2) Democratic Gathering Bloc (Jumblat), 16 seats, (3) Development and Liberation Bloc (Berri), 15, (4) Bloc of the Faithful for the Resistance (Hizbollah), 14, (5) Aoun Bloc, 14, (6) Lebanese Forces Bloc, 6, (7) Popular Bloc in Zahle, 5, (8) Tripoli Bloc, 3, (9) Qornet Shouhwan Bloc, 6, (10) Metn Bloc, 2, (11) Nationalist Bloc, 2, (12) Renewal Bloc, 1, (13) Democratic Leftist Bloc, 1, (14) Kataeb Bloc, 1, (15) Ba'th Bloc, 1, (16) Independents, 5. According to electoral list alliances, Hariri's bloc could muster 70 seats, Hizbollah 35, and Aoun 21. See *As-Safir* (2005, June 19, 20). It is noteworthy that Lebanon's newly elected parliament voted overwhelmingly to free LF leader Samir Geagea from prison. Simultaneously, the parliament also voted to release several dozen Sunni Islamic fundamentalists from northern Lebanon accused of attacking Lebanese army troops in 2000.

48. At the time of this writing a new government was formed. Headed by Prime Minister Fouad al-Sanioura, the new government included five

ministers from Berri's and Hizbollah's blocs. They obtained important ministries including Labor, Health, Agriculture, Energy, and Foreign Affairs. Significantly, an active senior member of Hizbollah, Muhammad Fneish, became minister of energy and water. Though the U.S. State Department supported the new government and lauded its formation as another step toward democratic reform, it asserted that it would not deal with any representative of Hizbollah. Meanwhile, the new Foreign Minister Fawzi Saloukh stated that the new government would deal with Resolution 1559 according to Lebanon's national interests and certainties. See *As-Safir* (2005, July 20, 21).

49. Hizbollah is not the only party with weapons in Lebanon. Several Palestinian groups in refugee camps have arms. Most of these camps have become a refuge for fugitives and criminals. Even some groups, such as Ansar al-Islam in the Ain al-Hilweh camp, have had contacts with al-Qaeda. However, the ability of these groups to operate outside the camps is limited by the government's surveillance, which has issued arrest warrants for several Palestinians.

50. See Nasrallah's speech in *As-Safir* (2005, June 9). "The seven villages were incorporated into Palestine during the French Mandate period, when Lebanon's southern frontiers were drawn by France and Britain." See Kaufman, A. (2002, Autumn). Who owns the Shebaa Farms? Chronicle of a territorial dispute. *Middle East Journal, 56*(4). According to an e-mail message by Kaufman, "The seven villages became part of mandatory Palestine in 1923, following the finalization of the boundary between Lebanon-Syria and Palestine. The first boundary between Lebanon and Palestine was determined in 1920 in an agreement between France and Britain. However, this line was modified in 1923 and some territory that was considered to be part of Lebanon was given to Palestine. There were 24 villages within this territory, seven of them were Shi'ites. We know today only about the Shi'ite villages because it has become a political issue, first of Amal and then of Hizballah. The seven villages became another arena for Shi'ite Lebanese to assert their place in Lebanese society."

51. Young, M. (2005, June 30). Is God really on Hizbullah's side? *Daily Star*.

52. In late July 2005, the new government of Fouad al-Sanioura issued a statement declaring its domestic and foreign policy positions. An outcome of compromise, the statement did not mention U.N. Resolution 1559 while at the same time confirming the government's abidance by international law. In reference to Hizbollah, the ministerial statement emphasized that "the government considers the Lebanese resistance a truthful and natural expression of the national right of the Lebanese people to liberate his land and defend his dignity in the face of Israeli threats, ambitions and aggressions, and to work to resume the liberation of Lebanese land." See The ministerial statement of the government of "reform and revival." (2005, July 26). *As-Safir*. A few days later, on July 29 the U.N. Security Council issued Resolution 1614, which called on the Lebanese government to "fully extend and exercise its sole and effective authority throughout the south,

including through the deployment of sufficient numbers of Lebanese armed and security forces, to ensure a calm environment throughout the area, including along the Blue Line, and to exert control and monopoly over the use of force on its entire territory and to prevent attacks from Lebanon across the Blue Line." See U.N. Security Council S/Res/1614(2005) (2005, July 29).

53. For complete details see Rabil, R. G. (2003). *Embattled neighbors: Syria, Israel and Lebanon* (pp. 127–132). Boulder, CO: Lynne Rienner Publishers.

54. Ibid.

55. An adaptation of this section of the chapter appeared as an article for the Washington Institute for Near East Policy. See Rabil, R. G. (2005, March 28). Syrian strategy in Lebanon. *Washington Institute for Near East Policy, PolicyWatch 980.*

56. Significantly, pro-Syrian and pro-Lahoud Defense Minister Elias Murr was a target of an assassination attempt in mid-July 2005. Analysts emphasized that those behind the wave of subversive activities to destabilize Lebanon were no longer distinguishing between pro- and anti-Syrian politicians. See *An-Nahar* and *Naharnet* (2005, July 13, 14).

57. See *An-Nahar* and *Naharnet* (2005, June 11). Moreover, Jumblat gave a list of Syrian intelligence generals still operating in parts of Lebanon, among whom were former military intelligence chief in Lebanon, Rustom Ghazaleh, Brigadiers Ali Diab and Ali Jabbour, and security officers Jameh Jameh and Abu Michel. Quoting *An-Nahar* and Al-Mustaqbal, *Naharnet* wrote that three senior intelligence officers, Mohammed Khallouf, Nabil Hishmeh, and Khalil Zogheib had sneaked back into Lebanon to operate from Tripoli, Lebanon's second largest city, and Akkar, provincial capital of northern Lebanon's countryside. See *Naharnet* (2005, May 31).

58. Hatoum, M. (2005, June 10). Annan warns Syrian intelligence may still be operating in Lebanon. *Daily Star.*

59. See *An-Nahar* and *Naharnet* (2005, July 10).

60. Batatu, H. (1999). *Syria's peasantry, the descendants of its lesser rural notables, and their politics* (p. 292). Princeton, NJ: Princeton University Press.

61. Syria admits holding Lebanese "terrorists" in its jails. (2005, May 7). *Naharnet.* Supported by SOLIDE, relatives of hundreds of Lebanese missing or imprisoned in Syria have taken to the streets, calling for the Lebanese authorities, the U.N., and the Red Cross to intervene. Caretaker government of Najib Mikati established a commission to address the issue. See Ghazal, R. (2005, June 23). Mikati names head to latest detainee committee. *Daily Star;* and Epps, D. (2005, June 24). Detainees families call for action. *Daily Star.*

62. Zaaroura, M. (2005, April 20). Bush adamant on Hizbullah disarmament. *Daily Star.*

63. Ibid.

64. Rice tells Syria to "knock it off" after Hawi's Beirut assassination. (2005, June 22). *Naharnet.*

65. U.N. Secretary General Kofi Annan appointed Mehlis in mid-May to lead a probe into Hariri's assassination.

66. Associated Press. (2005, May 27). Chief UN investigator hopes to crack Hariri's murder "soonest possible." *Naharnet.*

67. Levitt, M., and Chosak, J. (2005, July 13). Freezing U.S. assets of Syrian officials. *Washington Institute for Near East Policy, PolicyWatch 1012.*

Chapter 8: Syria Postwithdrawal: Reform or Dictatorship?

1. The Faustian bargain was originally mentioned by Yassin al-Haj Saleh; see Don't rush the revolution. (2005, June 4). *New York Times.*

2. See House Resolution 1141, 109th Congress. (2005, March 8). *Lebanon and Syria Liberation Act.*

3. An adaptation of this section appeared as an article for the Washington Institute for Near East Policy. See Rabil, R. G. (2005, June 2). Baath Party Congress in Damascus: How much change in Syria? *Washington Institute for Near East Policy, PolicyWatch 1000.*

4. *Al-Thawra* (2005, May 3).

5. Moubayed, S. (2005, July 18). Bashar Assad ensured the Baath was here to stay. *Daily Star.*

6. Out of 21 members, 12 new members were inducted into the Regional Command, the highest office in the land. They included Bashar, then-Prime Minister Mustafa Miro, current Prime Minister Muhammad Naji Otri, Foreign Minister Farouq al-Shara, Ghiath Barakat, Ibrahim Huneidi, Farouq abu al-Shamat, Majed Shadud, Salam al-Yasin, Muhammad al-Hussein, Walid al-Bouz, and Muhammad Said Bakhitan. Vice-Presidents Abd al-Halim Khaddam and Muhammad Zuheir Mashariqa, deputy secretaries of the Ba'th party Suleiman Qaddah and Abdullah al-Ahmar, parliament speaker Abd al-Qader Qaddura, former Defense Minister Mustafa Tlas, Ahmad Dargam, Fa'z al-Naser, and Walid Hamdoun all kept their membership in the Regional Command. The Central Committee (90 members) gained 62 new members including Maher al-Asad, the president's brother, and Manaf Tlas, son of former Minister of Defense Mustafa Tlas. See Rabil, R. G. (2003). *Embattled neighbors: Syria, Israel and Lebanon* (p. 273). Boulder, CO: Lynne Rienner Publishers.

7. *As-Safir,* (2005, May 3).

8. It is noteworthy that before the Congress, Syrian first lady Asma al-Asad addressed the Woman in Business International Forum held in May in Damascus. She told the delegates that "Syria is shaping its business environment for today's global economy. This means major change at a sustainable pace, introducing the reforms necessary for a dynamic and prosperous enterprise economy." See Syrian First Lady urges reform. (2005, May 21). *Bahrain Tribune.*

9. See al-Asad's speech at Syrian Arab News Agency (SANA) (2005, June 8).

10. See al-Ghaoui, R. (2005, May 2). I'tiqal Nashitin fi al-Mujtama' al-Madani fi Suria 'Ashiat In'eqad al-Mu'tamar al-Qutri le-Hizb al-Ba'th [Detention of Civil Society Activists in Syria on the Eve of the Ba'th Party's Regional Congress]. *Ash-Sharq Al-Awsat, 5.* See Also *As-Safir* (2005, May 25). At the time of this writing the Atasi Forum members, with the exception of Abdullah, were subsequently released. According to the Arab Organization for Human Rights, Syrian authorities arrested Muhammad al-Abdullah, son of Ali al-Abdullah, on June 27, 2005. At the same time, according to the same organization, Syrian authorities arrested Yassin al-Hamawi, father of detainee Haitham al-Hamawi, for convening a meeting in his house in which he established a Committee for the Families of Detainees in Daria (10 km south of Damascus). See *As-Safir* (2005, June 28).

11. Agence France Presse. Syria blames "criminals" for Kurdish Sheikh's murder. *Daily Star* (2005, June 2). On May 10, the Sheikh disappeared while on his way to Damascus. Kurdish parties, including the banned Yeki-ti party, blamed Syrian authorities for his disappearance, and many Kurds demonstrated in Qamishli calling for his release. Qamishli was the site of the March 2004 riots. On June 1, Syrian authorities led the Sheikh's sons to his body, blaming the murder on criminals.

12. See Muslim Brotherhood's statement "Syrian 'Brotherhood' calls for 'total change.'" *As-Safir* (2005, August 6).

13. For complete details see *As-Safir* (2005, June 10).

14. Leverett, F. (2005). *Inheriting Syria: Bashar's trial by fire* (p. 102). Washington, DC: Brookings Institution Press.

15. Ibid., pp. 102–104; and Zisser, E. (2004, June). Bashar al-Asad and his regime—Between continuity and change. *Orient, 45*(2).

16. See Rabil, R. G. (2005, May 9). How is Syria ruled? *The Washington Institute for Near East Policy, PolicyWatch 992.*

17. See *As-Safir* (2005, June 10). Those removed from the RCC included Khaddam, al-Ahmar, Tlas, Qaddura, Miro, Mashariqa, and Qaddah.

18. See *As-Safir* (2005, June 17).

19. Young, M. (2005, July 7). Can Lebanon parry Syria's threats? *Daily Star.*

Conclusion

1. See text of speech in the *New York Times* (2005, February 3).

2. Kristol, W. (2004, December 20). Getting serious about Syria. *The Weekly Standard.*

3. See al-Bianouni's statements in *As-Sharq Al-Awsat* (2004, December 17).

4. In an interview with *An-Nahar*, Ali Al-Atassi, a civil society activist, emphasized that "It is time for the opposition parties to unite. They often live more in the past than the presence. The leftist and liberal groups as well as the Muslim Brotherhood have to make alliances and work on a

common democratic program. The opposition parties are currently working on a national conference to engage in a dialogue together. We are in need of new political figures who give voice to society's concerns." The interview is available at http://www.qantara.de/webcom/show_article.php/_c-476/_nr-383/i.html.

5. See Agence France Presse (AFP). (2005, March 30). U.S. talks with Syrian opposition group divides dissidents. *Daily Star*.

6. Ibid.

7. Hamidi, I. (2005, June 18). Dimashq Ta'lun 'an Khalaya Takfiriyah wa Da'awat ila Juhud Tanwiriyah...Syria al-'Ulmaniyah Tazdad Islamiyah [Damascus reports on infidel (unbelief) cells and calls for awareness efforts...Secular Syria grows Islamic] *Al-Hayat*. In an attempt to encourage moderate Islam, the Syrian government supported the building of some 80,000 mosques, over 22 higher-education institutions for teaching Islam, and many regional Shari'a schools, including al-Khaznawi school in al-Jazeera, Sheikhs Ahmed Hassan and Abu al-Qaaqaa schools in Aleppo, Sheikhs Mohammed Said Ramadan Hassoun and Muhammad Habash (a deputy in parliament) study circles, and Abu al-Nour complex in Damascus. Also in Damascus, the government created the Sheikha Munira a-Qaisi complex, named after a famous Damascene lady, in which about 25,000 girls are enrolled. Hamidi, I. (2005, January 12). Can Syria keep its Islamist genie in the bottle? *Daily Star*. See also Moubayed, S. (2005, August 11). The history of political and militant Islam in Syria. *Terrorism Monitor, 3*(16).

8. Moubayed, S. (2005, August 11). The history of political and militant Islam in Syria. *Terrorism Monitor, 3*(16).

9. Hamidi, I. (2005, June 6). Dimashq: Tafkik 'Khaliyah Irhabiah min Tanzim Jund al-Sham lil-Jihad wa al-Tawhid [Damascus: Dismantling a "terror cell" of the organization of the "Army of Damascus for Jihad and unification"]. *Al-Hayat*.

10. Blanford, N. (2004, November 8). Hizbullah launches drone into Israeli airspace. *Daily Star*.

11. Ibid.

12. Nasrallah: al-Mirsad-1 Sana'tha al-Muqawama wa Ladayna Akthar Min Wahida [The resistance made the Mirsad-1 and has more than one]. (2004, November 13). *An-Nahar*.

13. Syria, Iran to form a "united front" to face intense US threats. (2005, February 16). *Naharnet;* see also *An-Nahar* (2005, February 16).

14. Agence France Presse. (2004, January 8). Bashar visit crowns Turkish rapprochement with Syria.

15. By signing agreements with Turkey on promoting trade and investments, al-Asad officially recognized Turkish sovereignty over Hatay, for the agreements contain the following definition: "The term 'Turkey' in this agreement means the sovereignty area that Turkey owns, its territorial waters, as well as the sea areas where it has judicial powers or sovereignty rights, in accordance with International Law, for prospecting, exploiting

and protecting the natural resources." It is noteworthy that Syria's Prime Minister Mustafa Miro had declined to sign these agreements during his official visit to Turkey in July 2003.

16. Of the most important issues bringing the two countries to work together is the Kurdish question. Turkey and Syria are both concerned about Kurdish separatist movements in their own countries. The Kurdistan Workers Party (PKK) has resumed its terror activities against Turkey. Significantly, on December 31, 2004, PKK members ambushed Turkish security officers in the Sirnak province in southeastern Turkey, near the Iraqi border. The PKK maintains its headquarters in northern Iraqi Kurdistan. On the other hand, encouraged by the newly assertive role and quasi-independence of their brethren in Iraq, Kurds in Syria, deprived of civil rights, have become bold enough to challenge Syrian authorities. In fact, both Syria and Turkey have been eager to participate in the meetings of the foreign ministers of Iraq's neighbors so as to have a say in shaping postwar Iraq. Interestingly, Syria attended the Brussels conference on Iraq, which was organized by the United States and the European Union. Secretary of State Condoleezza Rice chided the Syrians by stating that "let's not have more words about what they're [Syrians] prepared to do about Iraq, let's have actions." While promising to fully cooperate with the Iraqi government to secure the border, Syria's Foreign Minister Farouq al-Shara emphasized that U.S. sanctions have negatively affected Syria's ability to protect the Syria-Iraq border. For PKK activities see Cagaptay, S., and Uslu, E. (2005, January 10). Is the PKK still a threat to the United States and Turkey?" *Washington Institute for Near East Policy, Policy-Watch 940.* For the Brussels conference see Associated Press. (2005, June 24). Syria must help stop terrorists, US says. *Boston Globe.*

17. Asad describes his visit to Syria as "historic." (2004, June 21). *As-Sharq Al-Awsat.*

18. Ibid.

19. Agence France Presse. (2005, January 25). Syria looks to Moscow for stronger regional role. Quoted by *Daily Star.*

20. Russia writes off $9.8 billion of Syrian debt. (2005, January 2). *Daily Star.*

21. Ibid. A few days later, Moscow reversed its denial and confirmed that it was, indeed, selling Damascus new missiles.

22. Prados, A. B. (2003, October 10). Syria: U.S. relations and bilateral issues. *Congressional Research Service* (p. 3). Washington, DC: Library of Congress.

23. See President al-Asad's interview with *Al-Hayat* (2003, October 7).

24. See MacFarquhar, N. (2003, December 1). Syrian pressing for Israel talks. *New York Times.*

25. Agence France Presse. (2004, November 24). Syria ready to resume Israeli talks "without conditions." *Daily Star.*

26. Ibid. Although some Israeli officials, including the president of Israel, asked the Sharon government to sound out the intentions of Syria, the

Sharon government remained unswayed in its belief that the offer was "nothing more than a maneuver designed to alleviate international pressure on the regime in Damascus." Agence France Presse. (2004, December 1). Egypt backs Syrian overture to Israel. *Daily Star.*

27. See SANA (2004, December 1).

28. Discussions with Professor Asher Susser at Florida Atlantic University on February 12, 2005.

29. Shaaban, B. (2004, June 5). The Neo-anti-Semitism of the Neoconservatives. *Daily Star.*

30. See the author's response to Shaaban in the *Daily Star.* Rabil, R. G. (2004, August 4). Feeding an Arab sense of victimization. *Daily Star.*

31. For more details see Rabil, R. G. (2005, January 21). The Salafists versus Liberals: The struggle for Islam. *In The National Interest.*

32. Hourani, E. (2004, November 11). Fadlallah accuses US of continuing crusade against Islam. *Daily Star.*

33. Shaaban, B. (2004, December 24). A culture of peace links Africa and the Middle East. *Daily Star.*

34. For more details and analysis see Rabil, R. G. (2005, February 2). Arabs must apply their political culture in the process of change. *Daily Star.*

35. Syria's population and growth rate are, respectively, 18.2 million and 2.4 percent. Syria's GDP and per capita GDP are, respectively, $20.5 billion and $1,165. See U.S. Department of State. (2004, August). *Background note: Syria.* Washington, DC: Bureau of Near Eastern Affairs. In 2001, Syria's percentage of population under age 19 was 53.8, and according to 2000 estimates Syria's inflation rate was 0.54 percent. See Office of the Prime Minister, *Statistical abstract 2001,* Central Bureau of Statistics, Syrian Arab Republic, first quoted from George, A. (2003). *Syria: Neither bread nor freedom.* London: Zed Books. According to 2001 estimates, Syria's unemployment rate ranged between 25 and 30 percent. See U.S. Department of State. (2002, February). *Background note: Syria.* Washington, DC: Bureau of Near Eastern Affairs.

36. Abdulhamid, A. (2005, February 22). Reform starts with a Lebanon withdrawal. *Daily Star.*

37. Among the hard-liners in the top echelon of the Syrian regime, as revealed by the regime's clampdown on the reform movement and recent appointments, are former Vice-President Abd al-Halim Khaddam, former Defense Minister Mustafa Tlas, General Asef Shawqat (President al-Asad's brother-in-law) who was recently appointed head of Military Intelligence, General Bahjat Suleiman, former head of the internal division of General Intelligence Directorate, and Hassan al-Khalil, former head of Military Intelligence. For more details, see the previous chapter. According to a report by the Arab daily *Al-Seyassah,* Shawqat, Suleiman, and pro-Syrian head of Lebanon's General Security, Jamil Sayyid, were behind the assassination of former Lebanese Prime Minister Rafiq Hariri. See *Al-Seyassah* (2005, February 19).

—— Selected Bibliography ——

Official Documents, Autobiographies, and Other Sources By State Officials

Abdel Nasser, G. (1955, January). The Egyptian Revolution. *Foreign Affairs, 33* (2).

Aflaq, M. (1963). *Fi Sabil al-Ba'th* [For the sake of the Ba'th]. Beirut: Dar al-Tali'a.

Aflaq, M. (1958). *Ma'rakat al-Masir al-Wahid* [The battle of one destiny]. Beirut: Dar al-Adab.

Aflaq, M. (1975). *Al-Nidal Didd Tashwih Harakat al-Thawra al-Arabiya* [The struggle against the disfiguring of the Arab Revolutionary Movement]. Beirut: Dar al-Tali'a.

Al-Asad, H. (1984). *Kadhalika Qala al-Asad* [Thus al-Asad said] (statements compiled by General Mustafa Tlas). Damascus: Tlas Press.

Al-Hindi, H., and al-Nasrawi, A. I. (2001–2002). *Harakat al-Qawmiyyin al-'Arab: Nash'tuha wa Tataworiha (ibr Wathaiqaha, 1951–1968* [The Arab nationalist movement: Its emergence and evolution through its documents, 1951–1968] (Pts. 1–2). Beirut: Institution of Arab Research.

Baker, J. A., III. (1995). *The politics of diplomacy: Revolution, war and peace 1989–1992*. New York: G. P. Putnam's Sons.

Ben-Tzur, A. (Ed.). (1968). *The Syrian Baath Party and Israel: Documents from the Internal Party Publications*. Givat Aviv: Center for Arab and Afro-Asian Studies.

Bureau of Public Affairs, Department of State. (1975). *U.S. policy in the Middle East: December 1973–November 1974* (No. 12). Washington, DC: Government Printing Office.

Bureau of Public Affairs, Department of State. (1976). *U.S. policy in the Middle East: November 1974–February 1976* (No. 4). Washington, DC: Government Printing Office.

Bush, G. W. (2002, September). *The national strategy of the United States of America,* http://www.whitehouse.gov/nsc/nss.html.

Central Bank of Syria (1997). *Quarterly Bulletin, 35*(1–2).

Clinton, W. (2004). *My life.* New York: Alfred A. Knopf.

Congressional Information Service. 1992 House Resolution 4546, 102nd Congress House Resolution 4546; 1997 House Resolution 3080, 105th Congress House Resolution 3080; 1998 House Resolution 4569, 105th Congress House Resolution 4569.

Davis, H. M. (1953). *Constitutions, electoral laws, treaties of the states in the Near and Middle East.* Durham: Duke University Press.

Djerejian, E. P. (1993, October 15). *Current developments in the Middle East.* Washington, DC: Government Printing Office.

Documents of the Arab Ba'th Socialist Party (Arabic). (1963). *Nidal al-Ba'th* [The Struggle of the Ba'th] (Vols. 1 and 6). Beirut: Dar al-Tali'a.

Dulles, J. F. (1957, January). *Economic and military cooperation with nations in the general area of the Middle East.* Washington, DC: Government Printing Office.

Eisenhower, D. D. (1963). *Mandate for change: The White House years 1953–1956.* New York: Doubleday.

Hearing before the Subcommittee on International Organizations and Movements of the Committee on Foreign Affairs House of Representatives. (1974). *Treatment of Israeli POW's in Syria and their status under the Geneva Conventions.* Washington, DC: Government Printing Office.

Hearing before the Subcommittee on Europe and the Middle East of the Committee on Foreign Affairs House of Representatives. (1989). *The situation in Lebanon, July 1989.* Washington, DC: Government Printing Office.

Hearing before the Subcommittee on International Operations of the Committee on Foreign Affairs House of Representatives. (1990). *American Hostages in Lebanon.* Washington, DC: Government Printing Office.

Hearing before the Committee on Foreign Affairs House of Representatives on July 22, 1992. (1992). *To consider release of dual-use export licenses to Iran and Syria pursuant to Section 12(c) of the Export Administration Act.* Washington, DC: Government Printing Office.

Hearing before the Committee on International Relations House of Representatives. (1996). *Syria: Peace partner or rogue regime?* Washington, DC: Government Printing Office.

Hearing before the Subcommittees on Arms Control, International Security and Science, Europe and the Middle East of the Committee on Foreign Affairs House of Representatives. (1992). *Conventional arms sales policy in the Middle East.* Washington, DC: Government Printing Office.

Hearing before the Subcommittee on the Middle East and Central Asia of the Committee on International Relations, House of Representatives. (2003, September 16). *Syria: Implications for U.S. security and regional stability.* Washington, DC: U.S. Government Printing Office.

Hearing before the Committee on Foreign Relations. United States Senate. (2003, October 30). *Syria: U.S. policy directions.* Washington, DC: U.S. Government Printing Office.

Hurewitz, J. C. (1956). *Diplomacy in the Near and Middle East: A documentary record 1914–1956.* Princeton: D. Van Nostrand Company, Inc.

Kissinger, H. (1982). *Years of upheaval*. Boston: Little, Brown and Company.

Kissinger, H. (1979). *The White House years*. Boston: Little, Brown and Company, Inc.

Kissinger, H. (1994). *Diplomacy*. New York: Simon & Schuster.

Laqueur, W., and Rubin, B. (Eds.). (1995). *The Israel-Arab reader: A documentary history of the Middle East conflict* (5th ed.). New York: Penguin Books.

McGovern, Senator G. S. (1975). *Realities of the Middle East*. Washington, DC: Government Printing Office.

Ministere Syrienne des Affairs Etrangeres (1956, 1957).

Muallem, W. (1997, Winter). Fresh light on the Syrian-Israeli peace negotiations. *Journal of Palestine Studies, 26*(2).

Muallem, W. (n.d.). Beyond the brink of peace: Syria's chief negotiator responds to Itamar Rabinovich's *The Brink of Peace*. Damascus: (n.p.).

Nixon, R. M. (1978). *RN: The memoirs of Richard Nixon*. New York: Grosset & Dunlap.

Paterson, T. G. (1989). *Major problems in American foreign policy Volume II: Since 1914, documents and essays*. Lexington: DC Heath and Company.

Peres, S. (1995). *Battling for Peace*. New York: Random House.

Prados, A. B. (1992, May 12). Syrian-U.S. relations. *Congressional Research Service*. Washington, DC: Library of Congress.

Prados, A. B. (2003, October 10). Syria: U.S. relations and bilateral issues. *Congressional Research Service*. Washington, DC: Library of Congress.

Rabinovich, I. (1998). *The brink of peace: The Israeli-Syrian negotiations*. New Jersey: Princeton University Press.

Reagan, R. (1990). *An American life*. New York: Simon & Schuster.

Report to the Committee on Foreign Relations United States Senate by Senator James M. Jeffords and Senator Hank Brown. (1993). *Trip to Croatia, Syria, Jordan, Israel and Egypt*. Washington, DC: Government Printing Office.

Ross, D. (2004). *The missing peace: The inside story of the fight for Middle East peace*. New York: Farrar, Straus, and Giroux.

Savir, U. (1998). *The process: 1,100 Days that changed the Middle East*. New York: Random House.

Staff Report Issued on November 23, 1992 by the Subcommittee on Crime and Criminal Justice of the Committee on the Judiciary. (1993). *Syria, President Bush, and drugs—The administration's next Iraqgate*. Washington, DC: Government Printing Office.

Syrian Arab Republic. (1993, 1995, 2001). *Statistical abstracts*. Damascus: Office of the Prime Minister, General Bureau of Statistics.

The Higher Command of the Islamic Revolution in Syria. (1980). *Declaration and program of the Islamic revolution in Syria*. Damascus: (n.p.).

Tomeh, G. J. (Ed.). (1975). *United Nations resolutions on Palestine and the Arab-Israeli conflict, Vol. 1: 1947–1974*. Washington, DC: Institute for Palestine Studies.

Truman, H. S. (1955). *Memoirs: Years of decisions* (Vol. 2). New York: Doubleday.

UNDP, (2002, July). *The Arab human development report 2002*. New York: UNDP.

U.S. Department of State. (1965, 1977). *Foreign relations of the United States: Diplomatic papers 1944, 1949* (Vols. 5 and 6). Washington, DC: Government Printing Office.

U.S. Department of State. (1957). *American foreign policy 1950–1955: Basic documents*. Washington, DC: Government Printing Office, Vol. 2.

U.S. Department of State. (1961, 1964, 1967, 1969, 1984, 1985, 1986, 1989, 1991). *American foreign policy: Current documents 1957, 1961, 1964, 1966, 1981, 1982, 1984, 1988, 1990*. Washington, DC: Government Printing Office.

U.S. Department of State. (1983). *American foreign policy: Basic documents 1977–1980*. Washington, DC: Government Printing Office.

U.S. Department of State. (1995, April; 1996, April; 1997, April; 1998, April; 2003, April; 2004, April). *Patterns of global terrorism 1994, 1995, 1996, 1997, 2002, 2003*.

U.S. Department of State. (1996, March). Israel Human Rights Practices, 1995, and Syrian Human Rights Practices, 1995.

U.S. Department of State. (2003, March 31). *Syria: Country reports on human rights practices—2002*. Washington, DC: Bureau of Democracy, Human Rights, and Labor.

U.S. Department of State. (2004, February 25). *Lebanon: Country reports on human rights practices—2003*. Washington, DC: Bureau of Democracy, Human Rights, and Labor.

U.S. Department of State. (2002, February; 2004, August). *Background note: Syria*. Washington, DC: Bureau of Near Eastern Affairs.

U.S. Department of State. (2004, November). *Background note: Lebanon*. Washington, DC: Bureau of Near Eastern Affairs.

U.S. Department of State Bulletin. (1957, 1964, 1973, 1977, 1979, 1982, 1983, 1984, 1985, 1986).

U.S. Department of State Dispatch. (1989, 1990, 1991, 1992, 1993, 1994, 1995, 1996).

Weekly compilation of Presidential documents (U.S.). (1983, 1984, 1985, 1991, 1992, 1993, 1994, 1995).

Arabic Newspapers

Al-'Ahd. Beirut, official organ of Hizbollah.

Al-Ahram. Cairo.

Al-Anwar. Beirut.

Al-Ba'th. Damascus, Official Daily.

Al-Hayat. London, pan-Arab.

Al-Nadhir. Official organ of the Syrian Muslim Brotherhood, 1981–1990.

An-Nahar. Beirut.

Al-Quds al-Arabi. London, pan-Arab.

As-Safir. Beirut.

As-Sharq al-Awsat. London, pan-Arab.

Al-Thawra. Damascus, Official daily.

Tishrin. Damascus, Official daily.

Articles

Al-Hafiz, Y. (1963). *Fi al-Fikr al-Siyasi* [About the experience of the Ba'th party] (Vol. 1). Damascus: Dar Dimashq.

Atasi, J. (1963). *Fi al-Fikr al-Siyasi* [Arab socialism and the myth of [its] special qualities] (Vol. 1). Damascus: Dar Dimashq.

Batatu, H. (1981, Summer). Some observations on the social roots of Syria's ruling military group and the causes of its dominance. *Middle East Journal 35*(3).

Ben-Tzur, A. (1968, July). The Neo-Ba'th Party of Syria. *Journal of Contemporary History, 3*(3). London: Institute of Contemporary History.

Byrd, Senator R. (1992, Summer). Senator Byrd on loan guarantees and U.S.-Israeli relations. *Journal of Palestine Studies, 21*(4).

Cendar, G. (1997, August). Sura li-Turkeya Mina al-Dakhel [A picture of Turkey from the inside]. *Shu'un al-Wasat* (No. 64).

Dalila, A. (1997). Al-Siyasat al-Iqtisadiya wa al-Ijtimai'ya wa al-Maliya fi Suriya [Economic, social and fiscal policies in Syria]. *Dirasat Ishtirakia,169*. Damascus.

Eisenstadt, M. (1997). Turkish-Israeli cooperation: An assessment. *Policy Watch* (No. 262). Washington, DC: The Washington Institute for Near East Policy.

Falken, R., and Eisenstadt, M. (1998). Iran and weapons of mass destruction. *Special Policy Forum Report.* Washington, DC: The Washington Institute for Near East Policy.

Ghadry, F. (2005, Winter). Syrian reform: What lies beneath. *Middle East Quarterly, 12*(1).

Gresh, A. (1998, Spring). Turkish-Israeli-Syrian relations and their impact on the Middle East. *Middle East Journal, 52*(2).

Heller, P. B. (1974, Winter). Document: The permanent Syrian Constitution of March 13, 1973. *Middle East Journal, 28*(1).

Heydmann, S. (1992). The political logic of economic rationality: Selective stabilization in Syria. In H. Barkey (Ed.), *The politics of economic reform in the Middle East.* New York: St. Martin's Press.

Hinnebusch, R. A. (1995). State, civil society, and political change in Syria. In A. R. Norton (Ed.), *Civil society in the Middle East.* Leiden: E. J. Brill.

Howard, H. N. (1974). The Soviet Union in Lebanon, Syria and Jordan. In I. J. Lederer and W. S. Vucinich (Eds.), *The Soviet Union and the Middle East: The Post-World War II Era.* Stanford: Hoover Institution Press.

Jouejati, M. (1996). Water politics as high politics: The case of Turkey and Syria. In H. J. Barkey (Ed.), *Reluctant neighbor: Turkey's role in the Middle East.* Washington, DC: United States Institute of Peace.

Jumayil, P. (1970). Lebanese nationalism and its foundations: The Phalangist viewpoint. In K. H. Karpat (Ed.), *Political and social thought in the contemporary Middle East.* New York: Praeger.

Kaufman, A. (2002, Autumn). Who owns the Shebaa Farms? Chronicle of a territorial dispute. *Middle East Journal, 56*(4).

Khalidi, W. (1998, Spring). Selected documents on the 1948 War. *Journal of Palestine Studies, 27*(3).

Khalidi, W. (1998, January 30). The American factor in the Arab-Israeli conflict. *Middle East International*.

Khoury, F. J. (1963, Winter–Spring). Friction and conflict on the Israeli-Syrian front. *Middle East Journal, 17*(1 and 2).

Khoury, P. S. (1985, July). Divided loyalties? Syria and the question of Palestine. *Middle Eastern Studies, 21*(3).

Kober, A. (1996). A paradigm in crisis? Israel's doctrine of military decision. In E. Karsh (Ed.), *Between war and peace: Dilemmas of Israeli security*. London: Frank Cass.

Levy, A. (1973). The Syrian Communists and the Ba'th power struggle, 1966–1970. In M. Confino and S. Shamir (Ed.), *The U.S.S.R. and the Middle East*. Jerusalem: Israel Universities Press.

Little, D. (1990, Winter). Cold War and covert action: The United States and Syria, 1945–1958. *Middle East Journal, 44*(1).

Ma'oz, M. (1972, Autumn). Attempts at creating a political community in modern Syria. *Middle East Journal, 26*(4).

Maksoud, General A. K. (1996, May–June). Al-Stratigiyah al-Israiliya fi al-Tis'inat [Israel's Strategy in the Nineties]. *Al-Fikr al-Askari*.

Middle East Watch. (1992, Summer). Human rights watch world report 1992: The Israeli-occupied West Bank and Gaza Strip. *Journal of Palestine Studies, 21*(4).

Murqus, I. (1963). *Fi al-Fikr al-Siyasi* [Collapse of the Parliamentary System] (Vol. 2). Damascus: Dar Dimashq.

Nachmani, A. (1998, June). The remarkable-Turkish Israeli tie. *Middle East Quarterly, 5*(2).

Perthes, V. (1994). The private sector, economic liberalization, and the prospects of democratization: The case of Syria and some other Arab countries. In G. Salame (Ed.), *Democracy without democrats? The renewal of politics in the Muslim world*. London: I. B. Tauris Publishers.

Perthes, V. (1994, Fall). From front-line state to backyard? Syria and the economic risks of regional peace. *The Beirut Review* (No. 8).

Polling, S. (1996). Syria's private sector: Economic liberalization and the challenges of the 1990s. In G. Nonneman (Ed.), *Political and economic liberalization: Dynamics and linkages in comparative perspective*. Boulder: Lynne Rienne Publishers.

Rabil, R. G. (2001, September). The Maronites and Syrian withdrawal: From "isolationists" to "traitors"? *Middle East Policy, 8*(3).

Robinson, G. E. (1998, January). Elite cohesion, regime succession and political instability in Syria. *Middle East Policy, 5*(4).

Seale, P., and Butler, L. (1996, Autumn). Asad's regional strategy and the challenge from Netanyahu. *Journal of Palestine Studies, 26*(1).

Zisser, E. (1995, October). The Maronites, Lebanon and the State of Israel: Early contacts. *Middle Eastern Studies, 31*(4).

Zisser, E. (1998, February). Decision Making in Asad's Syria. *Policy Focus* (No. 35). Washington, DC: The Washington Institute for Near East Policy.

Zisser, E. (1995, September). The succession struggle in Damascus. *Middle East Quarterly, 2*(3).

Zisser, E. (2004, June). Bashar al-Asad and his regime—Between continuity and change. *Orient, 45*(2).

Books

Ajami, F. (1986). *The Vanished Imam: Musa al Sadr and the Shi'a of Lebanon.* Ithaca: Cornell University Press.

Al-Azm, K. (1973). *Mudhakkirat* [Memoirs] (Vol. 2). Beirut: Al-Dar al-Taqadumiya lil-Nashr.

Al-Jundi, S. (1969). *Al-Ba'th.* Beirut: Dar al-Nahar.

Al-Khair, H. (1996). *Akram Hawrani: Bayna al-Tanaqulat al-Siyasiya wa al-Inqilabat al-Askaria* [Akram Hawrani: Between political movements and military coup d'etats]. Damascus: New Orient Press.

Anderson, T. A. (1993). *Den of lions: Memoirs of seven years.* New York: Crown Publishers, Inc.

Antonius, G. (1969). *The Arab awakening: The story of the Arab national movement.* Beirut: Librairie du Liban.

Audo, A. (1988). *Zaki Al-Arsouzi: Un Arabe Face a la Modernite.* Beirut: Dar al-Mashreq SARL.

Azoury, N. (1905). *Le Reveil de la Nation Arabe dans L'asie Turque.* Paris: Plon-Nourrit.

Bar-Yaacov, N. (1967). *The Israel-Syrian Armistice: Problems of implementation, 1949–1966.* Jerusalem: Magnes Press.

Batatu, H. (1999). *Syria's peasantry, the descendants of its lesser rural notables, and their politics.* Princeton, NJ: Princeton University Press.

Be'eri, E. (1970). *Army officers in Arab politics and society.* New York: Praeger.

Brookings Middle East Study Group. (1975). *Toward peace in the Middle East.* Washington, DC: Brookings Institution.

Brown, S. (1994). *The faces of power: Constancy and change in United States foreign policy from Truman to Clinton.* New York: Columbia University Press.

Carter, J. (1985). *The blood of Abraham.* Boston: Houghton Mifflin.

Clark, R. C. (2004). *Against all enemies: Inside America's war on terror.* New York: Free Press.

Clawson, P. (1989). *Unaffordable ambitions: Syria's military build-up and economic crisis.* Washington, DC: The Washington Institute for Near East Policy.

Copeland, M. (1969). *The game of nations.* London: Weidenfeld & Nicholson.

Dawn, C. E. (1991). The origins of Arab nationalism. In Rashid Khalidi, Lisa Anderson, Muhammad Muslih, and Reeva S. Simon (Eds.), *The origins of Arab nationalism.* New York: Columbia University Press.

Deeb, M. (2004). *Syria's terrorist war on Lebanon and the peace process.* New York: Palgrave MacMillan.

Devlin, J. F. (1976). *The Ba'th Party: A history from the origins to 1966.* Stanford: Hoover Institution Press.

Diab, I. a.D. (1998). *Akram Hawrani...Kama A'ariftahou* [Akram Hawrani... How I Knew Him]. Beirut: Beisan Press.

Donovan, J. (1964). *U.S. and Soviet Policy in the Middle East: 1957–66.* New York: Facts on File, Inc.

Drysdale, A., and Hinnebusch, R. (1992). *Syria and the Middle East peace process.* New York: Council on Foreign Relations Press.

Eisenstadt, M. (1992). *Arming for peace? Syria's elusive quest for "strategic parity."* Washington, DC: The Washington Institute for Near East Policy.

Faour, M. (1993). *The Arab World after Desert Storm.* Washington, DC: United States Institute of Peace Press.

Feldman, S. (1996). *The future of U.S.-Israel strategic cooperation.* Washington, DC: The Washington Institute for Near East Policy.

Feldman, S. (1997). *Nuclear weapons and arms control in the Middle East.* Cambridge, MA: MIT Press.

Fisk, R. (1990). *Pity the nation: The abduction of Lebanon.* New York: Atheneum.

Friedman, T. L. (1989). *From Beirut to Jerusalem.* New York: Farrar, Straus, and Giroux.

George, A. (2003). *Neither bread nor freedom.* London, Zed Books.

Gibb, H. A. R. (1947). *Modern trends in Islam.* Chicago: The University of Chicago Press.

Haig, A. M., Jr. (1984). *Caveat: Realism, Reagan, and foreign policy.* New York: Macmillan.

Haim, S. G. (1962). *Arab nationalism: An anthology.* Berkeley: University of California Press, Ltd.

Hamizrachi, B. (1988). *The emergence of the South Lebanon security belt.* New York: Praeger.

Hinnebusch, R. (1990). *Authoritarian power and state formation in Baathist Syria: Army, party, and peasant.* Boulder: Westview Press.

Hinnebusch, R. (2002). *Syria: Revolution from above.* London: Routledge.

Human Rights Watch. (1998). *Israel's record of occupation: Violations of civil and political rights.* New York: Human Rights Watch.

Jumblat, K. (1977). *Lubnan wa Harb al-Taswiya* [Lebanon and the war for a settlement] (n.p.) Center of Socialist Studies, The Progressive Socialist Party.

Jumblat, K. (1978). *Hadhihi Wasiyati* [This is my will]. Paris: Stok.

Jumblat, K. (1962). *Fi Majra al-Siyasah al-Lubnaniya* [In the course of Lebanese politics]. Beirut: Dar al-Tali'a.

Kelidar, A., and Burrel, M. (1976). *Lebanon: The collapse of a state.* London: Eastern Press.

Khoury, P. S. (1983). *Urban notables and Arab nationalism.* Cambridge: Cambridge University Press.

Khoury, P. S. (1987). *Syria and the French Mandate: The Politics of Arab Nationalism, 1920–1945.* Princeton: Princeton University Press.

Kienle, E. (1991). *Ba'th versus Ba'th: The conflict between Syria and Iraq, 1968–1989.* London: I. B. Tauris.

Kliot, N. (1994). *Water resources and conflict in the Middle East.* London: Routledge.

Lesch, D. W. (1992). *Syria and the United States: Eisenhower's Cold War in the Middle East.* Colorado: Westview Press.

Lewis, B. (2003). *What went wrong? The clash between Islam and Modernity in the Middle East.* New York: Harper Collins.

Lowi, M. R. (1993). *Water and power: The politics of a scarce resource in the Jordan River Basin.* Cambridge, Great Britain: Cambridge University Press.

Malik, H. C. (1997). *Between Damascus and Jerusalem: Lebanon and Middle East Peace.* Washington, DC: The Washington Institute for Near East Policy.

Ma'oz, M. (1995). *Syria and Israel: From war to peace-making.* Oxford: Clarendon Press.

Ma'oz, M. (1988). *Asad: The Sphinx of Damascus, a political biography.* New York: Weidenfeld & Nicolson.

Middle East Watch. (1991). *Syria unmasked: The suppression of human rights by the Asad regime.* New York: Vail-Ballou Press.

Nasrallah, F. (1992). *Prospects for Lebanon: The questions of South Lebanon.* Oxford: Centre for Lebanese Studies.

Netanyahu, B. (1995). *Fighting terrorism: How Democracies can defeat domestic and international terrorists.* New York: Farrar, Straus, and Giroux.

Netanyahu, B. (1993). *A place among nations: Israel and the World.* New York: Bantam Books.

Owen, J. (1996). *Akram al-Hawrani: Dirasa Hawla al-Siyasa al-Souriya Ma Bayn 1943–1954.* Beirut: (n.p.).

Pakradouni, K. (1992). *La'nat Watan: Min Harb Lubnan ila Harb al-Khalij* [Curse of a fatherland: From the Lebanese War to the Gulf War]. Beirut: Trans-Orient Press.

Peres, S., and Naor, A. (1993). *The new Middle East.* New York: Henry Holt and Company.

Perthes, V. (1995). *The political economy of Syria under Asad.* London: I. B. Tauris.

Pipes, D. (1990). *Greater Syria—The history of an ambition.* Oxford: Oxford University Press.

Pipes, D. (1996). *Syria beyond the peace process.* Washington, DC: Washington Institute for Near East Policy.

Porath, Y. (1974). *The emergence of the Palestinian-Arab national movement: 1918–1929* (Vol. 1). London: Frank Cass.

Puschel, K. L. (1992). *U.S.-Israel strategic cooperation in the Post-Cold War Era: An American perspective.* Tel Aviv: Jaffee Center for Strategic Studies.

Quandt, W. B. (1993). *Peace process: American diplomacy and the Arab-Israeli conflict since 1967.* Berkeley: University of California Press.

Quandt, W. B. (1977). *Decade of decisions: American policy toward the Arab-Israeli conflict, 1967–1976.* Berkeley: University of California Press.

Quandt, W. B. (1986). *Camp David: Peacemaking and politics.* Washington, DC: The Brookings Institution.

Rabinovich, I. (1991). *The road not taken: Early Arab-Israeli negotiations.* New York: Oxford University Press.

Rabinovich, I. (1972). *Syria under the Ba'th 1963–66: The Army-Party symbiosis.* Jerusalem: Israel Universities Press.

Rabinovich, I. (1985). *The war for Lebanon: 1970–1985.* Ithaca: Cornell University Press.

Rabinovich, I. (1999). *Waging peace: Israel and the Arabs at the end of the century.* New York: Farrar, Straus, and Giroux.

Rathmell, A. (1995). *Secret war in the Middle East: The covert struggle for Syria, 1949–1961.* London: I. B. Tauris Publishers.

Rubin, B. (2003). *The tragedy of the Middle East.* Cambridge: Cambridge University Press.

Safran, N. (1981). *Israel: The embattled ally.* Cambridge: The Belknap Press of Harvard University Press.

Safran, N. (1969). *From war to war: The Arab-Israeli confrontation, 1948–1967.* Indianapolis: The Bobbs-Merrill Company, Inc., Publishers.

Seale, P. (1965). *The struggle for Syria: A study of post-war Arab politics 1945–1958.* London: Oxford University Press.

Seale, P. (1988). *Asad of Syria: The struggle for the Middle East.* Berkeley: University of California Press.

Schiff, Z. (1993). *Peace with security: Israel's minimal security requirements in negotiations with Syria.* Washington, DC: The Washington Institute for Near East Policy.

Shalev, A. (1994). *Israel and Syria: Peace and security on the Golan.* Boulder: Westview Press.

Shalev, A. (1991). *The Intifada: Causes and effects.* Boulder: Westview Press.

Tauber, E. (1993). *The emergence of Arab movements.* London: Frank Cass.

Tessler, M. (1994). *A history of the Israeli-Palestinian conflict.* Bloomington: Indiana University Press.

Tibi, B. (1990). *Arab nationalism: A critical enquiry* (2nd ed.). New York: St. Martin's Press.

By a number of researchers under the supervision of Tlas, General M. (1985). *Al-Ghazu al-Israili li-Lubnan* [The Israeli invasion of Lebanon]. Damascus: Tlas Press.

Tlas, General M. (1997). *Mar'at Hayati: Al-Aqd al-Awal-1948-1958* [Mirror of my life: The first decade 1948–1958] (2nd ed.). Damascus: Tlas Press.

Van Dam, N. (1996). *The struggle for power in Syria: Politics and society under Asad and the Ba'th Party.* London: I. B. Tauris Publishers.

Wedeen, L. (1999). *Ambiguities of domination: Politics, rhetoric, and symbols in contemporary Syria.* Chicago: The University of Chicago Press.

Woodword, B. (2004). *Plan of attack.* New York: Simon and Schuster.

Yariv, A. (1992). *War in the Gulf: Implications for Israel.* Boulder: Westview Press.

Zeine, Z. (1958). *Arab Turkish relations and the emergence of Arab nationalism.* Beirut: Khayat's.

Index

Note on Arabic names: The prefixes "al-" and "el-" have been retained but ignored when the entry is alphabetized, so that "al-Shara" is listed under "S." "Bin is treated as a primary element and appears under "B."

About the Author

Robert G. Rabil is Assistant Professor and Director of Graduate Studies in the Political Science Department at Florida Atlantic University, Boca Raton. The author of *Embattled Neighbors: Syria, Israel, and Lebanon* (2003), he writes frequently for the Washington Institute for Near East Policy, a think tank founded in 1985 to promote understanding of America's interests in the Middle East.